LUTHER FOR AN ECUMENICAL AGE

LUTHER FOR AN

Essays in Commemoration

SAINT LOUIS · LONDON

ECUMENICAL AGE

of the 450th Anniversary of the Reformation

Carl S. Meyer, Editor

CONCORDIA PUBLISHING HOUSE

Concordia Publishing House, St. Louis, Missouri

Concordia Publishing House Ltd., London, E. C. 1

© 1967 Concordia Seminary, St. Louis, Missouri

Library of Congress Catalog Card No. 67-30472

MANUFACTURED IN THE UNITED STATES OF AMERICA

This publication was made possible because of a generous grant from

Lutheran Brotherhood, Minneapolis

in recognition of the 125th anniversary of the founding of Concordia Seminary, St. Louis, Missouri (9 December 1839), and its observance on four consecutive Reformation Days — 1964, 1965, 1966, 1967.

CONTENTS

7

CONTRIBUTORS

James Atkinson, Ph. D., D. theol.

Professor of Ecclesiastical History, University of Hull, Hull, England; editor and translator of *Luther's Early Theological Works,* Vol. XVI in the *Library of Christian Classics;* editor of Vol. XLIV of *Luther's Works: The Christian in Society;* author of *The Great Light (Luther and the Reformation).*

Robert Bertram, Ph. D.

Associate Professor in the Departments of Historical and (Chairman) of Systematic Theology, Concordia Seminary, St. Louis, Missouri; editor of *The Lively Function of the Gospel* and of *Theology in the Life of the Church.*

Heinz Bluhm, Ph. D., M. A.

Department of Modern Languages, Boston College, Massachusetts, and Sometime Leavenworth Professor of the German Language and Literature at Yale University, New Haven Connecticut; Fellow of the Newberry Library in Chicago; author of *Martin Luther: Creative Translator.*

Harold J. Grimm, Ph. D., Litt. D.

Chairman of the Department of History, Ohio State University, Columbus; author of *The Reformation Era, 1500–1650,* and of *Martin Luther as a Preacher;* editor of Vol. XXXI of *Luther's Works: Career of the Reformer, I.*

9

Franklin H. Littell, Ph. D., D. D.

President of Iowa Wesleyan College, Mount Pleasant; Adjunct Professor, Chicago Theological Seminary; author of *The Anabaptist View of the Church* and of *Landgraf Philipp und die Toleranz;* editor of *Reformation Studies: Essays in Honor of Roland H. Bainton.*

Carl S. Meyer, Ph. D., D. D.

Director of the School for Graduate Studies and Professor of Historical Theology, Concordia Seminary, St. Louis, Missouri; author of *Elizabeth I and the Religious Settlement of 1559;* editor of *Cranmer's Selected Works;* author of *Log Cabin to Luther Tower.*

Norman Nagel, Ph. D. (Cantab)

Preceptor of Westfield House, Cambridge, England; translator of *Eucharist and Church Fellowship in the First Four Centuries* by Werner Elert.

Jaroslav Pelikan, Ph. D., Litt. D., D. D., LL. D.

Titus Street Professor of Ecclesiastical History, Yale University, New Haven, Connecticut; editor in chief of Vols. I–XXX of the American Edition of *Luther's Works;* author of *Fools for Christ; From Luther to Kierkegaard; The Riddle of Roman Catholicism; Obedient Rebels; Luther the Expositor.*

Arthur Carl Piepkorn, Ph. D.

Graduate Professor of Systematic Theology, Concordia Seminary, St. Louis, Missouri; author of *Historic Vestments of the Lutheran Church;* book review editor of *Concordia Theological Monthly,* lecturer, and theological consultant.

E. Gordon Rupp, Ph. D., D. D.

Principal, Wesley House, Cambridge, Sometime Professor of Ecclesiastical History, University of Manchester, Manchester, England; author of *The Righteousness of God: Luther Studies; Luther's Progress to the Diet of Worms; The Making of the English Protestant Tradition Chiefly in the Reigns of Henry VIII and Edward VI; Six Makers of English Religion, 1500–1700.*

Ernest G. Schwiebert, Ph. D.

Visiting Lecturer, Lutheran Theological Seminary, Gettysburg, Pennsylvania; author of *Luther and His Times; The Reformation from a New Perspective;* and *Reformation Lectures.*

10

Lewis W. Spitz, Ph. D.

Professor of History, Stanford University, Stanford, California; author of *Conrad Celtis: The German Arch-Humanist; The Religious Renaissance of the German Humanists;* editor of *The Reformation: Material or Spiritual?; The Protestant Reformation;* editor of Vol. XXXIV of *Luther's Works: Career of the Reformer, IV;* and coeditor of *Major Crises in Western Civilization.*

11

ABBREVIATIONS IN NOTES

CR – *Corpus Reformatorum.* Halle, 1834–1860.

LCC – *The Library of Christian Classics.* Published simultaneously in the United States and in Great Britain by The Westminster Press, Philadelphia, and the SCM Press, Ltd., London, 1953–1966.

LW – *Luther's Works,* American Edition. Fortress Press, Philadelphia, and Concordia Publishing House, St. Louis, 1955–.

WA – *D. Martin Luthers Werke.* Kritische Gesamtausgabe. Weimar, 1883–.

EDITOR'S PREFACE

P LANNING the observance of the 125th anniversary of Concordia Seminary, St. Louis, provided the occasion for the committee [1] to devise ways of connecting the anniversary [2] with the 450th anniversary of the Ninety-five Theses and of the Reformation. From 9 December 1964 to 31 October 1967 was not a long span to bridge. The committee soon came to the conclusion that a series of lectures and a book will provide the bridge.

Four lectures were delivered, the first and the last by alumni of the seminary, the second and third by two scholars of another communion. They were:

31 October 1964	Lewis W. Spitz
31 October 1965	Franklin H. Littell
31 October 1966	E. Gordon Rupp
31 October 1967	Jaroslav Pelikan

To these were added five other Luther scholars with contributions in written form: Heinz Bluhm, Harold J. Grimm, James Atkinson, Norman Nagel, and Ernest G. Schwiebert. They were joined by three

13

members of the faculty of Concordia Seminary: Arthur Carl Piepkorn, Robert Bertram, and the editor. The contributors have honored Concordia Seminary and paid tribute to Luther and to the church that bears his name.

The lecturers and writers were not assigned topics or given a theme to develop. Their interest in Luther, it was hoped, would give sufficient unity to the volume. As he studied the contributions of the various writers, the editor learned the meaning of Wilhelm Dilthey's observation that those who try to understand the course of historical events are themselves historical beings embedded in that course.[3]

What does the church of the last third of the 20th century ask the church of the first half of the 16th? The ecumenical concerns of 1967 are such that we need to listen to the voice of the Reformers. Littell has suggested that the dialog of the 16th century stopped too soon; men ceased to listen.[4] There were men of unity in that day: Martin Bucer and Philip of Hesse, Cranmer and Cassander and Contarini, Melanchthon[5] and — yes — Martin Luther. Although they did not listen to each other, the 20th century may be ready to listen to them.

Luther especially deserves to be heard. Ulrich S. Leupold has pointed out, for instance, that Luther wanted the Latin of the Mass retained in cathedral and convent churches "for ecumenical, academic, and musical reasons."[6] On 17 June 1525 Luther wrote "A Christian Exhortation to the Livonians Concerning Public Worship and Concord";[7] the word "concord" in the title of the tract is significant. Luther held that factions and sects cause differences in teaching and practice; people and preachers should therefore diligently seek to promote unity.[8] All have the same Baptism and the same Lord's Supper; as far as possible they should use the same rites.[9] Few passages from Luther surpass his insight into the meaning of a God-centered, functioning unity in the paraphrase of the opening petitions of the Lord's Prayer in the 1526 "German Mass":

> That God, our Father in heaven, may look with mercy on us, his needy children on earth, and grant us grace so that his holy name be hallowed by us and all the world through the pure and true teaching of his Word and the fervent love of our lives; that he would graciously turn from us all false doctrine and evil living whereby his precious name is being blasphemed and profaned.
>
> That his kingdom may come to us and expand, that all transgressors and they who are blinded and bound in the devil's kingdom be brought to know Jesus Christ his Son by faith, and that the number of Christians may be increased.[10]

14

Luther could sing in his version of the *Te Deum:* "All Christendom with one accord: exalt and praise their common Lord."[11] In his well-known hymn "Erhalt uns, Herr, bei deinem Wort," he prayed:

> O Comforter of priceless worth,
> Send peace and unity on earth.[12]

Peace, concord, and unity were cherished possessions of Christians, Luther held, which they should cultivate in church and society. He warned his followers not to call themselves by his name: "I hold, together with the universal church, the one universal teaching of Christ, who is our only master [Matt. 23:8]."[13] Through faithfulness to the Master the catholicity of the church would guarantee her peace and unity, a unity of the Spirit, which does not corrupt the doctrine of the Master.[14] The community of the faithful throughout the world, the assembly of all Christians, constitutes the one, holy, Christian church on earth,[15] Luther said in words which he echoed in the Large Catechism.[16] The Sacrament of Baptism and the Sacrament of the Lord's Supper are given to the church and by them the church is constituted and maintained,[17] and so the Christian carries on his vocation.[18] The church is in Christ.[19] In Christ the one, holy, Christian church is faithful to His Word; she is a house in which only the Word of God resounds.[20] Christ instituted Baptism; with that Baptism the early church and the Christians of his day had been baptized, Luther said. And with ancient Christendom "we eat and drink from one table" in the Holy Supper, he affirmed.[21] Thus he added continuity to the characteristic of catholicity as hallmarks of the one, holy church.

Luther's ecclesiology supported his theology of ecumenism, as Melanchthon's theology of ecumenism was grounded on his doctrine of the church.[22] However, it is not Luther's ecumenical stance that the present volume emphasizes, important as the topic is; it deserves an intensive study. This volume raises the larger question of the place of Luther's theology in the Ecumenical Movement. In this context Ragnar Bring treated the validity of the Lutheran doctrinal position over against other confessions with particular reference to the Lutheran emphasis on Law and Gospel.[23] Earlier Rupp spoke earnestly to the theological world about finding "healing for the nations" in Luther's theology.[24] In the year after the close of the Second Vatican Council he found the dialog profitable for Luther studies, warning that there would be limitations as well as rewards in a renewed appraisal of Luther.[25] Marc Lienhard has pointed out that Luther cannot be branded a museum piece in a 16th-century showcase, but that his witness must be heard and tested. He shows that Luther's

15

views on tradition, Christology, justification — three questions at the heart of Luther's theology — and Luther's attitude toward the *Schwärmer* have been studied seriously in recent research, and limitations in Luther have been pointed up, but Luther's thought, his person, and his times are all subjects for the dialog.[26]

The reappraisal of Luther by Roman Catholic historians and a reconsideration of the church of the late Middle Ages by Protestant historians have had fruitful beginnings. A survey of the extent and the findings of these studies lies beyond the scope of this introduction. Lienhard has described the work of Yves Congar, Louis Bouyer, Joseph Lortz, and Johannes Hessen.[27] Pesch has traced the development of the Roman Catholic reappraisal,[28] a study that amplified a popular reappraisal[29] of which he may not have been aware. However, an attempt to list even bibliographical studies of these developments would be of little profit in the light of new studies being made.

The question remains, however, as to the extent to which the present collection of essays is a genuine contribution to an understanding of Luther vis-à-vis an Ecumenical Era. This movement was given new direction by the adoption of the Dogmatic Constitution on the Church, *Lumen Gentium,* and the Decree on Ecumenism, *Unitatis Redintegratio,* on 21 November 1964, by the Second Vatican Council.[30] A brief glance at the essays in the light of this question may indicate an answer to the question.

The words "ecumenism" and "ecumenical" do not occur in Spitz's contribution. Focusing on anthropology, he does away with the outdated view that the Renaissance and the Reformation had diametrically opposed concepts of man. The Biblical view, the approach of the Greeks and Romans, the teachings of the Church Fathers with Augustine as a prime example, upheld the dignity of man. The dignity-of-man theme persisted throughout the Middle Ages; the Renaissance brought an emphasis to the theme evident in the writings of Fazio, Manetti, Mirandola, Pompanazzi, and Vives. Luther too recognized the dignity of man, as did John Calvin. If it is contended that the Reformers had a somber view of man, a view inherited from the Middle Ages, it must be granted that the human predicament cast its gloom over the humanists too. Petrarch knew the meaning of *accidia,* the melancholy concomitant with the pursuit of knowledge. To the men of the 15th and 16th centuries melancholy had varied manifestations as seen in the writings of Salutati or Bracciolini. The Florentine Platonists wrestled with the problem, and Vives tried to plumb it. The problem of modern man in his alienation is explored by Spitz,

16

and Luther's basic optimism and the manner in which he combatted melancholy are part of his delineation. Perhaps his treatment will help the reader see the relevance of knowing the full matrix of the thought in which the Renaissance and Reformation were akin rather than apart.

Rupp makes this evident in his essay on Luther's theology of the cross. Landeen's study of the *devotio moderna,* he indicates, needs to be supplemented by a study of Rhineland mysticism. Luther cannot be dissociated from the crosscurrents in the German religious climate of the late Middle Ages. An ecumenical age must concern itself with these movements as well as with the specifics of Luther's own theological development. If Luther's theology of the cross was foreshadowed already in his lectures on the Psalms in 1513–14, it emerged in 1516, just about the time when Luther was reading Johann Tauler and the *Theologia Deutsch.* The Explanations of the Ninety-five Theses in two years give ample proof of Luther's predilection for the *theologia crucis.* A study of the past has its place in an approach to today's questions. The Passion, death, and resurrection of Jesus the Christ had as their goal the uniting of all men to Him who said: "And I, when I am lifted up from the earth, will draw all men to Myself" (John 12:32 RSV). The theology of the cross has much to say for unity and ecumenism.

Will it be heard? Perhaps the 1523 dialog or conversation between the peasant father and his son, who had learned some theology at Wittenberg, will supply some kind of answer. Perhaps the dialog will merely seem like a propaganda pamphlet. It portrays abuses, and its realism in this respect is not an irenic note. Yet the 20th-century dialog must reckon with the faults of the past — violent protests and violent remedies. Protestant histories have said that strong medicine was needed to cure deep-seated ills. The existence of a tract of this kind already in 1523 lends weight to this contention without minimizing the positive accents coming out of Wittenberg. Generalizations are open to challenge. The popularization of the positive truths of the Christian tradition, the universal, or catholic, doctrines, must nevertheless form the core concepts of the dialog in an ecumenical age to which Luther speaks.

The Nürnberg Council listened in the 1520s. Are the citizens of St. Louis or Frankfurt am Main or Liverpool so different from the townsmen of 450 years ago? True, Nürnberg had its Lazarus Spengler. Grimm has shown Spengler's worth without drawing any parallels with possible 20th-century personages. To know a man like Spengler is an enriching experience in itself. To gain an insight from the records of the processes by which the Reformation won or gained its way has its intellectual rewards. It may be contended, however, that neither Spengler nor the Nürnberg Council was an advocate of unity; Grimm does not present them as such. He shows them as men of conviction, testing and weighing the doctrines emanating from Wittenberg.

Wittenberg's role in the 16th-century religious climate is the theme of Schwiebert's essay. But he does not force his presentation into a mold labeled "ecumenism" or brand it with an "Ecu Mov" stamp. Yet Wittenberg and Luther have much to say to this Ecumenical Movement, not only by way of their message — that becomes evident in other essays in this present volume — but particularly by way of their method, a Christian humanism, academic integrity, freedom to voice conviction, responsive and responsible patterns. That a small village near the frontier, divorced from the Commercial Revolution and seemingly removed from the Italian Renaissance, had such great influence exposes a deeper question about the hidden factors in history and in the making of a *Wundermann*. *Absconditus et mirabilis!* Will a 24th-century historian find these elements in the Ecumenical Movement of the 20th century as we find them in the Reformation of the 16th?

Luther's scholarship is shown by Bluhm in his investigation of the sources of Luther's early translation of the Scriptures. Luther, Bluhm shows, used the best tools available to him and set a pattern for the University of Wittenberg. Biblical studies are a meeting ground for scholars of the 20th century from both the Roman and the non-Roman churches. Bluhm traces the pattern that one man followed. He demonstrates Luther's indebtedness to Erasmus and Jerome. Here, not in Bluhm's essay, the ecumenical implications of Luther's example are raised. The reader of the essay may wish to interpret it by putting Luther into the vortex of 20th-century ecclesiastical movements; he need not. Luther's lack of scholarship, however, dare not be raised as a barrier in the dialog.

Luther's scholarship is an incidental but important point that emerges from Nagel's investigation of his use of *sacramentum et exemplum* in Luther's understanding of Christ. Augustine was of great significance for Luther here too. The contention has been made that the Church Fathers need to be studied in the ecumenical climate, not to supply "prooftexts" for positions being held or refutations for such positions, but to provide a common basis or a common ground

18

on which the participants in the dialog can meet. The reformers' use of the Fathers may provide helpful patterns. Perhaps an analysis of their use of patristics will make the depth of their theological insights more evident to both parties of the dialog. Luther ought not to be dismissed in this analysis.

If further proof is needed, Pelikan supplies it in his investigation of Luther's brief on infant Baptism (1528). He points to Luther's correlation of the testimonies from the natural order and from tradition with the Scriptures. This correlation is not a betrayal of the reliance on Scripture. "Without it we can grasp neither the historical importance of Luther's Reformation nor its ecumenical significance," the author states. Moreover, the topic "Infant Baptism" is itself of ecumenical significance. The Second Vatican Council affirmed: "All those justified by faith through Baptism are incorporated into Christ." [31] The promises and truth of God are of the essence of that statement. A study of Luther's theology can only contribute, we believe, to an understanding of its possible meaning for ecumenism.

In the concept "Luther's theology" we self-evidently included Luther's concept of faith — its relation to justification and to sanctification, the life of good works. Bertram examines especially Luther's exposition of Galatians 5 and 6 and finds Luther teaching that the goodness of the Christian's good works reflects the same distinctive inner structure that characterizes the Christian's being justified solely by faith. Luther tells us that as a monk he looked in vain for a true saint because he looked for him in the wrong places. He discovered him by the thousands in the most common and unpretentious places and walks of life. The true saints make up the church catholic, he learned — saints and sinners, *simul iustus et peccator coram Deo.* Phrases freighted with theological meaning, misunderstood perhaps for centuries, need to be studied in the total context of the theologian's writings. For Luther a part of that context is his *Galaterbrief.* What is distinctive about the life of the Christian — the victory of mercy over sin — is a life of eyes opened and a readiness for doing the "good." All under God's judgment, all under God's mercy, all with responsibilities to each other can listen to the voice of Luther speaking to all about sin, grace, faith, and good works. A presentation drawn from Luther's exposition of Paul's Letter to the Galatians need not belabor its ecumenical relevance. The exposition presents its credentials for the dialog solely by its substance.

Can the claim be made, indeed, that Luther's theology has its place in the dialog? Some of his writings are part of the distinctive Lutheran

Confessions and some are quoted in the Formula of Concord, for instance. Piepkorn does not discuss this problem in showing how the writers of the Lutheran Symbols used Luther. His study nevertheless concludes that the writers of the Confessions, especially of the Formula, believed that they stood in the Catholic tradition and under God's Word. If their confidence was not misplaced, then they and Luther might well be heard as significant voices. Possibly the pattern the editors of the Formula employed in their use of Luther must be studied even by the heirs of Luther, who call themselves after his name. In doing that their principles might gain clarity for themselves and for their partners in the dialog. Luther need not be set aside in an ecumenical age because he wrote Confessions and was cited by writers of Confessions.

Not a Lutheran but a student of Luther, Atkinson of Hull has sounded the *ecclesia reformata semper reformanda* cry, looking at the Reformation of the 16th century as a "responsible Reformation." Luther's recovery of the doctrine of the church, integrated with his theology of the cross, which Rupp discusses, and a reliance on the authority of the Scriptures made for Luther's responsible Reformation and that of the other reformers. A responsible 20th-century reformation must recognize a poverty in Protestantism, Atkinson believes, and the new vitality of the Roman Church. He writes: "Roman Catholicism and Protestantism belong to one another." If so, there is a clear case for Luther in an ecumenical age.

Littell's essay supports these contentions as he points up the concerns of the "Third Force" in the Reformation. Yet he goes far beyond them in a plea for unity that is of significance for the Ecumenical Movement. The accent on the work of the Holy Spirit has appeared in other writers; Littell brings it to the fore in his presentation.

In 1929 some 20 German contributors discussed Luther's ecumenical significance,[32] but their presentation has largely been forgotten. Possibly the climax of the present collection of essays, provided by Littell, will rescue it from a similar fate.

Pelikan has portrayed Luther as "the irenic churchman"[33] and "the irenic Reformer."[34] Luther was catholic, not sectarian; he wanted unity, not separation. To Pelikan this is "the real Luther." If he is correct — and I believe he is — the present tribute to the Reformer becomes a genuine contribution to the movement that seeks oneness in the Head of the church through the Spirit to the glory of God the Father.

There remains the pleasant duty of the editor to thank the contributors to this volume. Appreciation to the Lutheran Brotherhood for its part in this volume must be repeated. Behind-the-scenes typists, advisers and friends deserve words of gratitude. Among them the 125th anniversary committee and my life's companion are singled out especially. And thanks to Robert Kolb and Gary Galen for the emergency help they gave.   CARL S. MEYER

NOTES

1. President Alfred O. Fuerbringer appointed as members of the committee Robert Grunow, George W. Hoyer, Herbert T. Mayer, Edgar M. Krentz, Arthur M. Vincent, and Carl S. Meyer.

2. *Toward a More Excellent Ministry*, eds. Richard R. Caemmerer and Alfred O. Fuerbringer (St. Louis: Concordia Publishing House, 1964), a volume of essays by 11 members of the faculty of Concordia Seminary on the training of pastors to commemorate Founders' Day, 9 Dec. 1964; Carl S. Meyer, *Log Cabin to Luther Tower* (St. Louis: Concordia Publishing House, 1965), tells the history of Concordia Seminary; *Concordia Theological Monthly*, XXXV, 11 (Dec. 1964), brought six contributions by Concordia Seminary professors in commemoration of the 125th anniversary and an editorial by the editor of the journal, Herbert T. Mayer, "The Seminary and the Church."

3. Wilhelm Dilthey, *Pattern and Meaning in History*, ed. and trans. H. P. Richman (New York: Harper & Brothers, 1961), p. 74.

4. Franklin H. Littell, "A New Look at the Sixteenth Century," *Steps to Christian Unity*, ed. John A. O'Brien (London: William Collins Sons & Co., Ltd.; Fontana Books, 1964), p. 55.

5. John T. McNeill, "The Ecumenical Idea and Efforts to Realize It, 1517—1618," in *A History of the Ecumenical Movement, 1517—1948*, eds. Ruth Rouse and Stephen Neill (London: S. P. C. K., 1954), pp. 25—69; idem, *Unitive Protestantism: The Ecumenical Spirit and Its Permanent Expression* (Richmond, Va.: John Knox Press, 1964), pp. 131—254.

6. LW LIII, xvi. See also Luther's preface to "The German Mass and Order of Service," ibid., p. 63.

7. LW LIII, 45—50; WA XVIII, 417—21.

8. LW LIII, 48—49. In 1523 in his "An Order of Mass and Communion for the Church at Wittenberg," LW LIII, 31, he wrote: "And let us approve each other's rites lest schisms and sects should result from this diversity of rites. . . ."

9. LW LIII, 61.

10. LW LIII, 79.

11. LW LIII, 174.

12. The translation is Catherine Winkworth's.

13. "A Sincere Admonition by Martin Luther to All Christians to Guard Against Insurrection and Rebellion, 1522," LW XLV, 71.

14. "That These Words of Christ, 'This Is My Body,' etc., Still Stand Firm Against the Fanatics, 1527," LW XXXVII, 25—27.

15. "Confession Concerning Christ's Supper, 1528," LW XXXVII, 367.

16. *The Book of Concord*, ed. Theo. G. Tappert (Philadelphia: Fortress Press, 1959), p. 417.

21

17. "Confession Concerning Christ's Supper, 1528," LW XXXVII, 274—75: "So, too, the sacrament of the Supper must indeed prefigure and signify something, viz. the unity of Christians in one spiritual body of Christ through one spirit, faith, love, and the cross, etc."

18. To John 2:23-24, LW XXII, 269, 270: "When the church baptizes and is baptized, when the church administers the Sacraments, absolves and is absolved from all sin, hears the Word of God, receives and administers absolution, then all is right. There the true churches are to be found, for these are the true works of faith. . . . I say: I remain wherever the church remains, and I believe what the church believes. That is, with the church I believe the articles of the Christian Creed. I believe in God the Father, God the Son, and God the Holy Spirit. With the church I also pray the Lord's Prayer; and then I carry out my office, calling, and duty as a man or as a woman."

19. See, e. g., to Gen. 12:2, LW II, 255.

20. "Sermon in Castle Pleissenburg, Leipzig, 1539," LW LI, 306—7.

21. "Against Hanswurst, 1541," LW XLI, 194—95.

22. Carl S. Meyer, "Philip Melanchthon, Theologian of Ecumenism," *Journal of Ecclesiastical History,* XVII, 2 (Oct. 1966), 185—207.

23. Ragnar Bring, "Luthers Lehre von Gesetz und Evangelium in dem Beitrag der lutherischen Theologie für die Oekumene," *Luther-Jahrbuch, 1957* (Berlin: Lutherisches Verlagshaus, 1957), XXIV, 1—39.

24. E. Gordon Rupp, *The Righteousness of God: Luther Studies* (London: Hodder and Stoughton, 1953), p. 38.

25. Idem, "Luther: The Contemporary Image," Inaugural Lecture at the Third International Congress for Luther Research, Järvenpää, Finland, 11 Aug. 1966 (mimeographed), pp. 12—13.

26. Marc Lienhard, "La place de Luther dans le dialogue Protestant-Catholique actuel," *Positions Lutheriennes,* XIII (April 1965), 65—87. See also Herman Dietzfelbinger, "The Ecumenical Responsibility of the Reformation," *The Papal Council and the Gospel,* ed. Kirsten E. Skydsgaard (Minneapolis: Augsburg Publishing House, 1961), pp. 1—11; idem, "The Council and the Churches of the Reformation," *Dialogue on the Way,* ed. George A. Lindbeck (Minneapolis: Augsburg Publishing House, 1965), pp. 253—67.

27. Ibid.

28. Otto H. Pesch, "Twenty Years of Catholic Luther Research," *Lutheran World,* XIII, 3 (1966), 303—16.

29. F. M. Quealey, "The Changing Image of Luther," Ch. 17 in *Ecumenical Theology Today,* ed. Gregory Baum (Deus Book; Glen Rock, N. J.: Paulist Press, 1964), pp. 174—82.

30. Carl S. Meyer, "Vatican Council II Addresses Protestantism," *Concordia Theological Monthly,* XXXVIII, 2 (Feb. 1967).

31. Decree on Ecumenism *(Unitas Redintegratio),* I, 3.

32. Alfred von Martin, ed. *Luther in ökumenischer Sicht* (Stuttgart: Fr. Frommanns Verlag [H. Kurtz], 1929).

33. Jaroslav Pelikan, *Obedient Rebels: Catholic Substance and Protestant Principle in Luther's Reformation* (New York and Evanston: Harper & Row, 1964), p. 105.

34. Ibid., p. 136, heading of Ch. ix.

I

MAN ON THIS ISTHMUS

Lewis W. Spitz

T HE INCOMPARABLE Hegel said of Leopold von Ranke, the father of modern critical history, "Er ist nur ein gewöhnlicher Historiker!" Literati of all schools have been quick to agree with Aristotle's pronouncement in the *Poetics* that history is less philosophical than poetry. Moreover, historians are acutely aware of the inherent difficulties of their task, as Thomas Carlyle expressed it in one of his purple passages: "Listening from a distance of centuries across the death-chasms and howling kingdoms of decay, it is not easy to catch everything." A present-day Carlyle, Britain's late statesman-historian Sir Winston Churchill, in one of his less optimistic moments declared: "History with its flickering lamp stumbles along the trail of the past, trying to reconstruct its scenes, to revive its echoes, and kindle with pale gleams the passion of former days." [1] Contemporary philosophers such as Martin Heidegger in the *Holzwege* not only emphasize the mysterious nature of history but seem to revel in it. And even the keen and sober historian of early modern times, Jacob Burckhardt, who wrote the essay on the Italian Renaissance charac-

23

terized by Lord Acton as "the most penetrating and subtle treatise on the history of civilization that exists in literature," was not at all confident of the historian's ability to reach the inner core of historical happenings. "Mighty events like the Reformation," he confessed, "elude, as respects their details, their outbreak, and their development, the deductions of the philosophers, however clearly the necessity of them as a whole may be demonstrated. The movements of the human spirit, its sudden flashes, its expansions and its pauses, must forever remain a mystery to our eyes, since we can but know this or that of the forces at work in it, never all of them together." [2] In the presence of philosophers and historians all these difficulties, confessions of limitations, and fear of futility might well inhibit a hard-working, dirt-farming, garden-variety common historian. And yet the Reformation historian has the words of that bumptious young German humanist Ulrich von Hutten ringing in his ears, "Even if we do not succeed, there is merit in having tried!"

An occasion such as the 450th anniversary of Luther's epoch-making act on 31 October 1517, moreover, calls for a theme sufficiently grand to merit the attention of all whom Goethe has characterized as the "higher thinkers," which necessarily draws the historian away from the comforts of his own detailed and carefully circumscribed research to the larger arena of religious and cultural history. When confronted with the question of a suitable *terminus a quo* in his *Reflections on History*, Jacob Burckhardt settled on the problem of anthropology as the most suitable *Anknüpfungspunkt,* and a lesser historian may well emulate his example. "We, however," wrote Burckhardt, "shall start out from the one point accessible to us, the one eternal center of all things — man, suffering, striving, doing, as he is and was and ever shall be. Hence our study will, in a certain sense, be pathological in kind." [3] The problem of man is central for every historian who has a humanistic rather than a hominal view of history, that is, who views man as the subject of history as well as merely an object in history. The place of man in the total scheme of things is of singular importance for the historian of the Renaissance and Reformation period when Western man, for better or for worse, grew increasingly self-conscious about his position in the world and universe.

One badly dated way of viewing the phenomena of Renaissance and Reformation is in terms of a sharp contrast in their conceptions of man. One view of Western cultural history, widespread in popular literature and even in some purportedly scholarly writing to the present day, sees the Renaissance conception of man as one of lofty appre-

24

ciation and the Reformation view as one of abject denigration.[4] The picture of the Renaissance man as a lusty, amoral, ebullient type in contrast to the timid, inhibited, repressed Reformation man owes a great deal to Friedrich Nietzsche, for whom Burckhardt developed a distinct dislike when they were together at Basel. Upon hearing one of Burckhardt's lectures on his *Weltgeschichtliche Betrachtungen* (reflections on world history), Nietzsche paid him the compliment of saying that for the first time in his life he had enjoyed listening to a lecture. Considering Nietzsche's depiction of Renaissance man, it is doubtful whether he understood Burckhardt. Conrad Burdach, a serious historian of the Renaissance and an advocate of a theory of the northern origin of the phenomenon, has composed a montage of Nietzschean terminology that may well serve to mark one polar extreme of interpretation:

Renaissance Man is the free, genial personality, fresh and wanton in bold sinfulness, the type of an aesthetic immoralism, the domineering, fame-seeking, power-hungry, insatiable voluptuary, the frivolous despiser of religion, who nevertheless keeps peace with the church and its servants, because he views it as an indispensable device for managing the masses by deception.[5]

This portrait, coupled with Nietzsche's expressed regrets that the Reformation had unfortunately intervened to prevent the Renaissance popes from secularizing Western culture painlessly from on top, represents the extreme caricature of a contrast between the Renaissance and Reformation views of man that has been maintained in varying shadings of chiaroscuro. It is one that needs radical rethinking and adjustment. In reality, the synthesis achieved during the patristic period of the double aspects of man's dignity and misery, both having classical and Biblical sources, was maintained and reemphasized during the Renaissance and Reformation era. And if the balance has been disturbed in modern or postmodern times, it needs to be restored for the mental health and spiritual welfare of man.

The Biblical root of the conception of the dignity of man lay in the account of man's creation. In reason, moral judgment, free will, and immortality of the soul man was made in the image of God. The creation motif lies behind the psalmist's expression: "I have said, Ye are gods; and all of you are children of the Most High" (Ps. 82:6). The second Biblical basis for acclaiming the supreme worth of man was the incarnation, the appearance of the *Deus humanatus*. This guarantee of the genuine value of human flesh pointed to man as the chief object of God's concern. The New England poet Robert Frost

25

suggested a dimension of the incarnation that was important to the humanists in the lines:

> God's descent into flesh was meant
> As a supreme demonstration
> Of the merit of risking spirit
> In substantiation.

These are the double grounds for human worth capsulated in the *Formula missae* and intoned in parishes throughout Christendom through the long centuries, when during the preparation of the cup for Mass the priest murmured the words: "Deus qui humanae substantiae dignitatem mirabiliter condidisti et mirabilius reformasti," or: "God who has marvelously created the dignity of human substance and has more wondrously reformed it." Such a theme repeated before peasants and wool carders as well as before kings and prelates was sure to impress itself deeply upon the mind of the Latin West.

Classical antiquity served as a second major source of the cultural emphasis on man's supreme worth. Glorification of man was common in high Hellenic culture. A most striking statement of the awesomeness of man and his magnificent achievements comes from the second chorus of Sophocles' *Antigone:*

> Much is there passing strange;
> Nothing surpassing mankind.
> He it is loves to range
> Over the ocean hoar,
> Thorough its surges' roar,
> South winds raging behind. . . .
> Now bends he to the good, now to the ill,
> With craft of art, subtle past reach of sight.[6]

The radical anthropocentrism of Protagoras' *homo mensura* and the extreme views of the Sophists fed into a rhetorical stream of commonplaces lauding man. For Plato man was the midpoint of the universe, and in middle Platonism and Neoplatonism the philosophical notion of man as the microcosm was further developed. From Hellenic sources the rhetorical and philosophical traditions of the Latin West drew an exalted image of man. The Stoics saw in the universe a community of gods and men. The figure of Cicero loomed even larger in the later tradition than in his own times. For Cicero man is remarkable in his terrestrial achievements, building colorful and beautiful structures and cities and with the strength of his own hands establishing his own empire on earth. Man's reason desires to explore the secrets of a higher world. In one of his most famous passages in the

26

De natura deorum Cicero exclaimed: "Great and special endowments have been bestowed upon men by the gods. In the first place they made them tall and upright, raised aloft from the ground, that they might be able, through their gaze being turned upon the sky, to obtain a knowledge of the divine existence. For men are formed from the earth, not as mere inhabitants and occupants, but as spectators of the things above them in the sky, the spectacle of which is afforded to no other race of animate beings."[7] The poet Ovid in his *Metamorphoses* presented a picture of the formation of man reminiscent of the Genesis account. Prometheus constructs man out of earth and water after the image of the gods and teaches him to lift his face to the heavens. His upright position characterizes him as the ruler of the earth and its living essence. In his hymn of creation Ovid wrote:

> But something else was needed, a finer being,
> More capable of mind, a sage, a ruler,
> So Man was born, it may be, in God's image,
> Or Earth, perhaps, so newly separated
> From the old fire of Heaven, still retained
> Some seed of the celestial force which fashioned
> Gods out of living clay and running water.
> All other animals look downward; Man,
> Alone, erect, can raise his face toward Heaven.[8]

Ovid wrote of the "god within us," a phrase parroted faithfully by the Renaissance humanists and a thought given renewed emphasis by the microcosm-macrocosm dogma of the Neoplatonists of the Florentine school.[9]

The first great synthesis of Biblical and classical theological and anthropological motifs was made by the patristic writers, the Greek fathers in the first instance and the Latin fathers in the second. This fact needs reemphasis in this connection, not because it is unknown but because its great importance in the Renaissance and Reformation periods with the revival of Christian antiquity has not been sufficiently appreciated. If St. Paul's sermon on Mars' Hill became the *locus classicus* — and no pun is intended — for Christian humanism, then the expressions of the apologists spelled out precisely the positive attitude of the main-line patristic appreciation of classical culture that became programmatic for the fathers through the second to the fifth centuries. Justin Martyr's declaration that "whatever has been well said belongs to us Christians," or his reference to Christian theology as "the only philosophy which I find useful and adequate," are well known. In his first *Apology* he was very explicit: "We have

27

been taught that Christ was First-begotten of God (the Father) and we have indicated above that He is the Word of whom all mankind partakes. Those who lived by reason are Christians, even though they have been considered atheists: such as, among the Greeks, Socrates, Heraclitus, and others like them." [10]

The instrumental value of the classics for the Church Fathers in their monumental effort to rethink the universe in Christian terms was recognized by many. Gregory of Nazianzus, for example, declared that Julian the Apostate with his measure forbidding Christians to teach and study the classics openly declared himself conquered in advance. He wished to overcome the Christians in a spiritual struggle by robbing them beforehand of their weapons. That is as though a champion were to challenge all men to a duel except the strong, Gregory asserted. He could, to be sure, forbid the Christians to speak correct Greek, but he could not keep them from speaking the truth. [11] That great, comprehensive mind of Clement of Alexandria, himself a product of a milieu which had absorbed and integrated Greek thought with a culture of greater antiquity, laid out the program of cultural and religious synthesis most systematically. Philosophy educated the Greek people for Christ just as the Law did the Hebrews. Thus philosophy was a forerunner insofar as it prepared the way for him who would be enlightened by Christ. It is a "schoolmaster for Christ." [12] There were warnings in great number, of course, from all of the fathers against the lasciviousness of some classical writings and against the demonic nature of the antique gods. Tertullian, that dour rigorist, referred to the philosophers as the "patriarchs of heresy" and blamed Greek philosophy for the Gnostic deviation. He called Plato a "grocery store for all the heretics," and in the *De praescriptione haereticorum* he attacked Plato's greatest student: "Unhappy Aristotle who introduced dialectic for the benefit of heresy, the great master in building up and in tearing down, ambiguous in its sentences, forced in its conjectures, ruthless in its arguments; a work of contentions, a burden even for itself, it discourses on everything so as not to have discoursed on anything." [13] But even Tertullian spoke of an *anima naturaliter christiana*, which suggested that the divine *logos* had not left natural man without some light of truth.

One positive result of this synthetic approach to the Christian and classical traditions was the emergence in many of the Fathers of a euphoric assessment of the dignity of man. To personalize this general proposition, the example of Origen and Nemesius will prove to be illuminating. The Alexandrian Father Origen had discoursed

28

eloquently on the utility of Greek philosophy as a preparation for theology. He wrote:

I beseech you to draw from Greek philosophy such things as are capable of being encyclic or preparatory studies to Christianity, and from geometry and astronomy such things as will be useful for the exposition of Holy Scriptures, in order that what the sons of the philosophers say about geometry and music and grammar and rhetoric and astronomy, that they are the handmaidens of philosophy, we may say of philosophy itself in relation to Christianity.[14]

Man, as Origen saw him, is a free creature of reason gifted above all with the power of speech, ἐκούσιον καὶ λογικόν ζῶον. It was Origen's *Commentary on Genesis*, in turn, which inspired Nemesius, bishop of Emesa, to one of the grandest encomiums on the dignity and excellence of man in all patristic literature:

When we consider these facts about man, how can we exaggerate the dignity of his place in creation? In his own person, man joins mortal creatures with the immortals, and brings the rational beings into contact with the irrational. He bears about in his proper nature a reflex of the whole creation, and is therefore rightly called "the world in little." He is the creature whom God thought worthy of such special providence that, for his sake, all creatures have their being, both those that now are, and those that are yet to be. He is the creature for whose sake God became man, so that this creature might attain incorruption and escape corruption, might reign on high, being made after the image and likeness of God, dwelling with Christ as a child of God, and might be throned above all rule and all authority. Who, then, can fully express the pre-eminence of so singular a creature? Man crosses the mighty deep, contemplates the range of the heavens, notes the motion, position, and size of the stars, and reaps a harvest both from land and sea, scorning the rage of wild beasts and the might of whales. He learns all kinds of knowledge, gains skill in arts, and pursues scientific enquiry. By writing, he addresses himself to whom he will, however far away, unhindered by bodily location. He foretells the future, rules everything, subdues everything, enjoys everything. He converses with angels and with God himself. He gives orders to creation. Devils are subject to him. He explores the nature of every kind of being. He busies himself with the knowing of God, and is God's house and temple. And all these privileges he is able to purchase at the cost of virtue and godliness. But we must not let ourselves appear to any to be making out of place, a panegyric on man, instead of a straightforward description of his nature as we proposed to do.[15]

During the Renaissance period, as in medieval times, this work of

Nemesius was regularly ascribed to Gregory of Nyssa, the most prominent Christian philosopher of the fourth century. This was due in part to textual imprecision, but in large part also to the tone reminiscent of many of Gregory of Nyssa's flights of rhapsody about the human spirit. In his *Great Catechetical Discourse* and in his treatise *On the Creation of Man* Gregory depicted man as he was created in God's likeness, enjoying the gifts of intelligence, free will, charity, purity, and happiness. In the fifth chapter of his treatise *De hominis opificio,* he describes God in His own atelier, so to speak, busy painting His own portrait, omitting none of His perfections in His own likeness, human nature itself. Above all, the Divinity is intellect and reason.[16] In the Latin West the figure who cast his shadow over all the medieval centuries was St. Augustine. If, as Santayana once observed, no sermon is complete without a quotation from St. Augustine, then certainly no general chapter on Western intellectual history can pass him by. Augustine served as a primary channel for a certain expression of optimism and recognition of human worth during the Middle Ages, paradoxical though it might seem. His conviction that God had made man for man's own sake out of His own immense goodness, for the perfect God had no need of man for the Divinity's sake, reemphasized the creation basis for the primordial worth of man. He could speak of man as "opus eius tam magnum et admirabile."

In Book XIX of the *City of God* Augustine undertook to demonstrate Christianity's superiority over the pagan philosophies by helping man to transcend earthly sorrows and to attain to the eternal joys of heavenly life. Basically Augustine contrasts the miseries of this present life with the glories of the life to come, but in Chapter 24 he spells out the positive aspects of terrestrial life with such enthusiasm that taken alone without reference to the general argument the chapter constitutes a brief for the value of life in the here and now. In Chapter 24 of Book XXII Augustine came to speak again of the blessings with which the Creator has filled this life, obnoxious though it is because of the curse. The rich and countless blessings with which the goodness of God, who cares for all He has created, reflect His retributive justice, according to Augustine. The two major blessings are propagation and conformation, the first providing an ongoing genesis and the second assuring the continued sustenance of creation. Man's soul is thus gifted with a mind in which reason and understanding become capable of receiving knowledge and of understanding what is true and of loving what is good. By this capacity the soul drinks in wisdom and becomes endowed with those virtues by which in prudence, fortitude, temperance, and righteousness it makes war upon error and the other inborn vices and conquers them by fixing its desires on no other object than the supreme and unchangeable Good. Even in the body the goodness of God is apparent in the marvelous organs of sense and the rest of the members. And all the rest of creation with all its beauty and utility, the manifold and various loveliness of sky and earth and sea would fill a volume.[17] Augustine, to be sure, inserts these passages in the middle of a stream of thought with quite a different tendency. They have a grudging tone and are introduced with the concession that, if God had withdrawn His blessing completely and if man had lost his original image entirely, nothing would remain. This cannot be acclaimed as a bold humanistic assertion. Nevertheless, in the following centuries these statements were there for all to see.

One declamation of Lactantius, a Latin Father dubbed the "Christian Cicero," is reminiscent of the mood of the Greek Fathers. Lactantius had been a professor of rhetoric before his conversion to Christianity and became tutor to Crispus, the son of Constantine. His work on man as God's creation, then, stands in the rhetorical tradition and has roots in Latin as well as Greek antiquity. In his *De opificio Dei* Lactantius appealed to the creation motif as the ground for human dignity. "For that creator and father-God has given to man sense and reason, so that it might be apparent from this that we have been created by him, since he is himself intelligence, sense, and reason," he wrote.[18] He continued with a commentary on the superiority reason gives to man over the animal kingdom.

The tradition of Christian rationalism, with its culmination in St. Thomas Aquinas, kept reason central as man's basic claim to humaneness, for the final end is that knowledge of God which includes the faculty of intellect. Although with the ascendancy of the ascetic emphasis in medieval monasticism and with its Near Eastern source of origin and its Neoplatonic and partly Scriptural rationale, the assessment of the dignity of man in his natural estate under God's general providence was minimized. Even within the theology of the monks it remained an articulated theme. Bernard of Clairvaux might well serve as a striking example. He could refer to man as "celsa creatura in capacitate majestatis" and base such a lofty claim on man's dignity in creation, his rule over nature, and the power of his dominion.[19] In his *Meditationes piissimae* Bernard developed his ideas in a treatise entitled *De cognitione humanae conditionis,* with the first chapter *De dignitate hominis* making the argument for man's dignity on the basis of the persistence of the image of God in man and the advice for man

31

to look within himself to discover God there. Many people know many things, he argues, but they do not know themselves. They seek God through exterior things and desert their own interior realm, for God is within. Man should therefore return from the exterior to the interior things and ascend from lower to higher things and hence come to a knowledge of God. In making progress in a knowledge of himself, man gains a knowledge of God. Man is made in God's image and similitude, which God wished to give to no other creature, and man's creation in this image involves his possession of memory, intelligence, and will or love. His full manhood is realized in his knowledge and understanding of the Son, in whom God is revealed.[20]

While the dignity-of-man theme persisted in the medieval period to a much greater extent than is commonly realized, the basis of that dignity was almost universally held to be the religious ground of his being. The various medieval renaissances from the Iro-Celtic to the 12th-century Renaissance merely suggested the anthropocentric classical context for allegations of human worth, for they were predominantly classical in form rather than in norm. With the coming of the Italian Renaissance a perceptible shift in emphasis became evident. Due in large part to the new verve of bourgeois society, for taken as a whole the humanists in a city such as Florence represented the upper levels of the population in wealth and political power, a new appreciation of man's innate and acquired worth and a new confidence in man's ability to control his environment emerged.[21]

Petrarch, the father of Renaissance humanism, was a self-conscious and in some respects self-assured and highly individualistic person, though it is no longer in vogue to tag him as the "first modern man." In his *De sui ipsius et multorum ignorantia* (on his own ignorance and that of many others) Petrarch declared all knowledge of nature useless unless one knows man and his place in the universe; for that reason men should not neglect to know themselves. In his *Ascent of Mount Ventoux* he quoted Seneca to the effect that "nothing is admirable besides the mind; compared to its greatness nothing is great," a thought then nearing the end of its second millenium in longevity.[22]

In Boccaccio, Petrarch's contemporary and admirer, a programmatic note was struck for the Renaissance humanists. He was born in Paris, it must be conceded to the historiographical revisionists, and his *Decameron* did depend on the medieval *fabliaux*.[23] But his *De genealogia deorum gentilium*, which he began about A. D. 1350, is an Italianesque handbook of mythology without a medieval equal. In it Boccaccio introduced the second Prometheus theme into humanistic literature. If God as the first Prometheus created man as a natural being, the second Prometheus, the learned man, creates anew. He makes of natural man civil man, known for his morals, knowledge, and virtue. If nature produces man, learning forms him anew and reforms him.[24]

The engagement of such civic humanists in the *vita activa* as Coluccio Salutati, whose *De laboribus Herculis* as a handbook of mythological allegories was intended to supplement Boccaccio's work, was in itself testimony of the feeling of confidence in the individual's position and capacity to achieve in public life. In striving to maintain and extend republican ideals of statehood these *viri docti* reformed not only man but men in the collective. Salutati was the undisputed leader of the humanistic movement for some 32 years from the death of Petrarch in 1374, and it was Petrarch who initially inspired him to his passionate interest in the classics until his own passing in 1406. He handed the torch of civic humanism with its explicit recognition of the importance of the *vita civile* to his two most important disciples, Leonardo Bruni and Poggio Bracciolini, both of whom succeeded him in turn as chancellors of the city of Florence.

Leon Battista Alberti (1404–1472), himself a religious but of a well-established Florentine family, in the Preface to that famous handbook of bourgeois virtues, the *Della famiglia,* urged the importance of the activist response to life's challenges, declaring that "fortune places under a yoke only him who submits to her." Even though the stream of life may seem to be directed by fate or fortune, he asserted in the *Intercoenales* of 1443, much can be accomplished in human affairs through prudence and industry.[25]

Three archetypal discourses on the dignity-of-man theme in Italian Renaissance humanism illustrate the varying emphases within conventional statements on the same motif. The first, written about the middle of the Quattrocento, was Bartolommeo Fazio's (1400?–1457) *De excellentia et praestantia hominis,* written for "the first Renaissance pope," Nicholas V. Stating in the Preface that this work was intended to be a companion piece to Innocent III's *De contemptu mundi,* Fazio stressed the importance of the power of reason in man working in harmony with the senses to achieve the conquest of nature. God created man and endowed him with reason so that he could know, love, and possess the supreme good, which is God himself. The supreme end of man is to serve God for his own sake, but since man can add nothing to God's divinity, this service of God takes the form of service to man.[26] In words reminiscent of Cicero he rehearsed man's

33

achievements, for "men have known secrets, constructed cities, invented shelter and clothing, founded laws, apprehended the turnings of the heavens and the motions and course of the stars, discovered medicine, besides so many arts, so many sciences such as among the first, philosophy, that master and leader of good living which first incites and establishes in us the worship of God and thence all works of virtue." All the powers of man's mind should lead him to contemplate divine things.[27] In Fazio the human achievements are only of transient value, and the ground for optimism in the final analysis is metaphysical or religious.

The second even more renowned expression of the dignity-of-man theme was that of Giannozzo Manetti, born in Florence in 1396 and died as an exile in Naples in 1459. Had Manetti known in 1451 and 1452, when he composed the treatise, of his total ruin and disastrous flight from Florence, he might have written differently. Manetti was in the activist tradition of civic humanism, however, and once responded to a question of King Alphonso of Naples as to what comprises the whole duty of man with the answer: *Intellegere et agere* (to understand and to act). The *De dignitate et excellentia hominis* was dedicated to King Alphonso and stressed man's achievements as evidence of human worth. He rehearsed the achievements of man from the building of the pyramids in antiquity to the construction of the dome of Brunelleschi in his native Florence. The artists, rhetoricians, poets, historians, jurists, philologists, doctors, and astrologers through the long centuries have served as witnesses of man's great excellence. The climax of the treatise was reached in the grand encomium on human powers in these lines:

> The genius of man is such that all these things, after that first new and rude creation of the world, seem to have been discovered and completed and perfected by us with a certain unique and extraordinary acumen of the human mind. For things which are perceived are ours, that is, are human things, since they have been made by men, all houses, all towns, all cities, in short, all edifices on earth, which certainly are so great and such that they ought rightly to be considered the works of angels rather than of men, on account of this great excellence of theirs. Ours are the pictures, ours the sculptures, ours are the arts, ours the sciences.[28]

Once again the creation and the new creation by the *vir doctus* is stressed. In Book IV of the treatise Manetti went beyond Fazio, whose work he cited in the Preface, to undertake a detailed refutation of Innocent III's *De contemptu mundi*, urging the physical as well as the

34

mental and spiritual capacities of man as grounds for his value and the worthiness of life in the present world.

The third treatise, which may very well be the best-known document of Italian humanism, was Giovanni Pico della Mirandola's *Oratio de dignitate hominis.* He wrote it probably in 1486 as an introduction to the debate on his 900 propositions projected for January 1487, a disputation never held, thanks to ecclesiastical intervention. Pico, it is interesting to note, entitled his piece simply *Oratio,* and the subtitle *De dignitate hominis* was added by his editors, although it applies specifically only to the first part of the oration. The subject of the second half is that all conflicting schools of philosophy can be reconciled in a grand unity. As an admirer and understudy of Marsilio Ficino, Pico was familiar with his Neoplatonic approach to anthropology. Ficino had manipulated the traditional schemes in his *Theologia Platonica.* He had placed the rational soul at the center of the universe and had emphasized the importance of man's central position as the *copula mundi,* or midpoint in the totality of things, as well as man's universality. Man should dominate as lord and ruler, as the very rival of nature. Man can through astronomy even understand the heavenly sphere and his own place in the center of total reality. Pico stressed rather man's mobility and freedom, his potentiality for rising to great heights or for sinking to bottomless depths, sharing in the properties of all other things and finding his place where he wills it to be. It was this idea of man's freedom that drove Pico to put man outside the chain of being. Man must make the choices that will assure his upward movement to communion with angelic beings, an ascent aided by true philosophy, which recognizes the deep inner harmony of all sincere and genuine assertions of the mind.[29] The *Oratio* was composed, after all, in a burst of enthusiasm at a time when Pico was immersed in the study of Hebrew Gnostic literature and cabbalistic mysticism and was writing a treatise on love and beauty. The Hermetic literature was ecstatic about man, the great miracle who enjoys mental freedom.

The Italian Aristotelian Pietro Pomponazzi of Mantua (1462 to 1524) emphasized the humanistic conception of the dignity and worth of the individual soul. In his treatise *On the Immortality of the Soul* he argued that the excellence of man consists in his moral virtue and not in contemplation. In this emphasis he was not merely departing from the medieval ideal of the *vita contemplativa* but was differing with Aristotle, who in one passage in the *Nicomachean Ethics* had stressed the great value of contemplation. Pomponazzi knew little

Greek, and his humanist anthropology reflected the moralistic emphasis of the Latin classics and Italian humanism. It was, however, Pico's rhetorical statement that remained the Renaissance apotheosis of *homo sapiens* at its apogee, and that less than a decade before the disastrous invasion of Italy by Charles VIII and the beginning of a new time of troubles.

The *dignitas hominis* theme was reflected with varying brilliance also in septentrional, or transmontane, humanism. In following their Italian predecessors as well as the classical texts the German humanists lauded the *dignitas essendi,* the grandeur of the human spirit, and the "incredible power of the human mind." Among the French humanists Carolus Bovillus provides an excellent example of the lofty appreciation of man and above all of the learned man. In his *Liber de sapiente,* written in 1509 and published two years later, he developed the Prometheus theme once again. Following Pico's line, he held that man, being outside the order of all things, was free to become all things. Imitating Prometheus, man scales the heights of angelic intellection and governs the earth like a second god. Man resembles the divine Prometheus in his creative power and re-creates himself with learned wisdom. He is a man by nature because of his rational soul, and a true man by virtue because he is wise.[30]

A single example from Spanish humanism must suffice, the most obvious choice being Juan Luis Vives' *Fabula de homine,* an allegory portraying man as the son of Jupiter, born to play on the world-stage as he wills. The dependence on Pico's conception of the dignity of man is apparent throughout, stressing Pico's analysis of body and soul as equal parts of the human being, who is free to ascend or descend as he wills. Jupiter determines the creation of the world as a stage, prescribing no particular form to man, but gives to man an unlimited power of self-transformation. Man finally transforms himself into the person of Jupiter, thus becoming immortal. Once again the classical influence, specifically Cicero's *De legibus* and his *De natura deorum,* is evident, and the Biblical notions of the Creation and the Incarnation are suggested.[31] Vives (1492–1540) wrote the *Fabula* shortly after he first met Erasmus in Louvain in 1518, and it is intriguing to suppose that the prince of the northern humanists may have inspired him to do this Promethean allegory, for Erasmus was given to playing with mythology, such as the story of Cain deceiving the angel guarding the gates of Paradise and obtaining seed from which to grow outsized fruit, which Erasmus told at Colet's dinner table in November 1499. The statements on man's free will in the

De libero arbitrio were ambivalently mild compared with the ecstatic rhapsodies on the infinite resources of the human genius in the *Hyperaspistes* that followed the *Arbitrio*. In the *Enchiridion* he asserted that "the human spirit has never demanded anything of itself with vigor that it did not accomplish. A large part of Christianity is to wish to be a Christian with the whole heart." His whole confidence in the educability of man was in the tradition of the *vir doctus* as a second Prometheus.

The magisterial reformers had a loftier view of natural man in his natural estate than is often realized. Luther praised man's reason as the highest creation of the Almighty and marveled at the great achievements of man and the excellence of society and government also among the heathen. In his comments on Genesis 2:7 he referred to the creation as the primary basis of human dignity and worth:

> Here Moses returns to the work of the sixth day and points out whence the cultivator of the earth came, namely, that God formed him from a clod, as a potter forms a pot out of clay with his hands. For this reason he did not say above, as in the case of other creatures: "Let the earth bring forth man," but: "Let Us make a man," in order to point out the superiority of the human race and to disclose the unique counsel of God, of which He availed Himself when He created man, although after this man increased and multiplied in the same manner as the other beasts. For the semen congeals in the womb and is given form in an identical manner. Here there is no difference between a pregnant cow and a woman with child. But Moses shows that in their first state there was a very great difference, inasmuch as man was created by a unique counsel and wisdom and shaped by the finger of God.
>
> The difference between the origin of man and that of cattle also points to the immortality of the soul, of which we have previously spoken. Although all the remaining works of God are perfect objects of wonder and are very sublime, this nevertheless proves conclusively that man is the most outstanding creature: when God creates him, He takes counsel and employs a new procedure. He does not leave it to the earth to produce him, like the animals and the trees. But He Himself shapes him according to His image as if he were God's partner and one who would enjoy God's rest. And so Adam is a dead and inactive clod before he is formed by the Lord. God takes that clod and forms from it a most beautiful creature which has a share in immortality.[32]

Luther even adopted the humanists' imagery of man as the microcosm in a surprising passage on man as the *imago Dei:*

Here Moses does not employ the word "similitude," but only "image." Perhaps he wanted to avoid an ambiguity of speech and for this reason repeated the norm "image." I see no other reason for the repetition unless we should understand it for the sake of emphasis as an indication of the Creator's rejoicing and exulting over the most beautiful work He had made, so that Moses intends to indicate that God was not so delighted at the other creatures as at man, whom He had created according to His own similitude. The rest of the animals are designated as footprints of God; but man alone is God's image, as appears in the *Sentences* (Peter Lombard's). In the remaining creatures God is recognized as by His footprints; but in the human being, especially in Adam, He is truly recognized, because in him there is such wisdom, justice, and knowledge of all things that he may rightly be called a world in miniature. He has an understanding of heaven, earth, and the entire creation. And so it gives God pleasure that He made so beautiful a creature.[33]

In a fairly typical passage, Luther in fact lauded the new and pending conquests of nature with a verve characteristic of the humanists. Luther, like Aeneas Silvius and Erasmus, hailed the dawn of a golden age, a *güldene Zeit*.[34] In an unstudied and spontaneous expression of confidence in man's triumphs he exclaimed:

We are at the dawn of a new era, for we are beginning to recover the knowledge of the external world that we had lost through the fall of Adam. We now observe creatures properly, and not as formerly under the Papacy. Erasmus is indifferent and does not care to know how the fetus is developed in the uterus of the mother and is ignorant of the dignity of marriage. But by the grace of God we are beginning to recognize in the most delicate flower the wonders of divine goodness and omnipotence. Therefore we praise, bless, and give thanks to Him and we see in His creatures the power of His Word. He spoke and things stood fast. See that force display itself in the stone of a peach. It is very hard, and the germ it encloses is very tender; nevertheless, when the moment has come, the stone must open to let out the young plant that God calls into life. Erasmus passes by all that and takes no account of it and looks upon external objects as cows look at a new gate.[35]

Not only did Luther deliver a good many encomiums on the glories of human reason in the natural world, but he personally took the initiative in introducing the humanist curriculum into the University of Wittenberg as a replacement for the scholastic routine.[36] It is at the point of human-divine encounter that Luther most emphatically distinguishes between human and divine wisdom. There is no redemptive power in human knowledge and the arts:

> True it is that human wisdom and the liberal arts are noble gifts of God, good and useful for all sorts of things so that one cannot get along without them in this life. But we can never learn from them in detail what sin and righteousness are in the sight of God, how we can get rid of our sins, become pious and just before God, and come to life from death.[37]

Theology provides the infinite wisdom that cannot be learned.[38]

The case of Calvin and a humanistic view of man in the natural sphere of life has been made so well that it hardly needs retelling. Calvin as a young French humanist had edited a work of Seneca and had imbibed a large component of particularly Latin classical thought. It has been argued that this mental set remained with him after his religious conversion and affected his ethical and social thought. Recent scholarship has gone so far as to trace an increasing influence of Platonic thought in Calvin. Expressions of high regard for man's status as creature in the natural world are to be found not only in the young Calvin but also in the final editions of the *Institutes* and throughout his works.[39] Zwingli's *anderer Geist* was suffused with Erasmian anthropology to the point of extending instrumental reason to a magisterial role also in the realm of religion.[40] The optimism of 18th and 19th century Europe and 19th and 20th century America is so familiar as to make a full-dress rehearsal unnecessary.

If this euphoric view of life were the only or even the predominant one, the historian would find it a simple task to correlate a psychic and an intellectual ascending curve with the rise of the West in economic and political power. But at the high risk of easing the reader into a slough of despondency, it is mandatory to turn now to that other more somber view of man which has been a constant in Western culture from Biblical and classical times to the present. The very psalm of Asaph which called men "gods" and the children of the Most High continued with the somber reminder: "But ye shall die like men and fall like one of the princes. Arise, O God, judge the earth; for Thou shalt inherit all nations" (Ps. 82:7-8). This recognition of human frailty and mortality is a constant in the Biblical view of man, a view reflected upon more deeply and with greater agony in the struggles of Job and in the doubts of the Preacher. For St. Paul the body is the "body of this death." The ultimate hope of deliverance comes from the Beyond and points to the great Beyond.

In Hellenic and Roman classical culture the pessimistic view of man is not exclusively a characteristic of the decline or disintegration of classical culture. What is rather astonishing is the appearance of this corrosive mood at the very apogee of the golden ages. Among the Greeks rhetoricians, philosophers, and dramatists joined in a chorus of low notes. The Sophist antiphon argued that life should not be exalted as great and elevated since everything is small, mean, short, and mixed with misery. Not some ecstatic cultist of mystery and darkness but the measured and moderate Aristotle queried: "What is man? A true mark of weakness, the prey of the moment, a toy of fortune, a picture of sudden change, now subject more to envy, now more to misfortunes; the rest is slime and gall." [41] Aristophanes in *The Birds* echoed this sad refrain:

> Ye children of man! Whose life is a span
> Protracted with sorrow from day to day
> Naked and featherless, feeble and querulous
> Sickly, calamitous creatures of clay!

The Roman writers recognized that man's infirmities are both physical and psychological. In the Augustan age Vergil described the mood of the times not only in his paean of praise to Aeneas and the emperor but also in lines suggesting the coming of an early frost, killing flowers still in bloom. Pliny in his *Natural History* contrasted the physical weakness of man with the strength of animals, which are armed with natural weapons against their enemies and enjoy natural protection against the weather. Man alone sheds tears and begins life by crying. Nature asks a cruel price for her generous gifts, making it hardly possible to judge whether she had been more a kind parent to man or more a harsh stepmother.[42] Seneca, the author of so many humane treatises on kindness, gratitude, and graciousness, could yet advocate a necessary suicide. In many places, as in his *De consolatione ad Helviam matrem,* he lamented the great feebleness of the human body.[43] Plutarch in the *Moralia* has a witty dialog between Odysseus and Gryllus, his companion metamorphosed into a pig, entitled "Beasts Are Rational." In it he compares man unfavorably with the animals, arguing that animals are in full possession of all the virtues and even possess reason, but are free of all the desires that drive men through the world and lead them to make war on each other. He concludes that men are less fortunate than the animals.[44] And in the *Tusculan Disputations* Cicero added to the list of physical ills the psychic sufferings of man: "For nature has given to us infirm bodies and added to them intolerable sorrows and incurable diseases, and also gave minds suitable to the sorrows of the bodies and separately entangled in their own troubles and anxieties." [45]

The laments about the human predicament which can be heard even in the great age of Roman society increased to a mighty chorus during the centuries of imperial decline, dissolving at last in the tears of Jerome in Bethlehem for the fallen city. A necessary component for the health of Rome's body psychic as well as body politic was missing. Perhaps the lines of Matthew Arnold, who coined the beautiful phrase "sad lucidity of soul," are not too severe in depicting the Roman debacle:

> On that hard Pagan world disgust
> And secret loathing fell.
> Deep weariness and sated lust
> Made human life a hell.
> Stout was its arm, each thew and bone
> Seem'd puissant and alive —
> But, ah! its heart, its heart was stone
> And so it could not thrive! [46]

Dante in the *Convivio* relates that when he was in despair over the death of Beatrice, he turned to Boethius' *Consolation* and was like a man who looks for silver and finds gold. Boethius was not only a major formative influence upon the Middle Ages but also continued to be one of the most widely read and appreciated philosophers through the Renaissance period, particularly in northern Europe. Boethius in prison has Philosophy sitting down on the foot of his bed, beholding his dejected eye and his face disfigured with grief, and bewailing his wretched condition in the moving strains:

> Ah! hapless state of human race!
> How quick do all their pleasures pass!
> And too, too weak their minds to bear
> Life's varied scenes of woe and care.
> When grief's sharp thorn the heart assails,
> Of wisdom's sons the purpose fails;
> Their boasted vigour soon gives way,
> Dark melancholy clouds their day;
> The helm no longer reason steers,
> But lawless passion domineers.

The message seems to be that very few people die laughing. The medieval mood can hardly be characterized as hilarious, and the medieval image of man has been depicted in sufficiently grey tones often enough to do more than justice to this aspect of that phase of

41

Western culture. The great archetypal figure St. Bernard followed his chapter on the dignity of man with one entitled *De miseria hominis,* which reflected the major motifs in the melancholy dirge on man's transiency and frailty.

The most celebrated document of despondency over the human condition and the one against which Manetti was reacting specifically was Innocent III's *De contemptu mundi seu de miseria humanae conditionis,* in which he made the utmost of the dust-to-dust and ashes-to-ashes realities and rehearsed the most disgusting side of human life: the lice, spittel, urine, feces, the brevity of time, old age, the various labors and sorrows of mortals, the precariousness of life, the constant nearness of death, the many kinds of torments and sufferings of the human body, and his proclivities for sin and propensities for evil. It is true that Innocent planned to write the corresponding essay on the dignity of man, but he was caught up in administration and never rounded out the picture. Thus the total effect of this writing from such a lofty source was to underline in black the sorry side of human life.[47]

The closing epoch of the Middle Ages following the Black Death in the 14th century was the most gloomy in the history of all Europe. This age was more acutely aware than any before it of the brevity of life and the certainty of death. The suffering of the sick, the horrors of disease, the sudden, unpredictable coming of death were vividly described by popular pulpiteers such as Jacopo Passavanti and depicted in the paintings in murals and altarpieces.[48] At the very end of the era more was written about the *miseria* of human life than ever before. A characteristic expression of the depressed feeling of the time was Giovanni Conversino da Ravenna's (d. 1408) *De miseria humanae vitae.* Curiously the very advocates of Petrarchan humanism were major contributors to this body of gloom-filled literature.[49]

Eugenio Garin, the great Renaissance scholar at the University of Florence, once remarked that the Renaissance was a splendid but not a happy age. No longer is Petrarch, the father of Renaissance humanism, hailed as the first to embrace life in the world wholeheartedly. Petrarch is seen more as a man torn between conflicting world views, between a desire for the *vita activa* and the *vita studiosa* and even the *contemplativa.* He was a man full of self-doubt and agonized misgivings, given to serious reflection on central problems of existence in such treatises as his *De vera sapientia* or his *De vita solitaria.* His *Ascent of Mount Ventoux* is no longer understood as a new discovery and appreciation of nature but as a skillful literary artifice depicting

the meandering path of life and culminating in the introspective reflections on the summit as Petrarch reads and reflects on St. Augustine's
Confessions, where his eyes first fell upon the lines: "And men go to
admire the high mountains, the vast floods of the sea, the huge streams
of the rivers, the circumference of the ocean, and the revolutions of
the stars — and desert themselves." [50] He now, Petrarch relates, turned
his inner eye toward himself. Probably in June 1354 the prior of the
Milanese Certosa brought a letter to Petrarch from the Grand Prior
urging him to complete the unfinished treatise of Innocent III on *The
Dignity of Man.* Petrarch replied that he was preoccupied with a work
of his own on the remedies against the effects of fortune, *De remediis
utriusque fortunae.* In the *De remediis* he incorporated a dialog, *De
tristitia et miseria,* that brought to a head the opposition of Reason to
Sorrow and Fear, which are the children of Adversity, with Reason
contriving sufficient cause for considering life in spite of everything
as happy and pleasant. For Petrarch such a conclusion did not come
easily or with firm and lasting conviction.[51]

With Petrarch there entered into the body of Renaissance thought
the concept of the melancholy of the exquisitely cultivated isolated
individual, the special psychic anguish of the man of genius. In his
Secretum, or *De contemptu mundi,* which originally carried the subtitle of *De secreto conflictu mearum curarum* (the secret conflict of
my desires), Petrarch in three dialogs explored the agony of his soul
with St. Augustine, probing his difficulties and suggesting remedies,
some of which were not genuinely Augustinian. Particularly the second dialog analyzes the feelings of sin and guilt, and then he finally
comes to the heart of the matter, which is the problem of melancholy
and a despair that opens the way to destruction. He describes the state
of melancholy of the soul with the analogy to a besieged castle. This
melancholy is not the conventional *tristitia* (sorrow or sadness), but
rather *accidia* (deep melancholy). No longer is *accidia* the old *Kloster-
krankheit,* the monks' sin of sloth or malaise induced by routine living,
nor the vice defined by scholastic theology and berated by popular
preachers. In Petrarch it is related uniquely, if not exclusively, to the
pursuit of learning and wisdom.[52]

The concept of melancholy emerged in the Renaissance in at least
four basic modalities. The most easily defined was the medical notion
that identified *melancholia* and *mania* as a disease involving a disturbed balance of the humors, which should be medically treated and
is subject to physical correction. This Renaissance theory had Galenic
antecedents.[53] The second was the more traditional identification of

43

melancholy with the sin of sloth, and the way these two were combined to keep the catalog of cardinal sins within the prescribed limitation of seven is fascinating. Dante ingeniously suggested biting insects as the proper eternal retribution for sloth, and Thomas a Kempis suggested branding with red-hot pokers as a fitting reward. A third was associated with the struggle against the tyranny of *Fortuna,* a melancholy induced by the hopelessness of the struggle against the impersonal forces of *Fatum* or *Tyche Fortuna,* which was a nearly constant preoccupation of major Renaissance thinkers. Finally, melancholy was considered an all but inevitable concomitant of *ingenium,* or genius, which produced or was accompanied by an "enthusiasm" that was mystical and poetical in nature and either drove the intellectual into a state of restlessness, Augustine's *cor irrequietum,* or went so far as to reduce him to inertness and total immobility of mind and body. Although Aristotle formally associated genius and melancholy in classical times, the germ of this conception lay in Plato, especially in the *Phaedrus,* and this conception was reactivated through the agency of Marsilio Ficino.[54]

In Petrarch the third and fourth varieties of melancholy, the brooding over fortune and the pangs of genius, are clearly in evidence and subtly fused. A variety of reasons might be suggested for the misgivings and suffering of Petrarch. Quite obviously he was paying the price for the wider intellectual horizons his superior knowledge of the classical world revealed to him. Secondly, his psychic insecurity may well have resulted from an increasing individualism, for self-consciousness precipitated his self-doubts and a need for reassurance. Third, since the revival of Roman antiquity was not merely the revival of major classics but to a large extent a resurgence of late classical antiquity with the pessimistic cultural motifs far advanced, Petrarch may have absorbed attitudes characteristic of this declining epoch. Melancholy of the Aristotelian, Neoplatonic, or Hermetic-Magian kind shadowed the humanists through the Renaissance. The melancholy of Albrecht Dürer's famous woodcut of 1514, *Melancholia I,* was of the Saturnine type, influenced by the natural and spiritual magic of Agrippa of Nettesheim, whose popular book on the occult sciences Dürer knew well. The woodcut with the figure of Melancholy brooding, surrounded by all the instruments of learning but reduced to absolute inertness by *accidia,* may well serve to illustrate this dark stream running through Renaissance humanism. The difficulty of these cultural giants is pointed up in André Gide's clever lines: "When one has ability, one does what one wishes. When one has genius, one does what one can." [55]

The Italian civic and literary humanists took up the theme of human misery and the comforts of otherworldliness, all the more surprising in view of their general affluence and established position in the urban society of the Renaissance.[56] Coluccio Salutati (d. 1406), the celebrated Florentine chancellor, about 1381 wrote a treatise on the world and religion, *De seculo et religione,* designed to strengthen a Camaldolese monk in his determination to remain in his monastery. The first book deals with the evils of secular life and the second with the joys of the monastic life.[57] Salutati's two leading protégés, Leonardo Bruni and Poggio Bracciolini, each produced works discussing the limitations to human happiness. Leonardo Bruni (d. 1444) wrote an introduction to moral discipline which stressed the difficulty of achieving happiness while allowing for its possibility.[58] Poggio Bracciolini (d. 1459), who as an old man of 72 had already lived a successful life by worldly standards, composed a work on the misery of the human condition which complained about everything the world might offer man.[59] Poggio had been haunted by the ironic spectacle of grandeur and decay presented by the Roman ruins and describes them in his *De varietate fortunae.* It has even been plausibly argued that Manetti's optimistic work on man's dignity and excellence was just a shade removed from a fundamental pessimism and that the arguments were adduced more in a search for reassurance than from a natural conviction. He wrote it, apparently, at the height of his career and not long before he was ruined by confiscatory taxation and forced into exile, a development, as noted above, that might understandably have changed the emphasis of his work. The end of the *Quattrocento* with the triumph of factionalism within and the domination by barbarian invaders from without saw the depths of depression, strikingly expressed by Machiavelli or by Guicciardini (d. 1540), the historian of Italy in those last decades. Guicciardini wrote: "When I consider how many accidents and perils of infirmity, of chance, of violence, and in infinite ways, the life of man is subjected to . . . I marvel all the more to see an old man or a fruitful year." [60] He was the chronicler of the denouement of the Italian Renaissance.

To the Florentine Platonists goes the credit, however, of wrestling most seriously in metaphysical terms with the place of man in the total scheme of things. Marsilio Ficino himself suffered from acute melancholy for three years prior to entering the priesthood. He was the author of the *De vita triplici,* that "diatetic of the Saturnine man" which became a classical document of Platonic anthropology. But precisely because of his celebrated treatise on the dignity of man, it is Pico who startles the Renaissance student the most with his compensatory emphasis on man's dependency on God, to whom he is immediately related without being bound to the restricting limitations of nature as such. That Pico had strong ties with traditional scholastic theology has long been known, for it is evident in the structure of his *Conclusiones,* and in his famous letter to Ermolao Barbaro he made his enthusiasm for the scholastics explicit:

> I was so troubled by your remarks that I blushed and grew ashamed of my studies. What, six years wasted in trying to understand, with so much labor, a thing which you consider so foolish! On St. Thomas, Duns Scotus, Albert, Averroes, I have, then, squandered my best years! . . . Nevertheless, I tell myself as a kind of consolation, that if one of these philosophers returned, he would know very well how to defend himself, for they were men well equipped with arguments. Well and good; our scholastic is loquacious; he will offer you his apology with as little rudeness as possible. "We were famous in our time, Ermolao, and we shall remain so, not in the schools of the grammarians or with pedagogues, but in the circles of the philosophers and among the wise: there it is not a question of who was the mother of Andromache or the children of Niobe, and similar nonsense, but of the reasons of things human and divine. It was to study and unravel these things that we were so subtle, so sharp, so penetrating that we may seem to have been, here and there, too meticulous and pedantic, if indeed one can be too scrupulous in the search for truth. Let him who accuses us of dullness and heaviness come and fight with us. He will see that these barbarians had Mercury in their hearts, if not on their lips, and that in lieu of eloquence they had wisdom, that wisdom which, far from uniting itself to eloquence, ought to dispense with it." [61]

Years later Melanchthon still thought it useful in the interests of the humanist rhetorical tradition to compose a reply to Pico's letter. Familiarity with this aspect of Pico's thought helps one understand the turn toward high theology which Pico took and the deeply personal religious interest he developed. It comes as a great surprise to the casual student of the Renaissance to encounter in the brilliant Pico, archetype of Renaissance humanist individualism and lofty view of man, such moving expressions of man's complete dependence on God as the following statements. The first is taken from Pico's *Commentary on Psalm Sixteen,* the most complete of his exegetical writings on the Psalms:

Conserva me Domine. That is to say, keep me good Lord: which word "keep me," if it be well considered, taketh away all occasion of pride. For he that is able of himself anything to get is able of himself that same thing to keep. He that asketh then of God to be kept in the state of virtue signifyeth in that asking that from the beginning he got not that virtue by himself. He then which remembreth that he attained his virtue not by his own power but by the power of God, may not be proud thereof but rather humbled before God after those words of the apostle: *Quid habes quod non accepisti* — What hast thou that thou hast not received. And if thou hast received it, why art thou proud thereof as though thou had not received it? Two words then there be which we should ever have in our mouth: the one — *Miserere mei Deus,* keep me, good Lord, when we remember our virtue.

The second is the summary of Pico's *Exposition of the Lord's Prayer:*

All consideration of this Prayer is reduced to a consideration of Christ's cross and our own death. Our own death shows us truly that we are pilgrims on earth, and the death of Christ made us sons of God; so that, thinking neither of an earthly father nor of an earthly fatherland, we may rightly say: "Our Father, who art in heaven." Our death keeps us from seeking our own glory, for we shall soon be dust and ashes; and Christ's death makes us desire God's glory, for on our behalf He did not shrink from the disgrace of the Cross. Therefore we shall say: "Hallowed be Thy Name," as if we were saying: "Not to us, Lord, not to us, but to Thy name give glory." Moreover, if we remember that all men swiftly perish through death, we shall want Christ to rule among them.[62]

In the light of such expressions and making allowances for the influence of Savonarola upon him in the last years, Pico's famous *Oratio,* it might be argued, described man before the Fall and was not intended to eliminate the need for grace nor meant to assay how much supernatural help man needs in the fallen estate. Though Pico's *Oratio* was the apotheosis of man in the Renaissance, it cannot fairly be argued that his religious expressions constitute the nadir of the Renaissance regard for man.

In a twofold sense Pietro Pomponazzi represented a more modest evaluation of man's place within total reality, as is evident from the well known position taken in the *De immortalitate animae* that contrary to the assertions of the Platonists, the immortality of the soul must be accepted on the authority of the church and not upon rational or empirical proofs, and in the position that the excellence of man consists in his moral virtue, not in contemplation. Man cannot think outside the sensible world and can understand his life only from within the world. In this emphasis on the corporal confines of real man Pomponazzi was dependent on Alexander of Aphrodisias, who allowed even less room for the nonmaterial element in man than Aristotle, to say nothing of Plato. What man thinks has, therefore, only a relative and not an absolute value. Theoretical speculations must always remain unsatisfying. Only by limiting himself to the things he is capable of achieving, Pomponazzi continued, can man build a harmonious existence. To be satisfied with what comes to him and with what he can have must be the mark of the measured man. Because it is vain to fear the inevitable, man should "thank God and nature and always be ready to die and not to fear death." In Pomponazzi Italian humanism has clearly moved far from the ecstatic reaches of Fazio, Manetti, or Pico's treatises on the dignity of man.

In humanism beyond Italy two examples of the shadow side must suffice, the one surprising and the other well known. Juan Luis Vives was a fine Erasmian Spanish humanist and the author of the *Fable of Man* discussed above. Yet this secure Christian humanist had his dark side, for he believed that man's intellect was weak, that he can comprehend but little in this life, and that what he does understand is uncertain and obscure. Man's mind, imprisoned in the flesh, lies in darkness and ignorance, and his heart is filled with deep and somber secrets.[63] The example easy to anticipate is, of course, Montaigne, with intriguing turns of phrase such as "Who knows when I am playing with my cat but that my cat is killing time with me." Luther's own *Anfechtungen* and bouts with melancholy are so well known and the picture of man's shortcomings drawn by those sweaty realists, to use Huxley's phrase, the reformers, that an elaborate discussion is not really called for.[64] In the historical literature of recent decades the dark undertow of the age of the Enlightenment has been discovered, but for a cultural manifestation analogous to the humanists' *accidia* the intellectual historian must turn to Chateaubriand and the Romantics.

"Western civilization has begun to doubt its own credentials," wrote Andre Malraux in his *Psychologie de l'art*.[65] This mood of disenchantment and loss of confidence began to develop seriously in the course of the 19th century with such voices as the somber Sören Kierkegaard and with the wars and pending destruction accelerated enormously during the first half of the 20th century. In 1843 Kierkegaard wrote in this vein:

Our age reminds one vividly of the dissolution of the Greek city-

48

state: everything goes on as usual, and yet there is no longer anyone who believes in it. The invisible spiritual bond which gives it validity no longer exists, and so the whole age is at once comic and tragic — tragic because it is perishing, comic because it goes on. For it is always the imperishable which sustains the perishable, the spiritual which sustains the corporal.

It is as though man today were apprehensively echoing timid Erasmus' famous words: "Videmus fatalem quondam rerum humanarum mutationem!"

The secure and limited world of antiquity and the medieval periods has been badly shattered by four major successive blows: the Copernican revolution, the theory of Darwinian evolution, the Freudian discovery of the world of the subconscious, which Freud himself compared with the Copernican revolution, and post-Newtonian physics, which has unsettled the legal mechanics of the world machine. In writing his *Paradise Lost* John Milton presented a description of the Ptolemaic and Copernican systems, though he used a cosmological framework older than that employed by Dante. The question in early modern times weighed on sentient man's mind in a worrisome way. In 1611 John Donne, the English parson-poet, conceded to the Copernicans that "those opinions of yours may very well be true . . . (in any case they are now) creeping into every man's mind." In his poem on *The Anatomy of the World,* which represented "the frailty and decay of this whole world," Donne reflected the unsettling effect of Copernicanism:

> [The] new Philosophy calls all in doubt,
> The element of fire is quite put out;
> The Sun is lost, and the earth, and no man's wit
> Can well direct him where to look for it.
> And freely men confess that this world's spent,
> When in the Planets, and the Firmament
> They seek so many new; then see that this
> Is crumbled out again to his Atomies.
> 'Tis all in pieces, all coherence gone;
> All just supply, and all Relation:
> Prince, Subject, Father, Son are things forgot,
> For every man alone thinks he hath got
> To be a Phoenix, and that then can be
> None of that Kind, of which he is, but he.[66]

The impact of the new cosmology on man's view of his own position in the universe was given somber expression by Blaise Pascal when he wrote:

49

When I consider the short duration of my life, swallowed up in the eternity before and after, the little space which I fill, and even can see, engulfed in the infinite immensity of spaces of which I am ignorant, and which know me not, I am frightened, and am astonished at being here rather than there, why now rather than then? [67]

Modern man has learned to roll with the punches with greater skill than Donne or Pascal, but something analogous to the effect of Copernicanism on them is mirrored in the impact of the new physics on our own contemporaries. A precocious young poet, Barbara Baier Solomon, compressed the ideas, though overstating the case, into a few lines:

> Newton's world no longer exists
> In quantum paths chance persists
> Subtle device an extension
> Of random chance to man's intention.[68]

Very possibly, however, the new anthropologies of developmentalism and depth psychology have contributed equally to man's downward assessment of man, whether rightly or wrongly so. The worry about man himself was well phrased by New England's poet laureate Robert Frost when he said: "You cannot frighten me with your enormous spaces, It is the void in man that gives me pause."

The nestor of Renaissance historians, Jacob Burckhardt, was both prophetic and historical, it seems, when he raised the question in his *Reflections on History*, "Will optimism continue to survive and how long? Or, as pessimist philosophy of today might seem to suggest, will there be a general change in thought such as took place in the third and fourth centuries?" [69] The answer to his second question that wells up from the demimonde of intellectual life in our day is a shrill yes. Jacques Kerouac, spokesman for the ragged edge of the younger set, advertises his contempt for history as being neither true nor valuable. Norman Mailer defines a hipster as "a man who has divorced himself from history, who does not give a damn about the past." On a considerably higher level existentialist Sartre cites the reasons why man is not bound by history. For a large segment of the population, cut off from a serious bond with the past, whatever value and meaning there is in life is created by the self, while all outside belongs to the mysterious and impenetrable unpattern of an unreal reality. It could be plausibly argued that a Christian like Cardinal Newman and a pagan like Seneca had infinitely more in common than a large part of the postmodern generation (if the reader will forgive the use of this faddish term) has with either Christianity or paganism. It is no longer possible to ignore this loud chorus of "existential screaming," for it is both symptom and sickness.

What is, however, more decisive is the plaintive song of responsible intellectuals, particularly of the younger men. Without embarking on a discussion of the anatomy of revolution and the desertion of the intellectuals, we can at least suggest that the intellectuals have frequently proved themselves to be sensitive to great human problems and were their articulate heralds long before society had followed fateful tendencies toward final consequences. Only a few examples from the voluminous "viewing with alarm" literature will have to suffice. The key word is alienation.

A brilliant young Harvard-trained psychologist now at Yale, Kenneth Keniston, spoke out in the Phi Beta Kappa journal on the problem of Western man:

> This is an age that inspires little enthusiasm. In the industrial West, and increasingly now in the uncommitted nations of the East, ardor is lacking; instead men talk of their growing distance from one another, from their social order, from their work and play, and even from the values that in a perhaps romanticized past seem to have given their lives cohesiveness and direction. Horatio Alger is replaced by Timon, Napoleon by Ishmael, and even Lincoln now seems pallid before the defiant images of "hoods" and "beats." The vocabulary of social commentary is dominated by terms that characterize this distance: alienation, estrangement, separation, withdrawal, indifference, disaffection, apathy, noninvolvement, neutralism — all these words describe the increasing distance between men and their former objects of love, commitment, loyalty, devotion and reverence. Alienation, once seen as the consequence of a cruel (but changeable) economic order, has become for many the central fact of human existence, characterizing man's "thrown-ness" into a world in which he has no inherent place. Formerly imposed *upon* men by the world around them, estrangement increasingly is chosen *by* them as their dominant reaction to the world.[70]

The shift in literature from a preoccupation with the alienation of the outsider, the member of a minority group, to a concern for the alienation of the common man as a metaphysical malady is highly indicative. The American historian and presidential advisor Eric Goldman once commented sardonically that when the American Negroes have achieved all their realizable goals, they will discover what the emancipated Jews learned: that life itself is fundamentally empty. *Der Mann ohne Eigenschaften* was the title of Robert Musil's important Austrian novel which earlier in the century suggested the line

51

literature of despair would take. Contemporary man fears loss of self in the economic, social, and even cultural processes of mass society.

One very common diagnosis of the problem relates man as victim to the robotization and mechanization of man in an industrial society. The prolific journalist and articulate humanist Joseph Wood Krutch has emphasized this aspect of the problem. A montage of thoughts derived from his book *Human Nature and the Human Condition* will serve to bring out the concern of an honest contemporary social critic.

We lost what had been from about 475 B. C. until about seventy-five years ago the supreme conviction that what was best in man was that which was least like the machine.

Even though modern man may labor at the machine to provide the good things of life for others, he believes that these good things are the wealth and the power produced by the machine. During the two centuries just past more and more human beings have become accustomed to doubt that they are the sons of God and that they have immortal souls. Modern man regards himself as just another animal, another machine. He is only what circumstances and reflexes make him at any given moment. Reason is mere rationalization. Choice is an illusion. Standards are prejudices. Man is not Homo Sapiens, man the thinker, but merely Homo Faber, man the machine-tender.

He has become the master of know-how, but he is less and less capable of reason, wisdom and love. Even in the eighteenth century when men became more inclined to appeal to right reason than to revealed religion, they had ideals; they distinguished between right and wrong, purity and impurity, the courtly and the vulgar. But today's key words are wealth, power, progress, prosperity, welfare, adjustment, security and peace of mind. Love, whether considered as caritas or merely as eros, eludes us. Psychiatrists speak of the "incapacity to love." Millions are "alienated" from their world, unhappy strangers in their only home.[71]

Man is more than a metabolic engine merely reacting to his environment. On the other hand, he is never governed entirely by reason and by conscious aims. His whole being is intertwined with that of his family and associations, his religion and total culture. When the individual man is cut off from his own tradition and isolated from his own kind, the whole of human society is weakened. Where natural forms of association and sound influences from the higher life no longer provide the basic assumptions on which the reality of life is based, the way is opened wide for alien influences and corrosive forces to debilitate the individual and enfeeble all of society. If religion is in some sense the vibrant heart of a culture, then the question how well Christianity is maintaining its hold on Western society is a central concern.

A century ago the French historian and religious biographer Ernst Renan expressed his misgivings as to the future of Christianity in these words: "We are living off of the shadow of faith. We will be living on the shadow of the shadow, on the scent left in an empty bottle. Will it last?" [72] This challenge from an honest critic of the last century has become the militant theme of many bumptious crusaders in the 20th century. One German journalist, publisher, and public orator, Gerhard Szczesny, has attracted astonishingly large crowds of university students with his lectures announcing the end of the Christian era. He is taken seriously by the present generation of university youth. He declares:

> Today the real Christian creed, viewed in the broad, scarcely survives as a vitally creative force. The peoples of the West, as they live out their lives — and this takes into account the majority of those who call themselves Christians — in their thinking and behavior have ceased to pay the least attention to Christianity's idea of God and the hereafter, or the Christian notion of sin and grace. Christianity was once a faith that really pervaded human existence. But it has been supplanted by a kind of indifferent tolerance of that theological phraseology which, every Sunday, resounds from pulpit and loudspeaker.[73]

A fascinating development within the communist world has been the debate in recent years about alienation within a communist society. Marx had described alienation or the isolation of man from his environment and within it as a social phenomenon that was a product of capitalism, and until a short time ago good communists declared that alienation was impossible in societies of their creation. Now revisionists concede that communism has created forms of alienation peculiar to itself; and Eastern European writers, when liberated from the narrow dictates of the party, consistently turn to themes of solitude and despair.

In the democratic West the cultural and religious dislocations of our times are recorded with seismic sensitivity in both contemporary literature and the arts, in which traditional ideas and familiar forms are turned and distorted nearly beyond recognition. Empty sounds and meaningless lines symbolize the loss of content and meaningfulness in much of the life of contemporary man. It is plain irresponsible nonsense to characterize alienation and estrangement as universally

53

present in our society. There is much that is sound and solid in the cultural and religious body of Western man. It is, nevertheless, urgent to note that many intellectuals believe that our culture stands at one of those critical turning points marked by the breakdown of the old and the emergence of a new. The possibility that their analysis is accurate exists, and the probability of their warnings becoming self-fulfilling prophecies is high. An unwholesome paranoia of the leaders in thought can easily infect the multitude. In intellectual history the tendency or direction of movement is more significant than the quantified proportions of opinion at any given point. An ideology of despair in the midst of plenty and of melancholy profundity that repudiates the present and foresees illness in the future is to be taken seriously by all concerned men. The deepest theme in history, Goethe observed, has been posed by the conflict of faith and unfaith.

If the history of mankind teaches nothing else, it demonstrates that man is a durable and resilient creature. Western culture has twice gone through cultural crises that seemed to presage to men of those days the end of their culture and to promise only dark days for man. Friedrich Nietzsche, with insight becoming his brilliance, pronounced: "Before one seeks man, one must have found the lantern — must it be the lantern of the Cynic?"[74] During the first major crisis of Western culture, when the classical world was in noticeable decline, the golden age giving way to the silver and the silver age to lead and iron, and crepuscular shadows were enveloping the earth, the Church Fathers held aloft a lantern to send out light in the gathering gloom. Clement of Alexandria in his *Stromata*, that patchwork quilt of old and new thought, spoke for them all when he wrote:

> With the lamps of the wise virgins lighted at night in the great darkness of ignorance, which the Scripture signified by "night," wise souls, pure as virgins, understanding themselves to be situated amidst the ignorance of the world, kindle the light, and rouse the mind, and illumine the darkness, and dispel ignorance, and seek truth, and await the appearance of the Teacher.[75]

During the second major crisis precipitated by the deaththrows of medieval civilization, the Reformers with their rediscovery of the historical core of Christianity and a new declaration of its evangelical affirmations gave to the faith a new lease on life. Albrecht Dürer, whose *Melancholia I* symbolized the shadow side of the Renaissance, in the year 1516 did a drawing *Der Verzweifelnde* (the despairing man) which captured the anguish of his own and his fellowmen's uncertainty. When Dürer encountered Luther's proclamation of the

Kerygma (the glad tidings), he was swept along with the excitement of a new discovery. His response to the news after Worms that Luther had been killed was a disconsolate cry: "Who now will give us certainty?" A few characteristic expressions from Luther himself will bring out the tone as well as accentuate the theme of his message that "the Christian need not be melancholy."

Luther's assessment of the human situation was positive and rooted in the basic Christian optimism with its theological premise:

> We have more occasions for joy than for sadness; we believe in the living God, and Christ lives, and we, too, shall live. (John 14:19) Sadness is born in us. . . . But God is the Spirit of gladness. He saves us. . . . We must hold on to the fact that God does not desert his own. He did not create man with a head to hang down like the beasts but to be held erect so that man can look toward the heavens.[76]

In this final sentence Luther reverts to the thought of Ovid and Cicero on man, whose feet are planted on the earth but whose hands and head can be raised to the heavens.

In his commentary on Ecclesiastes Luther undertook to wrestle with the problems posed by skepticism and the theme of the vanity of all things. He was concerned to combat the view that the world is a *fatum* and that life is perpetually consumed by time, and stressed instead the need for personal faith and an activist engagement. Vanity does not lie in man's world, that is to say, in things *sub sole* (under the sun), but rather in the void, that is, within man himself — *vanitas in humano corde!* Luther's response to the total questioning of natural man is the universal answer of Christian faith. He recognized that epistemological skepticism is only one small twig on the large tree of doubt about life's meaning and purposes. In his famous reply to Erasmus, "Spiritus sanctus non est Scepticus," Luther was indulging in an unfair innuendo against Erasmus, but beyond that was offering his religious response to the doubt of an age.[77]

The man of faith must ideally take the good and the bad, the pleasant and the unpleasant things alike as from God's hands.[78] But to live in the midst of the world and to preserve a quiet and peaceful heart — that is an art![79] The great danger for the individual is to become isolated and turned in upon himself *(incurvatus in se)*. The man of faith has been recommissioned to care for all creation and to become a co-worker with God. This challenge to an activist program in the realms of social, political, economic, and cultural life is a most wholesome corrective and antidote to sloth, melancholy, and other sickness of the soul. Once faith has been implanted, Christians should be very busy toward the neighbor, zealous of good works, burning with love toward the neighbor. Thus life *coram Deo* leads to a constructive and meaningful life *coram mundo*.[80]

Luther spent a lifetime combatting melancholy and communicating a sense of confidence to his fellowmen. There is even a bit of bravado in his protestations of courage and Christian nonchalance, to borrow Reinhold Niebuhr's phrase. It came to the surface particularly in crisis situations, as in 1522 when desertions from his cause were numerous and he wrote to Elector Frederick of Saxony:

> Have a little confidence in me, fool though I am, for I know these and other like tricks of Satan. I do not fear him because I know that this hurts him. Yet all of this is only a beginning. Let the world cry out and pass its judgments. Let those fall away who will — even a Saint Peter or persons like the apostles. They will come back on the third day, when Christ rises from the dead. This word in II Cor. ch. 6, must be fulfilled in us: "Let us approve ourselves in tumults," etc.[81]

Or again, during the trying days of the Augsburg Diet in 1530, Luther allegedly wrote on the wall in the Koburg the words of the psalm for his own encouragement: "Non moriar sed vivam et narrabo opera Dei." He found it necessary to encourage Melanchthon and the less stalwart evangelicals at the Diet:

> I am displeased with your miserable worries, with which you write you are consumed and which rule so in your heart. This shows the magnitude of our unbelief, not the magnitude of our cause. For the same cause was greater in the time of John Hus and many others than it is with us. But just as the cause is great, so is its author and initiator, for the cause is not ours. Therefore, why do you continually and without intermission weaken? If the cause is false, let us renounce it. If it is true, why do we make him a liar in such great promises with which he commands us to be of a calm and quiet mind? [82]

Luther's correspondence is studded with letters of a *Seelsorger* combatting depression and melancholy in men who have turned to him for help. Luther sent Matthias Weller a characteristic bit of advice on the problem of his psychological depression.

> Grace and peace in Christ.
> Honorable, kind, good Friend:
>
> Your dear brother has informed me that you are deeply distressed and afflicted with melancholy. He will undoubtedly tell you what I have said to him.
>
> Dear Matthias, do not dwell on your own thoughts, but listen to

what other people have to say to you. For God has commanded men to comfort their brethren, and it is his will that the afflicted should receive such consolation as God's very own. Thus our Lord speaks through Saint Paul, "Comfort the fainthearted," and through Isaiah: "Comfort ye, comfort ye my people. Speak ye comfortably." And elsewhere our Lord indicated that it is not his will that man should be downcast, but that he should rather serve the Lord with gladness and not offer him the sacrifice of sorrow. All this Moses and the prophets declared often and in many places. Our Lord also commanded us not to be anxious, but to cast our cares upon him, for he careth for us, as Saint Peter taught from Ps. 55. . . .[83]

In the Table Talk Luther reverted to this theme frequently, as though he perceived an infectious malady spreading through society. Especially throughout the last 15 years of his life he warned that solitude produces melancholy and urged comradeship and social contacts as a cure, together with playing the lute, prayer, and a host of common-sense devices.[84] Luther was candid enough to admit that for all the sound advice he freely dispensed, he found that applying the same to himself was another matter. To Conrad Cordatus he wrote: "This is in accord with the saying, 'Good cheer is half the battle,' and, 'A merry heart doeth good like a medicine: but a broken spirit drieth the bones.' I give you this advice although I confess that I do not take it myself."[85]

That was Luther in another day and another age, at the end of the Middle Ages, which the medievalist Norman Cantor has described with the rubric "the life and death of a civilization."[86] The problem confronting contemporary man may very well be that of Albrecht Dürer's "Who now will give us certainty?" With Erasmus we too see a certain fatal mutation in human affairs, but need it be fatal?

The audacious survey now happily completed of man's view of man and his prospects through the long millenia of Western history at least suggests, if it does not confirm, certain tentative conclusions. A time-line perspective of the problem of man's ambiguous position in the total scheme of things and of man's ambivalent assessment of that position suggests that the range of human possibilities is fortunately limited at the extremes of both pessimism and optimism. The human habitation is provided with both a floor and a ceiling. As Hegel once reminded his lady friend and future wife, Marie Tucher, "In all not superficial minds a sense of sadness is linked with all sense of happiness," and the reverse is fortunately also usually true.[87] In the grand sweep of Western history there have been periods of decline in which the general mood was depressed and periods of ascent in which the mood was exuberant. But in each period the counterpoint of expectation or despondency found expression through some articulate spokesmen and was recorded for our contemplation. This chiaroscuro treatment of the human landscape displays broad areas of light and shadow. But close study of the detail reveals also that many of the leading figures in pronouncing upon either the grandeur of man's dignity or the abjectness of his misery have in their own persons given expression also to the antithetical aspect. The picture in terms of broad cultural analysis is complicated in two ways, then: first by the fact that both motifs were present in varying degrees in at least the major figures referred to and, second, by the fact that both motifs were found in varying degrees in all the cultural epochs traversed. The line runs not merely among men but through each man, marking off sectors in history of varying areas.

From within his own historical perspective man remains a mystery to man. It is ironic, in fact, that the world of nature should seem to be more accessible to human understanding than the world of history, which man makes and in which he is intimately involved. Alexander Pope's lines have a kind of permanent validity, so far as the really important questions of human life are concerned:

> Placed on this isthmus of a middle state,
> A being darkly wise yet rudely great:
> With too much weakness for the stoic's pride,
> He hangs between; in doubt to act, or rest,
> In doubt to deem himself a God, or Beast;
> In doubt his Mind or Body to prefer,
> Born but to die, and reas'ning but to err;
> Alike in ignorance, his reason such,
> Whether he thinks too little, or too much:
> Chaos or thought and passion, all confus'd;
> Still by himself abus'd, or disabus'd;
> Created half to rise, and half to fall;
> Great lord of all things, yet a prey to all.
> Sole judge of Truth, in endless error hurl'd:
> The glory, jest, and riddle of the world! [88]

If the temper of our times is one of gathering darkness with all the attendant apprehension and anguish of soul, then some comfort can be derived from the fact that our civilization has responded twice before in a positive way to similar disintegrating maladies. Ideas have exercised a powerful force upon men who collectively make history. The quality of the ideas and the evocative and creative efforts of men acting upon those ideas will determine what man's past will come to be in the future.

ἄνωθεν τὸ φῶς (From above the light) is the motto of Concordia Seminary. The words of a forceful contemporary poet who has himself wrestled with the dark melancholy, meaninglessness, and alienation of our times, W. H. Auden, express this thought with beauty and power:

> Defenseless under the night
> Our world in stupor lies;
> Yet, dotted everywhere,
> Ironic points of light
> Flash out wherever the Just
> Exchange their messages;
> May we (I), composed like them
> Of Eros and of dust,
> Beleaguered by the same
> Negation and despair
> Show an affirming flame.

NOTES

1. Samuel Eliot Morrison, *Vistas of History* (New York: Alfred A. Knopf, 1964), p. 21.
2. *The Civilization of the Renaissance in Italy* (New York: Harper & Brothers, 1954), p. 342.
3. *Force and Freedom. Reflections on History* (Boston: Beacon Press, 1964), pp. 80—81. The section "Fortune and Misfortune in History," pp. 347—70, is a notable attempt to guard against wishful thinking in history.
4. Typical of this view is H. A. Enno van Gelder's *The Two Reformations in the 16th Century* (The Hague: Martinus Nijhoff, 1961), a book that reflects an interpretation more current thirty or more years ago than today.
5. *Reformation, Renaissance, Humanismus* (Berlin, Leipzig: Gebrüder Paetel, 1926), p. 90. The sober Dutch cultural historian Jan Huizinga described the humanists in similar terms: "If ever an elite, fully conscious of its own merits, sought to segregate itself from the vulgar herd and live life as a game of artistic perfection, that was the circle of choice Renaissance spirits," *Homo ludens* (London: Routledge & K. Paul, 1949), p. 180.
6. Sir George Young, *The Dramas of Sophocles Rendered in English Verse Dramatic and Lyric* (London and Toronto: J. M. Dent & Sons, 1931), pp. 11—12.
7. Marcus Tullius Cicero, *De natura deorum*, trans. Francis Brooks (London: Methuen & Co., 1896), Ch. lvi, p. 146. The preceding chapter describes the marvel of the human physical organism.
8. *Metamorphoses* I, 72—84, trans. Rolfe Humphries (Bloomington, Ind.: Indiana University Press, 1955), p. 5.
9. This dogma is found also in northern humanists, for example, *Der Briefwechsel des Konrad Celtis*, ed. Hans Rupprich (Munich: C. H. Beck'sche Verlagsbuchhandlung, 1934), Br. 275, pp. 499 ff., lines 121 ff.; Johannes Tolhopf to Celtis, Br. 101, p. 166, line 22.

10. Justin Martyr, J. P. Migne, ed. *Patrologiae Graecae,* (Paris: Apud Garnier Fratres, editores et J. P. Migne successores, 1884), VI, col. 397. Hereafter cited as either Migne, P. G., or Migne, P. L., *Patrologia Latina,* as the case may be. *Apologia* I, 46.

11. "Contra Julianum I," Migne, P. G., XXXV, cols. 535—38. See Herbert W. Rüssel, *Gestalt eines christlichen Humanismus* (Amsterdam: Akademische Verlagsanstalt Pantheon, 1940), p. 75. Marcel Guignet, *Saint Grégoire de Nazianze et lá Rhétorique* (Paris: Alphonse Picard et fils, 1911), pp. 43—70, depicts Gregory's attitude to the classics as ambivalent, even contradictory. St. Basil's "Exhortation to Young Men on How They Might Derive Profit from Pagan Literature," *St. Basil: The Letters,* trans. Roy J. Deferrari (Cambridge: Harvard University Press, 1950), IV, 378—435, argued for the utility of the classics on grounds similar to those of Gregory, even adducing the examples of Plato, Plutarch, and Seneca, who themselves expounded the old poets.

12. *Stromata* I, 5, *The Ante-Nicene Fathers,* eds. Alexander Roberts and James Donaldson (Grand Rapids, Mich.: Wm. B. Eerdmans Publishing Co., 1962), II, 305.

13. Tertullian, *De Praescriptione Haereticorum,* VII, 6, *Corpus Christianorum. Series Latina* (Turnholti: Typographi Prepols Editores Pontifici, 1954), p. 192. See his *Apologia adversus Marcionem* I, 1, for a Prometheus reference; also p. 442.

14. Origen really desired to be orthodox, moreover, as is evident from his statement in the *De principiis, praefatio* 2: "That alone is to be accepted as truth which differs in no respect from ecclesiastical and apostolic tradition." The way in which Origen's orthodoxy has been refurbished by recent scholarship is evident in Jean Daniélou, *Origen* (London and New York: Sheed and Ward, 1955), p. 310: "He is of that rare class of men whose genius is equalled only by their sanctity."

15. *De natura hominis,* Migne, P. G., XL, cols. 532C—533B. Translated in William Telfer, ed. *Cyril of Jerusalem and Nemesius of Emesa* (London: SCM Press Ltd., 1955); LCC IV, 254—56. This panegyric reflects the Posidonian doctrine that man is the apex of the natural order. A rhetorical commonplace, it is related or indebted to Cicero's *De natura deorum,* II, 153.

16. Alcuin A. Weiswurm, "The Rational Nature of Man," *The Nature of Human Knowledge According to Saint Gregory of Nyssa* (Washington, D. C.: The Catholic University of America Press, 1952), p. 62. See Gregory of Nyssa, "Restoring God's Image," *From Glory to Glory* (New York: Charles Scribner's Sons, 1961), pp. 112—17; Roger Leys, S. J., "Anthropologie," *L'Image de Dieu chez Saint Grégoire de Nysse* (Brussels: L'Édition Universelle, 1951), pp. 59—119.

17. Saint Augustine, *The City of God* (New York: Random House, 1950), pp. 850 to 855. In the *De doctrina christiana* Augustine asserts the utility of classical thinkers in a way reminiscent of the Greek Fathers: "If those who are called philosophers, especially the Platonists, have said things by chance that are truthful and conformable to our faith, we must not only have no fear of them, but even appropriate them for our own use from those who are in a sense their illegal possessors," *Christian Instruction,* Ch. 40, John J. Gavigan, O. S. A., trans. *Writings of Saint Augustine,* (New York: CIMA Publishing Co., Inc., 1947), IV, 112.

18. *De opificio Dei, vel formatione hominis,* Migne, P. L., VII, col. 14. In Book II, Ch. 10, of his *The Divine Institutes,* Lactantius opposes the Genesis creation account to the Prometheus legend. *The Fathers of the Church,* (Washington, D. C.: The Catholic University of America Press, 1964), XLIX, 138—43. Lac-

tantius, *Div. Instit.* II, 2: "Deus unicus qui universa condidit, qui hominem de humo struxit, hic est verus Prometheus."

19. Saint Bernard, *Opera omnia,* (Paris, 1839), I, cols. 284D, 2594A, 1332A. Of all the creatures under heaven man is nearest to God. Ibid., col. 2331C.

20. Ibid., Tomus V, volumen secundum, pars prior, cols. 661—64. William of St. Thierry (d. 1148), Bernard's precise contemporary, referred to the image-of-God idea in addressing man: "O image of God, recall your dignity; let the image of the author shine brightly in you," *Expositio altera super cantica canticorum,* Migne, P. L., CLXXX, col. 494C. On William see Etienne Gilson, *La Philosophie au Moyen Age* (Paris: Payot & Cie, 1952) pp. 300—01. In the East an 11th-century Byzantine poet John Mauropus could pray for Plato and Plutarch, for they were both closely related to Christ's laws in their teaching and ethic. The dignity-of-man theme persisted also there.

21. The growth of secularism and its effect on the spiritual and intellectual life of Europe is emphasized by the noted Renaissance scholar Wallace K. Ferguson in his article "The Church in a Changing World, a Contribution to the Interpretation of the Renaissance," *American Historical Review,* LIX (Jan. 1953), 1—18, as well as in his major text *Europe in Transition* (New York: Houghton Mifflin Co., 1962).

22. The Seneca passage is his *Epistles,* 8, 5, cited in Ernst Cassirer and others, *The Renaissance Philosophy of Man* (Chicago: University of Chicago Press, 1948), p. 44.

23. Johan Nordström, *Moyen Age et Renaissance* (Paris: Librairie Stock, 1933), adduces these facts to promote his northern and specifically French origin of the Renaissance thesis.

24. *De genealogiis deorum gentilium,* Book IV, Ch. 44, a cura di V. Romano (Bari: Gius. Laterza & Figli, 1951), I, 198—202: "Circa quos secundus Prometheus insurgit, id est, doctus homo, et eos tanquam lapideos suscipiens quasi de novo curret, docet et instruit, et demonstrationibus suis ex virtutibus insignes, adeo ut liquido pateat alios produxisse naturam, et alios reformasse doctrinam. . . ." See Georg Habich, "Ueber 2. Prometheus — Bilder angeblich von Piero di Cosimo," *Sitzungsberichte der Bayerischen Akademie der Wissenschaften, Philos. Phil. Klasse, 2. Abhandlung* (Munich, 1920), pp. 1—18.

25. See Berthold L. Ullman, *The Humanism of Coluccio Salutati* (Padua: Editrice Antenore, 1963), pp. 39—70. Leon Battista Alberti, *Intercoenales,* in ed. *Prosatori Latini del Quattrocento,* ed. Eugenio Garin (Milan: Riccardo Ricciardi Editore, 1952), p. 656: "Contra vero Fortunam esse duram sensi nobis qui eo tempore in fluvium corruissemus quo perpetuo in nisu undas nando superare opus sit: plurimum tamen in rebus humanis prudentiam et industriam valere non ignorabimus."

26. Charles Trinkaus, *Adversity's Noblemen: The Italian Humanists or Happiness* (New York: Columbia University Press, 1940), pp. 64—65.

27. Ibid., p. 96.

28. Giannozzo Manetti, *De dignitate et excellentia hominis,* in Eugenio Garin, *Filosofi italiani del Quattrocento,* Pagine scelte, tradotte e illustrate (Florence: Felice Le Mounier, 1942), p. 238. See the excellent article by August Buck, "Die Rangstellung des Menschen in der Renaissance: dignitas et miseria hominis," *Archiv für Kulturgeschichte,* XLII (1960), 61—75. See A. G. Auer, "Manetti und Pico della Mirandola, de hominis dignitate," *Vitae et veritate* (Duesseldorf: Patmos Verlag, 1956), pp. 83—102.

29. The contrast between Pico and Ficino is not fundamentally one of an immanent as opposed to a transcendant basis for the dignity of man as suggested by

Giovanni Semprini, *La Filosofia di Pico della Mirandola* (Milan: Libreria Lombarda, 1936), pp. 63—65. A superior treatment of the question is in Eugenio Garin, *Giovanni Pico della Mirandola: Vita e dottrina* (Florence: Felice Le Monnier, 1937). See also Paul Oskar Kristeller, *Eight Philosophers of the Italian Renaissance* (Stanford: Stanford University Press, 1964), pp. 54—71. Eugenio Garin gives a summary of his views in *Der italienische Humanismus* (Bern: Verlag A. Francke, 1947), pp. 123—25.

30. *De sapiente*, xix, 341, xxi, 369, cited in Eugene F. Rice, Jr., *The Renaissance Idea of Wisdom* (Cambridge, Mass.: Harvard University Press, 1958), pp. 119, 121. Rice's excellent chapter on "The Wisdom of Prometheus," pp. 92—123, is germane to the theme of the *vir doctus* as the second Prometheus.

31. Ernst Cassirer and others, *The Renaissance Philosophy of Man*, pp. 385—97. See Otis H. Green, "The Concept of Man in the Spanish Renaissance," *The Rice Institute Pamphlet*, XLVI (Jan. 1960), 49—50: Cervantes has Don Quixote express a Pico-like thought when he says, "I know who I am and who I may be if I choose." Book I, Ch. 5.

32. LW I, 83—84.

33. Ibid., I, 68.

34. WA XXXIX 1, 41: ". . . und ist ja itzund eine güldene Zeit, darin man wohl und reichlich auch leichtlich gelehrte und feine Leute erziehen kann."

35. Luther, WA, Tr I, No. 1160, pp. 573—74.

36. On this point see Kurt Aland, "Die theologische Fakultät Wittenberg und ihre Stellung im Gesamtzusammenhang der Leucorea während des 16. Jahrhunderts," *450 Jahre Martin Luther Universität Halle-Wittenberg*, (Wittenberg: Selbstverlag der Martin Luther Universität Halle-Wittenberg, 1952), I, 155—237. On Luther's appreciation of natural reason in its proper sphere, as distinguished from regenerate reason of the man of faith and the arrogant reason of the man of unfaith speaking to questions of faith, see two admirable monographs, Bernhard Lohse, *Ratio und fides. Eine Untersuchung "über die ratio in der Theologie Luthers* (Göttingen: Vandenhoeck & Ruprecht, 1958) and Brian Gerrish, *Grace and Reason: A Study in the Theology of Luther* (Oxford: Clarendon Press, 1962). Luther's disputation on man proposed theses on reason as operative on the natural plane and as blind with reference to God's inner nature and the true essence of ultimate reality, WA XXXIX/1, 175—80.

37. WA XXXXVIII, 78.

38. WA XXXX/3, 63, 17: "Ideo Theologia est infinita sapientia, quia nunquam potest edisci."

39. The pioneer study on this subject was Quirinus Breen's University of Chicago dissertation, *John Calvin: A Study in French Humanism* (Grand Rapids, Mich.: Wm. B. Eerdmans Publishing Company, 1931). Josef Bohatec, the Czech scholar who taught in his final years at the University of Vienna, argued in his *Budé und Calvin. Studien zur Gedankenwelt des französischen Frühhumanismus* (Graz: Verlag Hermann Böhlaus Nachf., 1950) that the humanistic orientation of Calvin's thought did not make a telling impact on his high theological concerns about God, freedom, and immortality. The two strongest assertions of a Platonic influence on Calvin's anthropology and on his theology in general are an article that has been the center of considerable debate, Roy Battenhouse, "The Doctrine of Man in Calvin and in Renaissance Platonism," *Journal of the History of Ideas*, IX (Oct.—Dec. 1948), 447—71, and a recent analysis of Calvin's "humanism," Jean Boisset, *Sagesse et sainteté dans la pensée de Jean Calvin. Essai sur l'humanisme du reformateur français* (Paris:

Presses universitaires de France, 1959), pp. 4, 222 f., 296, etc. The tendency to develop the humanist influence in Calvin is evident from the summary work of François Wendel, *Calvin. Sources et évolution de sa pensée religieuse* (Paris: Presses universitaires de France, 1950).

40. The tie between Zwingli and Italian humanism was made over a century ago by Christoph Sigwart, *Ulrich Zwingli. Der Charakter seiner Theologie mit besonderer Rücksicht auf Picus von Mirandola dargestellt* (Stuttgart: Besser Verlag, 1855). Early humanist influences on his anthropology are delineated in Arthur Rich, *Die Anfänge der Theologie Huldrych Zwinglis* (Zurich: Zwingli Verlag, 1949). See also the references in Bard Thompson, "Zwingli Study Since 1918," *Church History*, XIX (June 1950), 116—28.

41. See Jacob Burckhardt, "Der griechische Pessimismus," *Gesammelte Werke*, (Basle: B. Schwabe, 1956), V, 349—67, especially pp. 365, 370. In the *Nicomachean Ethics* VII, 15, 1154b, 7, Aristotle wrote: "To see and to hear are laborious, as natural discourses testify."

42. Pliny, *Natural History* (Cambridge, Mass.: Harvard University Press, 1942), p. 507—13.

43. L. Annaeus Seneca, *Opera* III, *Dialogi* IX, ed. Carolus Fickert (Lipsiae: Sumptibus Librariae Weidmannianae, 1845), 355—57. So also his *Ad Paullinum de brevitate vitae*, ibid., 267—312.

44. Plutarch, *Moralia*, (Cambridge, Mass.: Harvard University Press, 1957), pp. 487—533.

45. M. Tullius Cicero, *Tusculanarum Disputationum ad M. Brutum. Liber Quintus*, Ch. 1, lines 20—24; *M. Tullii Ciceronis Opera* (Turici: Sumptibus ac Typis Orellii Füsslini et Sociorum, 1861), IV, 331.

46. Matthew Arnold, *Poems* (London: Macmillan and Co., 1903), I, 306; from *Obermann Once More, Elegiac Poems*.

47. Innocent's treatise is in Migne, P. L., CCXVII, cols. 701—46. A new English publication provides a translation of both Innocent III's and Manetti's treatises in *Two Views of Man;* Pope Innocent III, *On the Misery of Man*, and Giannozzo Manetti, *On the Dignity of Man*, ed. Bernard Murchland (New York: Frederick Ungar Publishing Co., 1966).

48. See Millard Meiss, *Painting in Florence and Siena after the Black Death* (New York: Harper Torchbook, 1964), p. 74.

49. Hans Baron, "Franciscan Poverty and Civic Wealth as Factors in the Rise of Humanistic Thought," *Speculum*, XIII, 1 (Jan. 1938), 12. In n. 3 Baron locates Conversino's *De miseria* as Codex IX, 11, fol. 55v-57v, of the Querini-Stampaglia Library in Venice.

50. *Confessions* X, 8, 15, cited from Petrarch, *Ascent of Mount Ventoux*, Ernst Cassirer and others, *Renaissance Philosophy of Man*, p. 44.

51. See the account in Ernest Hatch Wilkins, *Petrarch's Eight Years in Milan* (Cambridge, Mass.: Mediaeval Academy of America, 1958), p. 66, and in his *Life of Petrarch* (Chicago: University of Chicago Press, 1961), pp. 138—40.

52. Siegfried Wenzel, "Petrarch's *Accidia*," *Studies in the Renaissance*, VIII (1961), 36—48, an excellent study, draws the lines too sharply, however, in concluding that Petrarch's *accidia* belongs no longer to the system of Christian moral theology but to the pursuit of secular wisdom.

53. See Richard Walzer, *Greek into Arabic. Essays on Islamic Philosophy* (Oxford: B. Cassirer, 1962), pp. 142—57.

54. See the unpublished dissertation (Stanford Univ., 1965) by Noel Brann, "The Renaissance Passion of Melancholy."

63

55. Of the extensive contemporary literature on melancholy in the Renaissance a few titles of special interest are: Lawrence Babb, *The Elizabethan Malady* (Lansing: Michigan State University Press, 1951); Rudolf and Margot Witt-kower, *Born Under Saturn* (New York: Random House, 1963); Raimond Klibansky, *Saturn and Melancholy* (London: Thomas Nelson, 1964); Erwin Panofsky and F. Saxl, *Albrecht Dürer*, 2 vols. (Princeton: Princeton University Press, 1945), I, 156—69. In the brilliant recent study of Frances A. Yates, *Giordano Bruno and the Hermetic Tradition* (Chicago: University of Chicago Press, 1964), pp. 102—3, 110—11, 144—45, the author stresses the Hermetic sources for the dignity-of-man theme in Pico. The Hermetic root of the melancholy theme might also be sought there.

56. Lauro Martines, *The Social World of the Florentine Humanists* (Princeton: Princeton University Press, 1963), documents the solid footing of the Florentine humanists in their society, using 11 full studies and 45 special cases to demonstrate that the humanists were men of means connected by family ties and position in the state to the upper classes of society. The work of Martines has in effect reduced to shambles Alfred von Martin's *Sociology of the Renaissance* (New York: Oxford University Press, 1944). The book of Trinkaus, *Adversity's Noblemen: The Italian Humanists on Happiness* (New York: Columbia University Press, 1940), while mistakenly still basing its explanation of the insecurity of the humanists on the older notions of their uncertain status in society, is still of great value in presenting systematically the humanists' treatises in a thorough survey of their writings on this theme.

57. Berthold L. Ullman, *Coluccio Salutati de seculo et religione* (Florence: In aedibus L. S. Olschki, 1957). For an analysis of this work see B. L. Ullman, *The Humanism of Coluccio Salutati* (Padua: Editrice Antenore, 1963), pp. 26—30, 90—92. Charles Trinkaus, "Humanist Treatises on the Status of the Religious: Petrarch, Salutati, Valla," *Studies in the Renaissance* XI (1962), 20—34, suggests that Salutati used new arguments classical in origin, such as the poverty and vigor of early Rome, to support the promonastic arguments and saw no contradiction between his humanist values and the received traditional views of medieval asceticism, as a layman willingly granting spiritual superiority to the regular life of the religious.

58. Hans Baron, ed. "Isagogicon moralis disciplinae," *Leonardo Bruni Aretinos humanistische-philosophische Schriften* (Leipzig, 1928), 20—41, cited in Trinkaus, *Adversity's Noblemen*, p. 43.

59. *De miseria humanae conditionis, Libri II, Opera omnia* (Basel, 1538), pp. 86 to 131, cited in Trinkaus, *Adversity's Noblemen*, p. 44.

60. Francesco Guicciardini, *Ricordi*, 161, cited in Buck, *Rangstellung*, p. 69.

61. Victor Michael Hamm, trans. *Pico della Mirandola. Of Being and Unity (De ente et uno)*, (Milwaukee: Marquette University Press, 1943), pp. 4 ff.

62. Both Pico selections are cited from the excellent article of John Warwick Montgomery, "Eros and Agape in the Thought of Giovanni Pico della Mirandola," *Concordia Theological Monthly*, XXXII, 12 (Dec. 1961), 743—45. For a systematic presentation of Pico's theology, including such concepts as his understanding of original sin, proceeding from Pico's view of man, analyzing his dependence on Platonic and patristic sources, and treating the more formally theological aspect of his thought, see the work of Engelbert Monnerjahn, *Giovanni Pico della Mirandola. Ein Beitrag zur philosophischen Theologie des italienischen Humanismus* (Wiesbaden: Franz Steiner Verlag GMBH, 1960).

63. Otis H. Green, "The Concept of Man in the Spanish Renaissance," *The Rice Institute Pamphlet, Renaissance Studies*, XLVI, 4 (Jan. 1960), 46. Jan Huizinga, *The Waning of the Middle Ages* (London: Edward Arnold & Co.,

1937), and Rudolf Stadelmann, *Vom Geist des Ausgehenden Mittelalters* (Halle/Salle: Max Niemeyer Verlag, 1929), have characterized the culture of northern Europe, France, the Court of Burgundy, and the empire in dour terms as one of disintegration, pessimism, skepticism, resignation, as well as partially of emancipation.

64. Paul Bühler, *Die Anfechtung bei Martin Luther* (Zürich: Zwingli Verlag, 1942) is a good example of the extensive literature on the question. An uncomplicated treatment is Roland H. Bainton, "Luther's Struggle for Faith," *Church History*, XVII (Sept. 1948), 193—206. Heinz Bluhm, "Luther's View of Man in His First Published Work," *Harvard Theological Review*, XL (April 1948), 103—22, describes the emergence of the Augustinian-Pauline view of man in Luther's *Die Sieben Busspsalmen*, spring 1517.

65. Cited in Eric R. Dodds, *The Greeks and the Irrational* (Berkeley: University of California Press, 1951), p. 254.

66. *Complete Poetry and Selected Prose of John Donne*, ed. John Hayward (Bloomsbury, Nonesuch Press, 1929), p. 202. See the chapter on "The Assimilation of Copernican Astronomy," Thomas S. Kuhn, *The Copernican Revolution* (Cambridge, Mass.: Harvard University Press, 1957), pp. 185—228.

67. *Pensées*, ed. Léon Brunschvicq (Paris: Librairie Hachette et cie, 1904), II, 126, fragment 205.

68. "Within the Indeterminate Universe," *Sequoia*, VII, 3 (1962), 29.

69. Burckhardt, *Force and Freedom*, p. 300.

70. "Alienation and the Decline of Utopia," *The American Scholar*, XXIX, 2 (Spring 1960), 1.

71. (New York: Random House, 1961), pp. 98, 101, et passim.

72. Adolf Harnack, *Martin Luther in seiner Bedeutung für die Geschichte der Wissenschaft und der Bildung* (Giessen, 1911), p. 28.

73. Gerhard Szczesny, "The Future of Unbelief," in *The Fate of Man*, ed. Crane Brinton (New York: George Braziller, 1961), p. 23.

74. *Menschliches, Allzumenschliches*, II, *Nietzsches Werke* (Leipzig: C. C. Naumann, 1900), III, 205; Zweite Abteilung: "Der Wanderer und sein Schatten," No. 18: *Der Moderne Diogenes*.

75. Bk. V, Chs. iii, iv, *The Ante-Nicene Fathers*, II, 448.

76. WA, Tr II, 2342a, cited in *What Luther Says*, ed. Ewald M. Plass (St. Louis: Concordia Publishing House, 1959), III, 1244, Nos. 3966—67.

77. WA XVIII, 605, 32.

78. "Summa summarum: res non sunt in manu nostra, sed Dei." WA XX, 47, 16.

79. WA XX, 190, 3 and 18 ff.: "Qui vult versari in medio mundo et servare *cor pacatum et quietum, das ist ein Kunst.*"

80. WA XX, 152, 6: ". . . cum plantata est fides, hoc agendum est, ut Christiani sint negociocissimi erga proximum et prorsus nullum hic agant Sabbatum sed sint Zelotae bonorum operum, ardeant in charitate erga proximum et Sabbatum tantum agant coram Deo." On Luther's commentary on Ecclesiastes see the excellent study of Eberhard Wölfel, *Luther und die Skepsis. Eine Studie zur Kohelet-Exegese Luthers* (Munich: Christian Kaiser Verlag, 1958), pp. 39, 52, 120, 173—74, 197, 232—33. See also Horst Beintker "Die Überwindung der Anfechtung durch den Glauben," *Die Überwindung der Anfechtung bei Luther* (Berlin: Evangelische Verlagsanstalt, 1954), 115—79.

81. Luther to Elector Frederick of Saxony, Feb. 24, 1522, *Luther: Letters of Spiritual Counsel*, ed. Theodore G. Tappert (Philadelphia: The Westminster Press, 1955), p. 140.

82. WA, Br V, 399—400. On this exchange of correspondence see H. Fausel, "Luther und Melanchthon während des Augsburger Reichstags," *Theologische Aufsätze. Karl Barth zum 50. Geburtstag* (Munich: Chr. Kaiser Verlag, 1936), 405—16.

83. WA, Br VII, 104—6, trans. in Tappert, *Letters of Spiritual Counsel*, p. 96. See also Luther's letter to Jonas von Stockhausen on fighting melancholy, Tappert, *Letters*, pp. 88—90.

84. WA, Tr IV, No. 4857, versus the *Vita solitaria;* WA, Tr II, No. 1270, on how God hates our afflictions when they drive us to despair.

85. WA, Br VIII, 79, 80, trans. in Tappert, *Letters*, pp. 99—100.

86. *Medieval History. The Life and Death of a Civilization* (New York: The Macmillan Co., 1963).

87. *The Philosophy of Hegel*, ed. Carl J. Friedrich (New York: Random House, 1954), p. xxxix.

88. *An Essay on Man* (London: Methuen & Co. Ltd., 1950), pp. 53—56.

2

LUTHER'S NINETY-FIVE THESES
AND THE THEOLOGY OF THE CROSS

E. Gordon Rupp

W HATEVER WE THINK of the events which did or did not take place in Wittenberg on 31 October 1517,[1] I am sure it is meet and right that we commemorate the 450th anniversary of what happened the previous year, on 31 October 1516. For on that day, the eve of the Dedication Feast of the Castle Church, Luther preached in Latin, as was the custom on festal days, on the theme of the repentance of Zacchaeus and in the course of his sermon made some animadversions on indulgences.[2]

A few months before, in a sermon on the Tenth Sunday after Trinity, he had attacked indulgences even more directly in a sermon,[3] and his words had not been welcomed[4] by Frederick the Wise. Understandably, for the indulgences attached to the collection of relics in the Castle Church brought an ever-diminishing financial return to the Saxon coffers (about 41 florins a year) despite the constant accretion of sacred particles. But what makes 1516 worth celebrating is, I think, the fact that at this time, in his letters and his sermons even more strikingly than in his lectures, there emerges clearly Luther's theology of the cross, which underlies in turn his Ninety-five Theses of the following year. Without going into the enormous complexities about Luther's "breakthrough" about the righteousness of God, it seems clear to me that in 1516 some new experience of the Gospel lay immediately behind him and finds its expression in a series of utterances about the peace and joy of the Christian Gospel.

In 1516 Luther had raised the whole question of the theology and scope of indulgences. He had already contrasted to the "cheap grace" of these ecclesiastical dispensations the "costly grace" of genuine repentance. "Instandum est crucifixioni membrorum et mortificationi principiorum peccatorum, hoc est concupiscentiarum . . . diligenter attendendum, ne indulgentiae, id est satisfactione, fiant nobis causa securitatis et pigritiae et damnum interioris gratiae." [5]

At first sight Luther says nothing that other moralists had not pointed out. To many, perhaps to most of the readers of the Ninety-five Theses, what was in question was an area of doctrine where great ambiguity existed (Lortz's *Unklarheit,* which he takes to be a note of the age): the scholastic definition of penance, the doctrine of purgatory, the papal plentitude of power which canonists took to forbid any questioning at all of papal actions. Of all Luther's opponents — Tetzel, Wimpina, Prierias, even Eck — only one, Cajetan, seems to have sensed that something much deeper was at stake. Of the 41 propositions attributed to Luther and condemned in the bull *Exsurge Domine,* none touch the real dynamite, the real explosive, which is the theology of the cross.

Walther von Loewenich in his classic essay on *The Theology of the Cross* rightly says that it is not an isolated chapter in Luther's theology.[6] It is perhaps not so much an exposition of truth as a proportion of truth, a series of stresses and emphases, so that it is more like the key signature at the side of a piece of music than a set of notes in the score. But it is an all-important proportion, for it focuses revelation and redemption and the whole nature of the Christian life.

It is a theology we can detect in the first course of lectures that Luther gave on the Psalms, where we find such phrases as "the cross of Christ runs right through the Scriptures," and where we find his distinction based on Is. 28:31 between Christ's strange work and his own or proper work, and where the poignancy of Christ's sufferings and spiritual dereliction on our behalf is constantly underlined.[7] And it is a theology which Luther never needed to unlearn. It is powerfully expounded in a sermon he preached in the Castle Coburg in 1530 on Christ's sufferings in relation to the cross of Christians, and in fact it underlies the very last sermon he preached in 1546.[8]

Nonetheless it is a theology that emerges in its first freshness in 1516 in letters, sermons, and lectures during that year. It underlies the Ninety-five Theses and finds its clearest expression in the Explanations of the Ninety-five Theses,[9] which Luther wrote early in February 1518 and which were no mere afterthoughts, and finally in the Heidelberg Theses,[10] which Luther prepared for the debate during the chapter of his Order in April 1518 and which are perhaps the real, first theological manifesto of the Protestant Reformation.

Leaving aside the impressive weight of evidence in Luther's lecture material on Psalms,[11] Romans,[12] Galatians [13] and Hebrews,[14] we may notice three letters which Luther wrote in 1516. His letters to his two best friends, John Lang of Erfurt and George Spalatin, are at this time mostly about business and books and people, things on the surface of his mind.[15] But when as prior and district vicar he wrote pastorally to his brethren, he spoke from his heart. Hence the famous lines in his letter to George Spenlein on 8 April: "Therefore my sweet brother, learn Christ and Him crucified, learn to pray to Him saying, Thou Lord Jesus art my righteousness, but I am Thy sin: Thou hast taken on Thyself what Thou wast not, and given me what I was not." [16]

In the same month he wrote to another brother, George Leiffer, bidding him beware of trust in our own reason, which is the root of all unquiet: "The cross of Christ is distributed throughout the whole world and to each there certainly comes his share. Do not therefore cast it aside but rather take it up as an holy relic, kept not in a golden or silver reliquary but in a golden, that is, a gentle and loving heart." [17] We shall see how this thought is echoed in Thesis 58 of the Ninety-five.

Even more striking is a passage in a letter addressed to the unfortunate Michael Dressel, prior of the Augustinians in Neustadt, and soon to be deposed, warning him that the true peace of Christ dwells in the midst of turmoil and the complaints of enemies: "You say, with Israel, 'Peace! Peace!' where there is no peace. Say rather with Christ, 'Cross, cross,' and there is no cross! For then the cross ceases to be a cross when swiftly and joyfully you say, 'O Blessed Cross, incomparable Tree!' " [18] These words, 18 months later, would form the climax of the Ninety-five Theses. Further proof, if it were needed, of Luther's developed theology of the cross is to be found in the sermon he preached on St. Thomas' Day, 21 December 1516:

[Christ] cannot come to this his proper work unless he first undertakes a work which is strange and contrary to himself. . . . God's

69

strange work is the suffering of Christ and sufferings in Christ, the crucifixion of the old man and the mortification of Adam. God's proper work is the resurrection of Christ, justification in the Spirit, and the vivification of the new man . . . conformity with the image of the Son of God.[19]

There follows, arising from this distinction, one of Luther's first expositions of his mature dialectic between Law and Gospel, the way by which, as Hans Ehrenberg used to say, God saves us by a kind of pincer movement. When we have been brought to awareness of our desperate and guilty plight by the Law, we hear the Gospel. And then Luther says: "It is impossible not to rejoice. But this happens when the forgiveness of sins is proclaimed to grieving consciences . . . this good news is the altogether sweet and delightful mercy of God the Father, the Christ who is given to us." [20]

By 1516 Luther had taken the lead in his university with a new theological program, repudiating scholasticism and returning to the Bible "and the Old Fathers, especially St. Augustine." [21] He moved farther and farther away from the schoolmen, but he did not put in their place the intricate humanist philosophies of the Platonists, of Cusa, of Le Fèvre. This was in part because he had met another spiritual tradition of the late medieval church, which was itself, in its own right, a theology of the cross.

The word "mystic" is nebulous and perhaps open to misunderstanding, and so I prefer to use the 18th-century word "inward religion" to describe the revival of late medieval spirituality in Germany, which seems to have been a conflation of two sets of influences: the one, that of the "modern devotion," the other, of German mysticism.

In a series of studies in the University of Washington, William A. Landeen has traced the infiltration into Germany of the Dutch "modern devotion" with its "imitation of Christ" piety focused by the Brothers of the Common Life, and which, entering northwest Germany, infiltrated south at least as far as Tübingen, where it deeply influenced Gabriel Biel.[22]

We perhaps need somebody to do for German mysticism and the "Friends of God" what Landeen has done for the *devotio moderna*. It is possible that we might need to distinguish between a German Rhineland mysticism with its emphasis on conformity to Christ, and an older Thuringian emphasis on the "wounds of Jesus" going back to the Gertrudes and Mechthilds of the 12th century. At any rate it is clear that this kind of mystical influence touched a number of South-German scholars and theologians, among them Wimpfeling,

Oecolampadius, and above all Luther's friend and teacher Johann von Staupitz.[23]

I have little doubt that it was from this stream of Christian tradition rather than from scholasticism, even Thomist Augustinianism, that Staupitz drew the succession of comfortable words that helped this brilliant young protégé, Luther, when he struggled in deep waters. It was very likely Staupitz who drew his attention (as he in turn directed Spalatin) to the edition of Tauler's sermons published in 1508.[24] At a striking point in his *Explanations of the Ninety-five Theses* Luther turns aside to pay tribute to Tauler:

> I know that this teacher is unknown to the schools of theologians and is probably despised by them; but even though he has written entirely in the German vernacular, I have found in him more solid and sincere theology than is found in all the scholastic teachers of all the universities or than can be found in their propositions.[25]

Interestingly, this provoked from John Eck and Ambrosius Catherinus the statements that they had never heard of Tauler — an illumination perhaps of the limits of the infiltration of this tradition, which had reached Augsburg but perhaps not Ingolstadt. Berndt Moeller says plausibly of Tauler and Luther that he was *beeindrukt* rather than *beeinfluszt* (impressed rather than influenced).[26] And it is true that Tauler's impact on Luther was not decisive and catastrophic, as the same book seems to have been on Thomas Muentzer. Nonetheless, as Moeller also suggests, Luther at this time incurred a debt to Tauler which he never repudiated.[27]

There are books we read but which affect us little. We pause and go on our way. But sometimes, perhaps at most half a dozen times in a lifetime, there are books that meet us, which seem to have been lying in wait for us and which meet us at just the right time and place. Six months before they would have meant nothing at all. Now they speak to our condition, and this not so much because they tell us something new but that they tell us something we have always known; they confirm our own gropings and intuitions, they illuminate, and life is never quite the same again. Perhaps this is how it was with Luther and Tauler's sermons.

His copy survived with its marginal notes, and the notes themselves are disappointing, concerned with mental prayer, with ecstasy, with the synteresis. But suddenly in one line we have the whole theology of the cross: "Thus we know that God does not act in us, unless He first destroys us (i. e., by the cross and sufferings)." [28]

And then there was the *Deutsch Theologie*, or the *Theologia Ger-*

manica.[29] This was Luther's own discovery, and he took it to be a kind of distilled essence of Tauler, though in fact it came from the Teutonic Order in Frankfurt and has some interestingly different nuances from Tauler. But Luther must have found it in a Thuringian monastery, and when he published the first edition in 1516, his own very first publication, the title embodies the theology of the cross: "A nobly spiritual book. Of the right distinction and understanding of what the old and the new man consists. What it is to be a child of Adam and of God, and how Adam must die in us and Christ rise again." [30]

It is interesting that the frontispiece of Tauler's sermons shows a picture of the cross. The first edition of the *Deutsch Theologie* of 1516 shows the crucifixion, but the first complete edition of 1518 shows Christ risen and ascended. Thus the two pictures embody Christ's strange work of the cross and His own work, the resurrection.

It is against this background of Luther's own thought and experience, his Biblical theology, to which he added the comments of Augustine, and now his contact with late medieval German spirituality, that we must set his Ninety-five Theses: no afterthoughts, no external affair of an ecclesiastical scandal, but something much deeper, a crisis of conscience, for one Christian man first and then for the whole church of God.

The first thesis rings out like the opening notes of *Ein' feste Burg:*

When Our Lord and Master Jesus Christ said "Repent!" he willed
the entire life of believers to be one of penitence.

This dominates the first five theses, and to it Luther will return at the very end of his disputation.

Here the whole Christian life is set under the sign of the cross, of repentance. "This recovery or hatred of oneself should involve one's whole life. . . . He who does not take his cross and follow me, is not worthy of me." [31]

Luther found his definition of "repentance" rather than the ambiguous *poenitentiam agere* of the Vulgate confirmed when he read the new Greek Testament of Erasmus. But in his earlier preaching in 1516 he had already glossed "repent" with "be converted." And in the famous letter in which he dedicated his exposition of the Ninety-five Theses to Staupitz, he explained the real occasion of his mental illumination at this point:

It sounded like a voice from heaven when we heard you say that
a true repentance begins only with the love of righteousness and of
God; and that this love which others hold to be the final end and

consummation of penitence is rather its beginning . . . these words of yours stuck in my mind like some "sharp arrow of the mighty." I began to look up the passages of Scripture which teach penitence and I soon found my heart flooded with happiness . . . for so God's commandments grow sweet indeed when we learn to read them not so much in books as in the Wounds of our Beloved Redeemer.[32]

But if Luther rejects in the next thesis the view that "repent!" indicates the threefold sacrament of penance as scholastically defined, he does not subjectivize it away but defines it in terms of the theology of the cross.

If a person's whole life is one of repentance and a cross of Christ . . . then it is evident that the cross continues until death. . . . The cross of repentance must continue until, according to the Apostle, the body of sin is destroyed and the inveterate first Adam along with its image, perishes, and the new Adam is perfected in the image of God.[33]

But if penitence begins when a man turns from himself to the wounds of Jesus, the annihilation of his own self-righteousness is no momentary thing. In the beginning of his lectures on Romans Luther declares this breaking down of human self-sufficiency and self-righteousness to be the whole theme of the epistle and of his own massive commentary.[34]

A number of essays by famous theologians have traced the development of this theme in Luther's early lectures from the Psalms in 1514 to Hebrews in 1518, from the Augustinian notions of self-hatred and accusation of self, throughout the disciplines of humiliation to true humility — until a complicated process described with many and changing technical terms is caught up in the great master word "faith," for Luther in these years moved from an amazingly subtle and complex scholasticism to an ever simpler, plainer Biblical religion.

Critics of Luther, in his own time and in our day, have suggested that he delighted too much in hyperbole and paradox. And it is true that this is a mark of 15th-century mystical literature: the writings of Nicholas of Cusa and the sermons of Tauler. But the paradoxes of the theology of the cross come from Scripture and lie at the heart of Luther's doctrine. God Himself, according to St. Paul, has revealed the wisdom of God in the foolishness of the cross, and His strength in weakness. There is, therefore, a hiddenness of revelation — God is *absconditus* at the very point where He is seen by faith but not by reason. There is the further paradox and contradiction between the wrath and the mercy of God, between His strange work and His

73

own work, since it is the one God at work all the time. There is the same ambiguity, the same hiddenness about the life of the church and the story of the redemption of each Christian man. To grasp this is indeed the very office of Christian faith, which believes against appearance and holds to things unseen.[35]

There are years of theological investigation and much distress of soul behind the short phrase, therefore, in Thesis 7: "God remits guilt to no one unless at the same time he humbles himself in all things." And he expounds this more fully in the *Resolutiones:*

> When God begins to justify a man, he first of all condemns him; him whom he wishes to raise up, he destoys; whom he wishes to heal, he smites; and the one to whom he wishes to give life, he humbles and terrifies him into the knowledge of himself . . . in short God works a strange work that he may work his own work.[36]

But the theology of the cross is also a theology of conscience: the conscience bruised by sin and under the wrath of God: the forgiven conscience at peace. (It is remarkable how often the word "peace" occurs in Luther's letters during this time.)

It is when a man believes the word of Christ, which is the absolution given by a priest but which Luther insists is primarily important as a Word from Christ, that he receives "this peace . . . that sweetest power, for which, from the depth of our hearts, we ought to give the greatest thanks to God."[37]

That the good fight of faith is a battle, often an agony, belongs to Luther's doctrine of *Anfechtung*. At this time he underlines the anguish that may come to souls in this life and which is a foretaste of eternal torment. Here he is debtor to Staupitz, whose teaching about a "resignation to hell" Luther expounds at some length in his lectures on Romans, as well as from Tauler. But this, too, is a Christocentric doctrine, for the sufferings of the human soul are related to the sufferings of Christ in our behalf. Luther attacked the externalization of the notion of punishment, especially in regard to purgatory, and regarded this as one of the most mischievous errors of the indulgence sellers. For Luther it is fear and despair that are the true pains of purgatory and hell. "Some individuals have tasted these punishments in this life, especially those of hell. . . . For what else does John Tauler teach in his German sermons than the sufferings of these punishments."[38]

There follows the famous "I knew a man" passage which some have thought to be the image of Luther's own experience, of an agony so great that

. . . if they had been sustained or had lasted for half an hour, even for one tenth of an hour, he would have perished completely and all of his bones would have been reduced to ashes. At such a time God seems terribly angry, and with him the whole creation. At such a time there is no flight, no comfort, either within or without, but all things accuse.[39]

Luther then discusses the fear of death, which he knows is such that a mere paper safeguard like an indulgence becomes frivolous and irrelevant and therefore engenders despair by failing in the moment of real *Anfechtung*. But this fear is the sting of punishment and it is overcome by love.

Punishment and death are not grievous to one who loves, because they have been overcome by love and the Spirit.

Indulgences do not remove fear but increase it. . . . However, God has purposed to have children who are fearless . . . but who through trust in his grace shall overcome and despise everything and make light of punishments and death. He hates cowards who are confounded by a fear of all things, even by the sound of a fluttering leaf.[40]

At Thesis 26 he returns to the theme of true repentance as distinct from remorse:

True sorrow must spring from the goodness and mercies of God, especially from the wounds of Christ, so that man comes first of all to a sense of his own ingratitude in view of divine goodness and thereupon to hatred of himself and love of the kindness of God. . . . Then he will hate sin, not because of the punishment but because of his regard for the goodness of God; and when he has perceived this he will be preserved from despair and will despise himself most ardently, yet joyfully.[41]

At Thesis 32 Luther puts the counterpoint of the true preachers against the indulgence sellers. "Above all," say the true preachers, "believe in Christ, trust in Him and repent, take up your cross, follow Christ, mortify your flesh, learn not to be afraid of punishments and death. Above all else, love one another, serve one another, even by neglecting indulgences." [42]

Thesis 37 affirms that the true Christian, living or dead, shares the benefits of Christ, and it moves Luther to a noble exposition:

A Christian can . . . claim all things in Christ. Righteousness, strength, patience, humility, even all the merits of Christ are his through the unity of the Spirit through faith in him. All his sins are no longer his; but through that same unity with Christ everything is swallowed up in him. And this is the confidence that Christians have and our real joy of conscience, that by means of faith our sins become no longer ours but Christ's upon whom God placed the sins of all of us. He took upon Himself our sins. . . . All the righteousness of Christ becomes ours. He places his hand upon us and all is well with us. . . . He spreads his cloak and covers us . . . blessed Savior throughout all ages. Amen.[43]

Then he adds, as it were, a footnote to this splendid passage: "Indeed, this most pleasant participation in the benefits of Christ and joyful change of life do not take place except by faith." [44]

Thesis 58 is another paradox of the theology of the cross:

. . . the merits of Christ and the saints . . . always work grace for the inner man, and the cross, death, and hell for the outer man.[45]

He returns to his dialectic of the true and of the strange work of Christ:

The merits of Christ perform an alien work . . . in that they effect the cross, labor, all kinds of punishment, finally death and hell in the flesh, to the end that the body of sin is destroyed. . . . For whoever is baptized in Christ and is renewed shall be prepared for punishments, crosses, and deaths. . . . Just so must we be conformed to the image of the Son of God.[46]

It is scholastic theology which has got it all upside down:

A theologian of the cross (that is, one who speaks of the crucified and hidden God), teaches that punishments, crosses, and death are the most precious treasury of all and the most sacred relics which the Lord of this theology himself has consecrated and blessed, not alone by the touch of his most holy flesh but also by the embrace of his exceedingly holy and divine will, and he has left these relics here to be kissed, sought after, and embraced. . . . Yet, so holy are these relics and so precious these treasures, that . . . these can only be preserved in heavenly, living, rational, immortal, pure, and holy vessels, that is, in the hearts of the faithful which are incomparably more precious than every piece of gold and every precious stone.[47]

Thus, while the "theologian of glory still receives money . . . the theologian of the cross . . . offers the merits of Christ freely." [48]

At Thesis 62, the noblest of them all, that "the true treasure of the church is the most holy gospel of the glory and grace of God," he comes to another fine outburst:

Christ has left nothing to the world except the gospel. . . . the gospel is a preaching of the incarnate Son of God, given to us without any merit on our part for salvation and peace. It is a word of salvation, a word of grace, a word of comfort. . . . Through the Law we have nothing except an evil conscience, a restless heart, a troubled breast because of our sins, which the law points out but does not take away . . . the light of the gospel comes and says . . . "behold the Lamb of God, who takes away the sin of the world" [John 1:29]. Behold the one who alone fulfills the law for you, whom God has made to be your righteousness, sanctification, wisdom, and redemption, for all those who believe in him [1 Cor. 1:30]. When the sinful conscience hears this sweetest messenger, it comes to life again, shouts for joy while leaping about full of confidence, and no longer fears death, the types of punishments associated with death, or hell.[49]

Thesis 63 affirms that this true treasure is hateful to men because it makes first things last:

The gospel destroys those things which exist, it confounds the strong, it confounds the wise and reduces them to nothingness, to weakness, to foolishness, because it teaches humility and a cross.[50]

The last four theses are a kind of coda to this symphony. They are left unexpended in the Explanations — and they were left unexpounded by Prierias, though they were part of the original theses. In fact they sum up the theology of the cross, and we have seen that they take up ideas and even words which Luther had used in earlier letters to his friends. Luther had insisted in his very first lectures that the great vice of contemporary religion was a false security, a false peace. It was this deadly thing which the indulgence sellers were offering, and it is the complete opposite of the theology of the cross, which calls the Christians joyfully to endure suffering.

92

Away then with all those prophets who say to the people of Christ "Peace, peace," and there is no peace! [Jer. 6:14].

93

Blessed be all those prophets who say to the people of Christ, "Cross, cross," and there is no cross!

94

Christians should be exhorted to be diligent in following Christ, their head, through penalties, death, and hell;

95

And thus be confident of entering into heaven through many tribulations rather than through the false security of peace [Acts 14:22].[51]

The theology of the cross stands, then, for a proportion of faith:

it is rooted and grounded in the New Testament and above all in St. Paul. If it found striking confirmation, genuine affinities, real cross-fertilization from the theology of the cross of German mysticism, it is because that too had its roots in the New Testament.

Thomas Muentzer also had a theology of the cross; but the proportions are different, as well as the consequences he drew from them. And it is in the contrast between Muentzer and Luther's use of Tauler and the *Theologia Germanica* that we see that behind Luther's theology there was the long period of research and study and prayer, the wrestling with the Bible and the study of St. Augustine. It was perhaps easy for Luther's opponents to miss the undertones of the Ninety-five Theses to which we have listened. But his abundant writings of the next years in the end enlightened them that here in the Ninety-five Theses is something deeper than a protest against an abuse and a scandal. There is a new awareness of the height and depth, the poignancy and joy of the Christian religion. It is in the light of it that the cheap graces of indulgences are shown to be trivial and shabby irrelevances. Here was a new, serious, earnest appreciation of the depth of the human predicament, a new assurance that God has provided the remedy which would win more and more numbers of men and women to listen to His message, to find for themselves the power behind the clarion call — "The Cross Is Our Theology."

NOTES

1. This essay is not concerned with the debate sparked off by Erwin Iserloh, *Luthers Thesenanschlag — Tatsache oder Legende?* Institut für Europäische Geschichte, Vortrag, No. 31 (Wiesbaden: Franz Steiner Verlag, 1962). Yet if Luther took this public step in 1516, is it not plausible that a year later, facing a vaster scandal, he should have turned from words to act, from a sermon to the posting of a disputation? Iserloh's strongest point, that by writing to Albert of Mainz Luther had made the matter *sub judice*, ignored the fact that Luther wrote to his archbishop concerning the "Instructions to Commissaries" which bore Albert's coat of arms.

2. WA I, 94 ff. The date is not absolutely certain.

3. WA I, 65 ff.

4. Luther refers to this sermon in his *Wider Hans Worst* (1541), WA LI, 469 to 572; *Against Hanswurst*, LW XLI, 185—256.

5. WA I, 66, 19.

6. *Luthers Theologia Crucis* (Munich: Chr. Kaiser Verlag, 1933). There is a good chapter in Giovanni Miegge, *Lutero: L'uomo e il pensiero finoalla dieta di Worms* (1483—1521), (Torre Pellice: Liberia ed. Claudiana, 1946), pp. 144—47. See also Philip S. Watson, *Let God Be God! An Interpretation of*

the Theology of Martin Luther (Philadelphia: Muhlenberg Press, 1947), Part IV, pp. 102—48; E. Gordon Rupp, *The Righteousness of God: Luther Studies* (London: Hodder and Stoughton, 1953), pp. 208, 218 ff. There is an interesting discussion of the evidence reviewed in this paper in Ernst Bizer, *Fides ex auditu: eine Untersuchung der Gerechtigkeit Gottes durch Martin Luther* (Neukirchen Moers: Verlag der Buchhandlung des Erziehungsvereins, 1958). See also Gerhard Pfeiffer, "Das Ringen des jungen Luther um die Gerechtigkeit Gottes," *Luther-Jahrbuch 1959,* ed. Franz Lau (Berlin: Lutherisches Verlagshaus, 1959), XXVI, 25—55.

7. WA III, 246, 19 ff.; also WA III, 63, 1.

8. "Sermon at Coburg on Cross and Suffering, 1530," LW LI, 197—208; "The Last Sermon, Eisleben, 1546," ibid., LI, 383—92; see also "Sermon at the Baptism of Bernhard von Anhalt, 1540," ibid., LI, 315—29, especially p. 329.

9. Now happily accessible in English in LW XXXI, 83—252.

10. WA I, 350—65; LW XXXI, 39—70; LCC XVI, 276—307.

11. WA III and IV. Luther lectured on the Psalms from the beginning of the summer semester of 1513 until the end of the winter semester of 1515.

12. WA LVI; LCC XV. Luther began his lectures on Romans at Easter of 1515 and completed them in early September 1516.

13. WA II, 451—618; LW XXVII, 163—410. Luther lectured on Galatians from 27 Oct. 1516 to 13 March 1517.

14. WA LVII/3, 1-238; LCC XVI, 29—250. Luther's lectures on Hebrews were delivered from March 1517 to March 1518.

15. See, e. g., ep. 6 to Spalatin, 24 Aug. 1516; ep. 10 to John Lang, 26 Oct. 1516. LW XLVIII, 17—18, 27—32.

16. WA, Br I, 35, 24; LW XLVIII, 12. To George Spenlein, 8 April 1516.

17. WA, Br I, 37, 15. To George Leiffer 15 April 1516.

18. WA, Br I, 47, 34. To Michael Dressel 23 June 1516.

19. WA I, 111; LW LI, 19; Elmer Carl Kiessling, *The Early Sermons of Luther and Their Relation to the Pre-Reformation Sermon* (Grand Rapids, Mich., 1935), pp. 96—97.

20. WA I, 113; LW LI 20.

21. Ernest G. Schwiebert, *Luther and His Times: The Reformation from a New Perspective* (St. Louis: Concordia Publishing House, 1950), p. 296; see pp. 294—96.

22. "The Beginnings of the *Devotio Moderna* in Germany," *Research Studies of the University of Washington,* XIX (1951), 161—202; 221—53; idem, "The *Devotio Moderna* in Germany," ibid., XXI (1953), 275—309; ibid., XXII (1954), 57—75. See also idem, "Martin Luther and the *Devotio Moderna* in Herford," *The Dawn of Modern Civilization: Studies in Renaissance, Reformation and Other Topics,* ed. Kenneth A. Strand (Ann Arbor, Mich.: Ann Arbor Publishing Co., 1962), pp. 145—64; Heiko A. Oberman, *The Harvest of Medievil Theology: Gabriel Biel and Late Medieval Nominalism* (Cambridge, Mass.: Harvard University Press, 1963).

23. In Ernst Wolf, *Staupitz und Luther: Ein Beitrag zur Theologie des Johannes von Staupitz und deren Bedeutung für Luthers theologischen Werdegang* (Leipzig, 1927), there is abundant evidence of Staupitz's use of the technical terms of the mystic *theologia crucis,* conformity with Christ, resignation to hell, and renunciation, or *Gelassenheit.*

24. For the best modern edition of Tauler's sermons see Johann Tauler, *Predigten:*

vollständige Ausgabe, ed. Georg Hofmann (Freiburg: Herder und Herder, 1961).

25. LW XXXI, 129.

26. "Tauler und Luther," *La mystique rhénane* (Paris Presses Universitaires de France, 1963), pp. 157—68.

27. Ibid. See also Robert H. Fife, *The Revolt of Martin Luther: A Biography Covering the Years until the Diet of Worms* (London: Oxford University Press, 1957), pp. 218—20, 232, 258. References to Tauler are given in WA LVIII, and Otto Scheel, *Dokumente zu Luthers Entwicklung,* 2d rev. ed. (Tübingen: Verlag von J. C. B. Mohr [Paul Siebeck], 1929), pp. 12, 24, 25, 26, 283, 296, 315.

28. WA IX, 98. See also WA I, 153; Luther, *Werke in Auswahl,* ed. Otto Clemen (Berlin: de Gruyter, 1951), V, 34 ff.; Emmanuel Hirsch, *Luther Studien* (Gütersloh, 1955), II, 99 ff.

29. See H. Hermelink, "Text und Gedankengang der Theologia Deutsch" in *Aus Deutschlands kirchlicher Vergangenheit: Festschrift zum 70. Geburtstag von Th. Brieger* (Leipzig, 1912).

30. See also "Preface to the Complete Edition of a German Theology, 1518," LW XXXI, 73—76; Georg Baring, *Bibliographie der Ausgaben der Theologia Deutsch* (Baden-Baden, 1963), where a fascimile of the first edition is given.

31. "Explanations," LW XXXI, 84.

32. *Reformation Writings of Martin Luther: The Basis of the Reformation,* trans. and ed. Bertram Lee Woolf (New York: Philosophical Library, 1953), I, 57. See also "Explanations, LW XXI, 160, Thesis 26: "True sorrow must spring from the goodness of God, especially from the wounds of Christ." In 1515 Staupitz published a tract "On the Imitation of the Voluntary Death of Christ," which Luther must have read. E. Wolf, *Staupitz und Luther;* Theodor Kolde, *Die deutsche Augustiner-Kongregation und Johann von Staupitz* (Gotha, 1879).

33. "Explanations," LW XXXI, 89.

34. LCC XV, 3; see WA III, IV, LV, LVI, LVII for the Romans commentary.

35. There are beautiful images of this in Luther's lectures on Hebrews at this time. WA LVII, 215, 1; 238, 1; etc.; LCC XVI, 213, 233 f.

36. "Explanations," LW XXXI, 99. See Heidelberg Thesis 4, LW XXXI, 44; LCC XVI, 283: "And this is what Isaiah calls 'the strange work of God that he may work his own work' Isa. 28:21), (that means, that he may humble us in our own eyes and make us despair of ourselves, so that in his mercy he may exalt us and make us men of hope)."

37. "Explanations," LW XXXI, 101.

38. Ibid., pp. 128—29.

39. Ibid., pp. 128—30, Thesis 5. The quotation is from p. 129.

40. Ibid., p. 144.

41. Ibid., pp. 160—61.

42. Ibid., pp. 180—81.

43. Ibid., p. 190.

44. Ibid., pp. 190—91.

45. Ibid., p. 212.

46. Ibid., p. 225.

47. Ibid., pp. 225—26.

48. Ibid., p. 227.
49. Ibid., pp. 230—31.
50. Ibid., p. 232.
51. Ibid., p. 251.

3

A DIALOG OR CONVERSATION BETWEEN A FATHER AND HIS SON ABOUT MARTIN LUTHER'S DOCTRINE (1523)

Carl S. Meyer, Translator

INTRODUCTION

NDULGENCES were the object of Luther's proposition for debate,[1] posted on 31 October 1517.[2] They continued to draw fire from various sources in the ensuing years. One such salvo is the dialog here translated, dating from the year 1523.

This dialog, however, is more than an attack on indulgences. It is anticlerical, antipapal, anti-Roman. Its anticlericalism is economic; the greed of the Roman clergy is attacked. It is theological, too, for the privileged position claimed by the churchmen to ban or excommunicate is censured. A tinge of social democracy can be detected in it, evidencing a dissatisfaction with the social superiority claimed by the clergy. Opposition to pilgrimages, votive candles, chantry masses, mortmain is discernible.

The opposition to indulgences is greater, however, than the opposition to any of these and is dramatized in the "Dialog" by the burning of the indulgence letter. Even greater is the opposition to work-righteousness or the hope of meriting salvation.

Salvation by grace through faith in Christ's righteousness is the dominant theological theme of the tract. *Sola fide* and *sola gratia* are stressed. The universal priesthood of believers finds its place in the positive theological tenets set forth. So does *sola Scriptura*. The profusion of Scriptural references and citations makes the tract almost a handy compilation of texts for supporters of Luther's cause. The divine character of Scripture, its authority, and the writer's willingness to rely on it are evident throughout. Even though the Scripture passages are frequently quoted inexactly and sometimes do not seem to fit the argument, the lack of dialectic argumentation and the straightforward insistence on the primacy of the Word are notable.

The theology of the tract is not sophisticated. It is an elementary introduction to Luther's main teachings — sin and grace, faith and works, prayer and hope. Time and again favorable notice is taken of Luther. There are in the tract two brief references to the scholastics and a castigation of John Eck and several other German opponents of Luther. No reference is made to the opposition of the Parisian theologians or the royal theologian of England, Henry VIII. None of the other reformers is named. Luther and his Scripture-based teachings are given the limelight.

Skillfully the dialog leads to the climax of the father's wholehearted agreement with Luther's doctrine. The son has returned to Thuringia from the University of Wittenberg. He has resolved to convert his father to Luther's teachings. The dialog is rapid; there are only a few long monologs. It is lively, though not without repetitions. A bit of coarseness and an understandable inclination toward force on the father's part are present. Here and there one finds a bit of humor or a touch of irony. The son generally displays a warm, evangelical attitude. Sometimes the sentences are incomplete and no pretense is made to grammatical preciseness. Nor is there a sustained effort toward delineation of character. The dialog, not the speakers themselves, is important to the author.

The name of the author is unknown. Whoever he was he knew Luther's writings and the Scriptures. Probably he was or had been a student at the University of Wittenberg. The piece belongs to the pro-Lutheran propaganda pamphlets of the early 1520s. It is one of the 215 books published in Germany in 1523 favorable to Luther's cause, the same year in which some 183 books were published with Luther as actual or alleged author.

The translation attempts to preserve the semiformal character of the conversation and to reflect the popular flavor of the piece. Contractions, therefore, are used frequently and the many "etc's" are dropped. Paragraphing has been added. The Revised Standard Version of the Bible is generally used for citations, although the paraphrases in the document are maintained where they occur. Faithfulness to the original demands this, for they become part of the argumentation.

The translation is based on the edition by Otto Clemen, issued by Rudolf Haupt in Halle in 1906. Originally it was printed by Michael Buchfürer in Erfurt.[3] It has not previously been translated into English.

THE DISCOURSE OF A FATHER AND SON

The son comes wandering into his father's house and says: "Peace everlasting be to this house; God help you, my dear father."

Father: God bless you! See, you are welcome,[4] my dear son! Where are you coming from, dear son?

Son: I come from the Christian town of Wittenberg, from the highly learned Dr. Martin Luther.

Father: I'm very happy to hear that, Son.[5] But what is considered so good about him and about Christ's doctrine, so I presume, about which he is now writing and publishing?

Son: You surely must know very well that it pleases the laity in part. However, it displeases those priests and clergy, especially the bishops [6] and abbots, dogs, as the Holy Ghost calls them in Isaiah 56 [v. 10],[7] who can no longer bark, who in good days have filled their bellies with the blood and sweat of the poor sheep.[8] But I trust in God's mercy that it'll soon get better.

Father: Son, you speak altogether too rudely. Don't you know that also priests are holy? The pious lords (restrain yourself) have not deserved it. Don't talk so much!

Son: O ho, Father, I too am a priest and consecrated. Christ says so, Matthew 5 [v. 13]: "You are the salt of the earth." He does not say, "The priests are"; no, "You are." I also can absolve as well as any priest or monk, "All that you bind and loose on earth shall be bound and loosed in heaven."

Father: Ah, Son, that pertains to the priests and not to us, the laity.

Son: You heard that we are all priests. Now, though you don't want to, listen anyhow. Were the apostles also priests, to whom Christ their master spoke, and also to us? Doesn't Peter say, 1 Peter 2 [v. 9]: "You are a royal priesthood," that is, by faith in Jesus? He says that to all men who believe in Christ.

Father: Nevertheless we must follow the old custom, which our forefathers observed.

Son: Ah, Father, isn't that the old custom, which God and the apostles taught? It isn't new that you must hear God, believe His Gospel, Mark 1 [v. 15], Matth. 17 [v. 5], and not the sectaries,[9] humanists,[10] and evil Christians. In Jeremiah 23 [v. 3] [11] God points out plainly that one should follow Him and not parents, if they do not speak God's Word. Alas! I cry to God in heaven because the very oldest is berated as being new! There the enemy of the Gospel has thrown evil weeds and new, bad seed into the good, ancient seed.[12] Oh, if we only had had genuine Turks,[13] in these misleading preachers (on whom God have mercy), instead of false pastors.

Father: Oh, Son, what are you saying? The Turks would slaughter us with many kinds of torture.

Son: Dear Father, if we only had good pastors, who would preach to us the Gospel unadulterated by the teachings of men, so that we would believe in Christ and love Him, we would not be afraid of any Turk. They can kill only the body, Matt. 10 [v. 28], but they cannot kill the soul. But false pastors and preachers lead both body and soul away from God, our Savior.

Father: You talk sense and the truth; I've got to agree with you. I'll admit that the priests no longer preach for nothing but their own welfare, no matter what happens to souls. They do not understand and read the Scriptures, and they are such uncouth clods that they can scarce sing a requiem. They oppress and fleece the poor sheep.[14]

Son: That's true, Father; you're on the right track. Peter laid down his life for the sheep, according to Christ's example, as He indicated, John 10 [v. 11].[15] Likewise, God entrusted His sheep to Peter, John 21 [vv. 15-17], when He said to him: "If you love Me, feed My sheep." But these shepherds slip their heads out of the noose and abandon the poor sheep. They may yet find it better. I hope that the sheep may yet show the shepherds the pasture, that is the Gospel. That already is happening here and there. But listen how the Holy Ghost threatens those shepherds who do not tend His sheep properly! Thus He says to them, Ezek. 3 [v. 18]: "If you do not say to the sinners that they shall convert themselves from their evil ways, then I will require their blood at your hands."

Father: Nevertheless, they do say much about great sins. Indeed they frighten us and teach us to flee from sin and avoid it.

Son: Yes, they do that, but not correctly, since they teach us how we should help ourselves, as if we did not need Christ; and such teaching is a sheer perversion.

Father: O, what a stout statement that is! Speak on. Don't let anything sidetrack you.

Son: Peter, and also Paul, wrote about such false preachers. Thus Paul says in 2 Tim. 3 [vv. 1-2, 5]: "You should know this that in the last times men will arise who love themselves, are of a proud and haughty spirit, and have an appearance of faith, but deny and avoid its power." This is what Paul said to Timothy. About such people Christ also spoke, Matt. 24 [vv. 4, 5],[16] Luke 17 [vv. 1, 23] [17]; and Mark writes about them in his 13th chapter [v. 22]. There God says: "And if it were possible, they would mislead also the elect." [18] Alas, God, that is now being fulfilled. Therefore, dear father, believe only the Gospel and not the Thomists [19] and Coquinists! [20] For the Word of God will not allow anyone to add to it or subtract from it, Deut. 4 [v. 2]. And if the preachers do not preach the Gospel, then you surely get it in the neck.[21] They cry out to you about the pope's indulgences and commemorating of souls: "Aye, give that, endow an eternal Mass, then your soul will be saved." And so they want to save souls by works. Woe be to them! And you should not believe them when they say: "Yes, the peasants do not understand this." Don't you suppose that the God of the masses can dwell among the poor, despised peasants as well as among the priests and monks although they do not lie around in the churches as much as the monks and other Pharisees do, since they will be, and we all also will be, the temple of God through faith, as Paul says 1 Cor. 3 [v. 16]? [22]

Father: That's true. After all He always ate and drank with the poor sinners.[23]

Son: The Scriptures are full of that, as you have heard from your pastor (so I suppose) and daily will hear.

Father: Son, let me tell you something! Our pastor has so much to do with his "bible," the cook, that he pays little attention to the Bible. If he were to preach that, he would chatter about the Gospel of the kingdom of grace so that no one could understand him. If that were told him, he would reply: "Tomorrow you must fast; today is a vigil." With that the Gospel is left to lie; I cry to God about that. Tell me, I am hungry for it.

Son: God be praised that I hear someone say that he is hungry for the Gospel! Just hand me my Bible from the bench and listen first to Matthew 9 [vv. 9-13]. There we are told that when God received Matthew as His disciple, He ate with him in his house. Then the hypocrites said to Jesus' disciples: "Why does your Master eat with public sinners?" For there were many of them sitting at the table. Jesus heard that and said: "Those who are well do not need a physician, but the sick need one." He also says there: "I did not come to call the righteous, but sinners and evildoers."

In the same way God ate with Mary Magdalene [24] and Lazarus, as He was about to enter into His suffering, John 12 [vv. 1-2]; in like fashion, with many others about whom we are told throughout the Gospel.[25]

It is well to believe that God also now feeds the hungry and the poor with His Gospel and disregards the highly learned fools and dumb dogs, as Mary sang in the Magnificat, Luke 1 [v. 53]: "He has filled the hungry with good things, and the rich He has sent empty away."[26] Christ also says to the Pharisees, Matthew 21 [v. 43]: "The kingdom of God will be taken away from you and given to a nation producing the fruits of it." That comes alone through faith.

Father: So I see right well that one could fast himself to death and buy indulgences, and still he wouldn't be saved. Faith is being preached now in many places, that it alone saves.

Son: That is indeed true; faith alone saves, as St. Paul says Romans 5 [v. 1] [27] and Galatians 2 [v. 16].[28] The heart is unclean and wicked to begin with, and yet you want to be saved by works; after all, that is impossible. Therefore Peter said Acts 15 [v. 9] that hearts are cleansed by faith.[29] And when a person has faith, he must prove it by works. You must hear Christ, as we are told.[30] Thus it is written in Matthew 17 [v. 5]: "This is My beloved Son, hear Him." God there does not say: "Hear the monks or the humanists."[31] No! "Hear My Son,[32] who overcame your sins on the tree of the cross," as is written in Isaiah 53 [vv. 4-5].

Father: Ought one not to listen to St. Augustine [33] and Jerome [34] and others?

Son: If they agree entirely with the Gospel. For they erred in part, as they themselves admit.[35] Paul, Peter, John have interpreted the Gospel clearly enough to us, which resulted from divine revelation, as Paul shows in Galatians 1 [v. 12] and says: "I did not learn that from a man but from the revelation of Jesus Christ." John also testifies to that, 1 John 1 [vv. 1-3]. Peter does the same. Therefore we may not make glosses on the Gospel,[36] for these writings of Paul, Peter, and John agree with the Gospel.

Father: Therefore by the grace of God I also will follow them and will be a good Martinist.[37]

Son: No, not that. You must glory in God, as Paul says [1 Cor. 1: 31],[38] and not Martinist or Petrine, etc.[39] None of them redeemed you.[40] We have been so completely misled that the name of Christ no longer abides among us.

Father: How then were the pastors so hardened that they did not preach the Word of God to us?

Son: Listen, we deserved that because of our sins. God could have punished us much more severely than with false preachers and rulers, as He did the Children of Israel in the Old Testament (as will presently be shown). Therefore Zechariah 11 [v. 16] says: "For lo, I am raising up in the land a shepherd who does not care for the perishing, or seek the wandering, or heal the maimed, or nourish the sound, but devours the flesh of the fat ones, tearing off even their hoofs." You see from that, it results from our sins. Therefore, it is high time to pray out of a true faith that God may let His light, which He is, John 1 [v. 4],[41] shine again upon us poor sheep, that we do not do as God Himself laments, Jeremiah 2 [v. 13], where He says: "My people have committed two evils: they have forsaken Me, the fountain of living waters, and hewed out cisterns for themselves, broken cisterns that can hold no water." Those surely are men's laws, which after all cannot save. O Thou gracious God, what a noble Fountain that is, for from it flows Thy Old and New Testament, and besides that all that is good! That we have forsaken!

Father: Son, with that knowledge you want to influence me to believe that Word of God and not men's laws. For I see that for the Gospel one surrenders body, life, and spirit, as the saints did. For there a person loses nothing, as I see it; but he finds his reward in God, his Lord.

Son: Don't you see that I came to you to put the breastplate and weapon of faith on you, so that you can quench the fiery darts of the devil, as St. Paul says Ephesians 6 [v. 16]? Therefore, Father, if a person follows Christ, the Captain, faithfully in the warfare against the enemy and the courtesans [42] of the Gospel, then he finds and receives a treasure in heaven (which the Captain promises and gives as pay, Matthew 6 [v. 20]), a treasure which is not consumed nor rusts away.

That Captain we want to follow now, to pitch our tents under Him, believe in Him with a truly staunch faith, for which we will pray Him, and He will surely give it to us. Thus says the Captain in Deuteronomy,[43] Leviticus,[44] and in many places,[45] "I am your Guide and Ruler, follow My ways."

Father: Son, I will follow that Captain and stand by Him, as He gives me grace and otherwise accepts me.

Son: Aye, you must have no doubt about it; He will accept you as His child; if you will believe in Him with that faith which I will reveal to you with the help of God. For everyone who will fight under Him, will never taste death, as it is written in Matthew 16 [v. 28] and Mark 9 [v. 1]

Father: O God; I will be most happy to hear about this faith. You are here giving me real consolation and reviving of my soul, which no preacher or monk has given me for a long time. For the preachers also did not carry out the command, which Christ gave them in Mark, the final verses [16:15-16]. I cry out to God about that. It reads: "Go ye into all the world and preach the Gospel, and whoever believes and is baptized is saved, whoever does not believe is condemned."

Son: Father, I notice that you, too, have paid attention to the Gospel.

Father: See, I have an old postil [46] there, which a monk once wrote. I read in that once in a while and study it.

Son: That's good. Now note the passage. God says: "Go; do not ride on big beautiful stallions, do not sit on soft pillows and velvet. No! Go forth! Preach! What? the Gospel and nothing else." Oh God, instead of that they permitted butter letters,[47] indulgence myths, and Romish grace,[48] lying unevangelical matters,[49] to be preached and proclaimed. So also Scotus,[50] Thomas Aquinas,[51] Aristotle, Ockham,[52] etc. And the message of Christ, rich in grace, which was given and sent for mankind, they threw under the bench for a footstool. They also will be Christ's footstool, when He sits on Judgment Day, as David shows Psalm 110 [v. 1],[53] with the fatbellies,[54] blood-suckers,[55] and their indulgences together with their laws and distinct tithes [56] (as they are called) to the Rhine! [57]

Father: Son, I still remember right well that four years ago the devil's official was here with his Cardinal. They sold indulgences and letters for those wicked lords [58] and allowed the eating of butter, and gave one [indulgence] for six Groschen and more. And I, poor man, had scarce six Groschen in my house, and I gave them up. I thought that I had done right and would be saved if I had one [indulgence]. I was already a Christian. He would not want my [money]. If they came to my door again and bilked poor me of my money, I would give them an indulgence with a good bludgeon [59] so that they would have to be carried home in an old scuttle.[60] Well, I deserved it.

Son: That's right, Father. Don't be too angry. Forgive him as a brother, since we are all brothers and have one Father in heaven, Matth. 6 [vv. 14, 15].[61] They will not do it again. But do you still have the letters?

Father: Yes.

Son: Get them. We will burn them.

Father: That's right! Wife, bring fire and blow it up for a while.

Son: Very good.

Father: I'll bring them.

Son: Throw them in!

Father: There you lie in the name of Eck,[62] Emser,[63] and Murner.[64] We praise Thee, O Lord.[65]

Son: That's right, Father. Those three devils have wickedly persecuted Martin [Luther]. Although they are my brothers, it nevertheless grieves me, that they dishonor God so and oppose the Gospel. I notice, too, that you can speak also a little Latin. We must talk a bit more about money-fools and money-fishers, how they deceived us and the whole host of poor people, about whom you heard a few things before. But I want to show you the Scripture, if God will grant me help, without whom we cannot do anything good, John 15 [v. 5].[66]

Father: Son, I too am a little bit learned.[67] I was once at a church dedication.[68] There was a good Gospel preacher there, but he was half and half. He said that he read in one of the prophets, that God said out of regard for His poor people: "My people, that is called blessed; aye, [they say] you are indeed a godly man. They deceive you, and also say that you stand of yourself. He robs, and the goods of the poor are in the houses of the rich or the priests, etc." [69] Son, you've read the Bible with diligence. Since you have it here on the table, tell me, is that it? What does it say, so that I remember it?

Son: It is written in Isaiah 3 [vv. 12-14]. There are also other passages [70] there about false preachers, who are after peoples' money. It is my advice, too, that you buy yourself a Bible, since it has now been put into German by Martin [Luther].[71]

90

Father: Aye, who knows what I'll do. But let's hear how God laments that they do not feed the poor sheep with the Word of Christ.

Son: Again, it is written, Jeremiah 2 [v. 8] that God says: "The priests did not say, 'Where is the Lord?' Those who handle the Law did not know Me." Also, Jeremiah 5 [v. 31]: "The prophets prophesy falsely, and the priests rule at their discretion; My people love to have it so, but what will you do when the end comes?" There in Jeremiah 5 [v. 13] God also says: " 'The prophets will become wind; the Word is not in them.' " Also in Ezekiel 34 [v. 2] God says: "Ho, shepherds of Israel who have been feeding yourselves," etc.[72] Oh, dear father, all the prophets are full of this.

Father: O, indeed, a heavy burden is laid by God on the shepherds if they do not feed the poor sheep, which God has entrusted to them.[73]

Son: That's true, if they'll only take it to heart. So our Captain Christ also says through Paul, Romans 1 [v. 25]: "They exchanged the truth about God for a lie." That's certainly true about them, although Paul speaks that way about the learned among the heathen. Whoever seeks his own gain, as the preachers have done up to this time, does not preach Christ, as Jeremiah says.[74] Dear father, admit or say: You have never before heard such comforting words of Christ preached.

Father: No, by the true God,[75] I've never heard them. No one preaches what displeases him, and yet one finds pious ones.

Son: Yes, one finds pious preachers in the sight of man. But they did not want to counter-attack,[76] and they have let Christ lie and preached their own opinions. If that is godly, then the devil is in command! Martin [Luther] and his followers do not do that. They [the priests] have kept silent about what might harm them and have preached what has paid off in money.

Father: Yes, the priests [77] shouldn't do that. If they can't preach us anything good, we can't know about salvation, for you know: As the shepherd, so also the sheep.[78]

Son: That's true. If they don't wish to preach to us, the peasants will soon have to step up and preach. Christ can give them grace and dwell in them as well as in the clergy, as you heard.

Father: But the priests say that it is not proper for us, we are not called to do that.

Son: Yes, good fellow, were Paul, Peter, and the other apostles also priests?

91

Father: No, they were fishermen and manifest sinners.

Son: Wasn't Paul a great persecutor of the Christians, as he indicates to the Galatians, the first [chapter, v.13]? Did not the grace of God move him to preach? Weren't Peter, James, and John fishermen? Didn't God say to them in Matthew 4 [v. 19]: "Come, follow Me, and I will make you fishers of men," and not "of money"? "You have received without pay, give without pay" Matthew 10 [v. 8]; Luke 10 [vv. 4, 5, 7, 8] and Mark 6 [v. 8].[79] Thus He teaches them that they should not preach His Gospel for the sake of money, as unhappily happens today. Didn't Christ command us that we should teach and instruct each other? If the priests don't want to do that, we ourselves must preach, for God did not send out great lords and bishops to preach His Word. Haven't you heard that we are priests and may absolve? After all, God can just as easily spread His Gospel through a poor plowjockey as through monks and priests. Thus says David: "The eyes of the Lord look always upon the poor." [80]

Father: In truth [81] I never heard that before, for the fat bellies with the red berettas [82] always maintained that God, who never acknowledged them, was with them, which might well be. God has always favored the poor. He looked also on Mary, the most blessed mother of God, instead of other maidens. She was a poor housemaid, therefore she sang in the Magnificat, Luke 1 [v. 52]: "He has put down the mighty from their thrones, and exalted those of low degree." [83]

Son: That's true, Father. You'll become well versed yet.[84] God has exalted the lowly and has attacked the exalted with earnest words. Therefore He says, Matthew 21 [v. 31]: " 'Truly I say to you, the unchaste women and sinners will go into the kingdom of heaven before you.' "

Father: I'd guess, though, because the impractical thinkers [85] understood the Scriptures, they'd be the first to be saved.

Son: Don't you know that the bigwigs always delay with their godliness until it's time to die? Then first they want to be pious with their eternal masses, vigils, and other external unchristian works, if they do not come out of a true faith. After all, Judas, too, knew about salvation. His faithful Master was constantly concerned to convert him. It didn't help and he [Judas] was damned. Had he believed, it would have gone otherwise with him, even if he betrayed Him [Christ]. God is merciful. One finds much more of the same concerning others.

92

Father: Son, you studied real diligently in Wittenberg.

Son: Do you suppose that this also happens there? There one studies only the Gospel.

Father: Before you called Wittenberg a Christian town. But there are a few people and disparagers of Martin [Luther], who say the same thing will happen to it that happened to Sodom and Gomorrah, which God burned with fire; you know anyhow where it's written.

Son: You'll find that in Genesis 19. But that won't happen to that city, for there the Word of Christ is preached and learned with His help. Let's pray no more than that God would give His grace, that it continues as it has begun. We have been silent too long. Let's ask God and He will give unto us, as He says Matthew 7 [v. 7], John 16 [v. 23].[86] But we must pray believing that it will happen to us. If we believe that it will happen, it will happen; if we do not believe that, then we dare not think that it will happen to us, as is written in James 1 [vv. 6-8].

Father: O, Thou gracious God, I see most clearly how we have prattled [87] in our Lord's Prayer. Also, we didn't understand one word; there was no faith there, and there was more diligence used on indulgence prayers, written in red ink,[88] than on the Lord's Prayer. If the indulgence was a prayer and a meritorious work, then we would have ascended into heaven like a cow into a mouse hole.[89]

Son: O, you stubborn ignoramus [90] with your indulgence. Pray Christ's true prayer, the Lord's Prayer, which He taught us, Matthew 6 [vv. 9-13], Luke 11 [2-4]. Buy the Lord's Prayer with its interpretation, which Martin [Luther] wrote,[91] and you'll find that is otherwise.

Father: I'll do that. I didn't know such things about that prayer. As I have been led, so I have followed betimes. If you had only told me that ten years ago!

Son: Dear father, you're right again; none of us knew that. Our blindness is at fault. Had we only read the Bible, we would have stood differently. But that chosen instrument [92] of Christendom, Martin [Luther], is now driving us beautifully in the Gospel's harness, God be praised. But isn't it to be pitied that Jan Hus,[93] that godly and righteous man, was helplessly burned with violence when he wanted to bring the Gospel into the light of day and wrote against the rich popes and the clerics enthroned in their Roman, wicked knavery? [94] But, O God of heaven, Thou knowest what a blessed death he had for the sake of the Gospel.

Father: What shall I say? For the sake of money the Papists and dogs befouled [95] Christians in their mouth, suppressed the Gospel and Paul. Those are messengers of the Antichrist. May God spare Luther's life, and they'll have to break wind once more.

Son: That's right, Father. I think you're drunk. Be careful, it's still early in the day! That's what the Pharisees did also to Christ. The priests and Murner's monks are enemies of Luther because by the Gospel (as Hus also did) he overthrew and published their knavery along with their statutes and opinions. But there are still other young Martins in the monasteries who dare not bestir themselves because of their priors.[96]

Father: Why don't they pull out? Because if one tells someone the truth, he thunders and excommunicates as he pleases. God is truth; He will certainly not lie; His doctrine also will not vanish,[97] as I hear and know. The clerics will look sour in their capes [98] when the Word of God takes control.

Son: Now, Luther came out well at Leipzig,[99] at Augsburg,[100] and at Worms.[101] No one has dared to get at him, since Eck disputed with him at Leipzig and got a fat sow from it.[102] He did the same at Augsburg with the pope's legate or messenger; likewise he disputed with other doctors and remained unvanquished. So also at Worms.

Father: What kind of man is that Eck?

Son: He is a priest and indulgence fool who wanted to sell Luther for a few gulden, as Judas sold Christ.[103]

Father: Nevertheless, he was not as greedy for money as Judas! [104] Eck wants to have much. If Judas took only 30 pennies, he must have needed money.

Son: Aye. Happy New Year! [105] What are you saying? Judas had to have money. But Geck (what's his name? Johannes Eck, the worthy one, quarterly payment)[106] is more pious than Judas. Eck takes a few pennies and sells Martin [Luther] with all of Wittenberg into death. That's sure, and what nobody can bring about, that's what such an incendiary [107] and devil's brew [108] accomplishes.

Father: How, if somebody would once use a club [109] and give him indulgence and merit on his tonsure, to whom would he confess it?

Son: No, not so. Go easy! With blows you bring no one to faith and to the Word of God. The apostles and Christ didn't do that. Dr. Martin [Luther] has also written that the Antichrist should be overcome without the sword.[110] A forced work is also not pleasing to

94

God. It must come about out of free love to God. Perhaps they will still be converted, if God wills it. Wasn't Paul, after all, a great persecutor of the Christian faith (as we have heard), yet God gave him grace. The same thing happened to many more.

Father: I must agree with you. I've experienced that with my hired hands; the more one curses them, the less they do.

Son: Therefore Martin [Luther] has pointed and urged clerics to the Gospel rather with the Word of God than with the sword, as he also shows.[111]

Father: Aye, thanks be to the Evangelical. We will stand by him and help him. Whoever wishes him anything evil would have to be a boor.[112]

Son: You'll find enough of them, nevertheless, both among the learned and the ignorant.

Father: What are they thinking then? They know and see that it is the Word of God, and they profane Christ thus?

Son: God knows that well. When the devil incites [113] someone, then after all he becomes an enemy of God and of the Gospel. Then also nothing helps until God by grace enlightens the hardened person. Swine and dogs should not be given the pearls and the holy Gospel, nor should it be preached to them, as Christ says Matthew 7 [v. 6]. They may ban and curse, as they please. They must vanish, but the Word of God remains eternally. It is certain what the Word of God is, John 1 [v. 1]: "In the beginning was the Word, and the Word was with God, and the Word was God."

Father: Dear Son, you are very serious about the Gospel, which is quite proper. But let us sit down at the table and eat! The priest comes in often. He is not favorable to the Martinian cause. If he hears about it, he will give us the ban and the devil.

Son: What harm can the ban and the devil do me? After all, God is still their master. For God did not command the priests that they should ban for the sake of the Gospel. There it is, Matthew 18 [v. 20], John 20 [vv. 22. 23], Luke 17 [vv. 3. 4]. There God says: "Where two or three of you are gathered together, then I will be in your midst." Also in Zechariah 8 [vv. 16. 17][114] God says: "Speak the truth and be not afraid." What then can he ban? Let him ban a knave.[115] They have plagued us a long time with that. They will no longer do that, I hope.

Father: Four years ago I owed our priest four bushels of corn, as you know, and I was so poor that I didn't have them. Then he banned me and cursed me before everyone, and I had to give it him, God knows. He had more than my thirty.[116] The devil could not fill his fat baskets.[117] He came and banned me still more; yet I didn't owe it, as my neighbors admitted.

Son: They take that away from you and your children by force, contrary to God. When a priest has his daily fare, he should be satisfied, as St. Paul writes 1 Timothy 6 [6-8].[118] Now the devil can't satisfy them. In former times the ban was used because of sin, as Christ indicates, Matthew 18 [v. 17], Luke 17 [v. 3]; now the ban is used for the sake of money and goods. Therefore, Father, if you are banned for the sake of money, when you are not obligated to give it, then give the rich priests, who ban you, nothing. I and your children need it, too.

Father: You're giving me good advice. For that reason I'll also buy myself a Bible and like an ape [119] I'll overthrow the spirituals (as they are called) with the spiritual; it cannot be otherwise.

Son: That once again is my advice. Do that and follow the Bible and you will live. Let pope, bishops, emperor, devils, and all men persecute you! Don't you know what Paul says, 2 Timothy 3 [v. 12]: "Indeed all who desire to live a godly life in Christ Jesus will be persecuted"? So Christ also says, Matthew 5 [v. 10]: "Blessed are those who are persecuted for righteousness' sake, for theirs is the kingdom of heaven." [120]

Father: I believe and will do that. Yet I cannot wonder enough that the monks and clerics are so greatly opposed to the Gospel and so put God to shame.

Son: Doctor Luther has brought that about; he makes them foolish and also tells them the truth. For you heard before that if anyone tells the rascal that his traffic in indulgence and filth will no longer produce money, then he curses and becomes an enemy of God and of the author who has written it. Don't you know that? God told the high priests the truth and was severe with them, and therefore He was nailed to the cross; the same also the apostles.

Father: Aye, so they remain; and may they have a good year! [121] I would have said it entirely otherwise. God will not dwell in their hearts and make them blessed; there also is no peace there.

Son: That's true. So it's written in Jeremiah 28 [vv. 8. 11]:[122] "There is no peace for the wicked." For they can have no peace; the devil has possessed them. All right, let's sit down at the table, eat our soup, and in the meanwhile talk some more about these matters; it's almost evening.

Father: That's likely correct, but you must be cautious. It can happen to us as Judas treated our Lord Christ. Someone will inform our bishop about us; then the devil will become abbot.[123]

Son: Yes, Father, the Word of God is not bound, as St. Paul indicates, 2 Timothy 2 [v. 9]. I'm not worried about the devil; the bishops will not harm me, as you have heard. Nevertheless, I'll give you a lesson and a short instruction for a "good night," which will be profitable for you and us all, if indeed we want to obtain eternal life, which God has promised to us, differently. And I will present you three articles, faith, love, and hope; and thereon your life shall be ordered, and therein is your salvation, and not in outward childish works, as some suppose. And note:[124]

When a person sins against God, his Savior, then the Law, as the Decalog, comes and holds it in front of his nose, so that he sees what he has done. Thus he recognizes that he has sinned grievously. Then he laments and complains. So the Law says curtly: "Give what you owe." [125] See, then a person cries to God and is ready to despair.

When he is in such anxiety, then God comes to him with grace and confronts him: "Do you believe that I can help you?" If he believes, he is helped already, and thus God awakens him by His grace, which is promised him in the Gospel, which he has received. Thereupon follows the right faith, that he believes God, who will help him, and then he must believe firmly that God was born, died, and was raised from the dead.[126] Therefore it is written Isaiah 9 [v. 6]: "For to us a Child is born, to us a Son is given." You must also believe that the righteousness of Christ is your righteousness, Christ's satisfaction is yours, Christ's mercy is yours.[127] And do not doubt that your sins are forgiven you and that God is kindly disposed and favorable and gracious to you. If you have that faith in God, then your sins are forgiven you. And therefore faith alone, confidence, and trust in God's mercy is salvation. Thus St. Paul says, Romans 1 [v. 17]: "The just shall live by faith." Also in Galatians 2 [v. 16] [128] and 5 [v. 5]:[129] "Faith alone justifies and not works." The same in many other passages. And therefore God came because of our sins, Matthew 9 [v. 13],[130] so that when you sin you should pray Him for grace and mercy. If, therefore, you now want to pray to Him, then you must believe in God's mercy, for His mercy is everlasting, Psalm 118 [v. 2].[131] If you believe that you are forgiven, then you are already forgiven. So God says through the Scriptures: "Go, and sin no more," as God said to the woman that was taken in adultery, John 8 [v. 11]. See, He will do that to all of us, if we believe Him, and therefore faith alone saves, as has been sufficiently explained.

If salvation were from works, then Christ would have shed His crimson blood in vain; God did not want that. And so, if you would present all the works of the saints, even these would not save you. And therefore God says to those, whom He heals: "Go in peace, your faith has saved you." [132] If you now believe that you have a benevolent, gracious, wholly merciful God, and follow Him, then you are saved; you may not run hither and yon,[133] buy this or that indulgence. No, seek faith from God! You will receive that by grace. You or your natural self [134] cannot accomplish it. And therefore faith is nothing else but to trust and to believe in all the words of God. And that comes about in no other way than through the grace and mercy of God. As long as we do not believe God, then there is no perception of divine mercy. For even if a person fulfills [135] all the works of the Law without faith, he nevertheless sins without ceasing. This is what Paul means in Romans 14 [v. 23], when he says: "Whatever does not proceed from faith is sin." And therefore there is nothing more unreasonable and more wicked than to evaluate the will and mercy of God on the basis of works. So it is written in Ecclesiasticus 32 [v. 24]: "In all of your works believe from the faith in your heart, that is the fulfilling and keeping of the commandments." [136] God is a gracious Father in heaven. Now since God thus praises and lauds faith, why don't we want to believe Him, with a faith which He must give us, and rely on His mercy?

Father: O, Thou benevolent God. What a beautiful, wholesome doctrine that is! Dear son, you've put me firmly in the saddle.[137] Up and carry on; I will be eternally grateful to you.

Son: Very well. You have had a brief instruction about faith, by which Adam, Abraham, Jacob, David, etc., were saved. Now, if you have such a faith, then love to God and your neighbor will flow out of it. And faith without love is nothing, as Paul says: "And if I have such a faith, so that I could put the mountains on top of each other, but have not love, I will be nothing." [138] Thus with faith there must be love, so that you love God and give Him in all a home,[139] let Him carry on and you do nothing against His fatherly will, and hold Him so dear that you can do all things out of love, then you fulfill [140] that [commandment]. And the same to your neighbor, that you love him as yourself, as the Gospel says,[141] do well to him, help him in body and soul, give him bread.[142] If you cannot do that, comfort him and

98

be hospitable to him, and do everything good for him. Those are the works which God has commanded. It often happens that your Christ comes to you in the guise of a beggar before your door, begs you for a piece of bread; you should deprive yourself of that and give it to him, so that He can say to you on the Last Day: "You have fed Me, given Me to drink, been hospitable to Me; go and possess the kingdom of My Father, which was prepared for you from the beginning of the world." Matthew 25 [vv. 34-36].

Father: O God, to whom it is given to be worthy, these are comforting words!

Son: You obtain that by grace and not from merit, as St. Paul says: "The kingdom of heaven and the gift of God are by grace, so that no one can tell himself:[143] 'Aye, I have earned that with my works.'"[144] Also you should not become pious in order that you will merit heaven. No, you should do so out of affection and love for God. It's impossible for you to become pious by works. For it is surely true as Christ says: "An evil tree brings forth evil fruit."[145] If a person was previously a rascal and wants to become pious by works, he is building on sand.[146] And therefore love God with your whole soul, and your neighbor as yourself.[147] This is what God wants and these works he requires. For "love is the fulfilling of the Law," as St. Paul says, Romans 13 [vv. 8, 10].[148]

If you do these works, then afterwards you will do other external works, such as going to church, setting up foundations,[149] offering candles,[150] dedicating bells, and observing other things as you please. If you do not observe them, you will not be damned because of that.

So it is written Psalm 9 [v. 10]: "And those who know Thy name put their trust in Thee." And thus you hope in God; you do all your works to please Him, that they may be pleasing to Him and His will, and thus you hope in His mercy and in your Savior. And even if He casts you into hell, you hope and do not despair of His mercy.[151] Aye, then the Lord God comes, helps you, and receives you kindly, as the father his lost son, Luke 15 [vv. 22-24]. Therefore be certain that the angels will rejoice over you;[152] there is an eternal rejoicing.

Solomon[153] also speaks about faith, love, and hope.

Father: Yes, where? Dear son, show me! For all my longings incline me toward that.[154]

Son: God be praised for that! It's written in Ecclesiasticus 2 [v. 6]. There we read: "Believe in God, and He will exalt you, and order your work according to Him and hope in Him."[155] And immediately after that [vv. 8, 9] he says: "You who fear God, believe in Him, and His mercy will be a rejoicing for you. Love, and He will enlighten your hearts." [156] See there, these are words of the wise man Solomon. And regard herewith this my instruction as a father from his son for good, as a "good night." Order your life according to it; believe in God; hope in God; love Him and your neighbor; do him good, as you have heard; follow Him; fulfill the will of the heavenly Father. Then you will be Christ's brother and friend, as He says, Luke 8 [v. 21] and Matthew 12 [v. 50]. [157] God comfort you with this and feed you with this Gospel, which all of us need. Pray God, too, that He may advance His Gospel, which has now begun, and that it will be brought to light for the poor captives in sins and conscience, [158] so that they will be free. We must eat the Gospel bread. [159] Also that He may enlighten Martin Luther with grace. [160] With this I want to be commended in your prayer, to ask God that He might enlighten me with His true faith. I will also do that. I'm going to bed.

Father: Aye, drink to St. John's blessing! [161]

Son: So be it. In the name of the Father, of the Son, of the Holy Spirit.

Father: And God be thanked for you and your instruction, which you have given me, poor layman! Be commended to God! Go in the name of the Lord!

Son: So be it, as St. Paul says, Colossians 3 [v. 17]: "Everything that we begin or do, that should be done in the name of Christ." If God wills, tomorrow we will exercise ourselves further in the Gospel and I will drive you deeper into the faith for a "good night."

Father: I will gladly hear that. Thanks be to God. [162] God be with us all! Amen.

So they went to bed and with great joy this conversation was brought to an end by these two. God's will be done by us at all times from everlasting to everlasting! Amen.

Psalm 18 [v. 44]:

Deliver me, Lord, from the strife of the people. [163]

The end.

NOTES

1. Carl S. Meyer, trans. *Luther and Zwingli's Propositions for Debate: the Ninety-five Theses of 31 October 1517 and the Sixty-seven Articles of 23 January 1523,* Latin and German texts with a new English translation (Leiden: E. J. Brill, 1963); C. M. Jacobs, trans., rev. by Harold J. Grimm, "Ninety-five Theses," LW XXXI, 17—33.

2. See Schwiebert's essay in this volume, pp. 122 and 139, n. 10.

3. "Eynn Dialogus ader gesprech zwischen einem Vatter unnd Sun dye Lere Martin Luthers vnd süst andere sachen des Christlichen glaubens belangende," *Flugschriften aus den ersten Jahren der Reformation,* ed. Otto Clemen, I, i, printed together with "Ain Sendbrief von aym Jungen Studentten zue Wittemberg, an seine oeltern jm land zue Schwaben von wegen der Lutherischen leer zue gesschriben" (1523).

4. *Benevenertis,* i. e. welcome. Clemen, p. 48, n. 1, and references cited there. See also Friedrich Kluge, *Etymologisches Wörterbuch der deutschen Sprache,* ed. Walther Mitzka, 19th ed. (Berlin: Walter de Gruyter & Co., 1963), p. 65, sub *benedeien,* to wish well. Cited as Kluge-Mitzka.

5. The idiomatic *lieber sun* and *du lieber sun* are usually translated simply "son."

6. Thümbhern, i. e. Domherrn, bishops. Jacob Grimm und Wilhelm Grimm, *Deutsches Wörterbuch* (Leipzig: Verlag von S. Hirzel, 1852—1954), II, 1235. Hereafter cited as Grimm.

7. "His watchmen are blind, they are all without knowledge; they are all dumb dogs, they cannot bark; dreaming, lying down, loving to slumber."

8. "Ain schöner Dialogus," *Satiren und Pasquille aus der Reformationszeit,* ed. Oskar Schade (Hannover: Carl Rümpler, 1856), II, 119, 18—20: "A man of much wealth is Luther's enemy and brands him a heretic; but the poor love him." See Clemen, p. 48, n. 2.

9. Members of a theological party. Ibid., p. 48, n. 3.

10. *Humanisten,* i. e., adherents to men's ordinances. The reference is not to those who favored the revival of Latin and Greek studies. Ibid., p. 48, n. 4.

11. This reference, ibid., p. 26, is incorrect. It probably should be Jer. 12:6: "Believe them not [your brothers and your father's house], though they speak fair words unto thee." (KJV)

12. Matt. 13:25, 29.

13. They were the chief external enemies of Christendom in the first half of the 16th century.

14. For other contemporary denunciations of the clergy see, e. g., *Satiren und Pasquille aus der Reformationszeit,* ed. Oskar Schade (Hannover: Carl Rümpler, 1856), 3 vols. The series published by Rudolf Haupt in Leipzig, in which the present tract is found, *Flugschriften aus dem ersten Jahrhundert der Reformation,* should also be consulted.

15. "I am the Good Shepherd. The good shepherd lays down his life for the sheep."

16. "And Jesus answered them, 'Take heed that no one leads you astray. For many will come in My name, saying, 'I am the Christ' and they will lead many astray."

17. "And He said to His disciples, 'Temptations to sin are sure to come; but woe to him by whom they come. . . . And they will say to you, 'Lo, there!' or 'Lo, here!' Do not go, do not follow them."

18. "False Christs and false prophets will arise and show signs and wonders, to lead astray, if possible, the elect."

19. *Summisten,* scholastics, especially the followers of the Dominican Thomas Aquinas (ca. 1225—74). His influence became even greater after the Council of Trent than it had been in the Late Middle Ages. In 1567 Pius V made him a Doctor of the Church. Leo XIII's encyclical, *Aeterni Patris* (1879) recommended the study of Aquinas' writings. In 1923 Pius XI in the *Stu-*

diorum Ducem emphasized them as authoritative. Aquinas stressed the primacy of reason and knowledge.

20. A corruption of "Aquinists."

21. *So hastu gewis am hals.* See Grimm, IV, ii, 245—57; Clemen, p. 48, n. 6. It may be translated, "You will surely hang by the neck."

22. "Do you not know that you are God's temple and that God's Spirit dwells in you?" Note the addition of "by faith" to the passage.

23. Luke 5:30; 15:2; 19:7.

24. The identification of Mary Magdalene with Mary, the sister of Lazarus, cannot be maintained, but this is not the point of the argument here.

25. Mark 2:13-17; Luke 5:27-32; Luke 15:1.2; Luke 7:34; Luke 19:7; Mark 14:3-9; Luke 7:36-50; Matt. 26:6-13.

26. Both the Latin and the German are given in the original.

27. "Therefore, since we are justified by faith, we have peace with God through our Lord Jesus Christ."

28. "[We] know that a man is not justified by works of the Law but through faith in Jesus Christ, even we have believed in Christ Jesus, in order to be justified by faith in Christ, and not by works of the Law, because by works of the Law shall no one be justified."

29. "He [God] made no distinction between us [the Jews] and them [the Gentiles], but cleansed their hearts by faith."

30. Matt. 17:5; Mark 9:7; Luke 9:35.

31. See n. 10 above.

32. See Martin Luther, "Von Menschenlehre zu meiden und Antwort auf Sprüche, so man führet, Menschenlehre zu stärken, 1522." WA X/2, 79—92; Clemen, p. 48, n. 7.

33. Augustine of Hippo (354—430) had a great influence on the theology of the Middle Ages, and the late 15th and 16th centuries saw a revival of Augustinianism. The Reformers generally had a high regard for him.

34. Jerome (ca. 342—420) was responsible for the Latin translation of the Scriptures called the Vulgate. His commentaries on the Biblical books were valued highly.

35. The reference is particularly to Augustine's *Retractiones.*

36. *Darumb darff man nit gloss vber das Euangelion.* For *Glosse* see Kluge-Mitzka, p. 262; *glossieren, deuten, glossare.*

37. A follower of Martin Luther.

38. "Let him who boasts, boast of the Lord." See Jer. 9:27; 2 Cor. 10:17.

39. See 1 Cor. 1:13: "Was Paul crucified for you? Or were you baptized in the name of Paul?"

40. See A. Götze, *Lutherische Zeitschrift für deutsche Wortforschung*, III (1902), 189 ff., according to Clemen, p. 48, n. 8.

41. "In Him [the Word] was life, and the life was the light of men."

42. *Curtisanen*, Grimm, II, 640.

43. See Deut. 32:7-14; 33:26-29.

44. See Lev. 19:1-4; 26:11-13.

45. E. g., Joshua 1:9; Ps. 46; Ps. 81; Is. 45:15-17.

46. Exposition of Biblical texts, the reading of which was already established, *post illa* (*textus verba*). Kluge-Mitzka, p. 560, sub *Postille.*

47. *Butterbrieff*, letters which permitted the eating of butter at any time. **Grimm**, II, 584, and references cited there.
48. Work righteousness.
49. Contrary to *sola gratia*.
50. Johannes Duns Scotus (ca. 1264—1308), Franciscan philosopher and theologian.
51. See n. 19 above.
52. William Ockham (ca. 1300—ca. 1349), Nominalist philosopher who strongly influenced Luther, advocate of the *via moderna*.
53. "The Lord says to my Lord, 'Sit at My right hand and I will make Your enemies Your footstool.' "
54. *Feisten beuchen. Feist, fett.* Kluge-Mitzka, p. 190. Luther used both terms. Ibid., p. 56, sub *bauchen, beuchen*, bellies.
55. *Blutkauffern* reads as *Blutsaugern*. See Grimm, II, 190; Clemen, p. 48, n. 9. "Tyranny" would be a permissable translation.
56. *Zinckis distinctis. Zins, census*, tribute, tax. Kluge-Mitzka, p. 887, sub **Zins**.
57. Regarding the Rhine in proverbs, especially in maledictions, see Grimm, VIII, 854—55; Clemen, p. 48, n. 10.
58. *Heingen*, read as *heinzen.* Grimm, IV, ii, 889—90; Clemen, p. 48, n. 11.
59. *Trumscheyt*, i. e., *trumelscheit.* See ibid., p. 48, n. 12, and references given there.
60. *Schüsselkorben*, i. e., a frame on which dishes are placed, used to designate a contemptuous object. Grimm, IX, 2075; see Clemen, p. 48, n. 12.
61. See also Matt. 18:21-30.
62. Johann Eck (1486—1543), professor of theology at Ingolstadt, debated against Carlstadt and Luther at Leipzig (1519). He procured the bull *Exsurge Domini* against Luther in 1520 and in 1521 published his *De primatu Petri adversum Ludderum libri III.*
63. Hieronymous Emser (1478—1527), secretary to Duke George of Saxony, a persistent enemy of Luther, who called him *der Bock von Emser.* Emser's main polemic against Luther was directed against Luther's New Testament translation of 1522.
64. Thomas Murner (1475—1537), satirist and humanist, a persistent opponent of the Lutheran cause.
65. The original is in Latin, *Te deum laudamus!* The use of this phrase by the peasant father heightens the dramatic quality of the scene.
66. ". . . for apart from Me you can do nothing."
67. *Gelidert*, i. e., *gelehrt.* Grimm, IV, i, 3018; see Clemen, p. 48, n. 14.
68. *Kirmes, kirmesse, Kirchweihfest.* Kluge-Mitzka, p. 370.
69. See Is. 3:12-14.
70. *Grumpen*, i. e., *Krumpen, Glumpen*, pieces. Grimm, V, 2467—68; Clemen, p. 45, n. 15.
71. The first edition of Luther's translation of the New Testament was printed in 1522. The complete Bible cannot be meant here, only the New Testament.
72. See Ezek. 34:1-10.
73. Ezek. 34:10; Jer. 23:1.
74. The reference is obscure. It may be to Jer. 23. See also Ezek. 34.
75. *Per deum verum.* Note the father's use of Latin.

76. The colorful expression in the original reads: sie habenn den fuechs, dennost nit woellen beyssen." Clemen, p. 48, n. 16; Ernst Thiele, *Luthers Sprichwörtersammlung* (Weimar: Hermann Böhlaus Nachfolger, 1900), p. 220, no. 218. To bite the fox back again, when he bites, i. e., to retaliate aggressively.

77. *Die sacerdotes.* Again a Latin word used by the father; here the term is obviously used with contempt.

78. Clemen, p. 48, n. 17; Thiele, pp. 94—96, no. 76, has a collection of similar proverbs.

79. Clemen, p. 48, n. 18, remarks correctly that Mark and Luke do not have the Matthean passage cited in the text. The additional references, however, are evidently given to extend the thought.

80. Clemen, p. 35, adds Ps. 10:5 here as a reference; it is incorrect. It should be Ps. 34:15: "The eyes of the Lord are toward the righteous." See Ps. 34:6: "The poor man cried, and the Lord heard him."

81. *In veritate.* Again the peasant father uses a Latin phrase.

82. *Baneden,* i. e., *Banetten,* according to Clemen, p. 48. n. 19. The reference is to the bishops.

83. The passage is given in Latin; again it is to be noted that the peasant father is giving the quotation.

84. *Du wuerst noch gut,* not morally but in his argumentation.

85. *Verkertten gelertten.* See Thiele, pp. 33, 34, and other references in Clemen, pp. 48, 49, n. 20. The phrase expresses popular contempt for impractical and unrealistic scholars.

86. See also Luke 11:9; Mark 11:24; John 14:13.14; Matt. 18:19; Matt. 21:22; James 1:5-8; 1 John 5:14.15; John 15:7.

87. *Gewaschen,* i. e., *geschwatzt.* Clemen, p. 49, n. 21. A typographical error is presupposed.

88. *Tincken, tincta, tinkte, Tinte.* Kluge-Mitzka, p. 779.

89. See Mark 10:25: "It is easier for a camel to go through the eye of a needle . . ."; Clemen, p. 49, n. 22.

90. Ölgoetz, Grimm, VII, 1278—81. Kluge-Mitzka, p. 522, and references cited there. See also the references cited by Clemen, p. 49, n. 23.

91. Clemen, p. 49, n. 24. *Auslegung deutsch des Vaterunsers für die einfältigen Laien . . .* 1519. WA II, 80—130.

92. *Das ausserwelt fass, vas electionis.* See Acts 9:15; Clemens, p. 49, n. 25.

93. Jan Hus (1369—1415), Bohemian reformer, condemned to death by the Council of Constance. He was burned at the stake on 6 July 1415.

94. *Römische Curtisanische buberey;* Grimm, II, 465, *scelus, scurillitas.*

95. *Gefisten,* Kluge-Mitzka, pp. 199, 200, sub *Fist, leiser Bauchwind.* See also Clemen, p. 49, n. 26.

96. Ibid., p. 49, n. 27; Schade, II, 123, 15—17: "One finds, nevertheless, many secret, young enemies; they do not dare let themselves be noticed for fear of the Jews, their prelates."

97. *Zurgehen,* i. e., *zergehen.* Zur and zer were both used. Kluge-Mitzka, p. 882, sub *zer.*

98. *Sawr sehen auss den koppen.* Kluge-Mitzka, p. 349, *Kappe, cappa, Mantel mit Kapuze.*

99. At the Leipzig Debate with Eck, July 1519. See LW, XXXI, 307—25.

100. In October 1518, when Luther met with the general of the Dominican Order and the papal legate Cajetan at Augsburg. See LW XXXI, 253—92.

101. At the Diet of Worms, 17 and 18 April 1521. See LW XXXII, 101—31.

102. Clemen, p. 49, n. 28; Schade, II, 152, 15, to 153, 19. In lines 34 and 35, p. 152, also the expression *und hab ain grosse sau davon getragen,* is used.

103. Matt. 26:14-16; Mark 14:10.11; Luke 22:3-6. In spite of this remark Eck's sincerity cannot be impugned. Clemen, p. 49, n. 29; Schade, II, 124, 18, to 126, 13. On p. 125, 3, Eck is designated *ablass nar;* p. 125, 16—19, he is compared to Judas Iscariot.

104. Spoken in irony.

105. Clemen, p. 49, n. 30; Thiele, p. 191, no. 186.

106. *Quitten,* i. e., *Quentchen,* according to Clemen, p. 49, n. 31. Kluge-Mitzka, p. 574, as *Viertellot.* Schade, II, 124, 26, *junkherr Eck oder Geck;* p. 126, 26, *junkherr Geck.* A *Geck* is a fox.

107. *Meidamacher,* i. e., *Meutmacher, Aufrührer,* Grimm, VI, 2166. See also Kluge-Mitzka, p. 477, sub *Meute.*

108. *Teuffels kopf. Kopf, Trinkgefäss, Hirnschale,* i. e., cup. Kluge-Mitzka, p. 392.

109. *Knüttel,* i. e., *Knüppel,* Grimm, V, 1517—18.

110. "Eine treue Vermahnung M. Luthers zu allen Christen, sich zu hüten vor Aufruhr und Empörung, 1522," WA VIII, 676—87.

111. George W. Forell cites Luther's letter to Spalatin, 16 Jan. 1521: "I do not want the Gospel to be contested by force and the shedding of blood. . . . Through the Word the world was overcome, through the Word the church was maintained, and through the Word she will again be restored." LW XXXII, xii.

112. *büffels kopff,* Grimm, II, 492, *caput bubalium; anas bucephala.* According to Kluge-Mitzka, pp. 108, 109, it was used in the 16th century for *Klotz, Tölpel.* See also reference given by Clemen, p. 49, n. 33.

113. *Der teufel reitt.* Perhaps *reitt* comes from *riten,* although the form *reizen* with "tt" instead of "z," etymologically possible, fits the sense much better. Cf. Kluge-Mitzka, p. 595, sub *reizen.*

114. "Speak the truth to one another, render in your gates judgments that are true and make for peace, do not devise evil in your hearts against one another, and love no false oath, for all these things I hate, says the Lord."

115. *Er ban einen Schalk!* The term *Schalk* was generally used for *Knecht,* servant. Kluge-Mitzka, p. 633.

116. *Mer den meiner dreissig.* The reference is to the 30 pieces of silver given Judas. See n. 103 above.

117. *Die feisten kötzen,* i. e., *Korb.* Kluge-Mitzka, p. 397; Grimm, V, 1903—4; Clemen, p. 49, n. 35.

118. "There is great gain in godliness with contentment; for we brought nothing into the world, and we cannot take anything out of the world; but if we have food and clothing, with these we shall be content."

119. Clemen, p. 49, n. 36, for references.

120. Cited incompletely in the text.

121. *Haben in ain güts jar!* See n. 105 above.

122. Sic. It should be Is. 48:22.

123. Clemen, p. 49, n. 37, notes that this passage is obscure. See references given there. Clemen paraphrases: "As Judas betrayed Christ and thus the devil

gained possession of him, so we are slandered to our bishop, and so people obtain rule who are least suited to it."

124. Ibid., p. 50, n. 38, points out that the following is based on Luther's *Von der Freiheit eines Christenmenschen*, 1520, WA VII, 20—38; *The Freedom of A Christian*. LW XXXI, 317—77.

125. See Matt. 18:28.

126. See Apostles' and Nicene Creeds.

127. See, e. g., Luther's sermon, "Two Kinds of Righteousness," LW XXXI, 298 to 299.

128. ". . . a man is not justified by works of the Law but through faith in Jesus Christ. . . ."

129. "For through the Spirit, by faith, we wait for the hope of righteousness."

130. "For I came not to call the righteous, but sinners."

131. "His steadfast love endures for ever." See also Ps. 118:29, the refrain of each verse in Ps. 136 et al.

132. See, e. g., Matt. 9:22; Luke 7:50; Mark 10:52; Mark 5:34; Luke 17:19; Luke 8:48; Luke 18:42.

133. On pilgrimages.

134. *Deine natur.*

135. *Verbrecht,* Grimm, XII, i, 158, for *verbrechen,* to transgress. The context demands, it seems, that it be derived from *verbringen,* i. e., *vollbringen.*

136. "He that believeth in the Lord taketh heed to the commandment; and he that trusteth in Him shall fare never the worse." (KJV)

137. *Du brengst mich gar in sattel.* For *sattel* see Kluge-Mitzka, p. 626.

138. 1 Cor. 13:2: "And if I have all faith, so as to remove mountains, but have not love, I am nothing."

139. *Gibst im alles heim.* Kluge-Mitzka, p. 299, sub *Heim.*

140. See n. 135 above.

141. See Matt. 19:19; 22:39; Mark 12:31; Luke 10:27. See also Lev. 19:18; Rom. 13:9; Gal. 5:14; James 2:8.

142. Compare Matt. 25:35.

143. *Sich kennen.* Kluge-Mitzka, p. 363, *erkennen* is reflexive, *sich wissen machen.*

144. Eph. 2:8-9: "For by grace you have been saved through faith; and this is not your own doing, it is the gift of God — not because of works, lest any man should boast."

145. Matt. 7:17.

146. Matt. 7:26; Luke 6:49; James 1:22-25.

147. See the references in n. 141.

148. See also Gal. 5:14.

149. *Testament stiften.* Kluge-Mitzka, p. 750, sub *Stift,* n., *gründen.*

150. *Kertzen machen.* Ibid., p. 364, *Kerze,* taper.

151. Job. 13:15: "Though He slay me, yet will I trust in Him." (KJV)

152. Luke 15:10: "Even so, I tell you, there is joy before the angels of God over one sinner who repents."

153. See n. 136 above and Ecclus. 2:6-9.

154. *Alle meine begird stet mir nach dem. Begird* or *begirde,* usually *girde, Verlangen.* Kluge-Mitzka, p. 60 and p. 257, sub *Gier.*

155. "Believe in Him, and He will help thee; order thy way aright and trust in Him." (KJV)
156. "Ye that fear the Lord, believe Him; and your reward shall not fail. Ye that fear the Lord, hope for good, and for everlasting joy and mercy." (KJV)
157. See also John 15:14.
158. Luke 4:18: " 'He has sent Me to proclaim release to the captives.' "
159. John 6:35: "Jesus said to them, 'I am the bread of life; he who comes to Me shall not hunger, and he who believes in Me shall never thirst.' " See also John 6:48-50.
160. In the context this can mean only: "Also pray God that with His grace He may continue to enlighten Martin Luther."
161. See references given by Clemen, p. 50, n. 40.
162. *Deo gratias.* Another Latin expression used by the father.
163. "Eripe me, domini de contradictionibus gentium."

4

LAZARUS SPENGLER,
THE NÜRNBERG COUNCIL,
AND THE REFORMATION

Harold J. Grimm

R EFORMATION scholars have done much in recent decades to clarify issues involved in the rise of Protestantism and to relate the movement to late medieval thought. Few historians today dispute the proposition that the Reformation had its origins in the development of an evangelical theology and in its application to conditions in 16th-century Christendom. Today's great desideratum is an analysis of the various social forces of the period to ascertain reasons for the phenomenal spread of the Lutheran Reformation, which was brought to people of all classes in sermon and broadside, music and art, drama and verse. Great lacunae and wide divergences of opinion exist in this area.[1]

To arrive at tenable conclusions about the spread of the Reformation, historians must begin with analyses of the motives and interests of individuals and manageable groups within the social classes of that day rather than with the assertion of broad generalizations and assumptions. The townsmen, for example, were not all cast in the same mold and did not all respond to the new evangelical theology in the same way, for there were among them great differences in social position, education, economic interests, and political loyalties.[2]

The part played by the first important lay leader of the Reformation, Lazarus Spengler (1479–1534),[3] and the city council of Nürnberg, of which he was the *Ratsschreiber* (council clerk), can throw considerable light on the motives that prompted leading townsmen of the city to come to the support of the Reformation, on ways and means used in its support, and on their solutions to the complex issues raised by their revolutionary activities.

When Spengler embraced Lutheranism, he was more than 40 years old and had established his reputation as a leader in economic and political matters both at home and abroad. It is therefore safe to assume that he was in many ways prepared for his role in the spread of the Reformation.

Spengler's family, life, and career were closely identified with the interests and ideals of the upper merchant class of Nürnberg.[4] His father Georg, a member of a merchant family of Donauwörth, which had received its coat of arms from Emperor Frederick Barbarossa, had served the city council of Nürnberg for 30 years, first as clerk of the chancellery and then as council clerk. Lazarus attended the University of Leipzig, where he studied law. He discontinued his studies in 1495, however, because of the terminal illness of his father. The next year he began his service in the city council, culminating in his appointment as council clerk, a position he held to his death in 1534. In 1516 he was admitted to the important group of families represented in the Great Council and called the *Genannte*.

At the beginning of the 16th century Nürnberg was a free, imperial city of about 20,000 inhabitants.[5] Among German cities it ranked second only to Augsburg in the extent and volume of its trade. Although its merchants dominated the city council and the craft guilds, industrial production was fostered in a variety of ways. At that time more than 250 merchants from Nürnberg lived in Venice, compared with only 62 from Augsburg and 5 from Strasbourg.[6] Merchants from other cities were given an exceptional number of privileges within its walls. The exchange of ideas accompanying the exchange of goods was reflected in a lively interest in learning, particularly of a practical, scientific character; in the encouragement of the fine arts; and in the rapid growth of the book trade.

The development of industry and trade was accompanied also by a growing demand for more local autonomy of the city within the empire. The emperors had favored Nürnberg for centuries. They

109

had visited the city and its imperial castle frequently, deposited the imperial regalia in the city for safekeeping, and permitted the council to expand its territory to the size of a small principality. During its struggles with German nobles, territorial princes, and the bishop of Bamberg (its ecclesiastical superior), its leading citizens developed a strong sense of civic pride and a feeling of responsibility for the entire community best expressed by the frequently used word *Gemeinwohl* (common welfare).[7]

The city council evinced its concern for cultural affairs by establishing and maintaining schools; by founding and developing a council library containing books on theology, science, mathematics, and the classics; and by patronizing literature and the fine arts. The leading citizens sent their sons to universities both in Germany and abroad.

Since Nürnberg was not an episcopal city, it seldom felt the strong hand of its bishop at Bamberg. On the contrary, the city council steadily increased its authority in religious affairs. By 1500 it shared with the bishop the appointment of the parish clergy, exercised administrative rights over its monasteries, supervised the morals of its people, and showed an interest in carrying out religious reform programs.[8] Like numerous other German cities, it resented the influence of foreign clergy on local affairs, the withdrawal of large sums of money from the city to Rome, and the immunity of the clergy from taxation and services for the common good.

Spengler's concern for the general welfare of the citizens of Nürnberg and the high standards of his social ethics are apparent in the advice he gave his sons when they were about to begin their business careers [9] and in his *Admonition and Instruction for a Virtuous Life* of 1520,[10] dedicated to his friend Albrecht Dürer. In these he lists for those with responsibility for serving the common welfare such virtues as fear of God, equanimity in suffering, reasonableness, friendship, loyalty, modesty, humility, discretion, restraint, trustworthiness, compassion, and love of peace. The chief vices for him are pride, desire for revenge, pleasure in seeing others suffer, flattery, gossip, boastfulness, and contentiousness. Although humanist and Stoic influences are apparent, there is strong evidence of burgher ethics.

The interest of the intellectual elite of Nürnberg in humanism, stimulated by the widely known Willibald Pirckheimer (d. 1530), was reflected in Spengler's life and work. He was a close friend of Pirckheimer; while still at an impressionable age he had gone with him on a number of diplomatic missions. His own writings illustrate his familiarity with the classics and his emphasis on style. Like many other humanists of his day, he found comfort in reading the Bible and patristic literature; Saint Augustine and Saint Jerome were his favorite church fathers. Among his early works was his translation of Eusebius' *Life and Death of St. Jerome,* published in 1514.[11]

The religious thought of Spengler and his friends was influenced by late medieval Christian mysticism, which minimized the importance of dogma and ritual, seeking instead expression in inner spirituality and ethical earnestness. It became particularly strong among the Augustinian eremites, who in the eyes of many represented "the spirit of progress" as opposed to "the scholastic sterility" of the Dominicans.

The Augustinian monastery in Nürnberg, which had carried out a rigorous reform program with the support of the city council, was looked upon as a model of piety. Its vicar general Johann von Staupitz frequently visited the city, where he was highly respected by all, particularly by men of piety and learning. He preached to large crowds of people of all classes; they were attracted by his profound yet simply stated theology, deep inner spirituality, common sense, emphasis on the Bible and God's love, and opposition to work righteousness. Spengler, among others, made extensive notes on these sermons.

Because Staupitz was a brilliant conversationalist and preacher, he was welcomed by the Nürnberg circle of intellectual elite, comprising among others Christoph Scheurl, Willibald Pirckheimer, Hieronymus Ebner, Kaspar Nützel, Albrecht Dürer, and Lazarus Spengler, a circle Scheurl called the *Sodalitas Staupitziana.*[12] After Luther's two visits to Nürnberg in 1518 [13] this circle came to be known as the *Sodalitas Martiniana,* one of the first nuclei of the Lutheran Reformation.[14] The leaders of this group, Lazarus Spengler, Hieronymus Ebner, and Kaspar Nützel, all influential members of the city council, eventually led the city through the difficulties of the early twenties to the formal break with the papacy in 1525.[15] The group frequently met in the Augustinian monastery, where they discussed Luther's works, his reformation activities, and other matters of common concern.

Practical experiences and observations also help explain Spengler's commitment to Lutheranism. In the first place, he was greatly moved by Luther's precipitous flight from Cajetan in Augsburg in 1518, convinced that the Reformer was being persecuted as a martyr to the truth. He always remembered Luther's statement of that time to the effect that if his cause were God's cause it would prevail, regardless of what happened to him. Like many others, Spengler considered this

111

episode similar to that in Reuchlin's life, which had aroused the ire of men interested in the search for truth and freedom of learning.

A second experience had to do with a well-documented scandal in 1515 which involved the prior of the Dominican monastery in Nürnberg and a nun in the Dominican convent in Engeltal, the supervision of which had fallen to the city council. Spengler was on the council's committee that investigated the affair and induced the council to dismiss both prior and nun.[16]

In the third place, experiences of the city council with the indulgence traffic, such as the draining off to Rome of much of the money gathered by an indulgence for building an addition to the *Neues Spital*, made Spengler sympathetic to Luther in his indulgence controversy with Johann Eck.

Finally, the treatment by Eck of both Spengler and Pirckheimer, which culminated in their excommunication together with Luther, so disgusted him with the manipulations of the papal curia that only the stirring events of the Diet of Worms in 1521 were needed to make him a devoted leader of the Reformation.

As lay leader of the Reformation in Nürnberg, Spengler maintained close relations with Luther, published books and pamphlets in behalf of the Reformation, and pursued a steady, consistent course as one of its leaders, supported by the city council. His friendship with Luther, begun in 1518, was sealed at the Diet of Worms, where he was one of the three representatives of the Nürnberg city council. In his report to the council, he contrasted Luther's deportment at Worms with that of the great majority of the clergy who drank heavily, gorged themselves, and gambled while the "Roman robbers" persecuted the Reformer.[17] In 1525 he visited Luther, Melanchthon, and other reformers at Wittenberg on official business for the city council, which frequently sought their advice on such matters as abolition of the Mass, the establishment of schools, the formulation of a church discipline, and the right to resist the emperor by force. The Wittenberg reformers, on the other hand, occasionally sought the city council's advice on political and economic matters. Luther's regard for Spengler is evinced in his dedication to him of his *A Sermon on Keeping Children in School*, published in 1530.[18]

Spengler's most important polemical work in behalf of Luther and the Reformation is his *Defense and Christian Answer of an Honorable Lover of God's Truth in Holy Scripture*, written in German and published in 1519.[19] In it he makes the following points: Luther's doctrines are so thoroughly grounded in Scripture that anyone who opposes them opposes Christ's precepts and examples. These doctrines are in conformity with good Christian order and natural reason, for it is contrary to order and reason to ignore Christian faith and love while insisting on outworn ceremonies, indulgences, and other abuses. Accordingly, the light of Luther's doctrines should not be hidden under a bushel by referring them to theologians for debate but should be put on candlesticks for all to see. In the unequal battle that has ensued, Luther is succeeding against great odds because Christ is his fencing master who has taught him how to use the Gospel as a shield against his enemies. Since this *Defense* was published in Augsburg, though against the author's will, Johann Eck of nearby Ingolstadt considered it a personal attack on him and accordingly included Spengler with Luther and Pirckheimer in the threat of excommunication in the bull *Exsurge Domine* of 1520.

A good example of Spengler's constructive religious writings is his *Comforting Christian Prescriptions and Medicine for All Adversities*, written in 1521 and dedicated to his sister Margaretha.[20] In it he concludes that it is impossible to have the sweet without the bitter, happiness without sorrow, good fortune without adversity, and well-being without temptation.

About the same time Spengler wrote his well-known hymn, *Durch Adams Fall* (Through Adam's Fall), the only one of his hymns still extant. Printed in 1525 in a collection of hymns with a preface by Luther, it gained great popularity and soon appeared in many languages.[21]

Spengler's *Short Excerpts from Papal Law* of 1529 was written in support of Luther in his conflict with those jurists who defended the primacy of the papacy through canon law.[22] In the introduction to this pamphlet he accuses the papacy of wanting "to execute Luther before judging him, to judge him before trying him."

Probably the most effective of the council clerk's writings was his *Confession of Faith*, attached to his last will and testament of 1533 and published at Luther's request.[23] The Reformer wrote the introduction to it in which he speaks highly of this "excellent, worthy man Lazarus Spengler" who during his lifetime as a Christian "accepted God's Word, believed in it with all his heart, and accomplished great things with its assistance. Now, on leaving this world, he confesses and confirms such a faith for the comfort and strength of all weak Christians who suffer misfortunes and persecutions for the sake of this same faith." [24] The confession is a clear statement of the main articles of faith as taught by Luther and includes his reasons for denying certain doctrines of Catholicism, Zwinglianism, and Anabaptism.

Spengler demonstrated his effectiveness as a Reformation leader also by his steady course during the critical years leading to the break with Rome. When threatened with excommunication by Eck, he bowed to the wishes of the city council by stating officially that he was a follower, not of Luther but of evangelical truth.[25] Later, when he learned that he had been included among those excommunicated by the papal bull of 3 January 1521, he dropped all pretenses and openly supported the Wittenberg reformer. The city council continued to sympathize with Luther while assuring the emperor that it was remaining loyal to him. When, for example, it officially received the Edict of Worms, it made known that Luther's books were to be burned but postponed announcing that Luther had been outlawed.

During the sessions of the *Reichsregiment* and the meetings of the three imperial diets of 1522–24 in Nürnberg, Spengler encouraged the city council to defend evangelical preachers and prepared written memoranda on a variety of critical issues.[26] By insisting that the evangelical preachers were presenting only Christ and the Word of God, not Luther's doctrines, and that suppression of Christian truth would cause Germans in Nürnberg and elsewhere to revolt, the council placed opponents of the Reformation in an awkward position. It prohibited the publication of Luther's books but did not enforce the prohibition.

When in March 1524 representatives of the South German cities met to draw up a common program of action, Spengler presented a carefully prepared memorandum in which he urged that the cities obey the emperor in all temporal matters but recognize Christ alone as their Lord in all matters pertaining to the soul and their consciences.[27] They should refer the papal legate, who was attempting to suppress the Reformation, to the imperial recess of 1523, which had recognized the right to preach the Gospel as interpreted by the church fathers.

In response to the imperial mandate of July 1524 forbidding the holding of the national church council projected by the diet of that year, Spengler issued a detailed opinion for consideration of the city council. In it he asserted his belief that plans were being made to place Nürnberg and other imperial cities under the imperial ban for not having enforced the Edict of Worms. But he added that this could not be done except by action of the Imperial Court of Justice. For this reason he urged the council not to act out of fear, for it had complied with the laws and had remained loyal to the emperor.[28]

Meanwhile, on Easter 1524, the parish pastors of Nürnberg administered the Lord's Supper in both kinds without prior council approval, read the Mass in German, and discontinued the use of holy water, the singing of the *Salve regina,* and the saying of masses for the dead. When Archduke Ferdinand, Cardinal Legate Campeggio, and the bishop of Bamberg demanded that the reforms be rescinded, the city council refused and declared that these had been made in compliance with Scripture. When the bishop publicly pronounced the provosts of the two parish churches heretics, the council disregarded the order to dismiss them, introduced further evangelical changes, and called for a religious colloquy to be held in March 1525. At this colloquy those monastic preachers who still opposed the reforms were declared in error and Nürnberg officially became Lutheran.

Spengler now turned his attention to the consolidation of the Reformation. Whereas he agreed with the council's policy of permitting the free preaching of the Word of God according to the imperial recess of 1523, he believed that the agitations of the Sacramentarians, Anabaptists, Spiritualists, and social reformers threatened good government and should therefore be suppressed.[29] Because of the sympathetic but firm attitude of the council in the treatment of its peasants and poor townspeople, the city was spared from violence during the Peasants' Revolt and achieved uniformity of religious faith and practice relatively early in the history of the Reformation.

To gain these ends, Spengler recommended to the city council the holding of a church visitation and the formulation of a church order in cooperation with Margrave George of Brandenburg, a Lutheran prince whose lands adjoined those of Nürnberg.[30] The persistence with which he pursued this matter is best illustrated by his relations with Andreas Osiander (d. 1552), his friend and parish preacher at the church of St. Lawrence, who had been appointed head of a commission of four to prepare such a church order. Osiander, however, irritated Spengler by postponing action unduly. When finally he submitted a draft without having consulted the other members of the commission, Spengler rebuked him for his vanity and stubbornness and let him know in no uncertain terms that he should proceed according to instructions.[31]

The council clerk also took a leading part in improving education and in establishing a special school to educate evangelical clergy and further culture in general. He visited Luther and Melanchthon in

Wittenberg in 1525 to discuss the founding of such a school. Although the council could not induce Melanchthon to become its head, it brought him to Nürnberg to help plan it and also to open it formally with a public lecture.

Particularly difficult was Spengler's task of defending Nürnberg's evangelical reforms at the imperial diets. He and the city council were instrumental in gaining concessions for the evangelical estates at the Diet of Speyer of 1526 which, in effect, legalized Nürnberg's reforms. When attempts were made at the Diet of Speyer of 1529 to revoke these concessions, he and the city council remained resolute in their adherence to the Gospel and in using in its defense "protestation, appellation, and provocation." [32]

Spengler played an even more decisive role at the Diet of Augsburg in 1530 through the official representatives of his city, maintaining close contact with them by a special postal service established for this purpose.[33] He was especially active when Melanchthon and others were prepared to make a number of critical concessions to the Catholic estates in the interest of peace. When his fellow citizen Hieronymus Baumgartner wrote him from Augsburg that Melanchthon was "more childish than a child," that Brenz was "not only tactless but coarse and rough," that Heller was "full of fear," and that these men were greatly confusing the pious Margrave George of Brandenburg,[34] Spengler wrote a letter to the margrave counseling him to remain firm in his faith and to trust in God's promise of assistance in this affair.[35] When he received another letter from Baumgartner urging him to induce Luther to intervene,[36] he wrote the Reformer, who promptly sent him a letter to transmit to Melanchthon. But since the news already had been spread that the emperor was preparing to bring the diet to a close, Spengler returned the letter to Luther, for he did not wish to cause the disheartened Melanchthon further anguish. Nürnberg's firm policy was responsible to a large degree for the refusal of the Protestants to grant concessions which, it was felt, would not have appeased the emperor and the Catholic estates at that time.

Although Nürnberg did not accept the imperial recess of 1530, it consistently refused to join the Schmalkaldic League against Charles V, who threatened to use force to bring the Protestants back into the Catholic Church. Spengler always believed that Charles was well intentioned but had been duped by the pope and Catholic princes. Like Luther, he maintained that the emperor retained his divinely given authority even though he had abused it by forbidding the free preaching of God's Word. A Christian should not deny his faith, but neither should he offer armed resistance. His only right, he insisted, was to accept the consequences of his faith and to trust in God alone for protection against an ungodly government.[37] Whereas Luther later reluctantly conceded to the argument of the Saxon jurists that the emperor was bound by oath to defend the laws of the empire and that if he broke his oath the princes might resist him, Spengler clung to his position for both religious and political reasons. He and the council continued to hope that Nürnberg would never take up arms against Charles.

By steering a consistent and moderate course in all matters pertaining to the Reformation, Spengler gained the solid support of his city council and the citizens of Nürnberg and earned an admirable reputation throughout Germany. He was highly regarded for his sincere piety, his activities in behalf of peace, and his diplomatic skill in bringing together for common purposes groups with widely divergent interests. Many reformers, including those at Wittenberg, valued his good judgment and frequently requested written memoranda from him. The elector of Saxony, the duke of Prussia, and the margrave of Brandenburg asked his advice on a wide variety of matters and always gave careful consideration to his proposals. As a remarkably successful lay leader he, with the support of the city council of Nürnberg, exerted a lasting influence on the Reformation.

NOTES

1. The need for further study of the social forces of the Reformation is discussed by Hajo Holborn, "The Social Basis of the German Reformation," *Church History*, V (Dec. 1936), 330—39, and Harold J. Grimm, "Social Forces in the German Reformation," *Church History*, XXXI (March 1962), 3—13. See also A. G. Dickens, *Reformation and Society in Sixteenth Century Europe* (London: Thames and Hudson, 1966).

2. Although there are many accounts about the spread of the Reformation to German cities and towns, few of them are more than narratives of religious or political events. Indicative of a rising interest in the interplay of the many forces involved in this spread are Johannes Schildhauer, *Soziale, politische und religiöse Auseinandersetzungen in den Hansestädten Stralsund, Rostock und Wismar im ersten Drittel des 16. Jahrhunderts* (Weimar, 1959), a Marxist interpretation; Bernd Moeller, *Reichsstadt und Reformation*, "Schriften des Vereins für Reformationsgeschichte," LXIX (Gütersloh, 1962); and Ruth Prange, *Die bremische Kaufmannschaft des 16. und 17. Jahrhunderts in sozialgeschichtlicher Betrachtung*, "Veröffentlichungen aus dem Staatsarchiv der Freien Hansestadt Bremen," XXI (Bremen, 1963).

3. The best and most detailed biography of Spengler, but covering his life only to the year 1524, is by Hans von Schubert, *Lazarus Spengler und die Reforma-*

tion in Nürnberg, "Quellen und Forschungen zur Reformationsgeschichte," XVII, ed. Hajo Holborn (Leipzig, 1934). Still useful because of the inclusion of much source material is Urbanus Gottlieb Haussdorff, *Lebens-Beschreibung eines christlichen Politici, nehmlich Lazari Spenglers, weiland vördersten Ratsschreibers zu Nürnberg* (Nürnberg, 1741). Theodor Pressel has provided an excellent biography with extracts of a number of Spengler's Reformation pamphlets in his *Reformation in der Reichsstadt Nürnberg nach den Flugschriften ihres Ratsschreibers Lazarus Spenglers* (Halle/Saale, 1926). See also Freiherr Georg von Kress, "Ein markgräflicher Kanzleirath über Lazarus Spengler," *Mitteilungen des Vereins für Geschichte der Stadt Nürnberg*, I (1879), 94—95.

4. The Spengler family history, begun by Georg and continued by Lazarus under the title *Geschlechtbuch*, is contained in the Spengler "Nachlass" in the Stadtarchiv in Nürnberg. I am grateful to Archivdirektor Dr. Werner Schultheiss and his staff for making the "Nachlass" and other materials available to me.

5. The most helpful accounts of the history of Nürnberg during the Reformation era are Adolph Engelhardt, *Die Reformation in Nürnberg*, 2 vols., in *Mitteilungen des Vereins für Geschichte der Stadt Nürnberg*, XXXIII—XXXIV (Nürnberg, 1936—37); Austin P. Evans, *An Episode in the Struggle for Religious Freedom; the Secretaries of Nuremberg, 1524—28* (New York, 1924); Eugen Franz, *Nürnberg, Kaiser und Reich* (Munich, 1930); E. Kusch, *Nürnberg: Lebensbild einer Stadt* (Nürnberg, 1950); Georg Ludewig, *Die Politik Nürnbergs im Zeitalter der Reformation* (Göttingen, 1893); Gerhard Pfeiffer, "Die Einführung der Reformation in Nürnberg als kirchenrechtliches und bekenntniskundliches Problem," *Blätter für deutsche Landesgeschichte*, LXXXIX (1952), 112—33; E. Reicke, *Geschichte der Reichsstadt Nürnberg* (Nürnberg, 1896); and Friedrich Roth, *Die Einführung der Reformation in Nürnberg* (Würzburg, 1885). The official action of the city council during this period is preserved in its *Protokolle*, *Ratsverlässe*, and *Briefbücher* in the Staatsarchiv in Nürnberg. Archivdirektor Dr. Fritz Schnelbögl and his staff went beyond the line of duty in making these materials available to me.

6. Hans Baron, "Religion and Politics in the German Imperial Cities during the Reformation," *English Historical Review*, LII (July 1937), 405—27; ibid., LII (Oct. 1937), 614—33. See especially p. 616.

7. Schubert, pp. 31—32, 92.

8. Ibid., pp. 35—36.

9. In the Spengler "Nachlass" is a copy of the council clerk's memorandum of 1526 to his son Lazarus in the latter's handwriting (No. 2), in which the senior gives excellent expression to his ethical concerns.

10. A copy of this rare work is in the library of the Germanisches Museum in Nürnberg. See Schubert, pp. 115—18, and Pressel, pp. 7—8.

11. Paul Kalkoff, *Die Reformation in der Reichsstadt Nürnberg nach den Flugschriften ihres Ratsschreibers Lazarus Spengler* (Halle, 1926), p. 6. The importance of humanism in the early spread of the Reformation is discussed by Bernd Moeller, "Die deutschen Humanisten und die Anfänge der Reformation," *Zeitschrift für Kirchengeschichte*, LXX (1959), 46—61. See also Lewis Spitz, *The Religious Renaissance of the German Humanists* (Cambridge, Mass., 1963).

12. Schubert, p. 142.

13. Pressel, pp. 15, 16.

14. Schubert, p. 163.

15. WA I, 689—710. Banner bearer of the group was Ebner, to whom Luther

dedicated his *Commentary on Psalm 110*. It was Nützel, second in authority to Ebner in the city council, who had Luther's Ninety-five Theses translated into German for publication and distribution in Nürnberg.

16. Schubert, pp. 131—38.
17. M. M. Meyer, *Spengleriana* (Nürnberg, 1830), pp. 13—62.
18. WA XXX/2, 508—88.
19. First published anonymously in 1519 and reprinted several times. Luther provided the introduction for one printing. See Kalkoff, pp. 6—9; Schubert, pp. 190—95; and Pressel, pp. 17—26, which contains the entire pamphlet.
20. Pressel, pp. 32—35.
21. Ibid., p. 49.
22. Kalkoff, pp. 103—18.
23. First published by Joseph Klug in Wittenberg in 1535 under the title *Bekendnis Lazari Spengler weiland Syndici der Stadt Nürnberg. Mit Vorrhede Dr. Mart. Luth.*, and by Jobst Gotknecht in Nürnberg under the same title. Both the first will of 1529 and the second of 1533 are given in their entirety in Haussdorff, pp. 468—508. See also Pressel, pp. 93—99.
24. Haussdorff, p. 504.
25. See the detailed accounts of the negotiations in Schubert, pp. 201—53, and Paul Kalkoff, *Pirkheimers und Spenglers Lösung vom Banne 1521* (Breslau, 1898).
26. Roth, pp. 104—52; Schubert, pp. 316—441; Engelhardt, I, 93—162.
27. Ibid., pp. 136—37.
28. Ibid., pp. 151—52.
29. See Spengler's correspondence with Theobald Billican concerning Zwinglianism in Haussdorff, pp. 213—70.
30. H. Westermayer, *Die Brandenburgisch-Nürnbergische Kirchenvisitation und Kirchenordnung 1528—33* (Erlangen, 1894); Karl Schornbaum, *Zur Politik des Markgrafen Georg von Brandenburg* (Munich, 1906), especially p. 30; and Engelhardt, II, 69—140.
31. The correspondence between Spengler and Osiander on this matter is given in detail in Haussdorff, pp. 271—316.
32. Engelhardt, II, 171.
33. For detailed accounts of the negotiations at Augsburg see Ludewig, pp. 109 to 131, and Engelhardt, II, 211—66. See also Wilhelm Vogt, "Die Korrespondenz des Nürnberger Rates mit seinen zum Augsburger Reichstag von 1530 abgeordneten Gesandten," *Mitteilungen des Vereins für Geschichte der Stadt Nürnberg*, IV (1882), 1—60.
34. This letter is given in its entirety in Haussdorff, pp. 71—77.
35. Ibid., p. 81.
36. Ibid., pp. 74—77.
37. These views are best expressed in one of Spengler's memoranda given the Nürnberg city council. Engelhardt, II, 272—73; Pressel, pp. 59—61.

5

THE THESES AND WITTENBERG

Ernest G. Schwiebert

Ⅰn LUTHERAN circles it has long been customary to hold Reformation festivals on 31 October; but the choice of that date as a symbol of the Reformation seems to have evolved gradually. Although there may have been earlier celebrations, the first recorded one occurred on 31 October 1617, when a group of Wittenberg professors gathered in the well-preserved *Lutherstube*, scene of the Reformer's labors for so many years, sang *Ein' feste Burg ist unser Gott*, and then marched in solemn procession to the *Schlosskirche* (Castle Church) to hold a religious service.[1] This 100th anniversary of the event seems, however, to have been unique. Such commemorations did not become annual festivals even in Electoral Saxony until 1668; in the remainder of the Saxon lands around Weimar and Jena not until 1718.[2] Since that time the custom has spread throughout Lutheranism.

The colorful 400th anniversary of Luther's nailing of his famous Ninety-five Theses, celebrated at Wittenberg, Germany, on 31 October 1917, was described by Max Senf, a former custodian of the *Luther-*

halle museum, as a triple celebration; the event was commemorated in three separate services.³ Although this was the final year of the First World War, Wittenberg was elaborately decorated. Early in the morning the people gathered in front of the *Katharinen-Portal* ⁴ of the *Lutherhaus.* Here they first heard a brief address before forming the customary religious procession in which they marched through the *Prediger Seminar* entrance, down *Collegien Gasse,* and along the *Schloss Gasse* to the *Schlosskirche.* A group of catechumens led the procession, followed by the seminary students, faculty, clergymen, and a number of distinguished visitors. The big bell in the *Stadtkirche,* which in Reformation times had so often been rung to announce doctoral promotions and on other special occasions, tolled once more as the solemn procession moved through the familiar streets to the recently rebuilt Castle Church.⁵

Principal speaker in the religious service in the Castle Church was Prof. D. Jordan, curator of the museum in the *Lutherhalle.* He recalled the past greatness of Wittenberg and of Luther, who lay buried beneath the floor below the pulpit of the Castle Church.⁶ This early morning service was followed by another in the *Stadtkirche,* the well-preserved Town Church where Luther had delivered so many of his stirring and powerful sermons for more than three decades. The Luther pulpit is no longer there, but otherwise few alterations have been made through the years. In the midst of war and hardship the speaker tried to console his hearers with the thought that the God of Luther's day was still living come what may and that they should hold firmly to the faith Luther had taught them.⁷

A third service was held in the *Grosse Hoersaal.* This large lecture room, capable of accommodating about 400 people, is on the second floor of the *Lutherhalle,* opposite the Luther study and directly above the monk's sleeping quarters.⁸ Here stood a *Katheder* similar to that used by Luther when he delivered his early lectures on the Psalms and Romans in this room. On this occasion Professor Jordan ascended the old *Katheder,* now a museum piece, and delivered the address. The exact origin of this particular *Katheder* is unknown; it may be from the 17th century, but some believe it is one of those which originally stood in the Castle Church and was used in various ceremonies. This one is about 9 feet tall, reaching almost to the ceiling. It has three levels joined by steps at either end and is elaborately and colorfully ornamented with pictures and the university seals. At the top level is a single seat that was occupied by the presiding official. On the second level were places for several professors or distinguished guests.

121

At the center of this level is a lectern from which participants addressed the audience. This is but one of many mementos collected in the Luther museum housed in his former home, the *Lutherhalle*. This museum was a magnet for Lutherans from all over the world prior to the Second World War.[9]

During the past years scholars throughout the world have expended much time and energy analyzing the various aspects of the Reformation, such as the Catholic indulgence traffic, the activities of John Tetzel and other agents employed by Albert of Mainz, the actual content and purpose of the Ninety-five Theses, and Luther's development as the Reformer. These fields have been extensively explored, and it would appear that the themes had been exhausted. Yet two recent studies have challenged the date of 31 October 1517 as the beginning of the German Reformation. Professor Hans Volz has thoroughly explored the indulgence story and the activities of Tetzel as the prelude to Luther's Ninety-five Theses, but in attempting to establish the date he disregarded all the clear Melanchthonian evidence, which stated definitely that the theses were nailed on the door of the Castle Church at 2 o'clock in the afternoon of 31 October 1517, and concluded that the event occurred on All Saints' Day, 1 November.[10] Nor did he consider the light thrown on the observance of All Saints' Day by the *Dialogus of 1507*,[11] which brings out the advisability of purchasing large wax candles at the *Apotheke* on the *Markt* the day before All Saints' Day because the Mass would begin at 6 o'clock in the morning. The candles should be large enough to last throughout the day while the pilgrims prayed before each of the many relics. It would seem to follow that Luther would not have been likely to nail his theses to the door on the day and at an hour when the visitors would already be inside and the festival nearly over. Erwin Iserloh has advanced the thesis that since there were no immediate references to the nailing in contemporary sources and since an actual recording of the event did not occur until decades later, the event is but a legend.[12] Scholars both here and in Europe have failed to react favorably to either the Volz or the Iserloh theses, and 31 October is a date still marked for worldwide Reformation festivals.

THE PHYSICAL ENVIRONMENT OF THE NINETY-FIVE THESES

The relationship between the Castle Church and the University of Wittenberg was an intimate one. The Castle Church had been a *Stift*, a richly endowed Catholic Church property administered directly by

Rome.[13] As an endowed feudal corporation, the funds of this *Stift* were sufficient to support 81 clergymen in the late Middle Ages.[14] Of course not all of these funds were immediately available to finance the university upon its founding in 1502; but after the *Stift* became a Protestant institution and the dependent clergymen gradually passed away, its funds could be, and were, diverted for the university's annual budget.[15] When the university was founded, the elector converted the Castle Church into the university chapel where religious services, convocations, promotions, and disputations were held. The castle proper, of which the church formed but one wing, was no longer used as a royal residence and was also diverted to university use. It housed the university library on the second floor;[16] the lower floor contained the lecture rooms of the law college.[17] Students using the library or attending the classes in civil and canon law passed through the main north door of the Castle Church and either up a corner stairway or across the inner courtyard to the library and classrooms. As a main point of entry, this door of the Castle Church was a logical location for the *Schwarze Brett,* or official university bulletin board, for official announcements of university events, including the posting of theses and announcing the date for all types of disputations.

The original Castle Church was destroyed by fire on 13 October 1760 during the Seven Years' War. It is therefore difficult to visualize the environment in which disputations were held. Faber in his *Historische Nachricht* of 1730 [18] left a brief description, and Giorgi in his *Wittenbergische Klagegeschichte* described its destruction and included in Plate III an interior view of the former beautiful Gothic structure.[19] A former Wittenberg professor, writing under the nom de plume of Charitius about 1740,[20] knew the original structure well. In an unpublished manuscript he described the door on which the theses were nailed, but was understandably skeptical about the nail still being exhibited as the one actually used by Luther. In more recent times Heinrich Heubner, custodian of the museum in the castle, described the interior of the former Castle Church and gave this description of the area where the disputations took place:

> When the Church became an academic university chapel, the Rector had a special *Katheder* in front of the altar; to its left, next to the wall, were the benches of the theologians, jurists, and medics, and these faced the benches of the philosophical faculty. Directly opposite the rector's *Katheder* at the west end of the church in front of the large pillar stood the doctor's *Katheder* which served for promotions toward the doctorate.[21]

123

Here many famous debates took place. Here, too, Luther hoped to debate his Ninety-five Theses with his fellow professors.

THE DISPUTATION IN MEDIEVAL ACADEMIC LIFE

Further light can be thrown on the circumstances surrounding Luther's Ninety-five Theses by a study of the academic environment surrounding the use of disputations and their application to various phases of university life. These lively debates were somewhat comparable to the College Bowl television shows of the present day, and also supplied the students with the entertainment afforded today by football games and other athletic contests.

Most medieval universities were patterned after either Paris or Bologna, and the University of Wittenberg was no exception.[22] At the University of Paris, commonly regarded as the "Mother of Universities," the use of disputations developed quite early. Both faculty and students participated, and such debates were highly regarded as an educational tool. Peter Abelard's famous *Sic et Non* (Yes and No) is an excellent illustration of the materials developed for such debates.[23] In it he placed side by side teachings of the Fathers which contradicted each other. It was his belief that these contradictions served to confuse the students and that such confusion made them examine and analyze the grounds on which the doctrines of the Roman Church rested. There were many stormy sessions at the University of Paris in the days of St. Thomas Aquinas, both inside and outside the classroom. Such debates were often concluded with fisticuffs in frequent street brawls between nations. Arab students, for example, bringing into St. Thomas' classes doctrines such as a denial of the immortality of the soul, furnished grounds for heated debates and many a student fracas.[24]

Later there emerged the well-regulated disputation controlled by university statutes which laid down exact rules governing the conduct of public debates. Professors were required to take their turn presiding over the debates, the order of participation being strictly according to rank and length of tenure. When a faculty member wished to hold a disputation, he drafted appropriate theses, chose an opponent, and scheduled the confrontation. Well-drafted theses were the foundation of a good disputation, and the deans took a lively interest in the subject matter to be covered, since through this medium students would be exposed to a broad view of the discipline. Some theses were purposely overstated to permit the respondent good ground for argument. This practice of overstatement explains why some of Luther's

Ninety-five Theses were so immoderate; so much so, in fact, that his friends were frightened. Luther revealed this fact in a letter to his former Erfurt professor, Jodocus Trutvetter, and later in a *Table Talk*. According to the latter source, Jerome Schurff, who was to serve as Luther's legal advisor at Worms, asked Luther what he was trying to do, start something with the papacy? [25]

DISPUTATIONS AT THE UNIVERSITY OF WITTENBERG

The University of Wittenberg, founded in 1502, was given regulations governing disputations by the *Statutes of 1508*.[26] They were drafted by the Saxon Court and, covering the traditional four faculties of philosophy or liberal arts, law, medicine, and theology, established disputations as a regular and accepted method of instruction at all levels. It is interesting to observe how carefully the rules were drawn, specifying the areas to be covered in each faculty, stipulating the number of times debates were to be conducted, drafting a schedule as to when the facilities of the institution would be available for disputations in the respective colleges, and specifying even the time of day and number of hours.[27] The high value ascribed by the authorities to disputations as an educational tool is also evident in the amounts of money budgeted each year by the Saxon Court for payment of the faculty participants. As has been noted, such an undertaking required considerable effort by the professor in drafting the theses, securing their approval and a suitable date, selecting the necessary participants, posting the theses, and presiding over the debate. The senior faculty members were quite well rewarded for such labors. In the upper faculties the professor in charge was paid the equivalent of $100, the respondents $50, and bachelors playing a supporting role were given $20. As these sums were bonus amounts paid in addition to the regular salaries, the efforts would seem to have been appreciated and financially quite rewarding.[28]

The amounts paid varied, however, among the several schools. In liberal arts the rewards were not as lucrative as in others; in fact, they seem too low. This may have been due partly to the fact that many of the faculty members in the liberal arts college were young and had not yet achieved the higher degrees; but Wittenberg's liberal arts faculty also had some very well trained and in some cases brilliant men, for example, Philip Melanchthon and the Hebrew scholar Mattaeus Goldhahn, more commonly known as Aurogallus. In this faculty the master who presided over a disputation received the equivalent of $20, the respondents each $10, and bachelors assisting received but $5. This difference may explain why, as the records indicate, it was sometimes difficult to obtain the participation of this faculty in the debates. Failure to participate, however, drew reprimands in the form of fines. In the early regulations the fine was $25, but it was later increased to $200 in the higher faculties and a comparable amount in liberal arts.[29] Since the reward in the liberal arts faculty was so low, the question naturally arises: Why was their fine the equal of the upper faculties? The *Statutes* did not explain that point, but were quite explicit on the method of discipline. Offenders were first reported to the dean, who reported quarterly to the rector. In stubborn cases the rector could take the matter before the entire faculty. If that failed to obtain the desired result, the case could be taken to the Saxon Court for appropriate action.[30]

Some exceptions were made. Some faculty members in later years, like Luther, Schurff, and Melanchthon, were getting on in years and had additional duties. Johannes Bugenhagen, the town pastor, had a large congregation to oversee. Some professors, notably Melanchthon, Luther, and Bugenhagen, did considerable traveling, and Melanchthon frequently represented the elector at important meetings. The authorities recognized these extenuating circumstances.[31] They also realized that the subject matter of some disciplines did not lend itself too well to such disputations; therefore, professors in rhetoric, poetry, and the Latin and Greek classics were not required to debate. Instead the faculty and students presented a declamation every other week in which they might recite from Demosthenes or Cicero or even present a Latin or Greek oration written by themselves. Graduate students were also asked to take part in such declamations.[32]

THE TYPES OF DISPUTATIONS

Disputations were of two general types: the educational or instructional type and the promotional type employed in the granting of advanced degrees. As an educational tool the disputation was a method of clarifying issues and training students; it should not be confused with the promotional disputation whose aim was to test the student's maturity and his qualifications for academic advancement, although procedures were similar in both instances.

Educational or instructional type debates occurred nearly every day and were not made a matter of official record. Promotional disputations, on the other hand, were carefully recorded by the deans of the four faculties. In the school of theology, with which we are here

126

principally concerned, such debates were recorded in the *Liber Decanorum,* or Book of the Deans.[33] But this official record does not contain one reference to the indulgence struggle. Nor would the world likely have learned anything about Luther's Ninety-five Theses had they not generated such a violent reaction in conservative Catholic circles.[34]

At the very lowest level of academic instruction were the practice disputations. These training exercises were usually held in the dormitories after the evening meal. No doubt the *aula* in the New Friderici College served as a convenient meeting place. The *Statutes* imply that these debates were in the field of liberal arts, covering themes similar to those of the classroom lectures and coordinated by the faculty and dean to aid the student in his grasp of subject matter and to provide practice in the art of debating.[35] The record is not entirely clear, but it is doubtful that these practice sessions counted as the regular disputations in which the faculty members were required to participate once a year. It is also possible that a similar type of closed or private, that is, within the university family, disputation was held in the promotion of students at lower levels as a means of determining whether the student was sufficiently mature to debate creditably in public.

Again the record is hazy, but it appears from sums paid for participation in such an affair that the "circular" type of disputation might also have been employed in these practice sessions, for the record mentioned the respondent, the opponents, and the bachelors who customarily took part in the circular disputations. In this type of disputation the candidate stood in front of the candidate's *Katheder* with two bachelors on either side. The presiding official would call on the participating faculty masters by rank. Each would step to the lectern and expound some aspect of the subject under dispute. The official would then call on the bachelors to debate these aspects. Some of them took the part of hecklers and deliberately tried to confuse the issues. The candidate was required to wait until all participants had had their say. Then the presiding officer called on him for a summation. This he was permitted to do at length and in detail. If he had a good memory, and indeed he needed one, he could refute point by point the issues raised. The other participants were then permitted a rebuttal. At the close the candidate would thank the audience for its patience and the participants for their assistance. He was expected to retain his equanimity throughout the ordeal and to be gracious to all concerned, though he was permitted the clever use of satire and humor, provided he was not malicious, when the occasion warranted.[36]

Another type of educational disputation was the regular faculty disputation, a much more formal academic exercise somewhat comparable to a faculty recital by members of a music faculty. The faculty debate served both to clarify thinking on specific themes by exposing them to the cross fire of a public disputation and to provide an example of procedure and tactics of defending a given thesis before a critical and informed audience. These debates were open to the public, and the entire faculty and student body were required to attend. To be effective, the disputation had to be well organized. Theses were formulated with great care, and the coming event was publicly announced. Procedure might be the same as in the student practice sessions or might be the circular disputation. Such a debate might last for several hours and was extremely valuable in clarifying issues, examining all sides of a controversy, and aiding the public, as well as the students, to become informed on the pertinent issues of the day — and providing rousing entertainment. These were the debates in which faculty members were required to participate at least once a year.

This was the type of academic disputation Luther had in mind when he posted his Ninety-five Theses. Had Luther's debate actually taken place, it would have been held in the Castle Church and preceded by the customary academic procession. After all had taken their prescribed positions in the church, the dean would arise and announce that Dr. Martin Luther, professor of theology, had drafted a set of theses as posted on the bulletin board, which the audience had no doubt seen, and that these propositions would now be debated by Dr. Luther and the several opponents whom the dean would introduce. As the proponent, Luther would sit at the top of the academic *Katheder,* facing the rector at the opposite *Katheder,* while the professors in order of rank would present certain groups of theses related to a common theme and call on the bachelors to discuss them pro and con. Following their presentation, Luther would enter the debate, and the ensuing lively interchange would cover all aspects of the Ninety-five Theses, analyze them thoroughly, and draw conclusions as to their validity. Had the debate been held, Luther's theses would have been subjected to a thorough scrutiny by his peers, their validity or falsity established, a conclusion as to Rome's responsibility for the activities of Albert of Mainz and his indulgence salesmen might have been reached, and the students would have most certainly gained new knowledge of and insight into the practice of indulgence sales and other abuses in the Roman Catholic Church.

One point to be remembered about this type of debate, however, is that no record was kept of these educational exercises, or at least none has been discovered. As noted above, a study of the *Liber Decanorum* reveals the regrettable fact that it does not contain a single reference to the Ninety-five Theses,[37] nor is there any mention of the subject of indulgences. This omission also explains why there was no record made of the posting of the *Theses* until Melanchthon mentioned the fact in his short *Vita Lutheri* written after Luther's death in 1546.[38] And it was not until much later that this act began to symbolize the beginning of the German Reformation.

The other type of disputation, the promotional, might be used at all levels, but it was particularly important at the graduate level. For example, in theology both the *Statutes* and the *Liber Decanorum* defined this type of disputation in considerable detail for the various degrees. The debates were scheduled on certain festival days and were always recorded in the dean's official report, but they did not count toward the obligation of each faculty member to participate in a debate at least once yearly as a method of student training.[39] The faculty members, however, were required to attend these promotional debates, for they acted as judges of the candidate's performance and voted for or against his promotion.[40] According to the regulations, they were enjoined to search their consciences before casting their vote lest an ignoramus be advanced unworthily to the shame of both faculty and institution.[41] The *Liber Decanorum* implied that the faculty might have been somewhat lax in its earlier evaluations but that by 1509 the higher requirements embodied in the *Statutes of 1508* were being enforced.

PROMOTIONAL DEGREES AT WITTENBERG

There were four steps toward the degree of Doctor at the University of Wittenberg as at most other European universities of that day. The first was the *Baccalaureus Biblicus,* or more informally, *Biblicus,* followed by the *Sententiarius, Formatus,* and *Licentiatus* before the Doctorate. The length of time required to obtain this degree varied with the ability of the candidate. For example, Martin Luther received the *Biblicus* degree at Erfurt in 1509 and completed his Doctorate at Wittenberg in the fall of 1512.[42]

Since the school of theology was a graduate school, the candidate for the degree of *Biblicus* presumably had already earned a master's degree in liberal arts. The *Statutes of 1508* estimated that from five to seven years of further study were necessary to achieve the degree of *Biblicus.* The student was required to attend two lecture courses on portions of the Old and New Testaments and also to attend a series of lectures delivered on certain special holidays. Some previous experience as an acolyte was desirable. The masters preferred that studies in theology be begun at a rather leisurely pace through reading and engaging in much relaxed reflection. The extent of the student's maturity was left to the judgment of the faculty. The record is somewhat contradictory as to when the student began the study of Lombard's *Sentences,* but Lombard was certainly the heart and core of his studies for the *Sententiarius* and of his advanced work toward the *Licentiatus* and the Doctorate.[43]

Lombard's *Sentences,* divided into four books, was the standard text for theologians of the Middle Ages. Peter Lombard preferred an approach opposite to that of Peter Abelard, mentioned earlier. Instead of trying to create confusion in the student's mind, Lombard, believing that the student was already confused enough, aimed to harmonize and simplify the doctrinal problems created by the different scholastic teachings and to use an orderly approach to an understanding of Roman Catholic doctrines. The first two books of his *Sentences* covered the great themes of God and the Holy Trinity, Creation, Angels, the Fall of Man, and the Grace of God.[44] Even though the student had attended lectures on these great themes before becoming a candidate for the *Biblicus,* he was certainly going to learn much more about Lombard's views as he advanced. Not only would he attend more lectures, but his mastery of the entire Lombard, both as to subject matter and his dialectical skill, would be tested in public disputation.

According to the *Statutes of 1508,* when the student believed he was ready for the degree of *Biblicus,* he arranged for an interview with the dean of theology. If the dean agreed that the student was ready, he assembled the masters who made up the senate and discussed privately with them the student's ability and maturity. If the consensus was favorable, the student was called before this august body of masters and took an oath in which he swore that there would be no hard feelings or reprisals should he not pass, and that during all examinations and debates he would be forthright in answering all questions honestly. On the other hand, the faculty members also promised by a show of hands that they would strive to be objective in the examination, but that they would not promote the candidate should they find him not qualified. It appeared that most *Biblicus* disputations were of the closed type with only a limited audience. If the student passed the test and disputation, he was made a *Biblicus*. This degree qualified him to teach in the *Studium Generale* of the philosophical college and to expound those books of the Old and New Testaments in which he had been examined and found qualified. Some exceptional students appeared to have been permitted to lecture also on the first two books of Lombard's *Sentences*.[45]

Following his promotion to *Biblicus,* the theological student widened his area of study. He now attended lectures on the entire Bible and covered all four books of Lombard. He deepened his knowledge of the first two books and added the great New Testament themes found in books three and four on the Incarnation, the Virtues, Sin, the Seven Sacraments, and the Last Things.[46] When the student had completed this course of study, he submitted to a private oral examination that might last all day. If the senate agreed that he was qualified, the candidate was subjected to the ordeal of a public disputation. The professor whose turn it was to do so drafted the appropriate theses and arranged for the debate. Should the masters who judged the debate find the candidate sufficiently knowledgeable on Lombard and possessing the necessary dialectical dexterity, the dean would present the student to the chancellor with the recommendation that the degree of *Sententiarius* be conferred. A convocation of the entire university was then arranged at which the chancellor delivered a stirring address, extolling the qualifications and accomplishments of the candidate, following which the degree was bestowed with appropriate ceremony. The degree of *Sententiarius* qualified the recipient to teach any aspect of Roman Catholic dogma as set forth in Lombard's *Sentences*. Martin Luther had reached this stage of his theological training when as an assistant to Professor Nathin he lectured at Erfurt from 1509 to 1511 on the *Sentences*.[47]

The requirements for the degree of *Formatus* are not very clearly defined in the *Statutes of 1508*. Apparently they entailed a further period of maturation by means of actual classroom teaching experience. The *Liber Decanorum* mentions young instructors trading assignments on Lombard's books. One might lecture for a time on the first two books and then trade assignments with someone lecturing on the last two. The senate appeared to regard this practice as wholesome training. In the case of Carlstadt,[48] the *Formatus* degree was a kind of trial to test both the maturity of the candidate in a public disputation and to measure his future promise. If the student performed well, he was encouraged to go on for the *Licentiatus* and the

Doctorate. If he was not too promising, he would be persuaded at this point not to attempt the higher degrees.

The two final degrees were decidedly difficult, and the examinations were so similar that the *Statutes of 1508* do not distinguish between them; yet, according to the *Liber Decanorum,* each involved separate senate action and required participation in a circular disputation. The student who withstood the ordeal of the *Licentiatus* usually went on to complete the Doctorate. Following the required ordeal of the circular disputation, the degree would be awarded on the following day with appropriate ceremonies as described above. The candidate had now successfully achieved the five steps in the field of theology and was regarded as a master of both the Bible and Lombard. Yet the theologian produced by this method may be regarded, in modern German terminology, as one of the *Altgläubigen* and not yet the *Neugläubigen* which would emerge from the German Reformation.

The *Liber Decanorum* was quite detailed in recording the promotions of two prominent candidates, Bodenstein von Carlstadt and "Martinus lueder." On 31 October 1510 all the professors of theology and the vice-chancellor of the university assembled at 8 o'clock in the morning in the *aula* of the Friderici College. In the opening address Dean Trutvetter spoke of Carlstadt's maturity as a scholastic theologian and stated that, in his opinion, Carlstadt should be granted the Doctorate.[49] Accordingly, on 12 November 1510 the customary vesper service was held with the venerable Doctor Polich von Mellerstadt in charge of the disputation. The next day Peter Lupinus conducted the ceremony granting Carlstadt the Doctorate while the great bell of the Town Church announced the event in solemn cadence. Many dignitaries were present, including some Frenchmen who later entertained the theological faculty, the new Doctor, and some guests at a sumptuous repast.[50]

An entry in the *Liber Decanorum* on 18 October 1512 recorded the promotion to the Doctorate of a member of the Augustinian Hermits and a *Licentiatus* in theology, one Martinus lueder. The early afternoon vesper service was led by the lord archdeacon of the Castle Church, the aforementioned Bodenstein von Carlstadt, in which the principal feature was the customary disputation for the Doctorate in the circular form and lasting this time for several hours. On the following day Carlstadt again officiated in ceremonies granting Luther the Doctorate. Passages were read from Holy Scripture, the candidate took the customary oath, was presented with a Bible, had the black biretta denoting a doctor of divinity placed on his head and a silver ring on his finger; and all the while the great bell sounded in honor of the occasion. Addresses were delivered by Wenceslaus Link, then dean of theology, and Nicholas von Amsdorf, the town pastor. At the close of the ceremonies Luther addressed the assembly, thanking them for their attendance and the officiants for their assistance. Within a few days he was formally presented to the university senate, an official act that made him a member of the faculty.[51]

Between the years 1503 and 1517 there were, by actual count, 104 promotions bestowed at Wittenberg in the school of theology and duly recorded in the *Liber Decanorum*. One of these is not identified, but the remainder are divided as follows:

Biblicus	30
Sententiarius	22
Formatus	17
Licentiatus	22
Doctorate	12

In some instances the record is more detailed than in others, but those cited above give the name of the candidate and frequently evaluate how well he performed.[52]

When the esteemed Erfurt professor Jodocus Trutvetter came to Wittenberg in 1509, he was immediately honored with the appointment as dean of theology. During his term some interesting entries appear in the *Liber Decanorum*. For example, a certain Brother Melchior was promoted to *Biblicus,* but the dean was apparently not too favorably impressed with his performance, for he made the following entry in the official record:

> On the same day, the second hour in the afternoon, with all the masters assembled in Mellerstadt's home, the faculty decided by a unanimous vote that no one in the future should be admitted to this degree who had been trained outside Wittenberg, unless that student's work had been done in a regular *Studien Generale,* in which there was at least one ranking professor, a master of theology, whose lectures he had attended; and, furthermore, unless in that university he had participated in disputations when scheduled by the professor in charge and had taken part in these practice debates.[53]

The entry states further that a student who came from another institution should be required to give proof of his faithfulness by the presentation of his lecture notes, testifying that they were his own and that he had made use of them in lectures delivered by himself.

The faculty also decided that only students with a master of arts degree in the school of philosophy would be eligible for advanced degrees in theology in the future.[54]

To summarize, the disputation as an academic tool might be used in several ways. When used as an educational tool, it might be public or closed, and it served both as a method of expanding the student's knowledge of the subject matter under discussion and as a training ground in the art of public debate, an accomplishment greatly admired. In the educational type the person who had drafted the theses was under fire and must defend his position, while other participants might assume positions either pro or con. The *Statutes* stated that the purpose of such a performance was not to demonstrate one's facility at debate but to elucidate the truth or falsity of a position; in other words, the debate was to establish whether certain viewpoints were tenable. In actual practice a skilled debater who defended his position in masterful fashion and exhibited considerable knowledge of his subject matter would be cheered by the students and even carried on their shoulders through the streets of the town after a particularly controversial debate.

The promotional type of disputation was quite different both in purpose and in execution. Now it was the candidate alone who was under fire. The theses were formulated by the professor and were designed to test the student's maturity both in the mastery of subject matter and in his dialectical skill in refuting his opponents, covering all the points raised and giving evidence of his worthiness to be granted the degree he was seeking. Such a debate taxed the student's memory, his stamina, and possibly at times also his temper.

From this examination of the various types and methods of disputations it becomes clear that Luther's Ninety-five Theses belong to the instructional type. He wished to hold a public disputation in which he would seek to defend the propositions he had formulated against the viewpoints and opinions of his colleagues. Such a debate would examine and weigh the issues surrounding the burgeoning indulgence sales then being conducted in the area by Albert of Mainz and his agents, and would serve to clarify Luther's own thinking and also draw the attention of others to the problem. The debate never took place because no opponent was ready or willing to debate this highly inflammatory issue,[55] and no record was made of it, nor of hundreds of similar debates that were actually held, because only promotional disputations were recorded.[56]

The change in the University of Wittenberg from a Roman Catholic to a Lutheran institution is clearly reflected in the *Statutes of 1533* drafted by Philip Melanchthon.[57] The courses in theology were now very different. Bible instruction embraced the new theology gradually introduced by Martin Luther in the period from 1517 to 1533. In this undertaking he had the close cooperation of Melanchthon and the entire Wittenberg faculty. In consonance with the change in theological instruction, the curriculum in the school of philosophy had been reorganized and reoriented by placing great emphasis on a mastery of Greek and Hebrew and a broad knowledge of the classics. Declamations designed to develop the student for later Biblical exegesis in the theological school had been introduced by Melanchthon as early as 1526. When the elector reinstated promotions and disputations in 1533, the theological faculty reexamined the type of degrees to be offered in theology.[58]

The *Statutes of 1533* established new rules in theology for Wittenberg, but outwardly much of the old system remained. The change was more of substance than of form. Lombard's *Sentences* were regarded as wholly unacceptable and were dropped entirely.[59] The Augsburg Confession was now the general norm in theological doctrine. Classroom lectures were almost entirely exegetical, and students were expected to be accomplished exegetes by the time they reached the doctorate level. In the disputations the student did not argue on the basis of Lombard but his own exegesis. The test was now on how well he could defend his interpretations by drawing substantiating passages from different books of the Bible and analyzing them in the original Greek or Hebrew.[60] His training in the liberal arts college had been heavily humanistic under Melanchthon's guidance, and in the graduate school he could build on this earlier foundation. He had participated in many disputations in the lower levels, had become proficient in Latin, Greek, and Hebrew, and could prepare his own orations for declamations, all of which made him well qualified to follow the lectures at the graduate level.[61]

The 1533 *Statutes* established four disputations yearly in the school of theology. The dean was to supervise the content of the theses to be debated, and in case of any unresolved disagreement as to the theses he could refer the matter to the rector; or in extreme cases the debate would be postponed until the entire faculty had examined the controversy and reached a decision whether to accept, modify, or reject the proposals.[62]

These *Statutes* stipulated that there would now be four degrees granted in theology, namely, *Biblicus, Sententiarius, Formatus,* and the Doctorate.[63] For the degree of *Biblicus* the student was expected to master St. Paul's Epistle to the Romans and St. John's Gospel on the Trinity, since these portions of the Scriptures contained a summation of all Christian doctrine.[64] A student well grounded in his belief as based on these sources was prepared to defend his position in examinations and disputations and was worthy of being granted the degree of *Biblicus*.

The title of the degree of *Sententiarius* presented the Reformers with a problem. Melanchthon pointed out that once it had been based on Lombard, but since the third book of the *Sentences* on "Justification" was in error and also departed from the pure word of the evangelists on the sacraments, the use of this scholastic work could not be tolerated. In the end it was decided to keep the name, since to change it might lead to confusion, but the subject matter was entirely revised. For this degree the student of the *Neugläubigen* was required to master all the doctrines set forth by St. Paul in his many epistles and should also be competent in parts of the Psalms and the Prophets. His proficiency would be tested in the usual examinations and a public disputation.[65]

The degree of *Formatus* followed a similar pattern and was a further testing of the student's maturity in public doctrinal disputation.[66] There were very basic changes in the requirements for the Doctorate. The new Lutheran theologian would approach this degree with the same reverence and respect as in approaching an altar. He was about to be entrusted with the mysteries of heaven and an explanation and judgment of divine teaching leading to heaven. For this degree character as well as intellectual maturity was important. Heavy emphasis was placed on the candidate's performance in the doctoral disputation by the *Statutes of 1536* and later amendments, and the heavy fines levied for failure to participate are evidence that in severity and a grueling test of the student's stamina the doctoral disputation had not changed much. The subject matter, however, now encompassed the entire material covered by the faculty in the exegetical courses on the Old and New Testaments.[67]

In liberal arts the subject matter did not change greatly, nor did the method of disputations. Those segments of the philosophical curriculum, such as rhetoric, poetry, languages, and the classics, which were influenced by the "Biblical Humanism" introduced by Luther and Melanchthon in the twenties, were not required to hold debates but could substitute declamations.[68] In law the courses in canon law had disappeared from the curriculum following Luther's bonfire of the books in canon law outside Elster Gate in 1520 (when he tossed in the papal bull as an afterthought). By the middle thirties Justus Jonas was introducing a new *Landeskirchenrecht* that covered those aspects of social and private life formerly regulated by Roman Catholic canon law.[69] In the field of medicine no changes were made in either subject matter or in procedures as a result of the Reformation, and the requirements set forth in the *Statutes of 1508* continued in force.[70]

The *Liber Decanorum* describes in detail a particularly festive occasion attending the granting of the Doctorate in 1533. There were three candidates, Bugenhagen, Cruciger, and Aepinus, and the ceremonies lasted for several days. As was customary, they began with an academic procession led by the rector dressed in ceremonial attire and escorted by the beadles of the university. He was followed by the chancellor, the prior of the Castle Church, the dean of theology, the dean of All Saints' Church, and the remainder of the faculty according to rank and all dressed in their distinctively colorful academic robes. Distinguished guests were included in the procession and, of course, the student body. The group proceeded from the university along the familiar streets to the Castle Church where they took their carefully appointed places. The church retained much of its earlier beauty, but the imposing array of relics had long since disappeared. On this specific occasion Elector John Frederick, his wife Sybilla, and other royal guests were interested spectators during the whole affair. Melanchthon had drafted special theses for each candidate to debate, embracing such themes as Faith, The Church, Tradition, and Human Literature. Throughout the debates Melanchthon and other faculty members actively participated in disputing with the candidates. After all had successfully concluded the disputations, a solemn ceremony was held at which Justus Jonas officiated and invested the candidates with the high honor of the Doctorate. Afterwards the elector was host at a "royal banquet" for the assembled guests, the candidates, and some 20 members of the faculty. The elector was so impressed with the performances that he reinstated promotions with disputations as a formal requirement at the University of Wittenberg.[71]

This study, it is hoped, will enable the reader to gain a new understanding of Luther's purpose in posting his Ninety-five Theses on 31 October 1517 on the university bulletin board mounted on the north door of the Castle Church. The circumstances surrounding the event would seem to remove from the act the bold defiance so frequently ascribed to it and place it in the context of the normal pattern of university life and teaching. Many years had passed before the act of posting the theses came to be regarded as the spark that kindled the Reformation.

A view of Luther's act in its true historical perspective demands its separation from the *processus inhibitorius* initiated by Rome, which only accelerated Luther's later unfolding as the Reformer by forcing him to examine the grounds of his belief.[72] Had Rome taken a different approach in the 1520s, the labors of Luther and his co-workers might have been channeled into constructive reforms from within the folds of the Roman Church and the external unity of the church might have been retained.

NOTES

1. Max Senf, *Die Reformationsfeier zu Wittenberg 1917* (Wittenberg, 1918), pp. 69—92. The three speeches delivered in the three services are included in this *Festschrift*.
2. Hans Volz, *Martin Luthers Thesenanschlag und Dessen Vorgeschichte* (Weimar: Hermann Böhlaus, 1959), p. 30 and n. 122. The author cited P. Graff, W. Stieda, F. Loofs, and G. Arndt for more detailed accounts of the development of Reformation festivals throughout Germany.
3. Senf, pp. 69 ff.
4. This *Katharinen-Portal*, given to Luther by his wife in 1540 as a birthday gift, has served as the entrance to the *Lutherhalle* since that time. For details see Schwiebert, *Luther and His Times: The Reformation from a New Perspective* (St. Louis: Concordia Publishing House, 1950), p. 228, n. 26, and Plate XXXIII.
5. For details about the Castle Church see ibid., pp. 235 ff.; also Schwiebert, "The Electoral Town of Wittenberg," *Medievalia et Humanistica*, III (1945), 106. Lucas Cranach the Elder included an artistic reproduction of this beautiful Gothic structure as the frontispiece of the *Wittemberger Heiligthumsbuch* of 1509. This building was destroyed by fire in 1760 during the Seven Years' War and again in Napoleon's day, Sept. 23—28, 1813, and was restored to its present form in 1892.
6. J. G. Walch, *D. Martin Luthers Saemtliche Schriften* (Halle, 1740 ff.), XXI, 295, stated that Luther was "buried near the pulpit." See Schwiebert, *Luther*, p. 752. In 1936, when the author last visited the grave, Prof. H. Heubner claimed to have been present when Luther's grave was opened in 1892 and saw in the coffin the mortal remains of the Reformer.
7. Senf, p. 76. According to Myconius, *Historia Reformationis vom Jahr Christi 1517 bis 1542* (Leipzig: Monitz Georg Weidman, 1718), p. 24, Luther delivered his early sermons in the small Augustinian Chapel next to the Black Cloister, but after he became the Reformer not even the Town Church, where he preached throughout his life, was adequate to accommodate the crowds.

8. Schwiebert, *Luther,* p. 230.

9. Senf, p. 92.

10. Volz, pp. 28 ff. See also his notes 115, 116, 117, and especially 118, where he cited the Melanchthon evidence: CR VII, 112, in 1552; VIII, 594—95, in 1558; IX, 956, in 1559. The author also cited Melanchthon's *Postille* of 1557, CR XXV, 777. He believed Myconius, Manlius, and others accepted the 31 Oct. date from Melanchthon's *Vita Lutheri* of 1546. Against Melanchthon, Volz cited two vague Luther sources (pp. 31—33, and notes 123, 128, 129). Luther's 1 Nov. 1527 letter to Amsdorf was dated "Witenbergae die omnium Sanctorum, Anno decimo Indulgentiarum conculcatarum," or "Wittenberg, All Saints' Day, ten years after indulgences were destroyed." This general statement makes no specific mention of the nailing of the Ninety-five Theses. WA, Br IV, 275. Again the cited WA, Tr II, No. 2455a and b, read: "Anno 17. in die omnium sanctorum incepi primum scribere contra papam et indulgentias," or: "In the year 1517 I began on All Saints' Day first to write against the pope and indulgences." Volz argued that Luther's is a primary source and Melanchthon's a secondary one. This argument might be more convincing had Luther been more specific. That Melanchthon made some errors in his *Vita Lutheri,* as in the date of the *Romfahrt,* is granted. It must be remembered, however, that Melanchthon was Luther's colleague, next-door neighbor, and intimate friend for many years and that, while he was not a participant in the journey to Rome, he was in Wittenberg by 1518 when the events of the previous year must have been quite vivid in the minds of his university colleagues. The research student must choose between Luther's general statements and Melanchthon's very exact designation of the day and hour as 2 o'clock in the afternoon of 31 Oct. 1517.

11. *Dialogus illustrate ac augustissime urbis Albiorenae, vulgo Wittenberg dicte, situm, amenitatem ac illustrationem docens tirocinia nobilium artium jacientibus editus, Andreas Meinhardi* (Leipzig, 1508), Sec. VIII; see Johannes Hauszleiter, *Die Universität Wittenberg vor dem Eintritt Luthers nach der Schilderung des Mag. Andreas Meinhardi vom Jahre 1507* (Leipzig, 1903), pp. 22—23. Only three copies of this rare work are extant, all in the Soviet Zone of Germany.

12. *Luthers Thesenanschlag Tatsache oder Legende?* No. 31 in *Institut für Europäische Geschichte Mainz Vorträge* (Wiesbaden: Franz Steiner Verlag, 1962), pp. 15 ff.

13. Schwiebert, *Luther,* pp. 257 ff.

14. *Annalen der Universität Wittenberg,* ed. J. C. A. Grohmann (Meissen, 1801), 2 vols. See I, 45 ff., for a good summary; also Schwiebert, "Remnants of a Reformation Library," *The Library Quarterly,* X (Oct. 1940), 495, n. 10.

15. See n. 14 above.

16. Schwiebert, *Luther,* p. 246; also Schwiebert, *Library Quarterly,* X (Oct. 1940), 508—9. At first it was on an upper floor.

17. *Dialogus of 1507,* Sec. VIII; see Hauszleiter, pp. 27—28.

18. H. Heubner, *Der Bau des Schlosses,* p. 14; also Schwiebert, *Luther,* Plate XXXIV.

19. Ibid.

20. M. D. Andreas Charitius, "Chronik des Wittenberger Archidiakonus" (ca. 1740), unpublished (formerly in the Max Senf Collection, Wittenberg, Germany), pp. 130—37. Present location unknown. See Volz, p. 104, n. 151.

21. *Der Bau des Schlosses,* pp. 12—14.

22. *Urkundenbuch der Universität Wittenberg,* ed. Walter Friedensburg (Magdeburg, 1926), I, 1—3 et passim.

23. J. de Ghellinck, "The Liber Sententiarium," *Dublin Review,* CXLVI (1910), 139 ff.

24. C. H. Haskins, "The University of Paris in the Sermons of the Thirteenth Century," *Studies in Mediaeval Culture* (New York: Frederick F. Ungar Publishing Co., 1958), pp. 36—37. For foreign students, see Hastings Rashdall, *The Universities of Europe in the Middle Ages* (London: Oxford University Press, 1951), I, 518 ff.; A. Budinsky, *Die Universität Paris und die Fremden an derselben im Mittelalter* (Berlin, 1876). Haskins says: "So prominent were the constitutional and theological aspects of the university and so violent the controversies which raged about it" that they really lost sight of the true purpose of a university.

25. WA, Tr III, 564, claims Jerome Schurff, a prominent Wittenberg law professor and close friend of Luther, asked, after reading the Ninety-five Theses: "Do you wish to write against the pope? What are you trying to do? It will never be tolerated." See WA, Br I, 170, for Luther's statement to Trutvetter, 9 May 1518.

26. Friedensburg, pp. 18—58.

27. Ibid., pp. 30—31, stated that liberal arts disputations were to be held on Saturdays and that the theological faculty should use the six holidays. In theological promotions the disputation for *Biblicus* would have 3 hours in the mornings of specified festival days, general holidays being excepted. Disputations for the intermediate degrees would be held on these festival days in the 3 hours before the evening meal. Disputations for the degrees of *Licentiatus* and the Doctorate would be held on these days beginning at the second hour of the afternoon and continuing for about 3 hours.

28. Friedensburg, I, 177—78. According to the *Statutes of 1536:* "Each paid faculty member, when his time comes, is obligated to hold a disputation and for his effort and energy expended he is to be paid $100; the respondent is to receive $50; and each student arguing pro or con is to be paid $12, if his effort indicates that worth." At these rates a single circular disputation cost the university some $250. The record (ibid., I, 202) noted some interesting sums paid to Martin Luther for presiding over disputations in the academic year 1538—39. For 34 disputations in which he served as chairman he was paid $573 and, later that same year, for acting as chairman in 20 disputations he received $407. The figures are comparable in law and medicine; but in liberal arts Professor Amerbach presided 15 times and received only $90, and Melanchthon received $102 for presiding 17 times. "Und soll ain ider president [in arts] von seiner gehaltenen disputation funf und der respondent vir, ein jeder opponent zwen groschen haben." These money values have been recalculated according to their modern buying power. See Schwiebert, *Luther,* pp. 257—68. The buying power of a gulden in 1966 would be roughly $50. If cows were worth three gulden and pigs one, this sum seems, if anything, conservative.

29. According to the *Statutes of 1508,* the fines in the schools of law, medicine, and theology for failure to participate in the required disputations were $25 for a doctor or *Licentiatus* and $12 for those holding the degrees of *Biblicus, Sententiarius,* or *Formatus.* In liberal arts the highest fine was but $12. Friedensburg, I, 37, 45, 50. The fines remained at that level in 1536, but in 1538 the faculty fines had increased to $100, and for a circular disputation to $200, which amounts would be deducted from the salaries. Ibid., pp. 177, 193—95. Why the fines should have been increased so drastically is not clear, for the

reports made each quarter indicate that the faculty performance was quite faithful.

30. Ibid., I, 204.

31. Ibid., pp. 203—4. An earlier record, ibid., pp. 193, 195, mentions the older faculty members who are too frail now to perform regularly, namely, Master Staffelstein, Master Vach, and the Hebrew lecturer Aurogallus, and are to be excused. Also Dr. Martin can do as he wishes: lecture or hold disputations; while Bugenhagen is also exempt because of his other duties. Master Philip may also do as he sees fit, while in law the aged Hieronymous Schurff is also relieved of this obligation.

32. Ibid., I, 124. See G. Bauch, *Die Einführung der Melanchthonischen Deklamationen*, pp. 10—14 (cited by Friedensburg).

33. *Liber Decanorum Facultatis Theologicae Academiae Vitebergensis*, ed. C. E. Foerstemann (Leipzig, 1838), pp. 3 ff.

34. Schwiebert, *Luther*, pp. 321 ff.

35. Disputations were already stressed for all the faculties in the *Statutes of 1508*. Friedensburg, I, 34—35, 42—44, 48, 53—55. During the disturbances of the twenties Carlstadt had dropped both the disputations and the formal promotions. In Melanchthon's *Statutes of 1533*, ibid., p. 156, under "De Promotionibus," the promotional type of disputation for advanced degrees in theology was reinstated. The *Statutes of 1536*, ibid., pp. 177—78, stipulated: "Because the holding of disputations in all the faculties is very important for student study and practice, it is desired that they be performed without interruption." In the higher faculties they were to be held once per quarter; these in addition to the regular ones held in connection with promotions, which were not to be counted. The *Denkschrift* of 1538, ibid., p. 193, states that the dean and rector were to regulate disputations so that they really contributed to the learning process.

36. Friedensburg, I, 14—15, 37—38; for the *Statutes* see p. 35.

37. *Liber Decanorum*, p. 20, records that Peter Lupinus gave up his position as canon of the Castle Church and became dean of theology during the period when Luther nailed his theses, but the account jumps to 11 Jan. 1518 to report the promotion of Petrus Fontanus, who was made a doctor on 12 January. There is no reference to the indulgence struggle. See Schwiebert, *Luther*, pp. 321 ff.

38. Volz, p. 29, and especially notes 115 and 118, where he treats in detail Melanchthon's alleged creation of the 31 Oct. 1517 date as a historic tradition. See n. 10 above.

39. Friedensburg, I, 34—35; *Liber Decanorum*, pp. 4 ff.

40. Friedensburg, I, 34—35, and especially p. 37: "At promotions and performances the theologians and masters must be present to serve as judges of how well the bachelors performed."

41. Ibid., p. 34.

42. *Liber Decanorum*, pp. 11—12.

43. Friedensburg, I, 34.

44. J. de Ghellinck, "The Liber Sententiarium," *Dublin Review*, CXLVI (1910), 160—61.

45. Friedensburg, I, 34.

46. Ibid. See Ghellinck, pp. 139 ff.

47. On Luther's lectures see Herbert Rommel, *Über Luthers Randbemerkungen von 1509 bis 10* (Kiel, 1931). See K. A. Meissinger, *Luthers Exegese in der*

Frühzeit (Leipzig: M. Heinsius, 1911), for an appraisal of the exegesis of the young Luther. For the actual text see WA IX.

48. *Liber Decanorum*, pp. 8—9.

49. Ibid. According to this record Carlstadt had been granted the degree of *Formatus* just shortly before on 25 Oct. 1510. He evidently did so well in the public disputation that the rector, Polich von Mellerstadt, recommended that the degree of *Licentiatus* also be granted. This was done on the following day.

50. Ibid. There is some confusion in the *Liber Decanorum* as to the exact date, but it seems most likely that the vesper service was held on 9 November with the degree being actually granted on 12 November.

51. Ibid., pp. 11—12. See Heinrich Boehmer, *Der junge Luther* (Gotha, 1925), p. 8. There are several additional details. The promotional service was held at 7 a. m. on 19 Oct. 1512. Luther was first presented with a closed and then an open Bible. The head covering was a black woolen beret. The silver ring is today in the Museum of Braunschweig. The title of Doctor was so revered that Luther's students carried him on their shoulders through the streets while the big bell rang out in his honor. He was presented to the five *senate* members on 22 Oct. 1512, an act that made him eligible for Staupitz's vacated chair of *lectura in Biblia*. The oath which Luther took on this occasion as a doctor of theology he as a Biblical exegete continued to hold sacred.

52. *Liber Decanorum*, pp. 4—20.

53. Ibid., pp. 5—6.

54. Ibid.

55. WA, Br I, 139: "Igitur cum in hanc arenam vocarem omnes, veniret vero nullus." Here Luther plainly implies that he wished to hold a disputation in the Castle Church, *hanc arenam*, but no one would venture to dispute with him. Luther wrote to Christopher Scheurl of Nürnberg on 5 March 1518 (*Ibid.*, pp. 151—53): "It was not the wish nor the plan to publicize these Theses but to discuss them with a few in our circle; and thus, upon discussing them, obtain their judgment as to whether to suppress them or to spread them outside" (the university circle).

56. See p. 129 and n. 35 above.

57. Friedensburg, I, 156, "De promotionibus."

58. *Liber Decanorum*, pp. 9, 28—30. In a speech at the banquet the elector announced his decision to reinstate disputations and promotions. The changes in the institution can be seen in the 1533, 1536, and 1545 *Statutes*, and disputations became a regular method of instruction. The *Statutes of 1536* (Friedensburg, I, 177—78) stipulated: "Because the holding of disputations in all the faculties is very important for student study and practice, it is desired that they be performed without interruption." In the higher faculties they were to occur once per quarter, in addition to the regular ones held in connection with promotions that did not count. The *Denkschrift* of 1538 (Friedensburg, I, 193) stated that the dean and the rector were to regulate disputations so that they really contributed to the learning process. For more details on Declamations and humanistic training in liberal arts see Schwiebert, "Education at Wittenberg," *The Springfielder*, XXVIII, 3 (Autumn 1964), 25 ff.

59. Friedensburg, I, 156.

60. Ibid., p. 154, on the Augsburg Confession as the new standard. For the new spirit in the school see Schwiebert, "Education at Wittenberg," *The Springfielder*, XXVIII, 3 (Autumn 1964), 27 ff.

61. Ibid., pp. 25 ff.

62. Friedensburg, I, 155.

63. Ibid., p. 156.

64. Ibid.

65. Ibid.

66. Ibid.

67. Ibid., pp. 155, 174—75.

68. Schwiebert, "New Groups and Ideas at the University of Wittenberg," *Archiv für Reformationsgeschichte,* XLIX (1958), 76—77. For *Statutes of 1536* on law see Friedensburg, I, 155—56.

69. Schwiebert, "New Groups and Ideas at the University of Wittenberg," *Archiv für Reformationsgeschichte,* XLIX (1958), 77.

70. Friedensburg, I, 47—51, 176.

71. *Liber Decanorum,* pp. 28—30. The elector announced his decision in a speech at the banquet in which he expressed his admiration for the entire performance and his desire that promotions, discontinued by Carlstadt during the "Wittenberg Disturbances" in 1523, should once more be a part of the Wittenberg academic life, Schwiebert, *Luther,* pp. 536—42. On the action of Carlstadt see *Liber Decanorum,* p. 27.

72. Schwiebert, *Luther,* pp. 331 ff.

6

THE SOURCES OF LUTHER'S
SEPTEMBERTESTAMENT: GALATIANS

Heinz Bluhm

N̲O ADEQUATE study of the sources of Luther's *Sep-tembertestament* of 1522 exists. Even the Weimar Edition of Luther's works fails the reader in this important respect. This is a serious state of affairs, since no effort to determine the full nature of Luther's translation of the New Testament can be successful until the question of the sources he used has been satisfactorily answered.

In the absence of a careful examination of Luther's sources, opinions about them range all the way from those that claim his straight and unabashed use of the Vulgate to others that postulate a complete and indisputable use of the Greek original. But these opinions are largely unsubstantiated and uncritically repeated over and over again. For this reason I have undertaken a close analysis of this basic aspect of Luther's translation of one of the most famous of the Pauline epistles, Galatians, to determine as exactly as we can the source or sources on which Luther's original rendering of 1522 is based.

What published sources were available to any translator of schol-

144

arly pretensions in the early 16th century? We need to set the date more precisely, however, because of the extraordinary importance of the year 1516 for any undertaking of this sort. A New Testament scholar working before that year would not have had the printed Greek text accessible to him, for it was only in 1516 that Erasmus, the foremost scholar of the age, published the first edition of the New Testament in the original Greek. Assuming that our hypothetical translator knew Greek (which was by no means certain in the first quarter of the 16th century), he would thus have had, from 1516 on, the use of the Greek text. In addition, he would have had one or more of the many editions of the Vulgate which had appeared in print since the Gutenberg Bible. He could also have availed himself of two important books by Laurentius Valla and the outstanding French humanist Faber Stapulensis. Both would have brought him closer to the Greek original than would the Vulgate.

The early Italian humanist Laurentius Valla, remembered best for his *De falso credita et ementita Constantini donatione declamatio*, wrote *Annotationes* to the New Testament (1440 to 1442). In 1504 Erasmus discovered these in Brussels and published them the following year as *Laurentii Vallensis viri tam graece quam latine linguae peritissimi in Latinam Novi Testamenti interpretationem ex collatione Grecorum exemplarium Annotationes*. Valla had also planned a new Latin translation of the New Testament from the Greek, but it is reported that the Pope frowned upon its execution.

Faber Stapulensis' *S. Pauli epistolae XIV ex Vulgata, adjecta intelligentia ex graeco, cum Commentariis* (Paris, 1512 I and 1515 II) was very important because in it the famous scholar called attention to a number of places where the Greek differed from the Vulgate. In addition, Faber did what Valla had not been permitted to carry out: he supplied a revised version of the Vulgate in small type next to the large-type church-approved Latin text.

There was another major source, the significance of which can hardly be exaggerated, although it has been strangely neglected by many scholars in this field. This was a new Latin translation made by Erasmus himself and published along with the Greek original in 1516. It was clearly and unmistakably done on the basis of the Greek and was not merely a revision of the Vulgate, as Faber Stapulensis' Latin translation had been. Erasmus made an independent, new rendering that differed materially from the Vulgate. Printed in large type as a second column in the epoch-making *Novum Instrumentum Omne*

145

of 1516, it was intended to strike the eye of everybody consulting the Greek text. It literally forced itself upon users of the famous new publication. One must also bear in mind that any aid extended by so revered an authority as Erasmus was sure to be welcomed.

By 1521 the number of publications in this field had increased by two: Erasmus brought out a second, revised edition of the *Novum Instrumentum Omne* (now entitled *Novum Testamentum Omne*) in 1519; and Nicolaus Gerbelius, a Strasbourg humanist and former assistant of Erasmus, reprinted the Greek text of Erasmus' second edition in 1521.

Finally, what was the situation in the modern languages? Germany, where the first Latin Bible was printed, also produced the first vernacular Bible. The earliest, a High German Bible, came out around 1465; it was revised more or less thoroughly in 1475 and again in 1483; the fourteenth and last redaction saw the light of day in 1518. Low German Bibles were published in 1478, 1494, and 1522, the last interestingly enough in the same year in which Luther's *September-testament* appeared, sounding the death knell of all 18 pre-Lutheran High and Low German Bibles. There were also vernacular Bibles in Bohemian, Dutch, French, and Italian, all of them somewhat later than the first German Bible. It is important to bear in mind that these vernacular Bibles were, without exception, based on the Vulgate. Translations of a translation, they were of only limited usefulness to an ambitious, scholarly translator eager to establish contact with the original text of the Bible.

These then were the printed sources available to would-be translators in the period under consideration: Erasmus' editions of the Greek and Latin text, Gerbelius' reprint of the Greek text of Erasmus' edition of 1519, Faber's and Valla's commentaries, the Vulgate, and the pre-Lutheran Bibles in the vernacular. Luther's achievement should be seen against this general background. Objectively speaking, all the sources just enumerated were as available to him when he began work on his *magnum opus* as to any other scholar of the age. Whether he had ready access to all of them is of course another matter. When Luther began translating the New Testament late in December 1521, two of the sources had already dropped out for him: Valla and Faber Stapulensis. After Erasmus' edition of the New Testament appeared, they were clearly antiquated and could be discarded with impunity.

What evidence does Luther's translation of Galatians present about the sources he used? So far we have indicated only what was objectively available to him. Now we shall want to know exactly what he did with the materials history had placed at his disposal. The question of paramount interest to us is naturally the extent to which he based his new rendering on the Greek text.

It will be necessary to begin at the very beginning. What is the relation between the Vulgate and the Greek original? How accurate a translation of the Greek text did the Vulgate furnish? If there are differences between them, what is their number and nature? We must have answers to these basic questions before we can proceed to our main topic.

This preliminary task is more complicated than has sometimes been realized. It would be fatal to take modern editions of the Vulgate and of the Greek text and base our calculations on them. In order to be fair to Luther, we must refer to the actual editions used by him, so far as they can be determined. Because of the many variants found in the different editions, an accurate answer to our questions demands a comparison on the basis of the texts actually consulted by Luther.

In the nature of the case it is easier to determine the Greek text he used than the edition of the Vulgate. There were only three editions of the Greek available to him at the time he undertook his monumental task: Erasmus' first and second editions of 1516 and 1519, respectively, and Gerbelius' reprint of 1521 of Erasmus' second edition of 1519. The number of printed Vulgates, on the other hand, was very large, and the texts they contained were by no means identical. Fortunately we are not completely in the dark here. It has been ascertained that Luther's copy of the Vulgate was a Basel edition of 1509. So far as the Greek text is concerned, there is general agreement among scholars that Luther had Erasmus' second edition or Gerbelius' reprint of it, or both, before him when he started to translate in December 1521.

It is therefore safe, as a working hypothesis at any rate, to make our comparison of the Greek and Vulgate versions of Galatians on the basis of the Erasmus and Gerbelius Greek texts of 1519 and 1521 on the one hand and of the Basel Vulgate of 1509 on the other. By comparing these specific editions we are likely to get as accurate a picture as possible of the relation of the Greek and Vulgate texts actually in Luther's hands during the months of his formal translation of the New Testament.

Taking these definite editions as our basis, what do we find? The answer to our question about the relation between the Greek original and the Vulgate is striking: There are more than 60 places where Erasmus' Greek text of 1519 diverges from the Vulgate of 1509. This figure, established by a careful comparison of the Epistle to the Galatians, is sufficiently large to allow us to determine the source or sources Luther followed. It is these differences between the Greek and Vulgate versions that I propose to examine. What was Luther's actual behavior in the face of these differences in the texts before him as he was engaged in his great task of translating the difficult Epistle to the Galatians?

To anticipate the results of this investigation briefly even before the actual data are presented and discussed: In the overwhelming majority of cases Luther clearly follows the Greek text; there are only six instances out of the more than 60 relevant passages in which Luther appears to agree with the Vulgate reading against the Greek text.

It will obviously be impossible, for lack of space, to discuss all the passages in which Luther is in agreement with the original Greek. I shall have to restrict myself to a number of the most important passages, examining, however, as closely as possible all cases in which Luther seems to side with the Vulgate against the Greek of the Erasmus and/or Gerbelius editions.

I. LUTHER AGREEING WITH THE GREEK ORIGINAL AGAINST THE VULGATE

A very real difficulty in the way of proving beyond the shadow of a doubt the claim that Luther followed the Greek text itself resides in the simple fact, not always recognized even by students of the subject, that the new Latin version furnished by Erasmus in connection with the Greek text is ordinarily in close agreement with the original and takes cognizance of the differences between that and the Vulgate. In other words, Erasmus' new Latin translation is, by and large, a faithful rendering of the original. It follows, therefore, that wherever the Greek text and Erasmus' independent Latin translation are in full agreement, it is not possible to state with absolute certainty that Luther based his own rendering on the Greek original rather than on Erasmus' scholarly new version. If two "sources," both of which are readily accessible to a translator, agree against a third (the Vulgate in this case), it cannot be determined with finality which of the first two he actually followed. Let us now look at some of the most important examples.

Galatians 1:3

The Basel Vulgate of 1509

. . . (pax) a deo patre nostro & domino jesu christo . . .

The Pre-Lutheran High German Bibles

. . . von got vnserm vatter vnd von dem herrn jhesu cristo . . .

Erasmus' Greek text of 1519

. . . ἀπὸ θεοῦ πατρὸς, καὶ κυρίου ἡμῶν Ἰησοῦ Χριστοῦ

Erasmus' Latin Translation of 1519

. . . a deo patre, & domine nostro Jesu Christo . . .

Septembertestament

. . . von Gott dem vater / vnnd vnserm hern Jhesu Christ . . .

What can be said with certainty about this passage is that Luther did not follow the Vulgate or any of the printed pre-Lutheran High-German Bibles obviously based on it. The difference between the Greek original and the Vulgate is such that one can definitely decide which of them the translator followed in this particular instance. The position of *nostro*, ἡμῶν, makes it abundantly clear, the Greek having it in the second phrase (κυρίου ἡμῶν vs. *domino*) and the Vulgate in the first (*a deo nostro* vs. ἀπὸ θεοῦ πατρὸς). Luther, in complete agreement with the Greek text, has the possessive adjective in the second phrase, "vnnd vnserm hern," and not in the first, "von Gott dem vater."

While there cannot be any question about Luther's parting company with the Vulgate in this passage, it is impossible to say whether his version is based directly on the Greek or merely on Erasmus' new Latin translation which, like the Greek and unlike the Vulgate, has the possessive in the second phrase, *domino nostro*, and not in the first, *a deo patre*. We can say that Luther's translation agrees with the Greek original, but we cannot say that it is based on it directly. The latter is probably true, but the nature of the sources does not allow us to establish this as an incontestable fact.

Galatians 1:17

The Basel Vulgate of 1509

. . . ad antecessores meos apostolos . . .

The Pre-Lutheran High German Bibles

. . . zu meinen furgenden botten . . .

From the Zainer redaction (1475) on, the following changes occur:
. . . gen meinen furgenden zwelffboten . . .

149

Erasmus' Greek text of 1519

. . . πρὸς τοὺς πρὸ ἐμοῦ ἀποστόλους . . .

Erasmus' Latin Translation of 1519

. . . ad eos qui ante me fuerant apostoli . . .

Septembertestament

. . . zu denen / die fur myr Apostel waren . . .

It seems fairly certain that Luther's rendering could not easily derive from the Vulgate or the pre-Lutheran Bibles translating the Vulgate most literally. On the other hand it cannot be stated categorically that the Greek text is the direct source. Erasmus' Latin version is a very smooth rendering of the Greek. This new Latin translation could be held to account, by and of itself, for Luther's German, which corresponds very closely to it. Again it is most difficult to draw the line between the Greek original and Erasmus' Latin rendering as the source of Luther's German version.

Galatians 2:3

The Basel Vulgate of 1509

Sed neque titus qui mecum erat / cum esset gentilis . . .

The Pre-Lutheran High German Bibles

. . . thyt . . . wie das er was ein heiden . . .

From the Eggesteyn redaction on, "thyt" became "tytus," and from Zainer on, "das" became "wol."

Erasmus' Greek text of 1519

. . . Τίτος . . . ἕλλην ὢν . . .

Erasmus' Latin Translation of 1519

. . . Titus . . . cum esset Graecus . . .

Septembertestament

. . . Titus . . . ob er wol ein krieche war . . .

The record shows plainly that Luther agrees with the Greek text against the Vulgate: "ein krieche" clearly goes back to ἕλλην, correctly translated as *Graecus* by Erasmus. But again we cannot state with finality whether Luther's "krieche" is based directly on the original Greek or merely on Erasmus' new Latin version. What we can say definitely is that the Vulgate's *gentilis*, rendered as "heiden" by all pre-Lutheran High German Bibles, cannot account for Luther's "krieche." Laurentius Diefenbach's *Glossarium Latino-Germanicum Mediae et Infimae Aetatis* (1857) contains no entry other than "heyde, heuden, heid" for *gentilis*. For Luther to use "krieche" as he did, it was necessary to consult the Greek original or Erasmus' accurate Latin rendering.

Galatians 3:6

The Basel Vulgate of 1509
sicut scriptum est: Abraam credidit deo . . .

The Pre-Lutheran High German Bibles
Als geschriben ist: abraham gelaubt gott . . .

Erasmus' Greek text of 1519
καθὼς Ἀβραὰμ ἐπίστευε τῷ θεῷ . . .

Erasmus' Latin Translation of 1519
Quemadmodum Abraham credidit deo . . .

Septembertestament
Gleych / wie Abraham hat Gotte geglewbt . . .

Luther, manifestly agreeing with Erasmus' Greek text and new Latin translation, omits the Vulgate's *scriptum est,* which the pre-Lutheran German Bibles retained as "geschriben ist." There can be no doubt about Luther's departure from the Vulgate. Again Erasmus' exact translation of the Greek original does not permit us to differentiate between the two as to Luther's indubitable source.

Galatians 3:12

The Basel Vulgate of 1509
Lex autem non est ex fide: sed qui fecerit ea viuet in illis.

The Pre-Lutheran High German Bibles
. . . wann der sy thut der lebt in ir.
From the Zainer redaction on, "ir" is correctly changed to "in."

Erasmus' Greek text of 1519
. . . ἀλλ' ὁ ποιήσας αὐτὰ ἄνθρωπος, ζήσεται ἐν αὐτοῖς.

Erasmus' Latin Translation of 1519
. . . sed qui fecerit ea homo, uiuet in ipsis.

Septembertestament
. . . sondern der mensch der es thut / wirt da durch leben.

It is clear beyond dispute that Luther's word "mensch" can be explained only on the basis of the Greek original's ἄνθρωπος, which Erasmus' Latin version faithfully reproduces by *homo.* The Vulgate, which does not have the noun, must be eliminated as a source of Luther's rendering.

151

Galatians 3:17

The Basel Vulgate of 1509

. . . testamentum confirmatum a deo / que post quadringentos & triginta annos facta est lex . . .

The Pre-Lutheran High German Bibles

. . . gezeug . . . geuestent von gott: das nach . . . wart gemacht die ee

From Zainer on, the following changes occurred:

. . . gezeugknuss . . . bestaetet von got. die dann . . .

Erasmus' Greek text of 1519

. . . ὑπὸ τοῦ θεοῦ εἰς Χριστὸν, ὁ μετὰ ἔτη . . . γεγονὼς νόμος . . .

Erasmus' Latin Translation of 1519

. . . a deo erga Christum, lex quae post annos quadringentos & triginta coepit . . .

Septembertestament

. . . das testament / das von Gott bestetiget ist auff Christum . . .

Luther's version is clearly in agreement with the Greek text: "auff Christum" is the indisputable evidence. Erasmus' Latin rendering of 1519, definitely based on the Greek original and differing from the Vulgate, also has this phrase. This fact once again prevents us, of course, from stating categorically that the Greek is the only source of Luther's translation. It is absolutely certain, however, that the Vulgate, which does not have these two words, is thereby eliminated as a source for Luther's translation.

Galatians 3:27

The Basel Vulgate of 1509

Quicumque enim in christo iesu baptiçati estis / christum induistis.

The Pre-Lutheran High German Bibles

Wann all ir do seyt getaufft in cristo: cristum habt ir geuasst.

From Zainer on, the following changes are found:

Wann woellich ir seyt getaufft in cristo: cristum habt ir angeleget.

Erasmus' Greek text of 1519

ὅσοι γὰρ ἐβαπτίσθητε, Χριστὸν ἐνεδύσασθε.

Erasmus' Latin Translation of 1519

Nam quicunque baptizati estis, Christum induistis.

Septembertestament

Denn wie viel ewr tauffet sind / die haben Christum angetzogen.

The simple fact that Luther omits the whole phrase *in christo iesu* is clear proof of his use of Erasmus, whether of the Greek text itself

152

or only of the Latin (or both) one cannot say in the nature of the case. But had Luther based his translation on the Vulgate, he would doubtless have included the extra phrase found in that version. With his deep attachment to Christ, it would never have occurred to him to omit a reference to the Savior.

Galatians 4:7

The Basel Vulgate of 1509
. . . quod si filius & heres per deum.

The Pre-Lutheran High German Bibles
. . . Vnd ob sun: vnd erbe zu gott.

Changes from the Zainer Bible on are as follows:
. . . Vnd ist er ein sun So ist er auch ein erb durch got.

Erasmus' Greek text of 1519
. . . εἰ δὲ υἱός, καὶ κληρονόμος θεοῦ διὰ Χριστοῦ.

Erasmus' Latin Translation of 1519
. . . quod si filius, & haeres dei per Christum.

Septembertestament
. . . Sinds aber kinder / so sinds auch erben Gottis durch Christon.

This passage also offers incontrovertible proof that Luther went beyond the Vulgate. His phrase "erben Gottis durch Christon" could never have been inspired by the Vulgate's *heres per deum*. It is impossible even to assume that the extra word in Luther's German could in any way derive from the Vulgate. Only the Erasmus texts κληρο-νόμος θεοῦ διὰ Χριστοῦ and *haeres dei per Christum* suffice as source or sources. So far as Luther's use of the plural is concerned, that appears to be due to verse 6. He may have preferred it to the singular for stylistic reasons. From a strictly philological point of view, the plural in verse 7 is of course inexact.

Galatians 4:14

The Basel Vulgate of 1509
. . . & temptationem vestram in carne mea . . .

The Pre-Lutheran High German Bibles
. . . euwer versuchungen inn meim fleisch:

Erasmus' Greek text of 1519
καὶ τὸν πειρασμόν μου, τὸν ἐν τῇ σαρκί μου

Erasmus' Latin Translation of 1519
. . . experimentum mei, quod erat in carne . . .

153

In Erasmus' first edition of 1516, *meum* occurs instead of *mei*.

Septembertestament
. . . vnd meyne anfechtungen . . .

It is clear beyond the shadow of a doubt that Luther does not base his translation of "meyne anfechtungen" on the Vulgate's *temptationem vestram* but indisputably on the Erasmus texts, both of which, the Greek original as well as the new Latin version, have the possessive in the first and not in the second person: μου and *mei*.

Galatians 4:18

The Basel Vulgate of 1509
Bonum autem emulamini in bono semper . . .

The Pre-Lutheran High German Bibles
Wann zeallen zeyten habt lieb das gut in gut . . .

This rendering of *emulamini* by "habt lieb," at first rather surprising, appears to be quite in keeping with medieval translations of this word as recorded in L. Diefenbach's *Glossarium Latino-Germanicum Mediae et Infimae Aetatis,* where "lieb haben" is actually the first entry.

Erasmus' Greek text of 1519
καλὸν δέ ἐστι ζητοῦσθαι ἐν καλῷ πάντοτε

Erasmus' Latin Translation of 1519
Bonum autem est aemulari in re bona semper . . .

Septembertestament
Eyffern ist gut / wens ymerdar geschicht vmb das gutte . . .

Again the difference between the Vulgate and the pre-Lutheran Bibles on the one hand and the Erasmus texts on the other is considerable enough to allow us to determine which Luther followed. His use of the infinitive "eyffern" rather than the imperative plural (*emulamini,* "habt lieb") makes it quite certain that it is Erasmus (ζητοῦσθαι, *aemulari*) whom he prefers.

Galatians 4:21

The Basel Vulgate of 1509
. . . Legem non legistis . . .

The Pre-Lutheran High German Bibles
. . . Last ir nit die ee?

Erasmus' Greek text of 1519
. . . τὸν νόμον οὐκ ἀκούετε;

Erasmus' Latin Translation of 1519
. . . legem ipsam non auditis?

. . . habt yhr das gesetz nicht gehoret?

There is an unmistakable difference in this verse between the Vulgate and Erasmus' Greek and Latin texts: two altogether diverse verbs are used. The pre-Lutheran Bibles, faithfully reproducing the Vulgate's *legere,* have "lesen." Luther on the other hand is in agreement with the original or at least with the new Latin version supplied by Erasmus himself: his "horen" must go back to ἀκούειν and/or *audire.*

Galatians 4:26

The Basel Vulgate of 1509
. . . que est mater nostra:

The Pre-Lutheran High German Bibles
. . . die do ist vnser muter.

Erasmus' Greek text of 1519
. . . ἥτις ἐστὶ μήτηρ πάντων ἡμῶν

Erasmus' Latin Translation of 1519
. . . quae est mater omnium nostrum.

Septembertestament
. . . die ist vnser aller mutter.

By reproducing in his German text the Erasmian πάντων, *omnium,* Luther clearly parts company with the Vulgate, which does not have this word. It naturally does not occur in the pre-Lutheran German Bibles either. Luther could have gotten it only from consulting Erasmus as his source.

Galatians 5:9

The Basel Vulgate of 1509
Modicum fermentum / totam massam corrumpit.

The Pre-Lutheran High German Bibles
Ein lútzeler hefel zerbricht allen samnung.

The Zainer redaction changes the older translation considerably:
Ein wieniger hefel zerstoeret den ganczen teyg.

Erasmus' Greek text of 1519
μικρὰ ζύμη ὅλον τὸ φύραμα ζυμοῖ.

Erasmus' Latin Translation of 1519
paulum fermenti totam massam fermentat.

Septembertestament
Ein wenig sawrteyg / versawret den gantzen teyg.

It would have been next to impossible for Luther to arrive at his word "versawret" if he had restricted himself to the Vulgate. There is no bridge leading from the Vulgate's *corrumpit* to Luther's "versawret." The pre-Lutheran German Bibles make that abundantly clear: "zerbricht" and "zerstoeret" are the natural and logical translations of the Vulgate's *corrumpit*. Luther's altogether different "versawret" can be accounted for only on the basis of the Erasmian ζυμοῖ and *fermentat*.

Galatians 5:16

The Basel Vulgate of 1509

Dico autem in christo: Spiritu ambulate . . .

The Pre-Lutheran High German Bibles

Wann ich sag in cristo: geet im geist . . .

Erasmus' Greek text of 1519 *

λέγω δέ, πνεύματι περιπατεῖτε . . .

Erasmus' Latin Translation of 1519

Dico autem, spiritu ambulate . . .

Septembertestament

Ich sage aber dauon / wandelt ym geyst . . .

Once again the difference between the Erasmian texts on the one hand and the Vulgate on the other consists in the absence or presence of a short phrase. Luther, by omitting the Vulgate's *in christo*, unmistakably places himself on record as preferring the Greek original, with which Erasmus' Latin version is in complete agreement.

Galatians 5:19

The Basel Vulgate of 1509

. . . opera carnis: que sunt fornicatio / immundicia / impudicitia / luxuria . . .

The Pre-Lutheran High German Bibles

. . . die werck des fleisches . . . : welche do seint gemein vnkeusch· vnreinikeit· arkeit· vnkeusch·

From the second Zainer redaction on, the following changes occur in the sins listed in this verse:

. . . eebrechung vnreynigkeit. vngeschaemige werck. vnkeusch

Erasmus' Greek text of 1519

. . . μοιχεία, πορνεία, ἀκαθαρσία, ἀσέλγεια . . .

* Gerbelius has no comma after δέ.

156

Erasmus' Latin Translation of 1519
. . . adulterium, scortatio, immundicia, lasciuia . . .
Septembertestament
. . . die werck des fleyschs / als da sind / eehbruch / hurerey / vn-
reynickeyt / geylheyt . . .

Luther is definitely in agreement with the Erasmian texts. His
first two words, "eehbruch / hurerey" are not likely to have been
derived from the Vulgate's single word *fornicatio*. Instead, Luther's
two words almost certainly go back to Erasmus' words μοιχεία, πορνεία,
which also occur in the new Latin version made by Erasmus, *adulterium, scortatio*. Similarly, where the Vulgate has two words, namely,
immundicia, impudicitia, Erasmus has but one, ἀκαθαρσία, *immundicia*
in the Latin text. Luther, following Erasmus against the Vulgate, has
only one word, "unreynickeyt." There can be little doubt that Luther's
rendering of this enumerative phrase is based on the new texts Erasmus made available. The Vulgate simply will not do as a source of
Luther's translation.

Galatians 6:16

The Basel Vulgate of 1509
Et quicunque hanc regulam secuti fuerint . . .
The Pre-Lutheran High German Bibles
Vnd alle die do nachuolgend dirr regel . . .
Erasmus' Greek text of 1519
καὶ ὅσοι τῷ κανόνι τούτῳ στοιχήσουσιν . . .
Erasmus' Latin Translation of 1519
Et quicunque iuxta regulam hanc incedunt . . .
Septembertestament
vnnd wie viel nach diser regel eynher tretten . . .

If Luther had been content to follow the Vulgate, he would have
used "folgen" or "nachfolgen" as the old German Bibles did. One
could easily argue that this would have resulted in smoother German
and a more natural, idiomatic phrase. Instead he employed the really
more awkward, at least more unusual, words "eynher tretten." It is
obvious that this rendering can derive only from the new texts that
Erasmus had put at his disposal: στοιχήσουσιν, *incedunt* are the sources
of Luther's translation. As in all examples quoted so far, it is impossible to tell whether Erasmus' Greek or Latin version is the ultimate
source.

The 16 passages that have been presented here as evidence of

157

Luther's breaking with the authority of the Vulgate have not, in the nature of the case, allowed us to differentiate between the Greek original and Erasmus' new Latin version. The latter is generally so closely rendered from the Greek text that one cannot decide which Luther followed.

There are, however, a few passages where Erasmus' Latin translation differs sufficiently from the Greek original to enable us to tell, with a measure of certainty, whether Luther took the Greek text itself or only Erasmus' Latin rendering as his primary source. It is to a consideration of these crucial passages that we now turn.

Galatians 1:15

The Basel Vulgate of 1509
Cum autem placuit ei qui me segregauit ex vtero matris mee . . .

The Pre-Lutheran High German Bibles
Wann do es dem geuiel der mich sundert von dem leib meiner mutter . . .

Erasmus' Greek text of 1519
ὅτε δὲ εὐδόκησεν ὁ θεὸς . . .

Erasmus' Latin Translation of 1519
Ast ubi deo . . . uisum est . . .

Septembertestament
Da es aber Gotte wolgefiel . . .

Two words in this brief phrase are of major importance for our problem. First, Luther has "Gotte" against the Vulgate's *ei* and the old German Bibles' "dem." It is clear that he agrees with Erasmus' ὁ θεὸς and *deo*. This word obviously does not permit us to identify the exact source, whether the Greek itself or only Erasmus' Latin. But the situation is different in the second word of interest to us in this phrase. Luther's "wolgefiel," which goes beyond the Vulgate's mere *placuit,* would appear to be derivable only from the Greek original itself, εὐδόκησεν. Erasmus' Latin version, which has *uisum est,* cannot be held to lead to Luther's "wolgefiel." It seems to me that nothing short of the original Greek compound verb can explain Luther's rendering. Only the Greek prefix εὐ can be the origin of Luther's "wol." In other words, Luther alone, against the Vulgate and even against Erasmus' Latin version, happens to express the full meaning of the Greek text. "Wolgefiel" corresponds one hundred percent to εὐδόκησεν. This exhaustive translation of the Greek compound verb by a German compound verb indicates the direct use of the original Greek source.

158

Galatians 4:30

The Basel Vulgate of 1509
Non enim heres erit filius ancille cum filio libere.

The Pre-Lutheran High German Bibles
Wann der sun der diern der wirt nit erbe: mit dem sun der freyen
(From the Zainer redaction on, the article "ein" is inserted before
the noun "erbe.")

Erasmus' Greek text of 1519
. . . ὄυ γὰρ μὴ κληρονομήσῃ ὁ υἱὸς τῆς παιδίσκης μετὰ τοῦ υἱοῦ τῆς
ἐλευθέρας.

Erasmus' Latin Translation of 1519
. . . non enim haeres erit filius ancillae cum filio liberae.

Septembertestament
. . . Denn der magd son sol nicht erben / mitt dem szon der freyen.

This passage also allows us to claim that Luther used the Greek
text directly. Both the Vulgate and Erasmus' Latin version employ
nouns: *heres* and *haeres*. Luther alone has a verb: "sol nicht erben."
This must go back to the original Greek text itself, where we also
find a verb, κληρονομήσῃ. Luther could not have derived his verb
from any other source except the Greek original.

Galatians 5:21

The Basel Vulgate of 1509
. . . quoniam qui talia agunt / regnum dei non consequentur.

The Pre-Lutheran High German Bibles
. . . die gewinnent nit das reich gotz.

Erasmus' Greek text of 1519
. . . βασιλείαν θεοῦ οὐ κληρονομήσουσιν

Erasmus' Latin Translation of 1519
. . . regni dei haeredes non erunt.

Septembertestament
. . . werden das reych Gottis nicht erben.

This phrase corresponds rather closely to the one just discussed,
except that the Vulgate in this instance differs radically from Erasmus'
Latin translation. What interests us chiefly in this connection is the
divergence between the Greek original and Erasmus' new Latin rendering. As in the previous passage, Gal. 4:30, Erasmus translates the
Greek *verb* κληρονομήσουσιν by a *noun, haeredes*. Luther could not
have arrived at his verbal rendering without consulting the Greek text

directly. Erasmus' Latin translation in and of itself does not lead to Luther's version. Only the Greek itself does.

Galatians 6:1

The Basel Vulgate of 1509
Fratres & si preoccupatus homo fuerit in aliquo delicto . . .

The Pre-Lutheran High German Bibles
Vnd bruder: vnd ob der mensch wirt bekumert in etlicher misstat·

Erasmus' Greek text of 1519
'Αδελφοί, ἐὰν καὶ προληφθῇ ἄνθρωπος

Erasmus' Latin Translation of 1519
Fratres, etiam si occupatus fuerit homo . . .

Septembertestament
Lieben bruder / so ein mensch etwa von eynem feyl vbereylet wurd . . .

This passage again indicates that Luther must have gone beyond Erasmus' Latin translation. Erasmus' *occupatus* leads just as little as the Vulgate's *preoccupatus* to Luther's "vbereylet." Only the original Greek, προληφθῇ explains Luther's translation. We cannot but conclude that Luther went directly to the Greek. No intermediate rendering suffices.

Galatians 6:12

The Basel Vulgate of 1509
. . . tantum vt crucis christi persecutionem non patiantur.

The Pre-Lutheran High German Bibles
. . . das sy allein nit leiden die iagung des kreutzes cristi.

From the Zainer redaction on, "iagung" is replaced by "durchaechtung."

Erasmus' Greek text of 1519
. . . μόνον ἵνα μὴ τῷ σταυρῷ τοῦ Χριστοῦ διώκωνται.

Erasmus' Latin Translation of 1519
. . . tantum ne ob crucem Christi persecutionem patiantur.

Septembertestament
. . . alleyn das sie nicht mit dem creutz Christi verfolget werden . . .

There can be no question of Luther's departure from the Vulgate. The version contained in the old German Bibles shows what a translation based on the Vulgate would be like. Luther's version differs materially.

First of all, his phrase "mit dem creutz" cannot derive from the Vulgate. So far as its relation to Erasmus' Latin translation is concerned, it is conceivable, though not too probable, that *ob crucem Christi* suggested it. It is much more likely that the actual Greek phrase τῷ σταυρῷ τοῦ Χριστοῦ is the source rather than Erasmus' free rendering.

Secondly, Luther's "verfolget werden" does not look as though it came from the Vulgate's *persecutionem . . . patiantur*. Erasmus' Latin rendering, which is exactly like the Vulgate in this instance, does not help either. Again it would seem that the actual Greek διώκωνται is responsible for Luther's "verfolget werden." Both the Greek text and Luther employ a simple verb in contrast to the circumlocution of the two Latin versions.

II. LUTHER AGREEING WITH THE VULGATE AGAINST THE GREEK ORIGINAL

We have presented only a selection of the most important cases of Luther's parting company with the Vulgate and following the Greek original. There are a few instances where Luther appears to agree with the Vulgate rather than with the Erasmian Greek text. They will all be discussed here.

So far as I know, these passages have never been pointed out or analyzed before. Although the editors of the relevant volumes of the Weimar Edition of Luther's works assure us that all cases of Luther's siding with the Vulgate against the Greek original have been called to the attention of the reader, they have failed to take cognizance of the following passages.

Galatians 1:10

The Basel Vulgate of 1509
Si adhuc hominibus placerem: christi seruus non essem.

The Pre-Lutheran High German Bibles
. . . Ob ich noch geuiel den leúten: ich wer nit der knechte cristi.

Erasmus' Greek text of 1519
. . . εἰ γὰρ ἔτι ἀνθρώποις ἤρεσκον

Erasmus' Latin Translation of 1519
Nam si hactenus hominibus placuissem . . .

Septembertestament
. . . Wenn ich den menschen noch gefellig were . . .

Contrary to the cases thus far discussed, we are here dealing with a very minor point. Luther does not translate the Greek γὰρ, correctly rendered by *nam* in Erasmus' Latin version. This omission makes Luther agree with the Vulgate, which does not contain this word. On the face of it, Luther is siding with the Vulgate against both Erasmian texts.

Why did he omit γάρ, *nam?* There are at least two possible explanations. First, an omission of this sort is in no way an unusual occurrence if we take Luther's translation as a whole. He rather frequently omitted little words, either because he translated hurriedly or because of his desire to provide a smoother rendering unencumbered by clusters of expletives and similar words. Second, there is a γάρ in the first half of this long verse, and Luther may very well have decided that one γάρ would do for the entire verse. In other words, it could be either negligence or deliberate choice that is responsible for the omission. All we can state with finality is that Luther's translation of this phrase agrees with the Vulgate rather than with the Greek original and the Erasmian Latin version.

Galatians 3:8

The Basel Vulgate of 1509
. . . quia ex fide iustificat gentes deus: prenunciauit abrae . . .

The Pre-Lutheran High German Bibles
. . . das got gerechthaftigt die heiden vom gelauben: er vor derkunt es abraham . . .

The second part of this passage underwent this change from the Zainer redaction on:
. . . Er verkuendet vor Abrahe . . .

Erasmus' Greek text of 1519
. . . προευηγγελίσατο τῷ ἀβραάμ . . .

Erasmus' Latin Translation of 1519
. . . prius rem laetam nunciauit Abrahae . . .

Septembertestament
. . . verkundiget sie dem Abraham . . .

Though this is again a relatively minor point, it is probably of more interest and significance than the one discussed in connection with the preceding passage. Luther, it is quite clear, failed to exhaust the full meaning of the Greek word in question, προευηγγελίσατο, translated carefully and correctly by Erasmus as *prius rem laetam nunciauit.* While Erasmus took notice of and gave expression to both the prefix προ and the infix ευ, Luther did nothing of the sort. Neither the Greek text nor Erasmus' explicit Latin rendering appears to have made an impression on him.

162

Still it could be argued that Luther, if given a hearing, might very well defend himself on grounds of style and usage. First, with reference to the omission of the prefix προ, he could mention that there is a "zuuor" earlier in the same verse and that for stylistic reasons he did not wish to repeat it. Second, "verkundiget" is by itself so rich a word, especially for Luther, that it may have implied for him the special infix ευ.

The various revisions of Luther's German Bible left this text fully intact. This is surely an indication that his somewhat condensed rendering, after it had been properly evaluated, was considered adequate. Also the Authorized Version, while retaining the prefix προ as "before," did not specifically translate the infix ευ, but limited itself to the simple "preached."

Still, whatever may be said in defense of Luther's abbreviation of the Greek text, the fact remains that from a strictly philological point of view both προ and ευ were left untranslated.

Galatians 3:13

The Basel Vulgate of 1509
. . . factus pro nobis maledictum . . .

The Pre-Lutheran High German Bibles
. . . er ist gemacht verflucht vmb vns . . .

From Zainer on, "gemacht" is replaced by "worden."

Erasmus' Greek text of 1519
. . . γενόμενος ὑπὲρ ὑμῶν κατάρα

Erasmus' Latin Translation of 1519
. . . pro uobis factus est execratio.

Septembertestament
. . . er wart eyn vermaledeyung fur vns . . .

It is apparent that Luther did not follow the Greek text as provided by Erasmus and Gerbelius or Erasmus' new Latin translation. He is rather in agreement with the Vulgate's *nobis*. This is a clear fact.

Why did Luther prefer the Vulgate reading? If one looks at the verse as a whole, it seems that "vns" makes better sense than the second person plural. Gal. 3:13 reads as follows: "Christus aber hat *vns* erloset von der vermaledeyung des gesetzs da er wart eyn vermaledeyung fur *vns*. . . ." It is quite possible that Luther did not like the shift from "vns erloset" to "eyn vermaledeyung fur *euch*" as he would have had to write if he had followed the Erasmian texts with absolute fidelity.

Luther, I venture to suggest, did not hesitate to decide against the Greek text and in favor of the Vulgate when the latter made better sense to him. It is also possible of course that there is no conscious choice involved here at all. If one bears in mind, as one always should, with what incredible speed Luther produced his translation, it is conceivable that, taking the verse as a whole, he more or less unconsciously put down what made the best sense to him.

Finally, Luther's preference for the first person plural actually turned out to be the right choice. The Complutensian Polyglot of Cardinal Ximenes, unfortunately not published until after Luther's translation was completed, does have ἡμῶν in lieu of Erasmus' ὑμῶν. The Complutensian reading has since been accepted and the Erasmian text rejected by Biblical scholarship. Thus Martin Luther, whatever the reason or reasons may have been that prompted him to depart from Erasmus, was actually on the right track after all.

Galatians 4:6

The Basel Vulgate of 1509
. . . misit deus spiritum filii sui in corda vestra . . .

The Pre-Lutheran High German Bibles
. . . gott der sante den geist seins suns in vnsere hertzen . . .

Erasmus' Greek text of 1519
. . . εἰς τὰς καρδίας ἡμῶν . . .

Erasmus' Latin Translation of 1519
. . . emisit deus spiritum filii sui in corda nostra . . .

Septembertestament
. . . hat Got gesand seynen geyst ynn ewre hertzen . . .

Again it is clear that Luther does not follow the Erasmian texts of 1519 (or the pre-Lutheran Bibles for that matter, which, strangely enough, have "vnsere"). The reason for Luther's preference of the *second* person plural in this case to the *first* person of the Erasmian texts is perhaps not too difficult to find. In fact, it appears to be quite similar to the one suggested for the preceding passage. If again we look at the verse as a whole, the *second* person simply makes better sense: "Weyl *yhr* denn kinder seyt / hat Gott gesand . . . ynn *ewre* hertzen/. . . ." As in Gal. 3:13, Luther does not appear to hesitate to depart from his Greek text in the interest of greater logic and more natural style. It should be noted that Erasmus' first edition of 1516 has the *second* rather than the *first* person plural in both its Greek and Latin texts, ὑμῶν and *vestra*. While it is not impossible that Luther

164

could have had the first edition in mind, it seems more plausible to me that his preference for the second person is based primarily on logical and stylistic considerations. In instances of minor importance, in which dogma was certainly not an issue, he apparently let reason be his guide. We should add, however, that again this may not necessarily have been a matter of conscious choice at all but simply the result of translating in a great hurry and not always looking at the text or texts word for word but sentence by sentence.

In conclusion, it is again interesting to call attention to the fact that the Complutensian Polyglot has ὑμῶν instead of Erasmus' second edition's ἡμῶν. Again Luther can be said to have "anticipated" what is accepted today as the better reading.

Galatians 4:7

The Basel Vulgate of 1509
Itaque iam non est servus, sed filius . . .

The Pre-Lutheran High German Bibles
Dorumb ietzunt ist er nit ein knecht . . .

Erasmus' Greek text of 1519
ὥστε οὐκ ἔτι εἶ δοῦλος, ἀλλ᾽ υἱός.

Erasmus' Latin Translation of 1519
Itaque iam non es seruus, sed filius.

Septembertestament
also ist nu hie keyn knecht mehr . . .

Without any doubt, Luther agrees with the Vulgate, which has the verb in the third person, whereas the Erasmian texts have it in the second. It is not very easy to put one's finger on the reasons that may have moved Luther to prefer the Vulgate to the Greek original. I am inclined to believe that Luther liked the generalizing effect of the third person. It reads like a universal truth, applicable to all men, not only to the one addressed in the second person. But we should not forget that this "error" may again be due to hurry rather than forethought. Whatever may be the ultimate explanation, the use of the third person makes good sense. In this particular instance the Complutensian Polyglot does not depart from the Erasmian reading.

Galatians 5:16

The Basel Vulgate of 1509
. . . desideria carnis non perficietis.

. . . vnd nit volbringt die begirden des fleisches.

Erasmus' Greek text of 1519

. . . καὶ ἐπιθυμίαν σαρκὸς οὐ μὴ τελέσητε.

Erasmus' Latin Translation of 1519

. . . concupiscentiam carnis non perficietis.

Septembertestament

. . . so werdet yhr die lusten des fleyschs nicht volnbringen . . .

Luther's plural "die lusten" agrees with the Vulgate's *desideria* against the Erasmian singulars ἐπιθυμίαν and *concupiscentiam*. It is not an unusual occurrence in Luther's translation of the New Testament as a whole to find the substitution of the plural for the singular and vice versa. Whichever number made more sense to him in the context appears to have been chosen. Luther, to be sure, made use of this "right" of the translator within reason.

Gal. 5:16 is an especially interesting case, for here is a difference between the Vulgate and the Erasmian texts. In all other instances in Galatians, where Luther makes a change of this sort, there is no difference between the original and the Vulgate.

So far as this particular verse is concerned, Luther agrees with the Vulgate against Erasmus' Greek and Latin texts. Whether he was so hurried that he did not look closely enough at his materials or whether he thought it more logical to speak of lusts rather than a single lust of the flesh, I cannot tell. I merely record that, from a philological point of view, his translation agrees with the Vulgate and not with Erasmus.

The results of our examination of the six passages in which Luther sides with the Vulgate and differs from the Greek original can be summarized as follows. In contradistinction to the many cases of major importance where Luther agrees with the Greek text and differs from the Vulgate, the cases where he agrees with the Vulgate and differs from the original are comparatively few and of minor significance. Three times he substituted another person of a pronoun or a verb; once he omitted a minor word; once he used the plural for the singular of a noun; once he did not exhaust the full meaning of a compound Greek verb, ignoring both a prefix and an infix. None of these cases has serious implications for his scholarship. Taken all in all, they imply and reveal that he was neither a literalist nor an ultrapatient translator with a superabundance of time on his hands. It is perhaps not idle to point out that Erasmus, a greater philologist with somewhat more time at his disposal, was not beyond occasional error either. If we rule out the three cases in which Luther, for reasons of structural and logical consistency, preferred the Vulgate reading, borne out in part by the then still unpublished Complutensian Polyglot, there remain but three minor passages in which he may actually have slipped, although even here a measure of doubt remains whether he may not have had good reason for what he did. As against the more than 50 cases where he followed the Greek original versus the Vulgate, these are very few indeed.

Luther's performance stamps him as a scholarly translator so far as the handling of his sources is concerned. But the record shows that he was, from a strictly philological point of view, not perfect in some little things. Yet even in these the question still remains whether these few "errors" may not ultimately be due to a conscious preference for the Vulgate reading, inspired by reasons of his own. This view, somewhat hesitantly advanced because of the virtual insolubility of such matters, is supported by the significant fact that these six passages remained unaltered throughout the many successive editions of Luther's New Testament and German Bible as a whole. Religious and literary considerations are part and parcel of his procedure as a "translator." He was most definitely not an automaton.

There are two further passages of more than passing interest that should be noted and discussed. The first has to do with the long-debated issue whether Luther used Erasmus' first edition of 1516 or the second of 1519.

Galatians 1:6

The Basel Vulgate of 1509
. . . ab eo qui vos vocauit in gratiam christi / in aliud euangelium . . .

The Pre-Lutheran High German Bibles
. . . von dem der euch rieff in die gnad cristi in einander ewangelium . . .

From the Zainer redaction on, "rief" is replaced by "hat gerueffet."

Erasmus' Greek text of 1516
. . . ἀπὸ τοῦ καλέσαντος ὑμᾶς ἐν χάριτι θεοῦ . . .

Erasmus' Latin Translation of 1516
. . . qui uocauit uos in gratia dei . . .

Erasmus' Greek text of 1519
. . . ἀπὸ τοῦ καλέσαντος ὑμᾶς ἐν χάριτι Χριστοῦ . . .

Erasmus' Latin Translation of 1519
. . . quod a Christo, qui uocauit uos per gratiam . . .

167

. . . von dem / der euch beruffen hatt durch die gnad Christi / auff
eyn ander Euangelion . . .

There are two problems in this verse. First, what could be the
origin of Luther's phrase "*durch* die gnad," from one edition of 1527
on replaced by "*in* die gnad"? It would seem to stem from Erasmus'
second edition of 1519, where the Greek reads ἐν χάριτι but the new
Latin translation *per gratiam*. In the *Adnotationes* of the second edition Erasmus states (p. 393) that the real meaning of the Greek phrase
is *per gratiam*. This translation and this interpretation are
found only in the second edition. In the first edition our passage reads
in gratia in the translation. There is no discussion of it at all in the
Adnotationes. From these facts it would appear that Luther must have
used the second edition of 1519 rather than the first of 1516.

This inference is reinforced by another important word. In the
first edition Erasmus has ϑεοῦ, *dei*, which Luther clearly did not use
in his translation. The *Septembertestament* agrees rather with the
second edition's Χριστοῦ. This passage makes it quite sure that Luther
relied on Erasmus' second and not on his first edition.

Galatians 2:19

The Basel Vulgate of 1509

Ego enim per legem / legi mortuus sum vt deo viuam . . .

The Pre-Lutheran High German Bibles

. . . das ich lebe zů gott . . .

From the Zainer redaction on, "zů" before "gott" is dropped.

Erasmus' Greek text of 1519

. . . ἵνα ϑεῷ ζήσω . . .

Erasmus' Latin Translation of 1519

. . . ut Christo uiuerem . . .

Septembertestament

. . . auff das ich Gotte lebe . . .

As was stated earlier in this essay, the possibility that Luther may
have translated simply from Erasmus' new Latin version instead of
from the Greek itself cannot be ruled out for all cases where the Greek
and Vulgate differ. On the whole, Erasmus' translation is good and
reliable so that one cannot tell whether Luther went back to the original itself or only to the new Latin version. We were, however, able
to point out a number of cases in which there is a difference between

the Greek and Erasmus' Latin, with Luther clearly following the Greek itself.

Gal. 2:19 contains another passage to support these findings. Why it was not taken up in connection with the other relevant verses is that the Vulgate in this instance does not differ from the Greek original.

Had Luther been content to translate from the new Latin version of Erasmus, he would have reproduced *Christo* as found in Erasmus' Latin rather than θεῷ as found in the Greek text. Whichever source he may have used in this verse, whether the Greek original's θεῷ or the Vulgate's *deo*, he certainly did not use Erasmus' new Latin translation. Our passage rules out this version as a source. This fact fully agrees with what we found earlier in this essay: the Greek text itself as furnished by Erasmus in 1519 appears to have been Luther's primary source.

The general results of this investigation of the sources of Luther's translation of 1522, the justly famed *Septembertestament,* can be summed up as follows:

1. There are more than 60 divergences between Erasmus' Greek text of 1519 and the Basel Vulgate of 1509.

2. In all but six of these Luther agrees with the Greek original against the Vulgate.

3. In the majority of these more than 60 cases it is impossible to tell whether Luther went all the way back to the Greek original or whether he merely used the new Latin translation which Erasmus brought out alongside the Greek text. In the few instances where there is a difference between the Greek text and Erasmus' new Latin version Luther followed the Greek original against Erasmus' new Latin translation. In the light of this important fact it is not amiss to give Luther the benefit of the doubt also in all cases where the Greek text and Erasmus' Latin rendering agree and to assume that the Greek original was the actual basis of Luther's work.

4. The six cases where Luther does agree with the Vulgate against the Greek original as printed by Erasmus are of minor importance. In general it can be maintained that Luther gave the nod to the version which made better sense to him. It was very definitely not a matter of uncritical preference of the Vulgate *qua* Vulgate. By exercising his right of choice Luther even anticipated several of the readings of the Complutensian Polyglot.

The most serious of these few cases of departure from Erasmus' Greek text involves Luther's failure to exhaust fully the entire meaning

169

of a Greek compound verb; Luther apparently did not catch a prefix and an infix, at least he did not reproduce them in German. He could, however, readily defend his procedure on grounds of usage and style.

5. One passage shows clearly that Luther used Erasmus' second edition of 1519 (the latest available at the time of the translation of the New Testament) rather than the first of 1516, which he had consulted from the day it became accessible to him while lecturing on Paul's Epistle to the Romans in Wittenberg in 1515 and 1516.

6. Another passage reinforces the view expressed in this essay that Erasmus' new Latin version was not the primary source. This had to be treated separately because, contrary to the six cases discussed above, there is no difference between the Vulgate and the Greek original in Gal. 2:19.

These results point to one fundamental fact: the first edition of Luther's translation of Galatians, an integral part of the *September-testament* of 1522, is a scholarly achievement so far as the sources are concerned. Taken as a whole, it is based on the Greek text of Erasmus' second edition of the New Testament of 1519. Yet Luther was not a mechanical translator even of the original. Where a Vulgate reading made better sense — in nondogmatic phrases to be sure — he did not hesitate to employ it. He himself appears to be the arbiter in such cases, a position of high privilege fully earned on the basis of having established himself as one of the greatest interpreters of Paul of all time. His insight into Paul's mind and style was such that Luther actually anticipated some of the Greek readings found in the Complutensian Polyglot, which furnished a better text than Erasmus' edition. Luther's translation is clearly the product of a scholar, but of a thinking scholar bold enough to prefer an occasional Vulgate reading that was to his liking and that more often than not turned out to be right when better texts became available. But by and large Luther's earliest official translation of one of the most famous epistles of the New Testament was based on the Greek text he had before him while engaged in this monumental task. This in itself was an epochal event, for it was the first time in more than a thousand years of West European intellectual history that a Christian scholar in making a translation into the vernacular broke with the Vulgate as the *textus princeps,* treating it for what it was — a translation — and proceeded to replace it by the original, the Greek text, henceforth the *textus princeps.*

Considered solely from the point of view of the sources used for this great venture, Luther's deed was a major accomplishment. *How,* i. e., how magnificently he translated is not the subject of this particular essay. We were here only concerned with Luther the scholar, not with Luther the artistic translator.* From a close examination of the *Septembertestament* Luther emerges as a scholarly translator into the vernacular, using the most recent tools the foremost scholar of the age had just made available. This claim to major distinction can now be made with confidence and assurance, resting as it does on what is, so far as I am aware, the first detailed examination of the sources of Luther's first translation of the Epistle to the Galatians undertaken and carried out in the year 1522, a year as great and significant in its way as the years 1521 and 1517 with the historic events of Worms and Wittenberg. The author of the greatest and most influential single version of the New Testament in a modern language is every whit as important as the intrepid figure who stood before the emperor in 1521 and the justly indignant religious genius who issued the Ninety-five Theses in 1517.

* Heinz Bluhm, *Martin Luther: Creative Translator* (St. Louis: Concordia Publishing House, 1965).

7

SACRAMENTUM ET EXEMPLUM
IN LUTHER'S UNDERSTANDING OF CHRIST

Norman Nagel

T HE PAIR *sacramentum et exemplum,* which has received some attention of late as an index of Luther's understanding of Christ,[1] appears for the first time in 1509 in Luther's marginal notes on Augustine's *De Trinitate.* The notes are quite sparse. Scheel suggests that this is because Luther found himself so much in agreement with what he read.[2] While we may acknowledge this agreement, we must add that had Luther been prompted to comment only when he disagreed, there would be very few comments at all. Both the paucity of comment and the comments themselves may then be adduced as evidence that Luther read the patron saint of his order most receptively.[3] Life and this essay are too short to enquire whether Luther was agreeing with Augustine or only with what he supposed Augustine was saying.[4] No definition of the pair will therefore be offered other than a functional one on the principle that a spade is to dig with. In this way we may avoid importing too much into the pair.

What there are of marginal notes are rather casual and pedestrian.

172

Luther was no new broom of a young professor. However, as childhood sayings of a famous man are sometimes recounted as portentous, so some of Luther's comments here are noteworthy.

His first long comment centers faith in Christ's humanity and incarnation, with His humanity given us in this life for life and salvation.[5] A summary of his early *theologia crucis* has been found in his comment on "strength in weakness." "That is in humility. When I am made weak, then am I stronger, that is when I am being humble." [6] Also, "Humility is the way of knowledge." [7] Aristotle talks frivolous nonsense.[8] We dare not be rash and brash when we deal with the ineffable Trinity.[9] God is hidden, but He can be known to be present by signs.[10] The way by which we see is our synteresis.[11] There is no mention of the forgiveness of sins. In his comments on Lombard from the same time Luther speaks of the guilt and punishment of sin. Baptism takes away the *culpa* of original sin. The *poena* remains as the burden to be borne through Luther's early understanding of the way of salvation as process. This answers for the concupiscence that remains after Baptism. The ultimate point of reference is God's *iudicium*.[12]

When Augustine speaks of the cry of dereliction as pertaining to the death of our soul, this is said to be as a *sacramentum* of the inner man. Luther marks the place in the margin with "Sacramentum." When Augustine continues with "Knowing that our old man is crucified at the same time," Luther comments: "The crucifixion of Christ is *sacramentum* because it signifies thus the cross of penitence in which the soul dies to sin. It is *exemplum* because it exhorts the body truly to proffer itself to death or cross." [13] When a little later Augustine has, "He has tranfigured the body of our humility," Luther tries his hand at Augustine's two-matching-one scheme — the single death of Christ has a double meaning. It redeems the soul from death, thus with death He murders death. It also makes the soul die to sin, and so we are crucified to the world and the world to us. Luther is not as good as Augustine at this sort of thing.[14] His effort here must come under the heading *sacramentum*, and there is nothing under *exemplum* to balance it. Indeed, these can hardly be called categories at all but are rather interesting ways of talking about the death and resurrection of Christ. The death engages Luther more than the resurrection, and his interest here is rather in what goes on in man than on Calvary.

Luther's next comment is a square of dots exercising Augustine's wondrous number six. If one wants to get much more from Luther's use of *sacramentum et exemplum* here, one has to read back into it what he later says with the phrase.[15] Indeed the question remains throughout: What does he say with the phrase? and not so much what the phrase itself says.[16]

Sacramentum et exemplum do not appear in the *Dictata*, although Luther refers to the place from which they come in Augustine with its two-matching-one scheme.[17]

What is one in Christ is always double in us. He did not suffer spiritually but only literally. This is because He was never in the evil of guilt but only in the evil of punishment. We, however, are in both and doubly so. We are in the evil of guilt and punishment, while He did not deserve even punishment: His punishment was for our sin. Therefore when He Himself pleaded to be freed from punishments, He was pleading that we be freed from sins and punishment, for He would have had no punishment were it not for our sins and our punishment.

While the relevant passage from Augustine is in Luther's mind, he does not use *sacramentum et exemplum*. Instead he has spiritually and literally. These should match interior and exterior and probably do, since Augustine says that Christ's suffering was that of His humanity alone. This was a suffering of punishment only, and this one of Christ matches our two: guilt and punishment.

Commenting on the setting sun of the Vulgate's Ps. 67:5, Luther says that the one of Christ's death matches our two of sin and death.[18] Christ was only in death and not in sin. He rises above our going down into sin through His faith, and this is by the going down of the flesh. It is difficult to know whether this last going down should come under *sacramentum* or *exemplum* or under spiritually or literally. There seems to be no sharp either/or in Luther's thinking here. Three deaths of ours are involved in this passage, and he does not work them neatly into Augustine's one-matching-two scheme. This lack of tidiness suggests that the scheme does not fully control his thinking here, rather that we have a collation of allegorical, tropological, and anagogical interpretations.

How loose a control *sacramentum et exemplum* have on Luther is shown by his failure to use them when commenting on the two-in-one *esca et memoria*.[19] Here the two sides of the matter are given by *sacramentalis et spiritualis*. Earlier we had "literally and spiritually" (Augustine). It would, however, be rash to equate "literally" with "sacramentally." Luther was not one to keep his terminological bookkeeping tidy and up-to-date. He tends to pile up terms rather than

174

keep them neatly sorted out. Nor does he move forward along the whole front, but rather by salients.

What Luther said just prior to *esca et memoria* (in the great passage on the wondrous works of God) relative to *sacramentum et exemplum* seems to fall under *exemplum*.[20] This not only indicates where the weight rests but also puts great strain on *exemplum*. It must swell in order to bear the weight, or rather, it in fact draws from its partner; and only after *sacramentum* has been replaced by *donum* and gone to its proper task, only then is *exemplum* relieved of the intolerable burden of carrying its own proper load.

"Example" will not altogether do as a translation. This reminds us too much of its bastard brother *imitatio Christi*. The subject of the critical verbs in the wondrous works passage is God. In the *Dictata,* what man must do retreats before the monergism of God, and so does syntheresis, although they have not yet left the field. Thimme would reproduce swollen *exemplum* with *exemplar,* and Erich Seeberg on the *sacramentum* side urges *Urbild*.[21] "Paradigm" might perhaps be better. What Christ went through the Christian is to be put through too. "Christ crucified" means not so much His unique cross as the cross seen in Him and the saints, the cross we are to bear and to which we are to be conformed.[22] The inward crucifixion is humility, hatred, and condemnation of self and spiritual descent into hell.[23] The outward crucifixion is submission to sufferings for the mortification of the flesh. Sufferings are to be accepted, welcomed, and sought.[24] As Augustine loved to say, there is community of goods between Christ and His members through union with Him.[25]

This is Luther's momentous tropological interpretation, which produces the *theologia crucis.* All the weight of this, *sacramentum et exemplum* are really not able to bear. They must certainly give up when Luther's theology of crosses is superseded by the theology of the cross.

The weakness of the suggested translations is their inability to convey the innate power of that which the term represents to effect itself. Pride of place as the conductor of this must be given to the Greek *mysterion*.[26] The translation of this with *sacramentum* meant constriction. Then flow was diffused through the four and more intrepretations. Luther's tropological interpretation built up high pressure. *Sacramentum et exemplum* proved to be of inadequate gauge. *Sacramentum* as *mysterion* did noble service, and full power is registered in what the mature Luther says of righteousness, Christ, Word, and Gospel; then he prefers *donum* to *sacramentum.* And any muddying is always due to the dirt of man-centered righteousness. But this is to anticipate — although Luther has already with help from Augustine acknowledged God as the sole author and effector of saving righteousness. The location of this is still, however, in man and not yet *extra nos* and *sola cruce Christi*. Divine monergism is not yet the Gospel.

The first extended statement of *sacramentum et exemplum* comes in 1515–1516 when Luther is expounding Rom. 6:3.

> The blessed Augustine says in the 4th book on the Trinity in chapter 3, "For our double death the Saviour puts his single death and to achieve our double resurrection he beforehand and before us put his single resurrection as *sacramentum et exemplum*. . . . He put on our mortal flesh and with that only he died, with that only he rose, with that only he matched what is twofold for us by making in it a *sacramentum* of the inner man and an *exemplum* of the outer. Regarding the *sacramentum* of the inner man we are given that word: 'Knowing that our old man is crucified at the same time with him so that the body of sin might be destroyed.' Regarding *exemplum* we have this (Matt. 10): 'Do not fear them who kill the body.' To this he greatly exhorts his own through this kind of death of his."
>
> It is clear from what the Apostle says (Col. 3) that the resurrection of the body of the Lord applies to the *sacramentum* of the inner man. "If you have risen together with Christ, seek those things which are above." To *exemplum* apply the words, "A hair of your head will not perish," and also the fact that he showed his body to the disciples after the resurrection. Therefore the Apostle speaks here of the death and resurrection of Christ inasmuch as they are *sacramentum* and not inasmuch as they are *exemplum*.[27]

This is not altogether pellucid. The execution of Augustine's scheme of Christ's one matching our two produces a puzzling singularity for Christ. His saving work is restricted to His mortal flesh and does not seem to involve His inner man, not to speak of His divinity. Although *exemplum* is not primary, its line is clearer: mortal flesh — outer man — the body. With the inner man of Christ excluded from the calculation we have His mortal flesh producing that one which matches our two. Our two that this one of Christ must match is provided by our inner and outer man. Our inner man lacks correlation with Christ's inner man, and its *sacramentum* is asserted by quotation of texts which do reluctant service to the one-matching-two scheme, which in turn does not serve very well what Luther is trying to say. For that we have to cast the net rather wider.

It is difficult to fit this passage into a picture of Luther wrestling in anguish or triumphing in the joy of the Gospel. He was lecturing. He was adding comments on the text in his lecture on that day, and the professor thought this quotation from Augustine would serve. Some latter-day professors seem prone to think of this activity a little too heroically. Not that they are not matters of great moment, however.

The effective significance of the death of Christ is at the heart of the matter. Since Rom. 6:3 deals with the death of the inner man, it is "quoad sacramentum non quoad exemplum." Luther continues with the observation of the twofoldness of death: temporal and eternal. Temporal death means the separation into the two of soul and body. Eternal death is also twofold. The one is the death of the damned. The other is the death of sin, the death of death, the separation of the soul from sin and the body from corruption and union with the living God through grace and glory.[28] A spiritual man undergoes this death in conformity with Christ. He appears to men and himself as Christ appeared to the Jews when He was buried and dead. The tune He plays to us we are to repeat back to Him in full.[29] As when Christ died He sensed no more of external things, so the spiritual man is in his heart turned away from all things and dead to them. He loathes all things of this life and joyfully glories that he is like a cadaver.[30] However, it is not necessary that all be found in this perfection. Such as go into this death joyfully were prefigured by Christ when He died with a mighty shout as bravest hero. Others have begun and are on the way. They travel on and move toward the goal.[31]

The death of Christ is quantitatively more than that of the saints, but theirs is to be a death of the same sort.[32] All His saints are to imitate His death. Some achieve more, some less. A man progresses according to how much he hates himself, or obversely, how much he loves God. Christ was raised from death and hell because of His love toward God. The man who does not fear death because of God certainly loves God above all things. Man cannot achieve this by himself, but it is rather a gift of God.[33] Man's ability does not reach beyond a *voluntatulam voluntatis*, and the will to be righteous is the whole of righteousness.[34] Conformity with the will of God brings peace to the conscience.[35]

Death and evil are overcome not by power or strength but by infirmity, weakness, and willing suffering. Christ teaches us by His example, for He went confidently to death and suffering. What is written of Christ is taught us so that we might imitate Him. We are not merely to think about it as referring to Christ but as example

177

for us. His example is there to show that whatever is of God must be crucified in the world. Until it is led to the cross (i. e., ignominious suffering), it is not recognized as of God.[36] This cross we are to accept.[37] God's people confess their sin, hate themselves, bear the judgment of the cross upon them, and unceasingly plead and sigh to God for righteousness.[38]

When Luther here propounds Christ as example, this may not simply be taken as a piece of *imitatio Christi*,[39] and yet there is in common a pattern and the necessity of its emulation with the decisive registration in man. There is, however, an important difference in the understanding of righteousness. For Luther this is not merely a quality to be cultivated in man with assistance from God, but first God's effective judgment of man and his spiritual death *(iudicium crucis, crux poenitentiae, accusatio vel odio sui, confessio, humilitas)* and the process *(transitus)* of becoming righteous by suffering and the mortification of the flesh from the hand of God. *Sacramentum et exemplum* are called upon to express all this, and the line between them becomes increasingly difficult to draw. When *exemplum* bears the whole weight, we may well, for all its brave show, look apprehensively to see if its knees are tottering.[40]

For the spiritual significance of a thing the scholastics used the terms *forma, idea, species, imago,* and *exemplar*.[41] These are the *abstractum* of Luther's statement in the *Dictata* that Christ is "ipse nostrum abstractum," [42] and in the *Lectures on Romans,* that "Christus Exemplum et Imago omnium nostrum." [43] The "nos ipsius concretum" of the *Dictata* is the *abstractum* made effective on earth in man. *Sacramentu*m belongs properly with *abstractum,* but Luther's usage is affected by his movement away from the dichotomy inherent here and his insistence on effective operation.

This effective operation moves more into the hands of *exemplum,* and this is made a point of contrast with *sacramentum*.[44] What Christ means pushes ever harder for vibrant expression. Vulcanologists can spot the fumaroles. This image, however, is apt only so long as the impelling force comes from God's *iudicium* and power. *Exemplum* and *exemplar* are rendered radioactive and *sacramentum* is carried along. In the end we do not have a volcano but a lowly stable set beside a little hill. Then *sacramentum* and *exemplum* are free to do each his own *opus proprium.*

We shall look to the scholia on Heb. 2:9 f. for Luther's understanding of Christ in early 1517 and then enquire how *sacramentum et exemplum* carry the load.

178

Here we are told that death is the saving medicine. It was not necessary for Christ to die, but He did so to provide an encouraging example. In the clause "that He might taste of death" Luther finds the emphasis on "taste." As Chrysostom says, it was only a taste because He stayed but a brief interval in death. As a physician He tasted the prescribed food to encourage the patient.[45] Here faith means taking your medicine, that is, death, and since this is presented as a process, it would better be called dying.

The scholium on Heb. 2:10 follows a nice stylistic observation in which Luther points out that in Paul's manner of writing we would not expect to find "through whom," used of the Father, but rather "out of whom" or "from whom." "Through whom" he uses of Christ. The ascription of Heb. 1:3 would in Paul be to the Father rather than the Son.

The authorship of salvation is more properly ascribed to God, obedience to Christ the man. Yet Christ can be called the cause of salvation to show the way we are saved, that is, through Christ as through archetype and example *(per ideam et exemplum)*, to whose image all are conformed who are saved, for God the Father made Christ to be a sign and archetype. Those who cling thereto through faith are transformed into the same image and drawn away from the images of the world. This gathering of the sons of God into one takes place in a manner similar to the way in which people flock to see a spectacle put on by the town council. Thus Christ is exhibited to the whole world by the Gospel as a spectacle, the knowledge and contemplation of which seize and draw men away from the things of the world. This is what it means to be transformed and made like Him. Thus Christ is said to be the cause and leader of salvation because through Him God draws and leads His sons into glory, or as people say, Christ is the instrument and means by which God leads His sons to Himself. In order that Christ be made this most perfect and absolute example, it was natural that God perfect Him through suffering. Suffering should be plural, as the Greek has it, and the Latin should be ablative of instrument without preposition. Without sufferings the perfection of the example would be lost by which He moves and draws us even to a love of death and suffering.[46]

The subject is God. Christ the man is *causa mediata salutis,* as they say. This is His way of being a sign that He is the cause of knowing and loving.[47]

How useful are *sacramentum et exemplum* for expressing this?

179

Do they match "knowing and loving," especially if the object here is death and sufferings? Bizer would tend to say yes,[48] Iserloh no.[49]

The big *sacramentum et exemplum* passage comes as a scholium on Heb. 2:3.[50] Here Luther distinguishes between Law and Gospel as external and internal, as many works and one work. The one work of the Gospel *(nova lex)* is faith. This *fides Christi* is not sterile like a human opinion, for Christ lives in it, and not only lives but works, rules, and triumphs in it. The consequent works named are patience and humility, which indicate a suffering of what God does rather than anything produced by man. Faith's patience and humility are tropologically transferred from Christ. The same may be said of righteousness, which elsewhere is equated with the theological virtues.

> For thus our patience is from Christ's patience, our humility from his, and other goods in the same way if we firmly believe that he has done *(fecerit)* all these things for us, and not only for us but also before us, that is, as blessed Augustine is wont to say, not only to provide a *sacramentum* but also an *exemplum*. Thus blessed Peter (1 Peter 4): "Christ suffered for us (that is the *sacramentum*) "leaving us an example." The *sacramentum* of Christ's suffering is death and the remission of sins, while the *exemplum* is the imitation of His sufferings *(penarum)*. Therefore whoever wants to imitate Christ as regards the *exemplum* must first with firm faith believe that Christ suffered and died as a *sacramentum*. They go wildly astray who would furnish obliteration of their sins with the works and labors of penitence. They begin from the *exemplum* when they ought to begin from the *sacramentum*. In a word, the Gospel is neglected by unbelief of the heart, the Law by disobedience of works.[51]

Working backwards we then have the following lineup:

Gospel	Law
faith of the heart	obedience of works
sacramentum	*exemplum*
death and forgiveness of sins *(culpa)* [52]	imitation of sufferings *(poena)*
pro nobis	*coram nobis*
faith	works
one work	many works
internal	external
Gospel	Law

The Gospel-Law sequence prompts many a reflection. If *sacramentum et exemplum* are inextricably involved in this sequence, they can scarcely hope to hold their job much longer, although their prospects are perhaps not so bleak as their workmates *culpa* and *poena* and internal and external. *Opera acta* and *opera facta* are already in retirement,[53] while *opus operatum* and *opus operantis* call for special arbitration. We may say at least that Luther's use of them would urge that Christ must make a difference, and not just a notional but an actual one. For the early Luther this difference must show in our embrace and experience of sufferings, that is, in our humility.[54] This is first of all internal in the heart, but to be genuine it must show external evidence in imitating the sufferings of Christ. The urgency and necessity of this imitation, which comes under *exemplum,* is inherent in the "not only but also."

As the dichotomies of man and sin weaken, we find in addition to contrast between *sacramentum et exemplum* also their flowing together, as in Luther's exposition of *transitus* at Heb. 10:19,[55] which is essentially a process that therefore blocks the way to the statements of Christ's complete and unique work in our stead. There are no scholia for Heb. 7:27; 9:12; or 10:10. In the passage before us the terms of our pair seem to oscillate, diverge, and coalesce.

Christ's crossing over gives us a *sacramentum imitandi Christi.* Both soul and body are to make their crossings over in imitation of Christ. His body signifies the weaknesses of our flesh, which are ours because of sin and in which we walk the old dead way following the lusts of the flesh. A new and living way must be prepared, and so concupiscence must be mortified.[56] The suffering of Christ's flesh, His death, and exaltation are a *sacramentum* for the conscience that must be mortified, and also for the new and living way of seeking and loving heavenly things with our whole heart.

The mystery and *exemplar* of Christ's suffering was achieved by Him according to the flesh, for He in no way makes the *transitus* from imperfection as we do because He always was and is in heaven. His one matches our two, as Augustine says. We make the *transitus* with flesh and spirit, Christ, however, only with the flesh. For the *transitus* of our flesh He is the *exemplum,* for we shall be like Him. The *transitus* of our spirit is signified as a *sacramentum* by the *transitus* of His flesh.

> The present life and death are the field where two other lives and two other deaths do battle, so that if charity lives, concupiscence dies, and this is what it means to live to God and die to the world. . . .
> To this new life the apostle provokes us with a double exhortation, for it is fearfully difficult and hard for those who at present

have little experience to set up everything in Christ and even life itself. He therefore first sets forth the *exemplum* of Christ our Leader, who fought in the front line. This was not necessary for Him. He went across as the first one and made level the rough way to strengthen our confidence. He not only shows an example of crossing over but reaches out His hand to those who follow. . . . Thus it is that we have no excuse for remaining behind since He could not do more for us than He does. Others can teach and exhort to make the crossing, but only this Christ is not only a companion but leader of the way, and not only a leader but a helper. . . . The man who faithfully leans on Christ is carried on the shoulders of Christ.[57]

It is difficult to see how the apostle is here beginning with the *sacramentum* unless it be that it has been swallowed up by the *exemplum*. If *sacramentum et exemplum* serve the view that living to God means the replacement of concupiscence by love, they can hardly rank as a constant in Luther's theology.

The warning was given that *sacramentum* must come first, but this is not enough by itself. Not only for us but also before us, not only *sacramentum* but also *exemplum,* not only faith of the heart but also obedience of works. Salvation by faith and obedience matches the Gospel-Law sequence.

If we further recall the spectacle passage, we see how most of that must fall under *coram nobis* and so under *exemplum.* This then has more of the center of the stage with the more moving speeches, but in the robes of *exemplar,* to which *sacramentum* has a more legitimate claim. *Sacramentum* has lost to *exemplum* the works and labors of penitence,[58] but it has gained remission of sins, which unfortunately, while it is cast with *exemplum,* it is hindered from bearing fully. Relevant to this forgiveness is also the *fecerit* above, which does not serve Christ's tropologically transferable attributes so well as it serves His unique works. The core of *sacramentum* is the death of Christ. *Sacramentum* is the loser to *exemplum* as long as His death is thought of paradigmatically and not as unique and vicarious. When Christ's death is first of all a saving death such as only He could die, and not first of all a death that provides the paradigm of dying, then its unique achievement can be fully apprehended.

In the short space of an essay it is difficult not to be exposed to the suspicion of setting up one's own Luther as the criterion. No one can really say, however, that he would repudiate our asking after the uniqueness of Christ's redeeming work, salvation full and free with its kindred bestowal, the *ordo salutis,* the distinction between Law and Gospel, and justification itself, distinct though not disconnected from sanctification. Strange things can happen when a single criterion is employed.[59]

In comparison with these, *sacramentum et exemplum* have only a bit part. They are brought on to echo the leading players. The leading role, Luther said, is played by righteousness, and after the clarification of righteousness in the 1518 sermons on righteousness they are hardly to be seen at all, except as by a fond mother looking for her boys in the crowd scene of a school play. *Sacramentum et exemplum* hardly get a word in, and when they do, it is an echo, but then of something different. Together they are as Rosencrantz and Guildenstern — inconstant and dispensable.

We find them jostled in a 1518 sermon on the Passion of Christ. The producer impatiently urges the players to their places. The spotlight is on Christ [60] and to His elbows come word and faith.[61] The intention of the spectacle is that we suffer the same passion in and with Christ.[62] We must identify with the suffering Christ.

"God has set up the cross, and who will lay it aside? He hangs His Son upon it, who will be free?" *Sacramentum et exemplum* are called on but really only *sacramentum* speaks. Christ's bodily death signifies our spiritual death and that effectively.

> Christ has killed the old man who had lived wickedly and awakened the new who had not been well dead. Thus as Christ is in the body, so we were and are in the mind or in the spiritual man. We must lament and weep so that we shall die and do die with the dying Christ. . . .
>
> If we learn this and it prevails over our weaknesses, we shall easily become mellow, patient, humble, worthless, compassionate, despise the world, and imitate the example of the Passion of Christ and moreover implore, as in Psalm 53 (54:5), "Turn the evil upon my enemies." Take the evil from my spirit and put it over on to the flesh with its senses, upon the old man. That is where my enemies are, for the Spirit says a man's enemies are those of his own house. . . . Here a sign of our misery is shown us which is faithful and does not lie. Whoever does not know or doubts who he is, let him look to this and he will see.[63]

We must bear in mind that

> all that is inflicted on Christ are the wounds and evils which are inflicted on our soul by the devil and sin and signify everlasting evils which must be inflicted upon us by the judgment (*iudicium*) of God. Whatever Christ is innocently accused of by the Jews we are to un-

183

derstand as our like accusation by the demons before God, our conscience concurring. From such fearful accusation we cannot be freed except by the injustice of the accusation of Christ. So for Jews understand devils, for Christ, the old man from Adam, the soul born and living in sins, for Pilate's tribunal, the judgment of God.[64]

We must acknowledge the accusation against us to be true.

> Then look to Christ who came down and suffered for you innocently. . . . The things against you no longer are but were, because they are not in Christ, in whom nevertheless are all things. And with this faith you will be saved, if you always acknowledge yourself to be such a one as Christ forms you. And so you flee from yourself to Him in true faith, seeing those things which are yours absorbed in Him and done away.[65]

Then "not only but also" is used to the advantage of *sacramentum,* which is wed with *mysterium,* and their reference is to the Christ who through His temporal and bodily Passion vanquished and crucified the spiritual and eternal passion of the old man.[66] Temporal punishments seem to remain especially if we are saved by God's commuting our eternal punishments to temporal ones.[67] However, the understanding of Christ that would go with this is more than bursting at the seams, and the faith that flees from yourself to Christ is not a *fides Christi* preoccupied with a paradigm and a conforming process. *Sacramentum et exemplum* do not seem to know very well what to do with such a Christ and faith. It is *sacramentum* that expresses the pressure while *exemplum* is rather at a loss what to say.

They have learned some new lines for their next appearance in the 1519 sermon on "The Contemplation of the Holy Suffering of Christ." These they have already practiced in declamation against Eck. Here it is the life of Christ that is *sacramentum* and at the same time *(simul) exemplum.*[68] We have then less of two departments and more of two sides of the same thing. *Sacramentum* is altogether of Christ and Gospel *(sine nobis),*[69] while *exemplum* still does legal service in seeking punishments,[70] although the way is opening for its freedom and vocational activity deriving from the Gospel.

In the "Contemplation" sermon the wrath of God on sin must first be recognized and we must know ourselves as those whose sins crucified Christ. When we are brought to despair of ourselves, we are to see through to the heart full of love that brought Christ to bear the heavy weight of our sin. Then we understand John 3:16, know God rightly, our faith and confidence stand sure, and we are born anew in God."[71]

184

The point on which everything turns is the fact that Christ bore our sins; it turns on the atoning death of Christ rather than His tropologically transferred attributes or the crosses we suffer. No longer do our sufferings answer for our sin as the *poena* we must suffer, Christ having answered for the *culpa*. The distinction between external and internal has also lost its former role. What Christ did must effectively be brought home to us and bear its fruit. This is the matter that *sacramentum et exemplum* are here called on to serve. All that Christ achieved and bestows comes under *sacramentum*. All that this means for our comfort and encouragement comes under *exemplum*, Heb. 12:3; 1 Peter 4:1 (which was earlier split between the two in the scholium on Heb. 2:3).[72]

Exemplum here remains centered in the Christian, but things cannot remain like this for long when salvation is Calvary-centered and no longer a process worked out in man. In the next sermon at which we shall look the bestowed fruits of Christ's death move out to the neighbor. *Exemplum* so far has been primarily between God and the individual. When Christ gives the all clear between God and the sinner, a man is freed from such personal preoccupation in his salvation process for serving his neighbor, who thus, so to speak, replaces God. When salvation is entirely a gift from God to us, this pushes on sideways with its fruits, and so indirectly toward God. *Sacramentum et exemplum* deal more directly and immediately toward God, with also a movement from us nearer to Him as the process of cleansing advances.

As Heinrich Bornkamm emphasized in 1966 at the Luther Research Congress at Järvenpää, until 1518 Luther's understanding of the world was quite Augustinian. In the sermon on "The Two Righteousnesses" Luther for the first time presents the Christian as a *Doppelperson*.[73] He is sent into the world. What he does there is not really his but belongs to his neighbor. This redirection of *exemplum* indicates its conversion to the Gospel, though Luther expresses doubts about this conversion. It has indeed lost its former power to *sacramentum*, but it may still carry the constriction that Christ serves in a way in which the saints also serve us. This is the case as long as Christ's sufferings are paradigms for ours and of the same sort. This is no longer the case when Luther stresses the uniqueness of Christ's suffering, death, and resurrection. When these are not only like those of the saints but also in the point of salvation radically differentiated, then *sacramentum et exemplum* have clearly had their day.

In Luther's Christmas sermon of 1519 — he was henceforward

always at his best at Christmas — we find *sacramentum* come into its own with the strange power that belongs to it as a birthright from *mysterion*. Poliander, who records the sermon, has a cross-reference to the exposition of Heb. 2:3 in the *Lectures on Hebrews* at the beginning of the first paragraph, where Luther says that the whole life of Christ and everything He did are to be dealt with in two ways: as *sacramentum* and then as *exemplum*. He condemns preaching that puts Christ before men's eyes as an example to be imitated, as may be done with any saint. From John you may ask an example of humility, but from Christ the virtue itself, and this He bestows.[74]

> Christ's humility becomes our humility even while we are yet in our sins. This is what I mean when I say sacramentally, that is, all the words, all the Gospel histories are sacraments, that is, sacred signs by which God effects in believers whatever those histories set out.
> "The birth of Jesus Christ." These words are a sacrament through which, if anyone believes, we are born again. In this way Baptism is a sacrament through which God makes a man new, etc. In this way Absolution is a sacrament through which God forgives sins. Thus the words of Christ are sacraments through which He works out our salvation.[75]

If we follow Poliander's reference, we find that in the Hebrews lectures, where Christ's humility becomes our humility, no such mediation is mentioned. From early on, Luther saw the words of Christ transferring their attributes. But the words were at first more general, and what they effected was a retributive righteousness that man was brought to accept and made to suffer for his sins and so to satisfy it. Such is humility. This view of the words, which cannot glory in their lowly externality, gives way to a fuller appreciation of particular words, most notably the words of absolution. When what they say is forgiveness achieved by Christ, then what they say and bestow is altogether Gospel.

Humility here recalls the old process way of suffering crosses so that man may gradually become more righteous and fit for God, but the echo is faint at most and is quite drowned out by the Christmas jubilation over the lowly Infant playing at the bosom of the Virgin. Here the Majesty does not terrify, for here is the One who is born for us, suffered for us, died for us, and made satisfaction for us.[76]

At the end of the sermon there are five lines of *exemplariter* exposition similar to that in the "Contemplation" sermon above, with the addition of the positive service of the neighbor. There is clearly a movement down — to ground level — and *extra nos,* even though this passage too, like so much in the *Lectures on Hebrews,* may also have to be interpreted under the sign of Janus.

The use of the pair in the *Operationes in Psalmos* of 1519–21 looks more backward than forward. Luther does not seem particular in which order they come and introduces them backwards: *exemplum et sacramentum.*[77] Augustine matched one to two, and Luther doubles two to four: faces of Christ or points of the cross: two for the pious and two for the impious. The two for the pious turn out to be *sacramentum et exemplum.* In the exposition of the first face of Christ we read that His Passion is spiritually known when with the full affection of faith you are seized into it and do not doubt that Christ suffered all these things for you so that they may not be noxious to you. Such as was the form of the suffering Christ in the eyes of men, such is to be your form in the eyes of God. What men did to Christ, the same is done to you by your sins and the demons. The Law reveals that this is salutary.[78]

The second face of Christ is the imitation of Christ by external example. This is the way they practice the Passion of Christ who today practice it best, although they be few indeed.[79]

On these two concepts hangs the wisdom of Christ's faithful. The first is the principal one because it belongs to faith. These two Augustine calls *sacramentum et exemplum: sacramentum,* by which hidden faith is nourished; *exemplum,* which the external life imitates.[80]

Luther holds to this hiddenness of faith all the way. But the hiddenness changes from that of the just God so fearfully above us, who yet puts us through suffering to save us, to the gracious God hidden for us in Mary's Baby and in the lowly words: water, wine, and bread.

The source of *sacramentum's* potency is clear for all to see in the sermon on "Christ's Testament" of Easter 1520, taken down by Melanchthon.[81]

> In the Mass the *sacramentum* is set forth, which signifies nothing other than Christ, the sign of the new testament and the forgiveness of offenses. This is the one, the very one, through whom you surely know that sin is done away. . . . There is no greater joy for us than the use of this sacrament.[82] O how great are faith's mysteries! [83]

Stringing together the pearls of this sermon we have *mysterium, promissio, testamentum, sacramentum, signum, Christus,* and in the same year Luther proclaims one sacrament, Christ, and three sacramental signs.[84]

All along Christ has provided a *sacramentum,* and the role of the words has been similar to Christ's role. The understanding of Christ has changed more than the role of the words, and the former effects the latter change. While Christ is first of all exemplification of God's *iudicium* upon sin, our taking of it meaning our *iustitia*,[85] it is these that the words effect with the transposition of attributes, which goes along with a more immediate and mystical way of thinking, and as long as saving righteousness is retributive, it tends to be irresistible.

As long as *sacramentum* is yoked with *exemplum*, it conveys only a part of salvation when thought of as a process. In this process *sacramentum*, which internally answers to *culpa*, is only the beginning. *Exemplum* carries the process of cleansing forward with sufferings for our sins, which answer to *poena*. Not only but also. When *sacramentum* is no longer yokefellow with *exemplum*, it bestows the entire gift, and its wholeness and "giftness" are reflected in the manner of its mediation. The lowly humanity of Christ is matched by the lowliness of the resistible and specific words, and with the words, the sacraments. Therefore the three sacramental signs: absolution, Baptism, and the Eucharist. Here is the bestowal of all that Christ did for our salvation — all the way to us where we as sinners are. It is an entire salvation, for it is entirely of Christ, and it is given in its entirety by His bestowal through means that reach us where we are, even to our ears, bodies, and mouths.

The ground for our forgiveness and joy is gloriously *extra nos* and altogether of Christ and what He did. *Sacramentum* has come into its own, and in so doing has slipped from the yoke that harnessed it to *exemplum*. Or rather it is *exemplum* that has slipped, having no more strength of its own to carry on. When Christ answers fully for our sins, the righteousness He bestows is complete and no longer partly to be effected by sufferings in us. When the *poena* under *exemplum* is abolished by Christ, *exemplum* is no longer part of the essential ground of salvation. Henceforward it is no longer partner with *sacramentum*, but servant.

In the *Christmas Postil of 1522* Augustine's pair do not appear together. *Sacramentum* is replaced by *donum*. It clearly is no yokefellow with *exemplum*, but rather pulls it along.

> You must not make a Moses out of Christ as if He did no more than teach and give an example as the other saints do, as if the Gospel were a book of instructions and Law. There you must grasp Christ, His Word, work, and suffering in two ways. On the one hand as an example that is put before you that you are to follow and do likewise, as St. Peter says, 1 Peter 4:1. . . . But this is the

least of the Gospel if indeed it may still be called Gospel, for then Christ is of no more use than another saint. His life remains with Him and still does not help you. In short, by this way no Christians are made, only hypocrites. . . . The chief part and ground of the Gospel is that first of all, before you grasp Christ as an example, you receive and recognize Him as a gift and present, given you by God to be your own, so that when you look to Him or hear that He does or suffers something, you are not to doubt that that same Christ is yours with all this that He does and suffers. You may place your confidence on this as much as if you had done it, yes, as if you were that same Christ. . . .

When you thus have Christ as the ground and highest good of your salvation, then follows the other part that you grasp Him as an example and give yourself to your neighbor as He gave Himself for you. See then how faith and love are in full swing, God's commandment fulfilled, and man glad and unafraid to do or suffer anything. Therefore mark well that Christ furnishes your faith and makes you a Christian, whereas Christ as an example exercises your works. They do not make you a Christian, but they come from you as one already made a Christian. The difference between gift and example is as great as that between faith and works. Faith has nothing of its own but only Christ, His work and His life. The works have something of your own about them, but they are not to belong to you but to your neighbor.[86]

Luther's commentary on Galatians of 1519, which he began in 1516, offers a contrast with that of 1531. Luther himself thought poorly of the earlier work, his "foolish Galatians." [87] If we are looking for *sacramentum et exemplum* "I am crucified with Christ" should be the place. Here in the earlier commentary we read:

He had said that he was dead to the Law; now he expresses the manner of the death, which is the cross of Christ. . . . Augustine teaches that the suffering of Christ is both a *sacramentum* and an *exemplum* — *sacramentum* because it signifies the death of sin in us and gives it to believers, an *exemplum* because we ought to imitate Him in bodily suffering and dying. . . .[88]

He says he is crucified with Christ in the manner of a *sacramentum* because he has mortified sin and concupiscence. . . . Those who seek to be justified by works of the Law in no way crucify their flesh, but even increase its concupiscence, and therefore cannot possibly be justified. . . . On the other hand the faith of Christ, loving the Law which forbids concupiscence, already does just what the Law commands, attacking and crucifying concupiscence.[89]

In 1531/35 our pair do not appear. Here being crucified with

Christ means first of all freedom from the Law.[90] "If Christ is crucified to the Law, then I too. How? Through faith."[91] Faith is not here first of all union or conformity with Christ and His lot. Its reference is not to a process in man but to what Christ did on Calvary. In 1519 it is *fides Christi;* 1531 has *per fidem in Christum* and "that sublime crucifixion." In 1519 it is "in me"; 1531, "in Christ, not in me."

Union and conformity with Christ are by no means discarded. They are relieved of an intolerable burden and so gain their liberty.[92] They are reassigned from work geared to the Law to gamboling with the Gospel. Then too imputation and union are children of the same father.

> Paul does not speak here of being crucified together in the way of imitation or example, because to imitate the example of Christ is to be crucified also with Him, and such a crucifixion applies to the flesh. . . . But he speaks here of that sublime crucifixion by which sin, devil, and death are crucified in Christ, not in me. Here Christ alone does everything, but when I believe that through faith I am crucified with Christ, then are they [sin, devil, death] dead and crucified for me.[93]

Under *sacramentum et exemplum* attention was drawn to what happened in me. My soul died to sin and my body was offered to death and sufferings. This is reversed when attention centers on what Christ did uniquely. Then it is sin, devil, and death that die. They have power and a role only so long as the Law does. They are crucified in that sublime crucifixion. If we look to where *sacramentum* used to be, we find only Christ and what He did. "In Christ, not in me," is the whole crux of the matter.

> Christ dies on the cross and bears my sin, hell, and the devil. This dealing with sin for me is the way I am justified. I receive what is not my work. Christ alone bears and kills sin in His body, my death He makes void and my hell. . . . These burdens which bore down on me now bear down on Him so that I may be free. There is nothing for me to do but believe, hear that these things are thus accomplished, and receive them with undoubting faith. If I am liberated from sin, death, and the Law, justified through Christ from death, hell, etc., then I do works . . .[94] love God, give thanks, and practice love toward my neighbor.[95]

Luther goes on saying this over and over again.

In his sermon on the Gospel for the Third Sunday in Advent of 1524 Luther is very much in his stride — the stenographer shows the strain. After the first and second uses of the Law we come to Christ as *donum* and then *exemplum.*

Donum is the chief thing. Don't believe it if anyone preaches otherwise. The devil can bear Christ being propounded as an example. He did this; therefore you must do it too. John and Peter did similarly. If you do not preach otherwise, of what use is Christ to me? [96] The devil has the victory if we take Christ's doctrine for Law and His life for example. Only Christ is a gift; other saints can be examples. He is above all others in that He is a gift.[97]

Works follow, of course. A Christian follows the example of Christ, but this does not make a Christian. He is a Christian who has the gift which is Christ.[98]

The Gospel is not the preaching of Christ as example, but proclaiming Him as gift.[99] Whether a man falls or stands he is a Christian if he has Christ. Looking for evidence elsewhere only brings uncertainty.[100] Cling only to the word.[101]

When Christmas comes, Luther rejoices that God always puts words with His work.

This nativity would have remained hidden if He had not had it proclaimed through the Word.[102] Christ is enclosed in this Word, which brings all the things He did for your sake, therefore rejoice. This is Gospel preaching. This is a picture of all preachers of the Gospel. We preach the same message and announce the saving nativity. The nativity does not set forth what we do but what we receive — surely a Savior, who is called ours.[103]

Donum has stepped into *sacramentum*'s place with *exemplum*. *Sacramentum*'s role of deep radiant cancer therapy is supplanted by the *verbum*'s bestowal through its lowly and external means in a way that is unmistakably *donum*. *Donum* and *verbum* take over from *sacramentum*, and in return *sacramentum* is furnished with the Gospel.

In the *First Disputation Against the Antinomians* in 1537 our pair are surrounded by such distinction between Law and Gospel that they cannot possibly carry their former burdens.[104] The same is true in the *Second Disputation*.[105] *Donum* has pride of place, and coupled with it *sacramentum* serves to underline the completeness of Christ's redemption.

It is enough to have Christ as gift, and we have besides His example to follow. . . .[106] To set Christ forth as an example is nothing other than to show how we are to live in obedience toward God, parents, and superiors and follow every good work and virtue as they are recited by Paul and Peter at the end of almost every epistle.[107]

There is nothing here of the *sacramentum* working our inward death or of our suffering the punishments for our sins in the likeness of

191

Christ. A little further on *donum* is equated with *redemptor.* Then *sacramentum* is linked with *mysterium.*[108]

> Christ is *sacramentum* for me because He redeemed me from sin, death, and the devil. My righteousness could not do this, neither could it be grasped by works but altogether by faith. This is what Christ says to me and all believers: "Do not fear the wrath of the Father or death. I have made satisfaction for you. You are saved already and are now set with me in heavenly places. Neither do you lack anything, unless it be what is not yet revealed. Now it only remains that, as this *sacramentum* signifies, it be mine alone, not John the Baptist's, not Peter's, not Paul's, not the Virgin Mary's, nor any saint's." [109]

In their day *sacramentum et exemplum* meant that the saints shared with Christ the role of showing the paradigm through which God puts His people in order to save them. Now the saints are excluded from the ground of salvation, which is only Christ. *Sacramentum* is now called upon to serve this fact, and there is nothing that by nature *sacramentum* would more willingly do.

When *sacramentum* is altogether of Christ's redeeming deed and bestowal, Augustine's one-matching-two is cavalierly reversed.[110] Christ's passion now gives the two: *sacramentum redemptionis* and *exemplum.* This matches the one in us of following the example. There is none of us in the *sacramentum.* We are not up to that. "In Christ, not in me." To the extent that *sacramentum et exemplum* put in an appearance here, they are like pterodactyls flying backwards.

Luther could never leave well enough alone. However, when he trots out *sacramentum et exemplum* for disputation, pedagogically this may be excused. And in his Table Talk we cannot insist that he mind his P's and Q's. Our pair occasionally appear there, but then they are like ghosts that must dance to a new tune. The catching tune lures one on to sing it, but this essay must fade away with its subject, and so it takes leave with the plea that the career of *sacramentum et exemplum* may throw some little light on the delineation of Luther's progress. They are part of that progress, but when yoked together, neither can be itself. Finally Christ outshines them. Then they derive their light from that great Light, the Christ who died and rose again to give us through the lowly sacramental signs the complete forgiveness and salvation that liberates us from the Law, sin, devil, and death.

NOTES

1. Erwin Iserloh, "Sacramentum et Exemplum, ein augustinisches Thema lutherischer Theologie," *Reformata Reformanda, Festgabe für Hubert Jedin,* eds. Erwin Iserloh and Konrad Repgen (Münster: Aschendorff, 1965), I, 247—64. Also his paper on "Luther und die Mystik" at the Third International Congress on Luther Research at Järvenpää, Finland, August 1966. The present study reproduces substantially a part of a thesis presented at the University of Cambridge in 1961.

2. Otto Scheel, "Die Entwicklung Luthers bis zum Abschluss der Vorlesung über den Römerbrief," *Schriften des Vereins für Reformationsgeschichte,* XXVII (1910), 145. Scheel also points (pp. 133 ff.) to some nominalizing of Augustine by the Sententiarius.

3. The first paragraph of Iserloh's published essay (p. 247) sums up Luther's progress beautifully. There are few who excel such separated brethren of the Roman obedience as interpreters of early Luther.

4. See Bernhard Lohse, "Die Bedeutung Augustins für den jungen Luther," *Kerygma und Dogma,* XI (1965), 116—35; Kurt Aland, "Der Weg zur Reformation," *Theologische Existenz Heute,* CXXIII (1965), 82 f.; *La Trinité,* eds. M. Mellet and Th. Camelot, *Oevres de Saint Augustin,* XV (Desclee de Brouwer, 1955), 582, n. 29; C. Couturier, "Sacramentum et mysterium dans l'oevre de saint Augustin," *Etudes Augustiniennes,* Coll. "Théologie," XXVIII (1953), 163—274: "Peut-on douter qui'il ne s'agisse ici du bapteme, avec son double effet de guérison immediate de l'âme et de promesse de résurrection pour le corps? Mais l' exégèse du nombre 6 entraine plus loin notre Docteur; il y discerne le rapport de 1 à 2; rapport qu'il retrouve dans le temps passé par le Christ au tombeau, image, comme nous l'avons expliqué, de l'effect de sa mort sur nous."

5. WA IX, 17, 12; see 23, 32; 39, 21.

6. WA IX, 18, 13.

7. WA IX, 22, 3. See Bernhard Lohse, *Mönchtum und Reformation* (Göttingen: Vandenhoeck & Ruprecht, 1963), p. 73.

8. IX, 23, 7.

9. WA IX, 20, 27; 16, 13; 43, 41; 47, 25.

10. IX, 21, 37.

11. WA IX, 18, 15. See Gordon Rupp, *The Righteousness of God* (London: Hodder & Stoughton, 1953), pp. 150 ff., 227.

12. WA IX, 74, 18—76, 4. See Werner Jetter, *Die Taufe beim jungen Luther* (Tübingen: Mohr, 1954), p. 166; Albrecht Peters, *Glaube und Werk* (Berlin & Hamburg: Lutherisches Verlagshaus, 1962), p. 39; Lohse, pp. 215 ff.

13. WA IX, 18—19: "Interioris enim hominis nostri sacramento": Sacramentum "vetus homo noster simul crucifixus": Crucifixio Christi

$$\text{Est} \begin{cases} \text{Exemplum} \\ \text{sacramentum} \end{cases} \text{quia} \begin{cases} \text{significat sic crucem poenitentiae} \\ \text{hortatur pro veritate corpus morti} \end{cases}$$
$$\begin{cases} \text{in qua moritur anima peccato} \\ \text{offere vel cruci.} \end{cases}$$

Prenter finds this thoroughly Augustinian. As an index of Luther's advance, his criterion of *vetus homo* is immediately more attractive than his *pro nobis,* which is already represented here, IX, 17, 13: *nobis data.* Regin Prenter, "Der barmherzige Richter," *Acta Jutlandica,* XXXIII, 2 (1961), 117, n. 346.

14. See his next unclear and unsymmetrical comment.

15. More enterprising expositions of the usage of the terms here are to be found in Otto Ritschl, *Dogmengeschichte des Protestantismus* (Leipzig: Hinrichs, 1912), II, 1, 43. "Bereits 1509 hat er den Grundgedanken seiner *theologia crucis* unter Verwertung eines von Augustin entlehnten Begriffspaares in voller Deutlichkeit ausgesprochen"; Jetter, pp. 136—44; Gerhard Ebeling, *Evangelische Evangelienauslegung* (Darmstadt: Wissenschaftliche Buchgesellschaft, 1962), pp. 237 f., 424 ff. Reinhard Schwarz, *Fides, Spes und Caritas beim jungen Luther* (Berlin: De Gruyter, 1962), p. 70, n. 161; Katharine Bornkamm, *Luthers Auslegungen des Galaterbriefes von 1519 und 1531* (Berlin: De Gruyter, 1963), pp. 81 ff.; Hans Thimme, *Christi Bedeutung für Luthers Glauben* (Gütersloh: Bertelsmann, 1933), pp. 51 f.; Adolf Hamel, *Der junge Luther und Augustin* (Gütersloh: Rufer, 1935), p. 23: "Doch läszt die äuszerste Knappheit der Randbemerkung diese Deutung als nicht mehr als eine Vermutung erscheinen." See Ernst Bizer, "Die Entdeckung des Sakraments durch Luther," *Evangelische Theologie*, XVII (1957), 65 f.

16. Albert Brandenburg, *Gericht und Evangelium* (Paderborn: Bonifacius, 1960), p. 10: ". . . dasz seine Worte als organische Worte gefaszt werden müssen, dasz man sie also nicht ungebührlich logisch preszt. . . . Man musz beim einzelnen Wort Luthers eine gewisse 'logische' Unschärfe präsumieren und musz aus der Fülle von Aussagen das, was er eigentlich will, erhärten." See Heinrich Bornkamm, "Äuszerer und innerer Mensch bei Luther und den Spiritualisten," *Imago Dei, Festschrift für Gustav Krüger*, ed. H. Bornkamm (Giessen: Töpelmann, 1932), p. 85.

17. WA III, 418, 20.

18. WA III, 392, 35.

19. WA IV, 243, 14. For Luther's *et* Jetter, p. 206, n. O, has *oder* and justifies Iserloh's stricture, p. 251, n. 14. Iserloh is certainly right in pointing to the proximity of the Mass to the matter of *sacramentum et exemplum*. The truly amazing thing therefore is that Luther so seldom mentions it, in the lectures on Romans scarcely at all. When he does mention it, it is put in harmony with his understanding of Christ as suffering paradigm (see n. 20 below). Although what he had learned of the Mass did not afford him much help forward, he was so reverential toward it that he simply let it stand and used what he could. Only when Christ is complete gift for him does his understanding of the Mass blossom. The buds break in his lectures on Hebrews. Thereafter *sacramentum* can hardly contain its vitality. It is then bursting with the Gospel come clean of the Law, which cannot always be said of the *signum efficax* urged by Iserloh, see WA LVII [3], 170, 4. James Atkinson, *Luther: Early Theological Works*, LCC XVI, 106; see also end of n. 58 below. WA IV, 236, 21: *"Escam" sacramentalem et spiritualem*. In his lectures on Romans we find *corporaliter* and *sacramentaliter*. LVI, 58, 19.

20. WA IV, 243, 7: " 'Memoriam fecit mirabilium suorum.' Ista sunt mirabilia: non tantum miracula que fecit, sed multo magis, quod mortem morte occidit et penas pena, passiones passione, ignominias ignominia, ita quod mors in Christo est ita preciosa in conspectu domini, ut sit eterna vita, pena sit gaudium, passio sit voluptas, ignominia sit gloria; et econtra vita sit mors, gaudium sit pena, voluptas passio, gloria ignominia, sed secundum differentem conspectum, dei scilicet et hominum. Sic enim 'mirificavit dominus sanctum suum.' Ista autem mirabilia radicaliter et causaliter in Christi passione sunt facta, ad cuius exemplum omnes formari necesse est. Ergo Sacramentum Eucharistie est passionis, id est mirabilium eius memoria. In quo reficiuntur et comedunt timentes eum. Veruntamen ista esca et memoria est duplex, scilicet sacramentalis et spiritualis." See WA III, 52, 9; 62, 36; 407, 19; 410,

36: "meditatione et excercitio crucis et passionis Christi"; WA IV, 8, 23; 87, 19; 271, 9: "Si igitur 'Mors sanctorum est preciosa &c.', ergo et quelibet poena pro Christo suscepta. Et hoc per benedictionem Christi habemus. Omnes autem accipere debent calicem domini, licet alii tantum intentionaliter, id est in memoria. Alii spiritualiter, id est crucifigendo carnem et concupiscentias eius, quod est [sacramentaliter] velut per sacramentum significatum per passionem Christi secundum Apostolum. Alii exemplariter, ut martyres, qui similia passi sunt cum Christo." Jetter suggests that Luther's crossing out of *sacramentaliter* may indicate that he had no sure grip of the terminology, p. 206, n. O. Compare how Luther uses Ps. 111:4 for the Sacrament in his lectures on Hebrews, WA LVII [3], 119, 16; LCC XVI, 160.

21. Thimme, p. 21 ff. Erich Seeberg, *Luthers Theologie: Christus Wirklichkeit und Urbild* (Stuttgart: Kohlhammer, 1937), II 72 et passim. See K. Bornkamm, p. 114, n. 289.

22. WA III, 613, 15; 614, 27; 617, 25; IV, 387, 28; III, 212, 34: "Pena eius nostram culpam significat"; IV, 52, 28.

23. WA IV, 363, 14; III, 437, 29; IV, 387, 26; III, 452, 29; III, 618, 5; Lohse, p. 256 f.

24. WA IV, 52, 37; 342, 27. See Hans Iwand, *Rechfertigungslehre und Christusglaube* (Darmstadt: Wissenschaftliche Buchgesellschaft, 1961), p. 24: "In diesem Gedankengang ist die *passio* und das Kreuz Christi nur Zeichen der göttlichen *iustitia*, Motiv zur Busze und Vorbild zur Imitation."

25. WA III, 167, 24; IV, 264, 29; 88, 4. See W. Wagner, "Die Kirche als Corpus Christi mysticum beim jungen Luther," *Zeitschrift für katholische Theologie*, LXI (1937), 42, 54; Holsten Fagerberg, "Die Kirche in Luthers Psalmenvorlesung 1513—1515," *Gedenkschrift für Werner Elert*, ed. F. Hübner (Berlin: Lutherisches Verlagshaus, 1955), pp. 109—18; Ernst Kohlmeyer, "Die Bedeutung der Kirche für Luther," *Zeitschrift für Kirchegeschichte*, XLVII (1928), 466—511; Prenter, pp. 126—27.

26. Günter Bornkamm, "mysterion," *Theologisches Wörterbuch zum Neuen Testament*, ed. G. Kittel (Stuttgart: Kohlhammer, 1941), IV, 826 ff.; A. Kolping, *Sacramentum Tertullianeum* (Regensberg-Münster, 1948), p. 53; Wilhelm Maurer, *Bekenntnis und Sakrament* (Berlin: Töpelmann, 1939), pp. 46 f.; Ernst Kinder, "Zur Sakramentlehre," *Neue Zeitschrift für Systematische Theologie*, III (1961), 147 f.; Karl Prümm, "*Mysterion* von Paulus bis Origines," *Zeitschrift für katholische Theologie*, LXI (1937), 391—425; Eduard Ellwein, *Die göttliche Wirklichkeit des Sakraments* (Neuendettelsau: Freimund, 1951), pp. 6 f., 19 f. In 1 Cor. 2:1, P [46] has *mysterion*, also the original Sinaiticus and Augustine (*MPL*, XXXIII, 874). Its replacement by *martyrion* does not suggest a dissimilarity in the potency of the terms. *Mysterion* certainly has equally good claims to take "faith" to wife, if not better, and as a convert would be more apt to keep her from compromising misalliances. *Mysterion* is more intractable, and one cannot but wonder whether there are not some prejudices working against its earliest attested reading. These might be what was indicated with the term *Verbismus* by Kinder and by the wicked comment overheard during the coffee break at Järvenpää, "For Ebeling everything can be sacramental except perhaps not Baptism and the Lord's Supper." So long as history is ostracized, *mysterion* with its saving facts must share the exile. It would, however, be rash for any tyrant to hope to keep them exiled from the city for very long.

27. WA LVI, 321, 23; Wilhelm Pauck, *Luther: Lectures on Romans*, LCC XV, 178—79.

28. WA LVI, 322, 11; LCC XV, 179.

29. WA LVI, 324, 5; LCC XV, 181. See Ernst Bizer, *Fides ex auditu* (Neukirchen: Erziehungsverein, 1958), p. 25.

30. WA LVI, 324, 9; LCC XV, 181.

31. WA LVI, 324, 15; 58, 1; LCC XV, 181. See Lennart Pinomaa, "Die profectio bei Luther," *Gedenkschrift für Werner Elert*, ed. F. Hübner (Berlin: Lutherisches Verlagshaus, 1955), pp. 119—27; Lohse, p. 258.

32. WA LVI, 392, 7; 79, 8, 19: "eadem, que Christus passus est"; 377, 4; LCC XV, 263, 242; WA LVII ³, 129, 8: "eodem modo"; LCC XVI, 60.

33. WA LVI, 360, 3; LCC XV, 223. *Donum* here does not reach beyond monergism.

34. WA LVI, 359, 20; 280, 15; 264, 16; 265, 18; LCC XV, 222, 135, 119, 120.

35. WA LVI, 365, 19; LCC XV, 229.

36. WA LVI, 194, 9; 377, 4; LCC XV, 43, 242.

37. WA LVI, 450, 5; LCC XV, 330.

38. WA LVI, 266, 9; LCC XV, 120.

39. See Thimme, pp. 21 f.; Erich Vogelsang, *Luthers Schriftauslegung* (Bonn: Scheur, 1935), p. 20; Ernst Wolf, "Die Christusverkündigung bei Luther," *Peregrinatio* (Munich: Kaiser, 1954), I, 37 ff.

40. WA LVI, 366, 3; LCC XV, 230.

41. See Thimme, p. 25, n. 1; LVII ³, 124, 10; 44, 11, 22: "Exemplar est, secundum quod aliud fit" (Gl. ord.: "ad cuius similitudinem fit").

42. WA IV, 173, 23.

43. WA LVI, 136, 12.

44. WA LVI, 51, 20: "Resurrectio et Vita Christi est non tantum sacramentum, Sed et causa i. e., efficax sacramentum nostre spiritualis resurrectionis et vite, quia facit resurgere et vivere credentes in eam, Ut infra: 'Si credideris in dominum Ihesum et confesses fueris, quod Deus illum suscitavit, salvus eris', quia in morte eius spiritualiter morimur." LVI, 296, 20: "Et resurrectio eius non tantum est sacramentum Iustitie nostre, Sed etiam efficit eam in nobis, si eam credimus, et est causa. De quibus infra latius. Hoc totum Scholastici theologici Vnam dicunt mutationem: expulsionem peccati et infusionem gratie." See n. 66 below; also Iserloh, p. 262.

45. WA LVII ³, 123, 18; LCC XVI, 55 f.; WA LVII ³, 12, 15. See V, 603, 38: "Quae autem absurditas Christo tribuisse conscientiam metuentem ad paulum tempus."

46. WA LVII ³, 13, 9; 124, 4; LCC XVI, 56.

47. WA LVII ³, 178, 1; LCC XVI, 116; Biel, *Sent.* IV, *dist.* 16, *qu.* 2.

48. *Entdeckung*, pp. 66 f.

49. Ibid., pp. 250 f.

50. WA LVII ³, 113, 21; LCC XVI, 145 f.

51. WA LVII ³, 187, 7; LCC XVI, 132.

52. Erich Vogelsang, *Luthers Hebräerbrief-Vorlesung* (Berlin and Leipzig: De Gruyter, 1930), p. 19.

53. Wilhelm Maurer, *Von der Freiheit eines Christenmenschen* (Göttingen: Vandenhoeck & Ruprecht, 1949), p. 130 ff.

54. WA IX, 18, 13.

55. WA LVII ³, 222, 12. LCC XVI, 196 ff.

56. See David Löfgren, *Die Theologie der Schöpfung bei Luther* (Göttingen: Vandenhoeck & Ruprecht, 1960), p. 117. The Augustinian connection between *poena* and *concupiscentia* points to the sphere of *exemplum* and the importance of what happens there. See also Hans Iwand, "Glaubensgerechtigkeit nach Luthers Lehre," *Theologische Existenz Heute*, LXXV (1941), 22.

57. WA LVII³, 223, 16—18, 24 ff.

58. WA LVII³, 114, 18; IX, 18, 20.

59. An illustrative example is a passage from a 1516 sermon on trusting in God. One geiger counter seems to register surprisingly, Jetter, pp. 147—48, while others scarcely flicker.

Christ is set forth as the example and author of hope. He is *sacramentum* because He was bound for us so that we who are bound *(ligati)* might be unbound in eternity. He is *exemplum* so that we might be bound by men and by ourselves with the chains of penitence on the old man. With the *sacramentum* He justifies the interior man and makes him a new man. With the *exemplum* He indicts the exterior man and shows up the old man, WA I, 76, 39. Here we have men old and new, the interior and the exterior in a sort of musical chairs. The critical question is according to what are we to sort things out. The safest criterion should come from a contemporaneous reference, although sermons lag behind lectures in Luther's theological advance. In the pulpit Luther is more conservative than otherwise.

From Schwartz's exposition of another sermon we learn of hope: "Es sei das Werk Gottes, wenn der Mensch in der Hoffnung in die verborgene Zukunft Gottes versetzt wird. Ohne sie können wir ebensowenig wie ohne die fides und die caritas vor Gott angenehm sein und etwas Verdienstvolles tun (p. 353)." This fits our passage and keeps us from interpreting the unbinding beyond the interior man who becomes the new man whose unbinding is in heaven. *Exemplum* continues the binding for the exterior man, for he is still in process of becoming new. By taking binding as the picture of suffering we blunt its punctiliar quality, which is discordant with Luther's process way of thinking of salvation at this time. The accident of this quality in the term may not permit us to bring the theology into conformity with it. Perhaps in the manuscript *solveremur* is abbreviated with an "o" that could be read as an "a."

On the other hand the punctiliar quality fits Baptism (n. 12), and since Augustine's *sacramentum et exemplum* come on the scene at Romans 6, this may well be riding along in Luther's use of the terms. This would then be a parallel to the way in which the potent matter of the Mass for so long a time flows along almost completely below the surface. When it does appear, it reflects Luther's understanding of Christ and of salvation. The reverse happens later. Something similar may be observed with Baptism, although it is earlier productive, and in this production we may count a good deal of the work of *sacramentum et exemplum*.

Unfortunately Jetter does not carry his investigation far enough. He stops before Baptism has really come into its own. Bizer chides him for this, although he himself also stops too soon — before Luther spoils his account of him. Bizer's review of Jetter's book is in *Zeitschrift für Kirchengeschichte*, LXVII (1955—56), 341—44, esp. p. 342.

See also James Atkinson, "Luthers Einschätzung des Johannesevangeliums," *Lutherforschung Heute*, ed. V. Vajta (Berlin: Lutherisches Verlagshaus, 1958), p. 50.

60. WA I, 331, 2. The scene opens with the cry *Ecce homo*.

61. WA I, 339, 21 & 7. Cf. Jetter p. 154. Rupp, p. 227.

62. WA I, 339, 23. See n. 32.

63. WA I, 337, 16—19; 337, 37—338, 1; 338, 9—11.

64. WA I, 338, 37

65. WA I, 339, 8.

66. WA I, 339, 17.

67. See n. 63 above; also WA IV, 343, 23; 243, 36.

68. WA I, 309, 18.

69. WA I, 309, 20. Prenter seems guilty of a doubtful antithesis or exclusive alternative when he says (p. 99, n. 271): "Ein 'exklusives' 'pro nobis' würde bedeuten, dass Christus wohl für uns gehandelt hat, aber ohne dass sein Handeln in unseren Lebenszusammenhang einbezogen wird." For Luther *sine nobis* is clearly not in conflict with *in nobis*. Prenter's subtlety in making *coram* mean *in*, though costing more effort, is even less persuasive than Thimme's understanding of *per* as "nach dem Bilde von" (p. 52, n. 1). The trouble lies perhaps in not using enough criteria — but then who will escape whipping? Against Prenter's estimation of LIV, 185—86, must be set Kinder's review of Bizer's *Fides ex auditu*, *Theologische Zeitschrift*, XV (1959), 67. See Peters, p. 28.

70. WA I, 307, 22. See n. 24.

71. WA II, 140, 30.

72. WA II, 141, 8.

73. See Peters, p. 35. "Erst dieses frohe und bewusste Ja zum Dienst in der Welt ergänzt und korrigiert die Stossrichtung der augustinischen Mystik. . . . In diesem inneren Ringen erschliesst sich ihm die Dimension des Wortes Gottes."

74. WA IX, 439, 19; XXVI, 319, 35; LW XXXVII, 209 f.

75. WA IX, 440, 1.

76. WA IX, 440, 33.

77. WA V, 637, 34.

78. WA V, 638, 15. See n. 32 above. See also Horst Beintker, *Die Überwindung der Anfechtung bei Luther* (Berlin: Evangelische Verlagsanstalt, 1954), pp. 85 f.

79. WA V, 639, 5.

80. WA V, 639, 14.

81. WA IX, 445, 3. Melanchthon held back from the equation of *sacramentum* and Christ. The writer is indebted for this point to Werner Neuser, as also for the following references: *Melanchthons Werke in Auswahl*, ed. R. Stupperich (Gütersloh: Bertelmann, 1962—63), 11 1, 141, 5; 143, 29; 144, 18; IV, 57, 14; 166, 14; 167, 16; 173, 23; 207, 1.

82. WA IX, 448, 13; XXIX, 184, 6: "Et sic sacramentum nihil aliud est quam ein ubung seins mittelampts. . . . Nihil est quam donum."

83. WA IX, 447, 23.

84. WA VI, 86, 7; 97, 18; 501, 37; 551, 9 & 19, LW XXXVI, 18, 93 f.

85. Peters, p. 36—37; Schwartz, p. 288, n. 16; Hans Dombois, "Juristische Bemerkungen zur Rechtfertigungslehre," *Neue Zeitschrift für systematische Theologie und Religionsphilosophie*, VIII (1966), 173: ". . . der Schuldige durch Annahme der verdienten Strafe justifiziert werde."

86. WA X/I 10, 20.

87. WA II, 437; WA XL/1, 2. The scholium on Galatians 2:19 in the *Lectures*

on *Galatians* of 1516 has: "Respondetur, quod omnes fideles sunt iusti propter Christum, in quem credunt et cui incipiunt fieri conformes per mortificationem veteris hominis. Ideo quicquid est reliquum nondum mortificati, Deus propter fidem et ceptam conformationem non imputat, WA LVII ², 74, 9. See Aland, pp. 75 f.

88. WA II, 501, 29; LW XXVII, 237—38.
89. WA II, 502, 3; LW XXVII, 238. Schwartz, p. 406; Bizer, *Fides ex auditu*, pp. 134—35.
90. K. Bornkamm, p. 116.
91. WA XL/1, 280, 4.
92. K. Bornkamm, p. 110: "Die unio Christi mit dem Glaubenden wird reicher und rückhaltloser beschrieben." She cannot be faulted for ordering Thimme off the field in 1531 (pp. 111 ff.), although the 1519 incident were better referred to a court of inquiry. As long as *sacramentum et exemplum* are going strong, Thimme may be no more than cautioned.
93. WA XL/1, 280, 25.
94. WA XL/1, 274, 6. Miss Bornkamm's *Tendenz* is showing, p. 110, when she raps Rörer over the knuckles for writing *gesta* and not *geri*. Luther would not argue with either.
95. WA XL/1, 275, 14; see Aland, pp. 57—58.
96. WA XV, 777, 15.
97. WA XV, 778, 1. See the 1516 sermon on the same text, I, 107, 29; Bizer, *Fides ex auditu*, pp. 131—32.
98. WA XV, 778, 28.
99. Ibid., 779, 4.
100. Ibid., 779, 23.
101. Ibid., 780, 4.
102. Ibid., 782, 17.
103. Ibid., 783, 14.
104. WA XXXIX/1, 356, 35.
105. Ibid., 462, 20.
106. Ibid., 463, 11.
107. Ibid., 464, 19.
108. Ibid., 465, 2, 12.
109. Ibid., 465, 12.
110. WA, Tr V, 216, No. 5526: "Iam sic distinguit Augustinus passionem Christi: Dicit esse duplicem, sacramentum et exemplum. Item nostram vocat simplam passionem, quam tantum exempli passio in nos convenit; Christi vero passionem vocat duplam, quia est sacramentum redemptionis et exemplum. Exemplo Christi nos conformes fieri oportet, sed sacramentum redemptionis esse non possumus; do sein wir zu gering dazu." It does seem a bit too much for Ebeling, p. 238, to ask this passage to live happily in the same footnote with the *sacramentum et exemplum* reference from a depressing sermon of 1516. WA I, 77, 1. Iserloh, p. 264, is reduced to the suggestion that the man who took down the dictum was too Protestant to get it straight. WA, Tr V, 327, No. 5711: "Inimici crucis Christi etc. Quia non credunt ipsius passionem esse sufficientem pro peccatis. Passio Christi et exemplum ist zweierla. Livore eius sanati sumus. Da gehoren wir nicht zu. Hoc modo nobis est inimitabilis. Suppleo, quod deest [id est]: Non implemus legem Dei."

8

LUTHER'S DEFENSE OF INFANT BAPTISM

Jaroslav J. Pelikan

THE ARGUMENTATION OF *VON DER WIDDERTAUFFE* 1528

O N 7 MAY 1943 Karl Barth delivered a lecture raising fundamental questions about the traditional practice of infant Baptism.[1] Coming at a time when all the churches were beginning to devote critical attention to the renewal of their doctrine and discipline, Barth's lecture has precipitated a vigorous discussion of the exegetical and the dogmatic, the pastoral and the liturgical issues involved in this practice.[2] For each of these areas of theological thought, infant Baptism raises special questions. Thus the exegetical debate has managed to force consideration of some of the fundamental problems of New Testament hermeneutics, for example, the problem of the typological use of the Old Testament in the interpretation of the New: What force is to be given to the supposed typology of circumcision and Baptism, which seems to be implied in Col. 2:11-12 but is not developed in detail within the New Testament itself?[3] Dogmatically, the very question of the sacramental nature of Baptism has been raised, not only by those theologians who question the idea of "Sacrament" as such,[4] but also by those who have asked whether the New

Testament contains any report concerning Baptism to correspond to the four accounts of the institution of the Lord's Supper, and, if it does not, what this implies for the ecclesiastical definition of a Sacrament.[5]

In the midst of such a widespread reexamination of infant Baptism the historians of the church and of its doctrine have also been obliged to make their contribution. The chronological area where this contribution has been the most significant is the first three centuries, during which both the practice and the theory of infant Baptism came to be regarded as essential components of orthodoxy. The collision between Kurt Aland and Joachim Jeremias is the most highly publicized of the historical controversies over the question.[6] Perhaps even more important is the attack which Geoffrey Lampe's study of the relation between Baptism and confirmation has directed against the theories of Gregory Dix and Lionel Thornton.[7] And I have elsewhere contended for the hypothesis, *pace* both Jeremias and Aland, that there was a practice of infant Baptism before there was an explicit theory of original sin sufficient to account for it, and that the doctrinal theory, set forth with amazing precision by Cyprian and codified by Augustine, was in a position to presuppose the practice with such assurance that no opponent, not even Pelagius, could gainsay it.[8] There is good reason for the predominance of patristic scholarship in the historical study of infant Baptism.

Nevertheless, it should not be forgotten that the problematical nature of infant Baptism was pointed out for Western Christian theology not by Karl Barth in 1943 or even by John Smyth in 1609, but by the Anabaptists in the 1520s. It is somewhat ironic that just when the issue of infant Baptism has become a central concern for theologians and churchmen whose denominations have felt able to ignore the problem for centuries, the historical interpretation of the Anabaptists has turned away from infant Baptism to other doctrinal and ethical themes. Scholars who have concentrated on Anabaptism have noted how crucial the doctrine of the church was for many leaders of the movement, who objected to infant Baptism because of their definition of the Christian community as an intentional fellowship of those who had committed themselves to Christian discipleship.[9] Others have located the central issue at stake between the Anabaptists and the mainstream of the Reformation in the relation between church and state and have argued that both Luther and Calvin opposed the left wing of the Reformation as resolutely as they did because it was not only heretical but also seditious.[10] Still others have called attention to the devout and simple faith of individual Anabaptists, as this is documented in the deeply moving accounts of their martyrdom.[11] The result of these new insights has been a picture of Anabaptism that is simultaneously more sympathetic and more accurate than the stereotypes in the textbooks on church history and comparative symbolics.

Yet for those textbooks, as for the Reformers themselves, the matter of infant Baptism was by no means a side issue, as it seems to have become for our picture of the controversy. And here it is essential, for the sake of methodological precision, to distinguish between, for example, Luther's picture of Anabaptism and the Anabaptists' understanding of themselves. The evidence is convincing, perhaps even overwhelming, that in the piety and (to the extent that the term is appropriate) in the theology of the Anabaptists the question of the mode and the subject of Baptism was not the central issue; nor could it be, for no Sacrament or outward ordinance was important enough to claim the central place. That much is an assured result of historical research, with which the historiography of the Reformation has managed to come to terms in an impressive fashion. Yet none of this changes the evidence, no less cogent, that to the "magisterial Reformers"[12] these radicals were indeed *Schwärmer* and *fanatici*, but that they were distinct from others of such ilk because of their insistence that men who had been baptized as infants in the papal, the Lutheran, the Calvinist, or some other unreformed church be baptized again as adults. In this insistence lay both their distinctiveness and their special perversity. Luther may not have understood the central religious intention of the Anabaptists, but he did understand where that intention attacked his theology and his churchmanship most directly: at his retention and defense of the traditional practice of infant Baptism.

Not only did Luther fail to understand the central religious intention of the Anabaptists; he probably knew very little about them at all. Careful study of the sources of his information about Anabaptism makes clear that he may never actually have seen a genuine Anabaptist face to face.[13] Moreover, he persisted in his identification of the Anabaptists with the heavenly prophets, with Münzer, and with Carlstadt even when he had the opportunity to become more precisely informed about the differences.[14] While Melanchthon and especially Menius did gather firsthand data about Anabaptist teaching and practice,[15] Luther seems to have been content with the rumors he got from others and the suspicions he had within himself; and on this basis he formed his judgments. But once more it is methodologically important to keep the question of Luther's knowledge of Anabaptism distinct from the question of his defense of infant Baptism; for the former could have been changed by more accurate reportage, but the latter could not have been changed by anything less drastic than a fundamental theological reorientation. Luther's defense of infant Baptism was not, as Harnack supposed, part of a "doctrine of the sacraments [in which] Luther abandoned his position as a Reformer, and was guided by views that brought confusion into his own system of faith"; nor is it accurate to contend, as Harnack did, that "if the fundamental evangelical and Lutheran principle is valid . . . then infant baptism is in itself no sacrament, but an *ecclesiastical* observance." [16] On the contrary, Luther's defense of infant Baptism, like his defense of the real presence in the Lord's Supper, was inseparable from "the fundamental evangelical and Lutheran principle."

That principle, however, was not simply the one which Harnack identified, "that grace and faith are inseparably interrelated," but the more subtle and complex one, that faith and the Word are inseparably interrelated, even and also in the means of grace, and moreover, that even and also in the means of grace "faith builds and is founded on the Word of God rather than God's Word on faith." [17] This was the fundamental issue in the controversy over infant Baptism, as Luther interpreted it. How Luther interpreted that controversy is, however, more difficult to determine in detail than one might expect, for in spite of many *obiter dicta* on the Anabaptists throughout his writings and lectures he actually devoted only one full-length treatise to the defense of infant Baptism, the essay *Von der Widdertauffe an zween Pfarherrn. Ein brieffe Mart. Luther,* written in December 1527 and January 1528 in response to the request of two otherwise unidentified pastors for arguments against the Anabaptist position.[18] Although the issue was, of course, to recur in later works of Luther, most notably in the Large Catechism of the following year, where he made use of some of the same arguments, the treatise of 1528 deserves to be analyzed in some detail within the context of Luther's theological development.[19]

THE ARGUMENT FROM THE FAITH OF INFANTS

A considerable part of the polemic in *Von der Widdertauffe* was devoted to the charge of the Anabaptists that faith was prerequisite to Baptism and that since children could not believe, they were not to be baptized. Luther claimed to have read that they were citing the words of Mark 16:16, "He who believes and is baptized will be saved," as proof of this charge.[20] But if they wanted to argue from this passage of Scripture that faith was prerequisite to Baptism, they also had to produce proof from Scripture that children were incapable of faith.[21] For his part, Luther found proof in Scripture, both in the Old Testament and in the New, "that children may and can believe, even though they have neither speech nor reason."[22] He was careful to point out that this proof did not yet establish that children did in fact have faith, only that they might and could. This presentation of Biblical evidence is an interesting case study of "commentary and controversy" in Luther's use of Scripture.[23] It is also a significant index to his affinities with the exegetical, dogmatic, and legal tradition of the Middle Ages. For the appropriate arguments from St. Augustine in defense of the thesis that children could believe had been assembled under Distinction 4 of the *De consecratione* in Gratian's codification of the canon law.[24] Artur Landgraf has shown how, on the basis of these arguments, the Biblical evidence had been exploited with increasing care and profundity by early scholasticism and had been carried as far as it could be, until the speculative doctrine of the infusion of faith provided exegetes with a method for gathering additional proof texts.[25] Despite his hostility both to canon law and to speculation, Luther seems in fact to have been drawing on this material in *Von der Widdertauffe*.

The first passage Luther cited was "Psalm 72,"[26] although his words suggest that he was, as so often, conflating two quite discrete passages. He seems to have been thinking of Ps. 73:13, 15, but he was actually quoting Ps. 106:38, "They poured out innocent blood." If the blood of the children sacrifed to idols was innocent, the children must have had faith. The second proof was taken from the story of Herod's murder of the children of Bethlehem. They, too, were "innocent," Luther argued.[27] Of course, the text of the Gospel does not say that they were, but they had acquired the title *Innocentes* in the liturgical usage of the church at Rome, being called simply *Infantes* in other orders and calendars.[28] And from this designation, embellished by medieval piety, Luther maintained that they were "holy and were saved" even though they had neither speech nor reason. The third passage was Matt. 19:14, "Let the children come to Me . . . for to such belongs the kingdom of heaven." Tertullian's polemic against the appropriateness of these words to infant Baptism suggests that they were already being applied that way.[29] Luther, following the established usage of pre-Reformation Wittenberg, had incorporated these words, in the version found in Mark 10, in the *Taufbüchlein* of 1523 and of 1526.[30] The fourth passage was the account of the Visitation, in which John the Baptist "in the womb leaped for joy" (Luke 1:44). The observance of the Visitation had finally received conciliar sanction a century before, and Luther's interpretation of the words of the Gospel reflected the traditional observance.[31]

From the researches of Karl Brinkel it is evident that the relation between the faith of infants and the Baptism of infants was a matter of continuing concern to Luther both before and after *Von der Widdertauffe*.[32] Part of Brinkel's purpose is to argue, in opposition to Paul Althaus, that Luther did not place less emphasis on infant faith during 1528 and 1529 than he had earlier.[33] Certainly, if Althaus meant that Luther was repudiating his earlier affirmations that children received the gift of faith through Baptism, Luther's constant reference to his earlier statements on the matter proves that no such repudiation was involved.[34] On the other hand, it is evident even from the argumentation in *Von der Widdertauffe* that Luther, in contradistinction to at least some parts of the dogmatic tradition, was not willing to let the entire defense of infant Baptism depend so utterly on the theory of infant faith that the two teachings would stand or fall together. Martin Luther may well have been, as various latter-day interpreters have claimed, the one theologian in the history of the church who, more than any other, elevated faith to the status of a normative principle in Christian theology; he himself seems sometimes to have seen his historic role this way.[35] But when it came to the relation between faith and the means of grace, or at any rate to the relation between faith and infant Baptism, he did not assign the decisive importance to faith but gave it to the structured mediation of divine grace in Baptism. And so, immediately after his recitation of the traditional exegetical proofs for infant faith, he declared: "Anyone who wants to use the faith of the person to be baptized as the basis for Baptism may never again baptize anyone; for even if you were to baptize the same man a hundred times in one day, you would not know a single one of those times whether he [really] believes." [36] Theologian of faith though he quite self-consciously was, Luther would not make infant faith the decisive issue in his defense of infant Baptism — even though, on the basis of Brinkel's research, it is clear that Luther had no qualms about ascribing faith to infants and that he would even go so far as to say, as he did in *Von der Widdertauffe*, that infant Baptism was surer than adult Baptism, for the very reason that made it so problematical to the Anabaptists — the absence of personal, subjective assent.[37]

If, then, the defense of infant Baptism could not be based solely on the assertion that infants could have faith, whether through the infusion of grace in Baptism itself or through the faith of their parents or through the faith of Mother Church, it became necessary to provide other grounds for the practice that would, if not indeed supplant, at least supplement the historic argument from the faith of infants. And though Luther was the theologian of faith, he was also, perhaps even more, the theologian of the means of grace, regardless of the way the modern histories of theology, for their own reasons, have emphasized the former at the expense of the latter. And as a theologian of the means of grace Luther made it a point to dissociate himself from those "subjective" theories of means of grace which tied the efficacy of the sacraments to the person of the priest or even to that of the recipient. The Donatists had begun "to base Baptism on the holiness of men, though Christ had based it on His Word and commandment."[38] But no one could ever be sure of his Baptism if he had to look into the heart of the one who baptized him; nor, for that matter, could his own state of heart be made decisive. For just as he was contending in this very year for the *manducatio indignorum* against all attempts to make the real presence in the Lord's Supper conditional on faith,[39] so he also maintained that the Baptism of one who did not believe was "a correct Baptism in itself, regardless of whether or not it was received rightly."[40] Neither the faith of the priest nor that of the candidate could affect the objective validity of the Sacrament of Baptism.

THE ARGUMENT FROM THE NATURAL ORDER

Another parallel between the controversy over infant Baptism and the controversy over the Lord's Supper was the attention devoted in both of them to the proper place of reason and of the natural order in theological discourse. But while the conflict with Zwingli was the occasion for some of Luther's most violent attacks on "the old witch, Lady Reason, the grandmother of alloeosis,"[41] he found himself contending in the conflict over infant Baptism against those who spurned any theological argument from the natural order. They repudiated infant Baptism, he said, because it made certainty about Baptism dependent on the witness of men rather than on the testimony of God. Anyone baptized in infancy had to trust the word of men.[42] Luther's opponents could throw his own words back at him and ask: "Have you not yourself taught that we should obey God and not man?" [43] Thus he was compelled to clarify what he had meant by the distinction between obeying God and obeying man and in the process to state what place the "natural" testimony of other men occupied in his sacramental theology.

It is significant that Luther, accurately or inaccurately, associated this denial of the natural order by the Anabaptists with their "intra-mundane asceticism" [44] about the structures of the world. Therefore he took the controversy with them as an occasion to affirm the integrity of those structures. In contrast to the Anabaptists' willingness to disrupt marriage, the state, and public order over the issue of rebaptism, Luther's Reformation "not only allows but commands that every estate should remain and be held in honor and that faith should exercise itself peaceably in love," [45] that is, that faith should not abolish or disrupt, but uphold and sustain, the structures and "estates" of the natural order. From the thesis of Holl and others, that Luther attacked the *Schwärmer* at least partly because they were seditious in the secular order and not only because they were heretics and schismatics in the spiritual order, it is understandable that part of his defense of infant Baptism should also be a defense of the natural order and that therefore the argument from reason should assume unwonted importance in his theology at this point.[46] As Brian Gerrish has shown, the conventional assessment of Luther's attitude toward reason has been based on his fulminations against the intrusion of the organic use of reason into the area of authority that belonged to the Word of God; but Luther continually emphasized, as his interpreters have sometimes forgotten, that reason had a constructive and instrumental function also in the work of the theologian as a servant of the Word of God.[47] Reason could not tell him what to think, but it could and did tell him how to think.

At least this much is implied in the reply of *Von der Widdertauffe* to the charge that infant Baptism was a case of believing man rather than God. For Luther did not base this reply only on an extensive analysis of the Biblical evidence but simultaneously on a series of "natural" analogies in which believing man was in fact a way (or *the* way) of believing God. Without developing a detailed methodological theory he seems to have meant that the authority of the Gospel was mediated through the authority of other men, so that the *reductio ad absurdum* of what he took to be the Anabaptist position would be the rejection of any Christian teaching, even of the person and work of Christ and the proclamation of the apostles, simply because it had been transmitted through other men.[48] At this point the transmission of the knowledge given by "revelation" was of a piece with the transmission of knowledge given by "reason." The Biblical principle that the testimony of two or three witnesses was evidence trustworthy enough to sustain a fact applied equally to revelation and to reason.[49] One's birth was a work of God, but when one believed the evidence of the witnesses who testified to it, one was believing God through them. The deeds of God were in the public realm and were to be verified in the public realm:

> God's works go on so publicly that neither devil nor man can controvert them, but every man can so know and declare them as he declares that you are alive. . . . In sum, when any one declares and bears witness to something which is the work of God and which is not the figment of man's imagination, and this can be controverted neither by the devil nor by man, then you are believing God and not man, for it is the work of God which He so publicly discloses that even the devil cannot deny it.[50]

Therefore the Biblical command to honor father and mother was reinforced by the evidence of human witnesses that this man and woman were one's parents. The Biblical imperative to obey the government took shape through the witness of other men that one was a citizen of this realm and was subject to its ruler.[51] Both parental authority and governmental authority were works of God, not merely works of men. But they "went on so publicly" that the experience of other men and the conclusions of reason about that experience could quite legitimately be cited in support of them. Reason agreed with revelation that a man "[has] to have a mother and father and [is] not sprung from a rock," as Luther said, quoting Homer and Genesis in the same sentence.[52] And it was perfectly legitimate, he maintained in opposition to the Donatism of some Anabaptists, when "St. Paul recognized the heathen poets Aratus and Epimenides and honored their sayings as a word of God."[53] Therefore it was also legitimate to cite the testimony of others about one's Baptism. It was an institution commanded by God, as were parenthood and the government. Others testified that Baptism has been administered, and by admitting one to the Eucharist they showed that they were persuaded both of the fact and of the validity of that Baptism. A refusal to accept this testimony was tantamount to a refusal to believe the authority of God.[54]

It would, of course, be a mistake to treat this argument from the natural order in isolation. Its context was still the theological and exegetical case which Luther was making in defense of infant Baptism. On the other hand it would also be a mistake to suppose that this

208

argument was no more than a response to the disparagement of the natural order which Luther thought he sensed in the Anabaptist position. The analogies to Baptism with which Luther was working in this argument were significantly all taken from the doctrine of creation — birth, parenthood, government. The positive evaluation of reason and of the natural order in *Von der Widdertauffe* was part of Luther's appreciation of the natural good in the creation, a good which sin could not defile and which redemption did not debase. As the Small Catechism of the following year was to say, Baptism was not merely plain water:[55] it was more than natural. But that did not make it less than natural, and therefore the argument from the natural order and from reason had a legitimate though limited place in the theological defense of infant Baptism.

THE ARGUMENT FROM CONTINUITY

The defense of infant Baptism involved Luther not only in a rather surprising assertion of the legitimate place of reason in theological discourse but also in a defense of tradition against the iconoclasm of the left-wing reformers. During these years he was defending tradition also against his opponents in the eucharistic controversies, who accused him of being "a good papist who believes that there is no wine in the Supper." To this accusation he replied: "Sooner than have mere wine with the fanatics, I would agree with the pope that there is only blood."[56] He claimed to discern a parallel between the Anabaptist position on infant Baptism and the position of Zwingli and Carlstadt on the Real Presence. The former claimed by their rebaptism "to spite the pope and to be free of any taint of the Antichrist," while the latter "want to believe only in bread and wine, in opposition to the pope, thinking thereby really to overthrow the papacy."[57] In both instances a hostility to tradition had produced an indifference to the need for continuity and a definition of the Reformation in negative terms. Or, in the words which Luther put into his opponents' mouths: "Whatever comes from the pope is wrong. If something goes on in the papacy in a particular way, we must do it some other way."[58]

Such statements seemed to Luther to be drawing not only a false definition of the Reformation but also a false conclusion from its identification of the pope as Antichrist. The pope did indeed demonstrate the aptness of that identification by persecuting, cursing, excommunicating, hounding, burning, and executing unfortunate Christians.[59] Luther was proud that he had come to recognize the papacy as the fulfillment within history of the prophecies of 2 Thess. 2:3-12.[60] But it was essential to this recognition that the "man of lawlessness" and "son of perdition" described in those prophecies was to be one who "takes his seat in the temple of God." Far from meaning that "whatever comes from the pope is wrong," therefore, the identification of the pope as Antichrist meant that "the Christendom that now is under the papacy . . . has the true Spirit, Gospel, faith, Baptism, Sacrament, keys, the office of the ministry, prayer, Holy Scripture, and everything that belongs to Christendon." [61] From this it even followed that "we are all still under the papacy," but still more that a continuity with the Christendom of the papacy was something to be cultivated rather than spurned. For "everything that is Christian and good is to be found [under the papacy] and has come to us from this source." This included all the gifts and marks of the true church just enumerated, including Baptism. If the papacy, as the seat of Antichrist, "is not a haunt of heretics, but true Christendom," then the conclusion was unavoidable that the papacy "must truly have a Baptism which is right beyond any doubt." [62] But that Baptism was infant Baptism, now vindicated by the very identification which had been used to attack it. Thus the pathos about which Friedrich Heiler has written in his discussion of the idea of the pope as Antichrist attended Luther's polemic as well.[63] As Luther put it half seriously and half mockingly:

> In fact both remain, the Antichrist sits in the temple of God through the action of the devil, while the temple still is and remains the temple of God through the power of Christ. If the pope will suffer and accept this dissembling of mine, then I am and will be, to be sure, an obedient son and devoted papist, with a truly joyful heart, and take back everything that I have done to harm him.[64]

But in any event the identification of the pope as Antichrist was an argument for continuity rather than discontinuity.

Luther found any discontinuity simply inconceivable which would assert that there had been no Baptism for the thousand years or more when only infant Baptism had been practiced.[65] The article of the creed about the church meant that the church would always continue. Yet if its Baptism was invalid, the church had been without Baptism and was therefore itself invalid. But since infant Baptism had been accepted and practiced universally throughout the church, this "gives rise to no probability that it is wrong, but rather to a strong indication that it is right." [66] By contrast, the sacrificial view of the Mass had not been accepted and practiced universally, for among the laymen the Mass still remained a sacrament; therefore the argument from continuity did not favor the doctrine that the Mass was a sacrifice. Similarly, the argument did not hold in the case of the papacy itself; "for not only has the Eastern church borne testimony against the papacy and opposed it, but so have also many subjects of the pope himself." [67] Therefore the authority of the papacy could not claim the sort of unbroken and unopposed continuity that could be cited in support of infant Baptism. So deeply impressed was Luther with that continuity that he was willing to formulate a general criterion: "No heresy endures to the end, but always . . . soon comes to light and is revealed as disgraceful." [68] The Bible, the Our Father, and the Apostles' Creed [69] all met this criterion, having continued from antiquity to the present. The papacy, however, had not; for it "is an innovation and has never been accepted by all Christians." The continuity of the church had been preserved in spite of the papacy, but because of infant Baptism. Thus it was evidence for the correctness of infant Baptism.

Further support from the continuity of the church was provided by the empirical evidence in the lives of the saints.[70] There had been genuine saints whose only Baptism was infant Baptism. To them God had given His great and holy gifts, thus confirming the gift conferred on them in their Baptism. If their very Baptism had been invalid and an act of disobedience to the divine command, He would not have commended it by these additional blessings. Just as the apostles had established from the gift of the Holy Spirit to the Gentiles that observance of the Mosaic law was not required, so the gift of the Holy Spirit to those baptized in infancy proved that rebaptism was not required. The only specific saint whom Luther named here was John Hus. In the Large Catechism of 1529 he repeated this argument, but expanded the catalogue of the saints:

> Since God has confirmed Baptism through the gift of His Holy Spirit, as we have perceived in some of the Fathers, such as St. Bernard, Gerson, John Hus, and others [who were baptized in infancy], and since the holy Christian church will abide until the end of the world, our adversaries must acknowledge that infant Baptism is pleasing to God.[71]

Thus the list of "fathers" came to include not only Bernard of Clairvaux, but John Hus and John Gerson, who had been on opposite sides at the Council of Constance. All of them were church fathers, and all of them had been baptized in infancy. They gave proof for the continuity of usage and for its validity.

Yet if the pretensions of the papacy — against which Bernard of Clairvaux, John Hus, and John Gerson had all protested, albeit in

211

quite different ways — were to be rejected, in spite of claims for papal continuity, on the grounds that the papacy was an innovation in the history of the church, the argument from continuity was incomplete without an argument from antiquity. "Our Baptism has been of this sort from the beginning of Christianity, and the custom has been to baptize children," Luther asserted.[72] And the antiquity of the usage argued for its retention. Enunciating a principle he had formulated in his defense of Catholic liturgical practice, he declared: "We should not discard or alter what cannot be discarded or altered on clear Scriptural authority."[73] But the first half of this sentence read: "Baptism did not originate with us, but with the apostles." And in the context "Baptism" would seem to mean "infant Baptism." Elsewhere in *Von der Widdertauffe* Luther did make the claim that infant Baptism was not only an ancient usage but an apostolic one. "Infant baptism," he stated, "derives from the apostles and has been practiced since the days of the apostles."[74] At that point he did not supply any evidence in support of the claim and was even compelled to admit that "from Scripture we cannot clearly conclude that you could establish infant Baptism as a practice among the first Christians after the apostles"; but earlier in the treatise he had done so — from St. Augustine! "For St. John in 1 John 2:14 writes to the little children, that they know the Father. And, as St. Augustine writes, infant Baptism has come from the apostles."[75] Once more it would appear important not to isolate such a statement from the total context of the argument from continuity, for to do so would be to make it an argument in a circle. But in that context the claim to antiquity formed part of an affirmation of tradition which shifted the burden of proof to the iconoclast. Even in the absence of explicit Scriptural warrant for the practice, "you can well conclude that in our day no one may reject or neglect the practice of infant Baptism which has so long a tradition, since God actually not only has permitted it, but from the beginning so ordered, that it has not yet disappeared."[76]

THE ARGUMENT FROM THE COVENANT

The argument from continuity was intended to shift the field of battle from the subjective to the objective, so that one did not look at the vagaries of his own faith but at the ordinances of God as given in the church and in its tradition. Yet Luther would not have been the Reformer he was if he had merely referred private faith to the church and its tradition. For he referred these, in turn, to the objec-

212

tivity of the commands and promises of God. As he put it in an axiom in the *Galatians* of 1535,

> This is the reason why our theology is certain: it snatches us away from ourselves and places us outside ourselves, so that we do not depend on our own strength, conscience, experience, person, or works, but depend on that which is outside ourselves, that is, on the promise and truth of God, which cannot deceive.[77]

Also in the defense of infant Baptism this "promise and truth of God, which cannot deceive," proved to be the final ground of the argument.

It was, in fact, "the very strongest and surest ground," [78] for it rooted Baptism not in the fluctuations of human faith and experience but in the foundation of the divine covenant. The divine covenant was universal in its validity, extending not only to adults and not only to children but to "all nations," as the Great Commission in Matt. 28: 19-20 said.[79] There "Christ commanded us to teach and baptize all heathen, without exception." The faith of any individual, even of the strongest Christian, was continually in doubt, and so was his private experience. The testimony of other Christians to his Baptism was therefore more certain than his own experience of it would have been. For the devil could easily have deluded him into supposing that it had been a dream or an apparition, but he could not so easily delude the entire company of Christian witnesses.[80] Similarly, the covenant of God was a stronger and a surer foundation for Baptism than the faith of the individual, for faith, too, was a sometime thing. How could one be sure, even in case of an adult, that his faith was authentic and sincere? Luther knew from the bitter experiences of his years of trial that one could not be sure that his repentance was authentic and sincere. He had sought one confession after another, one father confessor after another, relying on his repentance as he now found the Anabaptists relying on their faith — and with the same result, the loss of the very assurance which the Sacrament was intended to provide.[81] The source of that assurance could not be the subjective state of the individual. In fact, "it happens, indeed it is so in this matter of faith, that often he who claims to believe does not at all believe; and on the other hand, he who does not think he believes, but is in despair, has the greatest faith." [82]

But when one turned from the experience and faith of man to the command and promise of God, this fluctuation ceased. This was, for Luther, the significance of the parallel between Baptism and circumcision.[83] In both cases God had instituted a sign of His covenant by

213

which man could know that God was graciously disposed toward him. He had given circumcision to Abraham and to his descendants as a sign that His covenant with them would endure.[84] Concerning the faith of an individual, God had never said anything to anyone, so that one could not rely on faith. But the covenant was based on God's own command, which could not deceive. To this Abraham and his descendants were to look, not to their subjective state. The command was accompanied by the promise that God would be their God. Now if Abraham and his descendants in the people of Israel had the right to look to the command and promise of God as the ground of their covenant with Him, it followed *a fortiori* that in the New Testament the command and promise of God were an even surer ground. "This new covenant and sign must be much more effectual and make those a people of God who receive it."[85] But in the New Testament the subject of the command and promise of God was not the nation of Israel, but "all nations." Thus the command and the promise were universal, excluding no nation and no individual from the divine covenant. How then could any individual or any nation be excluded from the sign of the covenant, which was Baptism? Only those who excluded themselves by refusing to accept the sign and the covenant could be denied Baptism. Otherwise, "if we follow His command and baptize everyone, we leave it to Him to be concerned about the faith of those baptized."[86] The Gospel was the same for all nations and for all individuals, including children. Baptism, too, was the same for all, in accordance with the covenant of God, signed in His command to baptize and sealed in His promise.

The command and promise of God stood because they were the Word of God; the covenant stood because it was the work of God. And "when one sees a work of God, one must yield to it and believe it just as one does when one hears His Word."[87] That reciprocity between the Word of God and the work of God aptly summarizes much of the argumentation of *Von der Widdertauffe*, based as it was on a correlation between the authority of Scripture and the other testimonies from the natural order and from tradition. It was not inconsistent for Luther, the champion of *sola Scriptura*, to uphold such a correlation in a dispute with those who claimed to be applying the *sola Scriptura* more rigorously than he; for by it he was enabled to formulate his defense of infant Baptism as a conclusion derived directly from the Christian Gospel. Far from being a betrayal of "the fundamental evangelical and Lutheran principle," this defense of in-

214

fant Baptism was one of its most important and inescapable corollaries. Without it we can grasp neither the historical importance of Luther's Reformation nor its ecumenical significance.

NOTES

1. Karl Barth, *Die kirchliche Lehre von der Taufe*, Heft 14 of *Theologische Studien*, 2d ed. (Zurich: Evangelischer Verlag, 1943).

2. See Oscar Cullmann, *Die Tauflehre des Neuen Testaments*, Vol. XII of *Abhandlungen zur Theologie des Alten und Neuen Testaments* (Zurich: Zwingli-Verlag, 1948).

3. In the apt formulation of Arthur Darby Nock, "Baptism came to be regarded as that which replaced circumcision. There is a suggestion of this in Coloss. 2, 11-13, but circumcision was too controversial an issue in Paul's time for free development of the idea," *Early Gentile Christianity and Its Hellenistic Background* (New York: Harper & Row, 1964), p. 128.

4. Markus Barth, *Die Taufe — Ein Sakrament? Ein exegetischer Beitrag zum Gespräch über die kirchliche Taufe* (Zurich: Zwingli-Verlag, 1951).

5. On the problem of what is implied by dominical institution see the discussion of Karl Rahner, *The Church and the Sacraments*, Vol. IX of *Quaestiones Disputatae*, trans. W. J. O'Hare (New York: Herder and Herder, 1963), pp. 41 to 47.

6. Kurt Aland, *Die Säuglingstaufe im Neuen Testament und in der alten Kirche* (Munich: Chr. Kaiser Verlag, 1961); Joachim Jeremias, *Hat die Urkirche die Kindertaufe geübt?* 2d ed. (Göttingen: Vandenhoeck & Ruprecht, 1949).

7. Geoffrey W. Lampe, *The Seal of the Spirit* (London: Longman, Green, 1951).

8. Jaroslav Pelikan, *An Essay on the Development of Christian Doctrine.* Saint Thomas More Lectures for 1965—66, to be published by Yale University Press.

9. Franklin H. Littell, *The Anabaptist View of the Church: A Study in the Origins of Sectarian Protestantism*, 2d ed. (Boston: Starr King Press, 1958).

10. See the recent study of Claus-Peter Clasen, *Die Wiedertäufer im Herzogtum Württemberg und in benachbarten Herrschaften. Ausbreitung, Geisteswelt und Soziologie*, Vol. XXXII of "Veröffentlichungen der Kommission für geschichtliche Landeskunde in Baden-Württemberg," Reihe B (Stuttgart, 1965), esp. pp. 106—12.

11. See Ethelbert Stauffer, "The Anabaptist Theology of Martyrdom," *Mennonite Quarterly Review*, XIX (July 1945), 179—214.

12. Despite objections raised against this term, I find it extremely useful; see George Hunston Williams, *The Radical Reformation* (Philadelphia: The Westminster Press, 1962), p. xxiv, which defines it as roughly synonymous with "classical Protestantism."

13. John S. Oyer, *Lutheran Reformers Against Anabaptists. Luther, Melanchthon and Menius and the Anabaptists of Central Germany* (The Hague: M. Nijhoff, 1964), pp. 114—39; this was a dissertation for which I had the privilege of serving as coadvisor.

14. John S. Oyer, "The Writings of Luther Against the Anabaptists," *Mennonite Quarterly Review*, XXVII (April 1953), 100—10.

15. John S. Oyer, "The Writings of Melanchthon Against the Anabaptists," ibid., XXVI (Oct. 1952), 259—79.

215

16. Adolf von Harnack, *History of Dogma*, trans. Neil Buchanan (New York: Russell and Russell, 1961), VII, 248, 251.

17. *Von der Widdertauffe an zween Pfarherrn. Ein brieff Mart. Luther,* WA XXVI, 172, 20—21; LW XL, 260. Since this essay is essentially a "one-source paper," I shall not refer to *Von der Widdertauffe* by title each time, but shall simply refer to the proper volume, page, and line numbers from the Weimar Edition, adding the corresponding volume and page numbers from the American Edition. Wherever possible I have quoted the translation that appears in the American Edition, but in some instances (see n. 69 below) I have felt obliged to diverge from it.

18. See the introduction, WA XXVI, 137—44; LW XL, 227—28.

19. There is unfortunately no monograph for the later stages of that development to correspond to Werner Jetter's careful study, *Die Taufe beim jungen Luther: Eine Untersuchung über das Werden der reformatorischen Sakraments- und Taufanschauung* (Tübingen: J. C. B. Mohr, 1954).

20. WA XXVI, 154, 1—4; LW XL, 239.

21. WA XXVI, 156, 3—5; LW XL, 241—42.

22. WA XXVI, 156, 8—9; LW XL, 242.

23. See Jaroslav Pelikan, *Luther the Expositor: Introduction to the Reformer's Exegetical Writings* (St. Louis: Concordia Publishing House, 1959), pp. 109 to 134.

24. Aemilius L. Friedberg, *Corpus iuris canonici* (Leipzig: B. Tauchnitz, 1879), I, 1382.

25. Artur Michael Landgraf, *Dogmengeschichte der Frühscholastik*, Part III, *Die Lehre von den Sakramenten* (Regensburg: Gregorius-Verlag, 1954), I, 296 to 331.

26. WA XXVI, 156, 10; LW XL, 242.

27. WA XXVI, 156, 13—15; LW XL, 242.

28. See the summary comments of the liturgical scholar, Frederick C. Holweck, s. v. "Holy Innocents," *The Catholic Encyclopedia* (New York, 1913), VII, 419.

29. *Tertullian's Homily on Baptism,* ed. Ernest Evans (London: S. P. C. K., 1964), xviii, pp. 36—41, and the editor's comments, pp. 101—6.

30. *Das tauff buchlin verdeutscht,* WA XII, 45, 3—8; LW LIII, 98—99.

31. See Reintraud Schimmelpfennig, *Die Geschichte der Marienverehrung im deutschen Protestantismus* (Paderborn, 1952), pp. 30—31, on the Visitation in 16th-century Lutheranism.

32. Karl Brinkel, *Die Lehre Luthers von der fides infantium bei der Kindertaufe,* Vol. VII of *Theologische Arbeiten* (Berlin: Evangelische Verlagsanstalt, 1958).

33. Paul Althaus, "Martin Luther über die Kindertaufe," *Theologische Literatur-Zeitung*, LXXIII (Dec. 1948), 705—14.

34. WA XXVI, 144, 10—145, 3; LW XL, 229.

35. See Wilhelm Pauck, *The Heritage of the Reformation*, 2d ed. (Glencoe, Ill.: Free Press, 1961), pp. 19—28.

36. WA XXVI, 154, 22—25; LW XL, 240.

37. WA XXVI, 157, 37—158, 5; LW XL, 244.

38. WA XXVI, 163, 17—18; LW XL, 250.

39. *Vom Abendmahl Christi, Bekenntnis,* WA XXVI, 491, 13; LW XXXVII, 354.

40. WA XXVI, 159, 31—32; LW XL, 246.

41. *Bekenntnis,* WA XXVI, 321, 19—20; LW XXXVII, 210.

42. WA XXVI, 149, 10—12; LW XL, 234.

43. WA XXVI, 150, 11—12; LW XL, 235.

44. On the difficulty of translating the term *innerweltliche Askese* see the note of Talcott Parsons in his translation of Max Weber, *The Protestant Ethic and the Spirit of Capitalism* (London: George Allen & Unwin, 1930), pp. 193—94.

45. WA XXVI, 163, 6—7; LW XL, 250.

46. Karl Holl, "Luther und die Schwärmer," *Gesammelte Aufsätze zur Kirchengeschichte, Vol. I: Luther,* 7th ed. (Tübingen, 1948), 420—67, especially pp. 450—67.

47. Brian A. Gerrish, *Grace and Reason: A Study in the Theology of Luther* (Oxford: Clarendon Press, 1962), especially pp. 138—52.

48. WA XXVI, 150, 3—10; LW XL, 235.

49. WA XXVI, 150, 39—40; LW XL, 236.

50. WA XXVI, 151, 4—12; LW XL, 236.

51. WA XXVI, 151, 21—152, 14; LW XL, 236—37.

52. WA XXVI, 151, 24; LW XL, 236; quoting *Iliad,* XXII, 126, and Gen. 1:28.

53. WA XXVI, 163, 29—30; LW XL, 251.

54. WA XXVI, 153, 18—30; LW XL, 239.

55. *Der Kleine Katechismus,* WA XXX/I, 309, 23.

56. *Bekenntnis,* WA XXVI, 462, 4—5; LW XXXVII, 317.

57. WA XXVI, 146, 33—147, 2; LW XL, 231.

58. WA XXVI, 148, 23—24; LW XL, 233.

59. WA XXVI, 148, 1—3; LW XL, 232.

60. See Hans Preuss, *Die Vorstellungen vom Antichrist im späteren Mittelalter, bei Luther und in der konfessionellen Polemik* (Leipzig, 1906).

61. WA XXVI, 147, 35—39; LW XL, 232.

62. WA XXVI, 169, 3—7; LW XL, 257.

63. Friedrich Heiler, *Der Katholizismus: Seine Idee und seine Erscheinung* (Munich: E. Reinhardt, 1923), pp. 327—33.

64. WA XXVI, 148, 15—21; LW XL, 233.

65. WA XXVI, 168, 27—30; LW XL, 256—57.

66. WA XXVI, 169, 1—2; LW XL, 257.

67. WA XXVI, 153, 1—3; LW XL, 238.

68. WA XXVI, 167, 19—21; LW XL, 255.

69. The term *kinder glaube,* WA XXVI, 167, 29, seems to me to refer to the Apostles' Creed, the *fides quae creditur,* not as LW XL, 255, has it, to "faith of a child," the *fides qua creditur;* see, for example, my note, LW XIII, 296, n. 59.

70. WA XXVI, 168, 12—26; LW, XL, 256.

71. *Deudsch Catechismus,* WA, XXX/1, 218, 15—19.

72. WA XXVI, 155, 29—30; LW XL, 241.

73. WA XXVI, 167, 11—13; LW XL, 255.

74. WA XXVI, 166, 22—23; LW XL, 254.

75. WA XXVI, 159, 2—4; LW XL, 245.

76. WA XXVI, 168, 1—5; LW XL, 256.
77. *In epistolam S. Pauli ad Galatas commentariu,* WA XL/I, 589, 25—28; LW XXVI, 387.
78. WA XXVI, 164, 24; LW XL, 252.
79. WA XXVI, 158, 31—33; LW XL, 245.
80. WA XXVI, 153, 34—35; LW XL, 239.
81. WA XXVI, 155, 1—4; LW XL, 240.
82. WA XXVI, 155, 18—21; LW XL, 241.
83. See WA XXVI, 158, 17—19; LW XL, 244.
84. WA XXVI, 164, 30—32; LW XL, 252.
85. WA XXVI, 169, 24—26; LW XL, 257.
86. WA XXVI, 169, 29—30; LW XL, 257.
87. WA XXVI, 168, 5—6; LW XL, 256.

9

THE RADICAL DIALECTIC
BETWEEN FAITH AND WORKS IN LUTHER'S
LECTURES ON GALATIANS (1535)

Robert Bertram

1. *THEOLOGIA BREVISSIMA ET LONGISSIMA*

ALTHOUGH sinners are justified solely by their faith, that, as Luther knew, does not yet exhaust the description of them as "Christians." "He who wants to be a true Christian . . . must be truly a believer. But he does not truly believe if works of love do not follow his faith." [1] Here Luther is commenting on that controversial phrase from Galatians 5:6 around which the Roman opponents had recently built their *Confutatio* at Augsburg, "faith working through love." Against their interpretation — that Paul here identifies what is justifying about faith, namely, its love — Luther argues rather that "Paul is describing the whole of the Christian life in this passage: inwardly it is faith toward God, and outwardly it is love or works toward one's neighbor; thus a man is a Christian in a total sense." [2] "Not one of these things [whether 'a cowl or fasting or vestments or ceremonies,' by which the opponents 'want to give the impression of being Christians'], not one, makes a man a Christian; only faith and love do so." [3] But the same judgment applies a few verses later (5:13) to those non-Roman, nominal "evangelicals" who "are enjoying

219

the advantages of the Gospel to their own destruction and are worse idolaters under the name 'Christian' than they used to be under the pope." [4] "The form of the Christian life," says Luther, "is faith and works" — "the only true rule" (Gal. 6:16), displacing "the rule of Francis, of Dominic, and of all the others," describing the Christian completely as "inwardly righteous in the spirit and outwardly pure and holy in the flesh." [5]

Yet what is equally clear is that this "perfect doctrine of both faith and love" is "also the shortest and the longest kind of theology — the shortest so far as words and sentences are concerned, but in practice and in fact it is wider, longer, deeper, and higher than the whole world." [6] That, alas, is the problem. And for all its being a problem "in practice and in fact," it is not for that reason any less a problem in "theology." Indeed, just because Christians succeed so poorly at believing and loving "in practice and in fact," what kind of theology is there that could honestly call them "Christians" at all, or their works "good" — except perhaps a merely hypothetical theology? But a merely hypothetical theology would fail in both of theology's functions, both as *doctrina* and as *consolatio*.[7] Precisely for *theologia*, therefore, the relation of faith and work, both of which are essential to being Christian, does pose a massive problem.

At least part of the difficulty is what we might call a problem in predication. If justification is solely by faith, how good, really, are good works? If the human subject, being always a sinner, can be justified only by his faith and not by his work, how can his work ever be expected to achieve the theological predicate "good"? But if his work does qualify as good, as Luther insists it does, is his justification still solely by his faith and in no sense by his work? Isn't it so "that Christian teaching [namely, that we are justified by faith] undermines good morals and conflicts with political order" — in other words, disqualifies Christians' work from the predicate "righteous"? If not, if "to avoid this impression . . . the apostle also admonishes about good morals," [8] then doesn't the opposite conclusion follow? "When he says that the whole Law is fulfilled in one word, he seems to have forgotten the cause he has set forth in this entire epistle [that is, justification by faith] and to maintain the exact opposite, namely, that those who do works of love fulfill the Law and are righteous" — in other words, are not righteous solely by their faith.[9]

Nor is this problem in predication academic or an imaginary dilemma contrived by the opponents. As Luther admits: "if grace or faith is not preached, no one is saved; for faith alone justifies and saves. On the other hand, if faith is preached . . . the majority of men understand the teaching about faith in a fleshly way and transform the freedom of the spirit into the freedom of the flesh." [10] This is how men can ruin that "perfect doctrine of both faith and love in practice and in fact," though they ruin it by something so apparently trivial and academic as a misunderstanding of *doctrina*. "The majority of men understand the teaching about faith *[doctrina de fide]* in a fleshly way." And that is why even this "shortest kind of theology" — shortest "so far as words and sentences are concerned" — now has to expand in Luther's lectures to well-nigh "the longest kind of theology" — longest even "so far as words and sentences are concerned" — and why we shall now have to follow him through the entire length of the fifth and sixth chapters of Galatians. For here in the relation of faith and works, more seductively perhaps than at any other point, is the *doctrina de fide*, that heart of Luther's theology, subject to misunderstanding. And here the problem of predication, which haunts his whole theology — the problem, namely, how theology is about man: man the sinner, the man Christ Jesus, man the believer — comes to its limit in man the "Christian." What relationship between the human subject and the theological predicate, between the working sinner-believer and the ultimate goodness of his work, is involved in the covering name "Christian" ?

Luther's resolution of this problem of predication, if with one word we may anticipate what follows, lies in his "doctrine of *faith.*" "Even reason understands and imparts this part of [the apostle's] teaching to some extent [namely, his teaching "about morals"], but it knows nothing at all about the teaching of faith." (Conversely, we shall find in the end that in "the teaching about morals," what "reason" ought to perceive but no longer can is retrieved by "faith.") Accordingly, Luther concludes, Christians "teach morals and all the virtues better than any philosophers or teachers, because they add faith." [11] The expression "because they *add* faith" recalls a similar use of this same word by Melanchthon in the fourth article of his Apology to the Augsburg Confession. Melanchthon, saving his constructive treatment of faith and works until the climactic end of his argument (in this respect resembling Luther's progression in the Galatians lectures and Paul's before that), invokes against the Roman *Confutatio* his exegetical "rule" that truly good works emerge only when the Biblical *lex* has the *promissio* "added" to it. Luther's position is, in this respect at least, similar. Here also he finds the secret to Paul's "faith working through love": why, in other words, love is not love, good work is not good, unless it is the function of *faith* — that very faith which justifies.

The best way, consequently, for us to frame a large enough question to elicit the fullness of Luther's anticipated answer is to ask: Why is it that a Christian's works are "good," not in spite of his being justified by faith, not in addition to his being justified by faith, but solely *because* he is justified by faith? (A further question, as an "afterthought," will be: If this authentically good work does not justify, what is it good for?) If Luther's claiming so much for faith elicits also the Barthian scolding, Barth's warning against Luther's "extravagant view" of faith [12] (a stricture understandable of course from Barth's position), we shall here have to try all the harder to understand Luther from his own position.

2. *RIXA ET PUGNA*

To say, however, that what is good about a Christian's good work depends on his faith may easily overlook that very feature of his faith which makes his good work good, namely, his life-and-death struggle, his *rixa et pugna*, against his flesh. At the least, theology dare not bypass this hard fact of life, this struggle, by defining Christian good works in some ideal fashion and then consigning the obstacles they face in actuality to some extratheological realm of "fact and practice." No, for Luther the empirical fact of the Christian's struggle with his flesh is itself, right along with the Biblical data, one of the essential data of theology. But more than that, the Christian's "conflict and fight" is of the essence of — it defines — what is "good" about his good work. Without this conflict, his life being what it is, his work would simply not be good at all and he would be no Christian.

It is not yet an adequate definition of Christian good work, therefore, to say merely (though Luther does indeed say all these things) that it means "true faith toward God, which loves and helps one's neighbor," [13] or "a love that is unfeigned," [14] or to "love one another . . . on account of the indwelling of Christ and the Holy Spirit," [15] or "following the example of Christ," [16] or doing "spontaneously, without any legal constraint . . . more than the Law requires." [17] It is true of course that "a faith that is neither imaginary nor hypocritical but true and living . . . is what arouses and motivates good works through love." [18] But none of this yet allows for the grim fact that "you cannot produce anyone on earth who loves God and his neighbor as the Law requires," [19] and that "every saint feels and confesses that his flesh

resists the Spirit and that these two are opposed to each other." [20]
Much less, however, does any of this explain why for Luther the opposition itself between Spirit and flesh, despite the disappointingly par-
tial character of its victories, should be that very thing that characterizes the Christian's work as "righteous," "holy," "good."

What exactly is the Christian's conflict? Between what and what?
If we take into view the entire fifth and sixth chapters of Galatians,
two of the verses which for Luther seem to summarize well the two
poles of the Christian conflict are 5:1 and 5:13. On the one hand, says
Paul, "for freedom Christ has set us free; stand fast therefore, and do
not submit again to a yoke of slavery." On the other hand, "you were
called to freedom, brethren; only do not use your freedom as an opportunity for the flesh, but through love be servants of one another." This
bipolarity, as we shall see in a moment, is deceptive and might easily
be so misconstrued as to locate the conflict between the wrong antitheses, namely, between "a yoke of slavery" on the one hand and
"freedom as an opportunity for the flesh" on the other, that is, between
legalism and antinomianism. That would be an error, though an
understandable one.

Before we identify the precise poles of the conflict, or rather *in
order* to identify them, we might note those other verses in Galatians
in which Luther seems to find the conflict most clearly resolved. High
on his list is 5:16: "But I say, walk by the Spirit, and do not gratify the
desires of the flesh." A close second is 5:6: "For in Christ Jesus neither
circumcision nor uncircumcision is of any avail, but faith working
through love," or its parallel, 6:15: "For [in Christ Jesus] neither circumcision counts for anything, nor uncircumcision, but a new creation." "Walking by the Spirit," "faith working through love," "a new
creation" are all, in Luther's treatment, approximate synonyms. They
all represent, moreover, one pole, the affirmative pole, of the Christian's struggle. Knowing that should now help us see where Luther
does and does not locate the other pole.

If the one side, the upper hand, of the Christian's conflict is his
existence in the Spirit, then his other side, the under hand, may be
summed up as his fleshly existence under the Law. It is *both* "flesh"
and "under the Law." These two ingredients are together the unitary
lot of the sinner, and together they pose one antithesis to the Christian's existence by the Spirit. There is no flesh which is not under the
Law, and only that is under the Law which is flesh. This point cannot
be emphasized enough lest we misunderstand Luther. For reasons
which we shall explore later, the fleshliness that admittedly permeates

223

all of a believer's doing is still by itself not sufficient to render him a non-Christian or to despoil his work of its goodness. This happens only when, as flesh, he so despairs of his goodness that he loses faith and then altogether falls back "under the Law." This means then that BOTH the threatening *sub lege* AND the *caro* would only too willingly drag him under the *lex* which, together as a formidable alliance with the former, the Spirit opposes.

It might be all too tempting to mistake Luther as saying that the Christian's "walk" is a kind of tightrope between two apparent extremes, between the pitfall of carnal license on the one side and the pitfall of judaizing enslavement on the other, between antinomianism and legalism. It is not as though the antinomians alone are designated as "flesh" and the legalists alone as "under the Law." Both designations describe both types of sinner. In fact, for this present inquiry into Luther it is unwise to make much of the distinction between the two groups.[21] In his exegesis Luther interprets those judaizing Galatians who would impose again "a yoke of *slavery*" to be the same Galatians who would use their "*freedom* as an opportunity for the flesh." The same flesh which under the yoke of the Law justifies itself with "silly and fanatical ceremonial works" also wants enough "freedom" to prefer such works to a truly lawful and loving service of the neighbor.[22]

This same perverse combination of legalistic enslavement and fleshly freedom is still in force, Luther finds, "under the papacy . . . in the sectarians of our day and in their disciples, especially in the Anabaptists. [Even] in our churches, where the true doctrine of good works is set forth with great diligence," there is also, first of all, an "amazing . . . sluggishness and lack of concern."[23] But in addition to this "amazing" (*dictu mirum*) fleshly freedom from the law of love, there is also, presumably among the same Christians, an equally amazing enslavement to legalistic "superstitions." "It is amazing [*mirum*] that godly people have this trial: their conscience is immediately wounded if they omit some trifling thing that they should have done, but not if, as happens every day, they neglect Christian love and do not act toward their neighbor with a sincere and brotherly heart."[24] Antinomianism and legalism, not at all the opponents they might seem to be in the Christian's struggle, are rather but two faces of that one and same opponent against whom he struggles, his *caro*, which is always also *sub lege*. In fact, it is decisive for Luther's whole argument that "flesh" should mean not just the crass behavior of the evildoer but also that exalted religiosity that (whether in presumption or despair) yearns for justification under the Law. Otherwise the flesh would hardly need to be opposed by something like faith, the faith which justifies. It could just as well be opposed by the divine law or perhaps by some assist from the Spirit without justifying faith. But these do not suffice when the "flesh," as legalism, entails an entire contrary soteriology.[25]

We are now in a position to look once more at those passages from Galatians which seem, as we said, to identify the poles of the Christian's conflict. Contrary to initial appearances, the decisive Christian antithesis is *not:* "submitting again to a yoke of slavery" (5:1) on the one hand versus "using your freedom as an opportunity for the flesh" (5:13) on the other hand. Basically the same antithesis appears in both passages: the Christian's "freedom" on the one hand versus *both* the Law's "yoke of slavery" *and* "the freedom of the flesh" on the other hand. Already in his comments on 5:1, which warn against the "yoke of slavery," Luther shows how this slavery goes hand in hand with "the freedom of the flesh." The same "papists" who are "slaves" "use the freedom of the Gospel" as "Epicureans."[26] Likewise in his comments on 5:13 Luther refers to those who abuse their "freedom as an opportunity for the flesh" as "captive" and "slaves."[27] The Christian's conflict, his "good" fight, is between his free life in the Spirit and the fleshly existence under the Law. And this fight is the very thing about his faith that defines his work ("faith working through love") as good, though we have not yet explained why.

And isn't this the same conflict — between Spirit and flesh under law — that Luther finds described in the other passages: 5:16, 5:6, 6:15? "But I say, walk by the Spirit, and do not gratify the desires of the flesh." At first Luther's notion that the Christian's struggle is between Spirit on the one hand and not merely flesh but flesh under Law on the other hand is not convincing. For Paul seems to pit the Spirit against the flesh exclusively. "The desires of the flesh are against the Spirit, and the desires of the Spirit are against the flesh; for these are opposed to each other." But then Paul continues: "If you are led by the Spirit, you are not under the Law." Luther is aware that this opposing of the Spirit not only to the flesh but also to the *sub lege* is not quite the way one would expect the Christian struggle to be defined.

> Here someone may raise the objection: "How can it be that we are not under the Law? After all, Paul, you yourself teach that we have a flesh whose desires are against the Spirit, a flesh that . . . enslaves us. . . . This is surely what it means to be under the Law. Then why do you say, Paul, that we are not under the Law?

What "Paul" answers is, "Do not let this bother you." [28] Why not, remains to be seen.

Consider also 5:6: "For in Christ Jesus neither circumcision nor uncircumcision is of any avail, but faith working through love" — or as 6:15 puts it, "a new creation." Once again the diametric opposite of being "in Christ Jesus," of "faith working through love," of the "new creation" is not only the obvious opposite, the antinomian flesh of "uncircumcision," but always also that *sub lege* existence, "circumcision."

> The Jews . . . were perfectly ready to concede that uncircumcision did not count for anything . . . but to say the same about the Law and about circumcision was unbearable. . . . Today the papists . . . excommunicate us for teaching that in Christ Jesus these traditions do not count for anything. In the same way some of our followers, who are no less stupid than the papists, regard freedom from the traditions of the pope as something so necessary that they are afraid of committing sin if they do not violate or abolish all of them immediately.[29]

Luther does not deny that circumcision and uncircumcision — legalism and antinomianism, shall we say? — are mutually opposed. It is simply that both together stand at the farthest remove from the new creation. "They are, of course, contrary to each other, but that has nothing to do with Christian righteousness," [30] or with "a new creation . . . which is inwardly righteous in the spirit and outwardly holy and pure in the flesh." [31]

We have tried to show that according to Luther, in order to predicate "good" or "Christian" of the believer's existence, it is not enough to say idealistically that his existence, his works, must be the product of his faith. They must, of course. But what this easily overlooks is that the Christian's work is always also the product of his flesh, which the law of God condemns. Then how can the Christian's work be honestly "good" work? By faith, Luther answers, as it struggles against that flesh, which is so susceptible of the Law's tyranny and which shows itself not only as antinomianism but also as the most pious sort of legalism. But how, let us ask again, does such a prestigious predicate as "good" or "Christian" apply to this struggle against flesh under law, as admirable as that struggle admittedly is, though its ambiguous, sin-conditioned character becomes all the more glaring when we recall that it is still only a struggle? In pursuing the answer to that question it should become clear why it was so essential for Luther to place the *sub lege*, along with the flesh, at the opposite pole from faith's walking by the Spirit.

226

3. NUNC INTERPRETATUR LEGEM

Despite all we have said in proof of the Christian's opposition in the Spirit to the *sub lege,* an honest misgiving that might still lurk about our present reading of Luther is that he surely does (because Paul does) find in that same *lex* a genuine resource for the Christian's fight against the flesh. Remember how Paul, in order to combat the Galatians' abuse of "freedom as an opportunity for the flesh," appeals to the commandment of mutual love, the Law. "Do not use your freedom as an opportunity for the flesh, but through love be servants of one another." (5:13) Luther too is frank to call this admonition by its lawlike names. "The apostle imposes an obligation *[servitutem]* on Christians through this law *[legem]* about mutual love in order to keep them from abusing their freedom. Therefore the godly should remember that for the sake of Christ they are free in their conscience before God from the curse of the Law, from sin, and from death, but that according to the body they are bound *[servos]*." [32] That this is the Law and that the Law is a weapon against the flesh is unquestioned.

When Paul goes on in the next verse to explain: "For the whole Law is fulfilled in one word, 'You shall love your neighbor as yourself,'" Luther marvels at Paul's exegesis of Biblical law: "This is the real way to interpret Scripture and the commandments of God." [33] Not only does Paul compress "all of Moses into a brief summary," thus bypassing all "unnatural and superstitious works" and coming directly to the heart of the Law, neighborly love.[34] What is more, he identifies in turn what is the very heart of love: not, as the sophists coldly imagine, "to wish someone well" but rather to "be a servant" of one's neighbor. "It is as though Paul were saying: 'When I say that through love you should be servants of one another, I mean what the Law says elsewhere (Lev. 19:18): 'You shall love your neighbor as yourself.'" [35] True, it is impossible for a man to understand the Law as perceptively as that (even though it be what "we call the law of nature") unless he has first exchanged his legalism for faith.[36] Still, what his faith understands is just that, the law. Yes, the Law — not the existence *sub lege,* of course, but the *lex* — is definitely here aligned with the Christian against his flesh.

However, not only must a man's healthy opposition to the flesh be distinguished from a man's enslavement under the Law, but we must also distinguish between the Law's genuine capacity to oppose the flesh and its incapacity. The Law has its limitations, for one thing, because it is incapable of being lived up to except by recourse to something beyond the Law, the Spirit, who is had by faith in Christ. (At this level there is no conflict between the Law and the Spirit, and Paul can say of "the fruits of the Spirit": "Against such there is no Law.") For another thing, we bear in mind that the deadliest form of the flesh is that very legalism, that yearning for self-justification, which capitulates *sub lege*. This legalistic brand of fleshliness brings with it, of course, every other ethical fleshliness of "vainglory" and lovelessness; but, still worse, it makes Christ and faith and the Spirit "of no advantage." Against this ploy of the flesh the Law itself is not effective, but only the Spirit.

It is of interest to Luther, therefore, that Paul's interpretation of the Law does not stop where we last left it. Having explained that "you shall love your neighbor as yourself" means really "through love be servants of one another," he goes a step farther. Now in turn "he interprets what it means to be a servant of one's neighbor through love." [37] And he does this in 5:16 ff.: "But I say, walk by the Spirit, and do not gratify," etc. Yet in this farther step of his exegesis Paul steps quite outside the Law itself into the doctrine of the Spirit, justification by faith, "the doctrine of faith." It is this stage, I take it, in the apostle's admonition "about good morals and about honest outward conduct, the observance of love and harmony," that Luther had in mind when he said earlier that Christians "teach morals and all the virtues better than any philosophers or teachers, because they add faith." [38]

The way Paul now "adds" faith in his further exegesis of the law of love, namely, in his "walk by the Spirit," not only deepens our understanding of that law (if it does that at all) but actually transcends that law. It supersedes the Law with an altogether new solution precisely at the point where the Law fails. Here we recall again how determined Luther is that theology, though it must insist finally on calling the Christians' work genuinely good, dare not blink the realities of these same Christians' failures and sins. For it is a simple fact that the Law fails to be fulfilled even among the saints. "Because sin clings to you as long as you live, it is impossible for you to fulfill the Law." Therefore, "with the words 'walk by the Spirit' Paul shows how he wants his earlier statements to be understood: 'Through love be servants of one another' (5:13) and 'Love is the fulfilling of the Law'" (Rom. 13:10). Namely, "it is as though he were saying: 'When I command you to love one another, I am requiring of you that you walk by the Spirit. For I know that you will not fulfill the Law.'" [39] The statement by which Paul reveals that "I know you will not fulfill the Law" is really not so much his verse 16, "Walk by the Spirit," etc., as it is the next verse (which Luther is anticipating), "For the desires of the flesh are against the Spirit . . . to prevent you from doing what you would." All the same, as Luther sees it, it is because "you will not fulfill the Law" ("You shall love your neighbor as yourself," etc.) that Paul must now reinterpret that law by recourse to something quite different from the Law, namely, "Walk by the Spirit."

"Thus," Luther adds (though at first glance his "thus" is anything but obvious), "he [Paul] has not forgotten the matter of justification. For when he commands them to walk by the Spirit, he clearly [?] [40] denies that works justify." Does this follow so "clearly" as all that? What is the connection? How did the issue of justification get in here? Why should Paul's simple and direct admonition to "walk by the Spirit" be interrupted now by this detour into justification by faith? And why should it be this obtrusive doctrine of justification rather than the direct guidance of the Spirit, which resolves the Christian's failure to keep the law of love? These questions can hardly be answered in one sentence, but in anticipation of the longer answer which lies ahead, let us try.

"The more aware they [Christians] are of their weakness and sin, the more they take refuge in Christ . . . plead for His assistance, that He may adorn them with His righteousness and make their faith increase by providing the Spirit, by whose guidance they will overcome the desires of the flesh and make them servants rather than masters." [41] This much at least should be clear from this quotation: The Spirit's "guidance," which helps Christians "overcome the desires of the flesh and make them servants rather than masters," is not *immediate* guidance. Nor is it in the first instance for the Spirit's guidance but instead "for Christ's assistance" that "they plead." Indeed, it is through Christ's assistance that the guidance of the Spirit is mediated, that is, through that justifying "righteousness" with which Christ "adorns them," and through that "faith" which, though it is provided by the Spirit, means to "take refuge in Christ." [42]

But this taking refuge in Christ, which is but another way of saying justification by faith, still presupposes that in the whole struggle to walk by the Spirit — to love one's neighbor as oneself, to be his loving servant — even the question of one's justification is at issue. That is a presupposition, true, the very one which Luther mentions first of all in the above quotation when he says: "The more aware Christians are of their weakness and sin, the more they take refuge," etc. Still, being aware of their weakness and sin, what — rather than taking refuge in the righteousness of Christ — would be their alternative? Not simply capitulating to the flesh but doing so because in their awareness of weakness and sin they would have no prospect of being anything else but flesh. Luther's name for this is "despair," and for him this is strictly a problem of justification, of a man's worth before God.

Isn't that, after all, the condition which also Paul presupposes in his original admonition, "Walk by the Spirit and do not gratify the desires of the flesh"? "For," as he goes on to explain, "the desires of the flesh are against the Spirit, and the desires of the Spirit are against the flesh; for these are opposed to each other to prevent you from doing what you would" (5:16-17). For those sanguine "sophists" who "took the statement of Paul, 'Love is the fulfilling of the Law,'" to imply a *justification* by love, this fact of an inescapable, Spirit-frustrating opposition by the flesh should be rebuttal enough.[43] ("If we were pure of all sin," Luther concedes, ". . . then we would certainly be righteous and holy through love. . . . But [that] must be postponed until the life to come.") [44] However, for those who are only too well aware of this conflict — "in fact, the godlier one is, the more aware he is of this conflict" [45] — and who know clearly enough that they do not have enough love to justify them, there is the converse danger, *desperatio:* losing heart in their battle against the flesh, feeling undone by their relentless, inextinguishable impatience, lovelessness, grumbling, sexual desire, competitiveness, becoming downcast over their way of life, their social position, their work and routines, all so seemingly unimportant and displeasing to God. What else is that but the problem of a sinner's justification before God? When he despairs of that, he concedes the battle to his flesh, and that is the end both of his faith and of his love.[46] "Paul cannot forget about his doctrine of faith, but he keeps on repeating and emphasizing it, even when he is dealing with good works." [47] Isn't this what Luther means by "adding faith" to the "teaching about morals"?

Presumably, then, Paul reinterprets the Law ("You shall love your neighbor as yourself") not only by being more faithful to the intention of the Law ("through love be servants of one another") but also by recourse beyond the Law to the Gospel, to the doctrine of justification by faith ("Walk by the Spirit"), for the simple reason that the Christian's very struggle to do good works and to love is what raises recurrently the question of his justification before God. It is exactly the Law's obligating the flesh to loving, neighborly servanthood that then suggests, alas, his reverting again *sub lege*, whether for self-justification or in despair, and therefore demands some other resource than the Law — namely, the Gospel — both for his justification and for his good work.

4. QUATENUS LUCTAMUR, EATENUS IUSTI

But how, we now ask, is this purpose accomplished by Paul's exhorting, "Walk by the Spirit and do not gratify the desires of the flesh"? For after all even those who do walk by the Spirit and do not gratify the desires of the flesh continue always to have the flesh very much with them, opposing the Spirit in them and preventing them from doing what they would. If so, if every action of theirs is still muddied more or less by the incursions of their flesh, then it is difficult to see how their work may honestly be called good, even though they simultaneously "walk by the Spirit," more or less.

Still, Luther insists on calling Christian work just that — good. This is all the more perplexing in view of his unyielding determination to call sin — also Christian sin — by its name. "Sin is really sin, regardless of whether you commit it before or after you have come to know Christ. And God hates the sin . . . A believer's sin is . . . just as great as that of the unbeliever." [48] Moreover, as we have noted, Luther does not call Christian work good simply because it is possible to conceive of such good work ideally, even though actual Christian existence may afford no instances of it. "The Law prescribes and commands that we love God with all our heart, etc., and our neighbor as ourselves; but from this it does not follow: 'This is written, and therefore, it is done. . . .'" [49] Of course, as Luther never tires of saying, a Christian sinner is gratuitously righteous before God, by faith in Christ, and in that relationship at least — *coram Deo*, "inwardly" — he "remains godly." [50] But how about "outwardly"? That is, if his only righteousness is by faith, then why invoke at all the predicate "righteous" for his work, his love? If it is true of the unbeliever that "even his good works are sins," [51] why should that be any less true of the believer? Why even distinguish between "good" works and some other kind, between "the works of the flesh" and "the fruits of the Spirit"? Why not leave the matter in the conflict it is, a *rixa et pugna* between flesh and Spirit, rather than claim some kind of victory, some brand of Christian work allegedly good "in practice and in fact"?

Still, Luther does say that a Christian "fulfills the Law," not only "inwardly by faith (for Christ is the consummation of the Law for

231

righteousness to everyone who has faith)" but also "outwardly by works and by" something else, to which we shall return quickly, but nonetheless "by works." "Thus it [the Law] is completely abrogated for them [Christians], first in the Spirit, but then also in works." [52] This is so because they walk by the Spirit. "But those who perform the works of the flesh and gratify its desires are accused and condemned by the Law, both politically and theologically." [53]

Christians, however, do not "perform the works of the flesh and gratify its desires." But didn't Luther concede that Christians do have the desires of the flesh? "This does not mean that they do not feel its desires at all; it means that they do not gratify them." [54] And there is a vast difference. "Christians strive to avoid the works of the flesh; they cannot avoid its desires." [55] Luther sees here a decisive distinction between Paul's terms "desires" of the flesh and "works" of the flesh, between the "opposition" from the flesh, on the one hand (which would "prevent you from doing what you would"), and "gratifying" the flesh or "submitting" to it or "doing such things," on the other hand.

Because the saints have not yet completely shed their corrupt flesh, they are inclined toward sinning. They do not fear and love God enough, etc. They are aroused to anger, envy, impatience, sexual desire, and similar feelings; nevertheless, they do not carry out these feelings, because, as Paul says here, they crucify their flesh with its passions and faults, . . . not only . . . by fasting or other kinds of discipline, but when, as Paul said earlier (5:16), they walk by the Spirit.[56]

Luther says: "Here it is sufficient if you resist the flesh and do not gratify its desires, that is, if you follow the Spirit rather than the flesh." This does not mean that the Law has now conveniently been "reinterpreted" in the sense that it has been compromised — requiring, say, merely that "we try our best." Not at all. Still, Luther does say: "To the extent that by the Spirit we struggle against the flesh, to that extent we are outwardly righteous, even though it is not this righteousness that makes us acceptable in the sight of God." [57]

Luther's distinction between "feeling" the flesh's desires and "gratifying" them, etc., pictures the Spirit and the flesh as being engaged in something more than an inconclusive, even-draw, up-and-down struggle. It is not enough to say, in other words, that the Christian is *partly* flesh and *partly* spirit, or that he is *both* sinful *and* righteous. No, the one pole is in control, the other is not. The faithful "know that they have partly flesh and partly Spirit, but in such a way that the Spirit rules and the flesh is subordinate, that righteousness is supreme and sin is a servant." [58] Luther is not of course equating Christians with just any people whose "good side" (as we say) happens to prevail over their "bad side," nor is he equating the Christians' Spirit with their native reason, soul, conscience, or will. True, he does locate the Spirit in the Christian's "good will," but this "is, of course, the Spirit Himself resisting the flesh." [59] And "the will which is opposed to the flesh" [60] is that "new mind, a new will, new senses, and even new action," [61] the "new creation." Essentially, to "obey the Spirit rather than the flesh" means "by faith and hope . . . [to] take hold of Christ." [62]

Yet at the same time this is all a behavioral occurrence as well "in practice and in fact." It is as factual behaviorally as its opposite, "despair," which — in the case of the conscientious man who succumbs *sub lege* — is exactly what "gratifying the desires of the flesh" means. To "walk by the Spirit" is that behavioral fact of Christian life which is signaled by a struggle, but a struggle in which the one power has the upper hand, exercises the executive office of the ego, though perhaps not much more than that. In fact, Luther seems at times to say that the mere fact that there is any struggle at all, that the flesh is even so much as being frustrated and resisted ("in the wicked, of course, it has dominant control" [63]), is itself "victory" by definition, seeing who it is (namely the Spirit) that is doing the resisting. In behavioral terms, the resister is faith — not the Law, which is helpless against despair and in fact abets it.

5. QUID FIDES EST

But that, finally, explains also why the Christian's work, his love, qualifies as "good," why he "is a Christian in a total sense," not only "inwardly through faith in the sight of God" but also "outwardly"; namely, because his love (or at least so much of it as he can manage in his struggle against his loveless flesh) is *by faith,* just as is his justification. His love is "*faith* working through love." To be sure, this Pauline phrase "has not yet said what faith is." But hasn't it? Doesn't it say, by Luther's own admission, that faith "is the impulse and motivation of good works or love toward one's neighbor"? Yes, but that is faith in "its external function," not what faith *is.* In its "internal nature, power, and function . . . it is righteousness or rather justification in the sight of God." [64] Presumably, therefore, it is impossible for good works or love really to be good at all unless their "impulse and motivation" is that very faith (and nothing else) which is "justification in the sight of God." At that rate, if good works or love could some-how take their impulse and motivation from some other kind of "faith" — or even from the Holy Spirit Himself, though without that faith which is "justification in the sight of God" — and even if those good works or love somehow met the demands of this lovely law, "through love be servants of one another" (though for Luther of course none of this could happen), still the good works in that case would not be good and the "love" would not be love.

Why not? Because these good works or love would always simul-taneously be vitiated by that ruinous opposition from the flesh. Granted, but isn't that equally the case with those good works or love which issue from faith? Yes, "even the saints love in an imperfect and impure way in this present life, and nothing impure will enter the kingdom of God." [65] Still that is exactly where faith makes the differ-ence despite the fact that, as an "impulse and motivation," it is no doubt inextricably intertwined with the desires of the flesh. The dif-ference is that faith possesses Jesus Christ, the Mediator who inter-poses Himself between the believer's otherwise incriminating flesh and that Law which does the incriminating. That is why, "if you are led by the Spirit [which means not despairing, not gratifying the flesh, but taking hold of Christ], you are not under the Law." [66] The be-liever's flesh, never to be minimized in its sinfulness, is nevertheless also not to be predicated ("imputed") as *his*. That is, *he* is not *sub lege*, and his faith in Christ — the opposite of despair *sub lege*, of gratifying the flesh — is his hanging onto that freedom. "This is not because of a difference between the sins, as though the believer's sins were smaller and the unbeliever's larger, but because of a difference between the persons. For the believer knows that his sin is forgiven him on account of Christ, who has expiated it by His death." [67] That is Luther's con-fidence in saying of Christians that "when Christ has been grasped by faith, . . . the Law is completely abrogated for them, first in the Spirit, but then also in works."

This does not mean that there is no difference among works *qua* works. It is the mark of believers that they struggle to do those works which "God commands," not "self-chosen" or "superstitious" works. But that is not what makes their works "holy." "Spontaneously they do what the Law requires, if not by means of perfectly holy works, then at least by means of the forgiveness of sins through faith." [68] But neither is this the same as their being righteous "inwardly," as justified. Also "outwardly" they are righteous, but "by works *and* by the forgiveness of sins."

With the realization that the flesh, though still merely resisted and not extinguished, is nevertheless suffered out of existence ("expiated") by Christ, the Christian's struggle now comes full circle. He is renewed, "a new creation," also behaviorally. In his hands "even evil will have to cooperate for good. For when his flesh impels him to sin, he is aroused . . . to seek forgiveness of sins through Christ . . . which he would otherwise not have regarded as so important. . . ." Then in turn he becomes "a wonderful creator, who can make joy out of sadness . . . righteousness out of sin . . . despair . . . anger or sexual desire . . ." — love out of resentment. "Find out by experience," Luther encourages his students, "what a good and brave warrior you are." [69]

6. HOC OBIECTUM AMABILISSIMUM

Our original question — how the Christian's work, precisely as work, qualifies as "good" — has been answered. But there might still be room for the afterthought: What in turn is this good work, this outward righteousness, *good for,* if it is not that "righteousness that makes us acceptable to God"? It is good, in one word, for the neighbor — the *proximus,* the near one. It might of course also have benefits for the loving worker himself. Being provided in this interim with faith, hope, *and love,* he has the assurance of being "whole and perfect in this life, both inwardly and outwardly, until the revelation of the righteousness . . . which will be consummated and eternal," [70] when he shall no longer need faith and hope, since his love will then be enough.[71] Moreover, "although no work is able to grant the conscience peace before God, yet . . . we have need of this testimony of our conscience that we have carried out our ministry well and . . . lived a good life . . . to the extent that we know [our works] to be commanded by God and pleasing in his sight." [72]

However, the fundamental truth remains: God "does not need our works," our neighbors do. That, after all, is what righteousness "outwardly" means: *coram hominibus.* It is for our fellowmen, and they "do not derive any benefit from [our] faith but do derive benefit from [our] works or from our love." [73] But then the question of what (or rather whom) our love is good for, is hardly an afterthought. For if "the Law cannot be fulfilled without the Holy Spirit, and the Holy Spirit cannot be received without Christ," [74] then what else is "this freedom of the Spirit [for], achieved by the death of Christ"? It is "for [people] to be servants of one another through love." [75] And what

235

else does "the whole Law" finally amount to except that — which is likewise "the law of Christ"? [76]

Not an afterthought indeed. Actually, this could well be the beginning of any discussion of Luther on faith and love, of the goodness of Christian good works, so vast is the phenomenology of this servant-love which he finds in the fifth and sixth chapters of Galatians. True, he refers those students who desire detailed elaboration of Paul's catalog of vices and virtues to "the old commentary which we prepared in 1519," seeing that "our chief purpose this time has been to set forth the doctrine of justification as clearly as possible." [77] However, exactly because of this heightened interest in justification, "even when the apostle is teaching good works" [78] — this "adding faith" to the "teaching about morals" — it is all the more revealing how one sort of Christian love after the other reflects the same structure within it as does the believer's own justification before God. One example will have to suffice, namely, the eye-opening advantages which such compassionate, burden-bearing love brings in the form of new appreciation of the commonplace in God's creation.

The prototype of this compassionate *epieikeia* occurs already when Paul reinterprets "You shall love your neighbor as yourself" to mean "Walk by the Spirit, and do not gratify the desires of the flesh": "When I [Paul] say that, . . . I am not requiring of you that you strip off the flesh completely or kill it, but that you restrain it." For "God wants the world to endure until the Last Day. This cannot happen unless men are born and reared; and this, in turn, requires that the flesh continue." But it also requires "that sin continue, since the flesh cannot be without sin." [79] This kindliness toward the flesh extends even to one's own. "For just as we should not be cruel to other people's bodies or trouble them with unjust requirements, so we should not do this [in this case enforced celibacy] to our own bodies either." [80] "In the church faithful pastors see many errors and sins which they are obliged to bear. In the state the obedience of subjects never lives up to the laws . . . ; therefore if he does not know how to conceal things, the magistrate will not be fit to rule." Likewise "in the family." "If we are able to bear and overlook our own faults and sins . . . let us bear those of others as well, in accordance with the statements: 'Bear one another's burdens' and 'You shall love your neighbor as yourself'" — "and so fulfill the Law of Christ." But "to carry the flesh, that is, the weakness, of the brethren" "a Christian must have broad shoulders and husky bones." [81] And that is what the "outward" righteousness — not just outer but outward, outer-directed — is for.

But then notice what eye-opening appreciation this good-neighborly love brings with it, what powers of discernment, of recognizing goodness in the most unlikely places and people — for instance, within the church, that communion of so-called saints. "When I was a monk, I often had a heartfelt wish to see the life and conduct of at least one saintly man" [82] — but in vain. Now, however, "I am happy to give thanks to God for His superabundant gift, which I sought when I used to be a monk; for I have seen, not one saint but many, in fact, innumerable genuine saints." [83] "Saints are all those who believe in Christ," "not those who lead a celibate life, who are abstemious. or who perform other works that give the appearance of brilliance or grandeur. . . . They are not all of equal firmness of character, and many weaknesses and offenses are discernible in every one of them; it is also true that many of them fall into sin. But . . . on no account . . . am I to jump to the conclusion that [they] . . . are unholy, when I see that they love and revere the Word, receive the Lord's Supper, etc." [84]

The same perceptiveness of love sees through the apparent inequalities in social status, refusing to evaluate one vocation as inferior to another. "In the eyes of the world, of course, these ways of life and their positions are unequal." "A monk does not concede that the works which a layman performs in his calling are as good and acceptable to God as his own." Neither does a nun in comparing her life with that of a married woman. Similarly "the Anabaptists imagine today" that the status of those who "suffer need, hunger, cold, and tattered clothing" is superior to that of "those others who own property, etc." But "no godly person believes that the position of a magistrate is better in the sight of God than that of a subject." Nor will he "distinguish between the position or work of a father and that of a son, or between that of a teacher and that of a pupil, or between that of a master and that of a servant." Instead, he will insist that "both are pleasing to God if they are done in faith and in obedience to God." [85]

Finally, this same appreciative faith working through love reappropriates that splendor to which, in God's violated creation, "reason" has become blind: above all, that splendid creation, the neighbor — man. "Men are completely mistaken when they imagine that they really understand the commandment to love" [86] — that is, "You shall love your neighbor as yourself" — "even though this principle and others like it, which we call the law of nature, are the foundation of

human law and of all good works." [87] To the corrupted reason, however, just as that "shortest" theology, "Believe in Christ," seems to be
a "stingy and paltry phrase," so "serving another person through love
seems . . . to mean performing unimportant works" like "teaching the
erring . . . bearing with [the neighbor's] rude manners and impolite-
ness, putting up with annoyances, labors, and the ingratitude and
contempt of men in both church and state . . . being patient in the
home with a cranky wife. . . ." But in truth these loving works in the
neighbor's behalf are incomprehensibly "outstanding and brilliant." [88]
Thereupon Luther follows with an extolling of man that rivals Pico's
or even Feuerbach's: "No creature toward which you should practice
love is nobler than your neighbor . . . more pleasant, more lovable,
more helpful, kinder, more comforting . . . more necessary . . .
worthier of love in the whole universe. . . ." "Even one who has done
me some sort of injury or harm has not shed his humanity on that
account or stopped being flesh and blood, a creature of God very much
like me . . . my neighbor." [89] But that is the sight which Christians
behold when, in their "teaching about morals," "they add faith." [90]

NOTES

1. LW XXVII, 30; WA XL/2, 37. This and all subsequent quotations from
   Luther are from the lectures on Galatians delivered in 1531 and which in the
   form of Georg Röhrer's edition of his own and others' class notes were first
   published in 1535, together with an authorizing preface by Luther himself.
   The WA carries at the top of each page Röhrer's original class notes, designated Hs. (for *Handschrift*), and at the bottom of each page the version which
   finally appeared in print, designated Dr. (for *Druck*). All quotations will cite
   both LW and WA, the latter referring (unless specifically designated Hs.) to
   the Dr. version. It so happens that the comments Luther makes on this
   present verse, Gal. 5:6, do not come either from Röhrer's class notes or from
   Luther's class lectures but are rather from a special manuscript on this verse,
   done in Luther's own hand and inserted by Röhrer into the published commentary. See WA XL/2, 34, n. 1.
2. LW XXVII, 30; WA XL/2, 37, 26—28.
3. LW XXVII, 31; WA XL/2, 38, 30—31.
4. LW XXVII, 51; WA XL/2, 64, 15—22.
5. LW XXVII, 30, 141; WA XL/2, 37, 30—38, 5.
6. LW XXVII, 59; WA XL/2, 74, 25—27.
7. For examples of how the two terms or their equivalents are paired see LW
   XXVII, 25, 31—32, 33, 39, 46—47; WA XL/2, 30, 17; 39, 17 and 40, 7; 41,
   18; 48, 28; 58, 14—22.
8. LW XXVII, 47; WA XL/2, 59, 24—27.
9. LW XXVII, 63; WA XL/2, 78, 28—31.
10. LW XXVII, 48; WA XL/2, 60, 27—31.

11. LW XXVII, 47; WA XL/2, 59, 23—24, 29—30. The words *quia fidem addunt* do not appear in Röhrer's Hs. (59, 4—12), but the same sense is there. *Doctrina nostra (fidei)* (of which Luther says *nihil scit mundum*) *melius docet bonas mores quam ulli gentium philosophi.*

12. Karl Barth, "An Introductory Essay" in Ludwig Feuerbach, *The Essence of Christianity,* trans. George Eliot, Harper Torchbook (New York: Harper & Row, 1957), p. xxiii.

13. LW XXVII, 31; WA XL/2, 38, 28—29.

14. LW XXVII, 54; WA XL/2, 68, 18.

15. LW XXVII, 93; WA XL/2, 117, 19—21.

16. LW XXVII, 114; WA XL/2, 146, 16.

17. LW XXVII, 96; WA XL/2, 121, 15.

18. LW XXVII, 30; WA XL/2, 37, 13—15.

19. LW XXVII, 64; WA XL/2, 79, 25—26.

20. LW XXVII, 75; WA XL/2, 94, 31—33.

21. True, Luther does seem to describe these two groups (for example, "the papacy" and "the unspiritual men") as a kind of Scylla and Charybdis, but only because they are the obverse results of a single heresy, namely, the urging of faith or works to the exclusion of each other — which after all is really no genuine theological option. "If works alone are taught, as happened under the papacy, faith is lost. If faith alone is taught, unspiritual men will immediately suppose that works are not necessary," LW XXVII, 63; WA XL/2, 78, 22—23.

22. LW XXVII, 52; WA XL/2, 66, 18—32.

23. LW XXVII, 53; WA XL/2, 67, 19—24.

24. LW XXVII, 54; WA XL/2, 68, 25—28.

25. LW XXVII, 87—90; WA XL/2, 110, 13—113, 26.

26. LW XXVII, 4, 8; WA XL/2, 2, 28 ff. and 9, 19—20.

27. LW XXVII, 49, 50; WA XL/2, 61, 30 and 62, 34.

28. LW XXVII, 77; WA XL/2, 97, 19—24.

29. LW XXVII, 138; WA XL/2, 176, 23—30.

30. LW XXVII, 137; WA XL/2, 176, 18—19.

31. LW XXVII, 141; WA XL/2, 179, 34—35.

32. LW XXVII, 49; WA XL/2, 62, 13—16.

33. LW XXVII, 51; WA XL/2, 64, 31—32. See Hs., 62, 7—8: "Quid sit servire . . . man kans am aller besten declarirn per decalogum."

34. LW XXVII, 56, 57; WA XL/2, 70, 24—25 and 71, 29.

35. LW XXVII, 51—52; WA XL/2, 64, 29—65, 22.

36. LW XXVII, 53; WA XL/2, 66, 30—32, 36—37.

37. LW XXVII, 62; WA XL/2 78, 15—16.

38. LW XXVII, 47; WA XL/2 59, 26—30. See n. 11.

39. LW XXVII, 65; WA XL/2, 81, 26—31.

40. LW XXVII, 65; WA XL/2, 81, 33—82, 13.

41. LW XXVII, 86—87; WA XL/2, 108, 28—109, 11.

42. "And when we say 'Spirit,' we do not mean a fanatic or an autodidact, as the sectarians boast of the Spirit; but our Spirit is 'by faith,'" LW XXVII, 20; WA XL/2, 23, 22—24.

43. LW XXVII, 63 ff.; WA XL/2, 79, 15 ff.

44. LW XXVII, 64—65; WA XL/2, 80, 31—34.
45. LW XXVII, 74; WA XL/2, 94, 14—15. "The wicked do not complain about their rebellion, conflict, and captivity to sin; for sin has powerful dominion over them," LW XXVII, 71; WA XL/2, 89, 19—20.
46. LW XXVII, 72—74, 70; WA XL/2, 90, 33—94, 17; 88, 25—26.
47. LW XXVII, 77; WA XL/2, 97, 18—19.
48. LW XXVII, 76; WA XL/2, 95, 27—96, 8.
49. LW XXVII, 63—64; WA XL/2, 79, 23—25.
50. LW XXVII, 76; WA XL/2, 95, 29—96, 16.
51. LW XXVII, 76.
52. LW XXVII, 96; WA XL/2, 121, 18—24.
53. LW XXVII, 96.
54. LW XXVII, 74; WA XL/2, 93, 13—14.
55. LW XXVII, 85; WA XL/2, 107, 21.
56. LW XXVII, 96; WA XL/2, 121, 29—122, 11.
57. LW XXVII, 72; WA XL/2, 91, 22—23; 90, 30—32.
58. LW XXVII, 74; WA XL/2, 93, 19—21.
59. LW XXVII, 75; WA XL/2, 95, 13—14.
60. LW XXVII, 77; WA XL/2, 97, 25—27: ". . . be led by the Spirit, that is . . . obey the will which is opposed to the flesh and . . . refuse to gratify the desires of the flesh; for this is what it means to be led and drawn by the Spirit."
61. LW XXVII, 140; WA XL/2, 179, 12—13. " . . . by 'flesh' Paul means whatever there is in man, including all . . . powers of the soul." LW XXVII, 89; WA XL/2, 111, 32—33.
62. LW XXVII, 73; WA XL/2, 91, 28. "Whatever there is in us beside Him [Christ] — whether it be intellect or will, activity or passivity, etc. — is flesh, not Spirit. . . . 'But we,' Paul says, 'go far beyond all this to live in the Spirit, because through faith we hold to Christ . . . ' " LW XXVII, 25; WA XL/2, 30, 20—26.
63. LW XXVII, 54; WA XL/2, 68, 13.
64. LW XXVII, 30; WA XL/2, 37, 26—38, 10.
65. LW XXVII, 64; WA XL/2, 80, 17—19.
66. LW XXVII, 78; WA XL/2, 98, 20 ff.
67. LW XXVII, 76; WA XL/2, 96, 10—12.
68. LW XXVII, 96; WA XL/2, 121, 18—21.
69. LW XXVII, 74, 26; WA XL/2, 93, 23—94, 14; 31, 27—28.
70. LW XXVII, 25; WA XL/2, 30, 14—16.
71. LW XXVII, 64; WA XL/2, 80, 25—26.
72. LW XXVII, 121; WA XL/2, 155, 17—21.
73. LW XXVII, 30; WA XL/2, 37, 29—30.
74. LW XXVII, 131; WA XL/2, 168, 15—16.
75. LW XXVII, 49; WA XL/2, 61, 32—36.
76. LW XXVII, 114; WA XL/2, 145, 15—16.
77. LW XXVII, 87; WA XL/2, 109, 30—110, 12.
78. LW XXVII, 78; WA XL/2, 98, 14—16.
79. LW XXVII, 68; WA XL/2, 85, 27—86, 13.

80. LW XXVII, 69; WA XL/2, 87, 26—27.
81. LW XXVII, 113—14; WA XL/2, 144, 22—145, 16.
82. LW XXVII, 81; WA XL/2, 103, 12—13.
83. LW XXVII, 83; WA XL/2, 104, 18—20.
84. LW XXVII, 82; WA XL/2, 103, 18—104, 16.
85. LW XXVII, 61—62; WA XL/2, 76, 15—77, 18.
86. LW XXVII, 56; WA XL/2, 71, 22—23.
87. LW XXVII, 53; WA XL/2, 66, 36—37.
88. LW XXVII, 56; WA XL/2, 70, 27—71, 21.
89. LW XXVII, 58; WA XL/2, 72, 31—73, 28.
90. "Without [faith] one cannot understand what a good work is and what is pleasing to God," LW XXVII, 53; WA XL/2, 66, 31—32.

10

THE LUTHERAN SYMBOLICAL BOOKS AND LUTHER

Arthur Carl Piepkorn

THE CATHOLIC Christian who is committed to the Augsburg Confession finds frequent cause for melancholy reflection in the name that his branch of Christendom commonly bears. Of all the major Christian traditions the Lutheran Church is the only one that has not succeeded in shuffling off a designation that links it to a man. "Zwinglian," "Calvinist," "Campbellite," and half a dozen others are recognized generally as impolite epithets that in this day of ecumenical considerateness one does not use in referring to other denominational traditions. Even "Socinian," "Irvingite," "Swedenborgian," and "Millerite" are viewed as being in bad taste.

But not "Lutheran"! Nor can the Lutheran take much comfort from the fact that "Wesleyan" is officially the name of some Methodists, and that the Roman Catholic Church has its Order of St. Benedict, its Brothers Hospitalers of St. John of God, its Hermits of St. Augustine, and its Oratory of St. Philip Neri. "Lutheran" comes so much closer to being a universal designation than any of these others.

Actually the name "Lutheran" — first applied to the conservative

Reformation by its enemies as a badge of heresy, like "Donatist," "Pelagian," "Sabellian," and "Mohammedan" — gives the false impression that Luther is somehow the source and norm of Lutheran teaching.

The theological mind of the Lutheran Church finds expression in the Book of Concord. As is well known, this moderately bulky volume contains, in addition to a preface, the three so-called Catholic or Ecumenical Creeds, the Augsburg Confession, the Apology of the Augsburg Confession, the Treatise on the Authority and Primacy of the Pope, and the Epitome and Solid Declaration of the Formula of Concord. Luther wrote none of these. Together they constitute well over three quarters of the text of the Book of Concord. The three documents in the Book of Concord that Luther did write — the Smalcald Articles, the Small Catechism, and the Large Catechism — come to well under one quarter of the total.

Furthermore, in the hierarchy of symbolical authority established by the Formula of Concord the so-called Catholic or Ecumenical Creeds stand as possessed of the "very highest kind of authority" *(summae auctoritatis)*[1] next only to the Sacred Scriptures. The preeminent Lutheran particular creed, "the common confession of the reformed churches" and "our symbol in this epoch,"[2] is the Augsburg Confession. The remaining documents — including the three by Luther — are supplementary "witnesses" *(Zeugen, veritatis testes)* which antedate the era of the controversies that the Formula was designed to settle and to which no person committed sincerely and unreservedly to the Augsburg Confession would object.[3]

One might even say that in terms of bulk and of direct influence the work of Philip Melanchthon — primary author of the Augsburg Confession and sole author of the Apology and of the Treatise — exceeds that of Luther, particularly if one remembers that three of the most influential authors of the Formula of Concord — Martin Chemnitz, Nicholas Selneccer, and David Chytraeus — were Melanchthon's protégés and reflected many of his basic attitudes, his methodology, and his temperament.

Nevertheless, the measurable impact of Luther on the Book of Concord — measurable, that is, in terms of references to him and appeals to his theological position in quotations and citations — is formidable, even apart from the Smalcald Articles and the Catechisms. The purpose of the present inquiry is to assess this measurable impact by taking up the 16th-century symbolical documents (other than the three by Luther) one by one.

Formally the Augsburg Confession (1530) is a political document, signed by estates of the Holy Roman Empire and submitted by them to the emperor. It is understandable that it nowhere refers to Luther by name.[4]

The references to Luther in the Apology of the Augsburg Confession (1531) reflect the situation. Although the Lutheran estates in September 1530 had submitted what became an early draft of the Apology as their official reply to the so-called Confutation, Melanchthon prepared the final version of the document as his personal defense of the Augsburg Confession and his personal rebuttal of the charges that the Confutation had leveled against the reforming party.

In echoing the charge of heresy that Leo X in his bull *Exsurge Domine* (1520) had raised against Luther,[5] the Apology asserts, the opponents are deliberately and slanderously misrepresenting his position. True, he taught that original sin remains after Baptism. At the same time he had consistently taught that Baptism takes away the guilt of original sin. What remained of original sin in the human being was its "matter," *concupiscentia.* This was good scholastic doctrine. The assertion that the matter of original sin was sinful — and not merely a penalty of sin or an indifferent matter *(adiaphoron)* as Luther's opponents taught — was one that St. Augustine had made before him.[6]

In connection with the discussion of justification Luther comes in for an indirect mention when Melanchthon reminds his readers that *Exsurge Domine* had anathematized a highly necessary article that all Christians hold and believe.[7] This tenet is that we ought not to trust that we are absolved on account of *our* contrition but on account of the words of Christ, "Whatever you bind and so forth."[8]

At the beginning of the Reformation, according to the Apology's article on confession, Luther had received the highest praise of all good men with his teaching that it is the command of God — indeed, the very voice of the Gospel — that we are to believe the absolution that is spoken over us and to entertain as a certain opinion the conviction that God gives us the forgiveness of sins on account of Christ and that through this faith we are truly reconciled to God. This teaching affords a sure and solid comfort for consciences, whereas before the teaching about works had smothered the whole power of absolution, inasmuch as the Schoolmen and monks taught nothing about faith and gratuitous forgiveness.[9]

In speaking of repentance, the Apology declares that all good men, including the theologians, admit that Luther's teaching on this subject had brought clarity and certainty to an area that previously had been marked by confusion and uncertainty.[10]

Luther is again referred to by indirection when the Apology in the same article [11] once more cites *Exsurge Domine* as condemning the teaching that we obtain the forgiveness of sins through faith on account of Christ and not on account of our own good works.[12]

Luther, says the Epilog to Part I of the Apology, was not the first to call publicly acknowledged abuses into question. When he arose, those who sided with him did so because on the one hand he was extricating the minds of men from the labyrinths of scholastic theology and canon law and on the other was setting forth teachings that contributed to genuine piety.[13]

Without explicitly saying so, Melanchthon's discussion of monastic vows seems to see in the rise of Luther the fulfillment of the prophecy of the unfortunate Franciscan, John Hilten, when he warned his fellow monks that in the year of our Lord 1516 another would come whom they would not be able to resist and who would destroy them.[14]

In the final epilog to the Apology, Melanchthon takes cognizance of the charge that when Luther's teaching about Christian liberty was inculcated into the common people, it had stirred them up to fatal and highly perilous sedition. Melanchthon replies with an argument *ad hominem:* If all these scandals that the Lutheran movement had allegedly evoked were rolled into one, the single article of the forgiveness of sins for Christ's sake through faith would bring so much that is advantageous that it would cancel out everything disadvantageous. Originally this gained for Luther the good will not only of those who still support him but even of many who now, alas, are opposed to him.[15]

In addition to these general references to Luther there is one direct citation of a work of his, *De votis monasticis iudicium* (1521).[16] Melanchthon states the issues in a series of eleven questions about the nature of the vows that religious took in the 16th century. He then proposes to summarize the arguments of the reforming party and in the process to refute the quibbles of the opponents. By way of providing a fuller explication of these arguments he observes that Luther had discussed this whole matter of the nature of monastic vows in the cited book. Accordingly Melanchthon desired that the statements of this brochure on the subject be regarded as repeated.[17]

Obviously this appeal does not cast the mantle of the Apology's symbolical authority over every statement that Luther makes in this work, but it invokes Luther's treatise as a fuller statement of the five arguments that Melanchthon produces: (1) It is not a legitimate vow if the person making it supposes that thereby he either earns forgiveness of his sins before God or makes satisfaction for his sins in God's sight; (2) obedience, poverty, and celibacy are, when they are not impure, useful disciplines but not essential ones; (3) monastic vows must not indispensably impose celibacy; (4) the abuses that mark 16th-century monasticism are in themselves grounds for dispensing religious from their vows (Melanchthon cites specifically the application of masses for the sins of the living and the dead, a kind of veneration of the saints that puts them in Christ's place and that exploits the credulity of the layfolk, teaching that the multiplied ceremonies of monastic worship earn the forgiveness of sins for the worshipers and others, and the peril that members of religious communities are forced to agree with the persecutors of evangelical truth); (5) the vows of so many religious are intrinsically not binding because of the misrepresentation and the duress that entered into their making these promises that one could argue for a general dispensation from vows to follow a life so full of hypocrisy and false opinions.[18]

The Treatise on the Authority and Primacy of the Pope (1537) understandably does not refer to Luther. Both its author, Melanchthon, and the Landgrave Philip of Hesse feared the political repercussions within the Smalcald League as well as within the Holy Roman Empire that would follow an effort to commit the league to Luther's almost truculently intransigent Smalcald Articles. Luther's illness at Smalcald conveniently assisted the efforts of the two Philips to divert the theologians present from the Smalcald Articles by involving them in a review of the Augsburg Confession and the Apology and in the preparation of a document that would repair an acknowledged defect of the Augsburg Confession, the lack of a statement on the papacy. Thus the theologian and the landgrave hoped to forestall a discussion that might very possibly have led to a division.[19]

THE FORMULA OF CONCORD IN GENERAL

Three decades lie between Luther's death in 1546 and the Formula of Concord (1577). By the seventies, when the work of unification began to proceed in earnest, time had thrust forward a new generation of Lutheran theological leaders. The protagonists of the "Gnesio-Lutheran" party — Matthias Vlacic (Flacius Illyricus), Nicholas von Amsdorf, Cyriacus Spangenberg, and Christopher Irenaeus among them — were either dead or had all but forfeited their diminishing influence by their heretical exaggerations and their theological excesses. At the other extreme of the continuum the progressive declension of the more radical Wittenberg disciples of Philip Melanchthon from the Lutheran norm was obvious to almost all but the wilfully blind. Indeed, it hardly required the denouement of 1574 to disillusion those who had mistakenly taken the "Philippists'" professions of genuine Lutheranism at face value.

There was widespread weariness with sterile theological bickering and an increasingly earnest desire for reunion. The stage was set for the type of leader that in general the six authors of the Formula of Concord — James Andreae, Chemnitz, Selneccer, Chytraeus, Andrew Musculus, and Christopher Cornerus — represented.

A homogeneous lot these six were not! In fact they diverged so widely in their individual theological views as well as in their personal temperaments that the likelihood that they could restore harmony to divided German Lutheranism seemed very often hopelessly remote. But they were one in their loyalty to the authentic Reformation tradition and in their recognition that harmony could not eventuate either from a one-sided commitment to the Luther image that the Gnesio-Lutherans had zealously fabricated or from a commitment to the Melanchthon that the Philippists had cast in their own likeness. Thus at the fruitless, futile conference of theologians at Zerbst in May 1570 there was agreement that the doctrinal standards on the basis of which theologians could seek for Lutheran reconciliation would have to be the Catholic Creeds, the 1530 edition of the Augsburg Confession, the Apology, the Smalcald Articles, and the Catechisms. The expansion of this canon by the addition of the works of Luther was accompanied by the addition in neat balance of the Melanchthonian *Corpus Misnicum* and Melanchthon's writings and of John Brenz's works.[20]

Pressures came from both sides. The letter that the four landgraves of Hesse, the heirs of Philip the Courageous ("Magnanimous"), none of whom ultimately signed the Formula, sent to Elector August of Saxony in October 1576, objected to the citation of any of Luther's works in the Formula on the ground that "the less one puts into matters of religion and faith the writings of human beings beside and next to the word of God, the better and more certain the word." [21] The theologians of Anhalt, whose orientation was toward the Reformed religion and whose princes also refrained from signing the Preface to the Book of Concord, in 1576 lamented the fact that the

Formula of Concord "forgets the ancient love and faithfulness, which we shall forever owe the dear sainted Philip Melanchthon, and even mounts frequent attacks on his views." [22] At the same time the conference of theologians that met at Lichtenberg in February 1576, apparently responding to pro-Lutheran and anti-Melanchthonian thrusts within its membership, indicated for the record a willingness to have Luther's commentary on Galatians added to the basic canon.[23] But in the next breath its actual recommendation significantly retreated to the Catholic Creeds, the 1530 Augustana, the Apology, the two Catechisms, and the Smalcald Articles (to which by this time the Treatise had attached itself as an anonymous German [!] appendix).

In the same year the chief theologians of the Duchy of Brunswick — Chemnitz among them — who met at Riddagshausen Abbey by command of Duke Julius, pronounced their verdict on the Torgau Book stage of the Book of Concord. They concurred in the rejection of the *Corpus Misnicum* (or *Corpus Philippicum*) as "a norm and rule of faith" both by the Lichtenberg theologians' conference and by a further theologians' conference that the elector subsequently convened at Torgau. But the Brunswick theologians pleaded that the *Corpus Misnicum* be allowed "to be and remain what it is intrinsically, a useful good book which ought to be read for its methodology and for the useful explications of a great many and very good matters that occur in it, and that one cannot in any way discourage from the churches and the schools. For we do not agree with those who would altogether reject and condemn the writings of Dr. Philip [Melanchthon], whether they be those contained in the *Corpus doctrinae* or others." [24]

The very similar proposal of the theologians of the Lower Saxon cities meeting at Brunswick three months later concluded by urging that the writings of Melanchthon might "be explicitly thus set down and called to people's attention either in the preface of this Formula or at the end or somewhere else," although with the qualification that Melanchthon's works are to be tested by the Formula and Luther's writings.[25]

As a result of these and other representations, the princes and municipal authorities that signed the Preface to the Book of Concord declare: "We do not want to have rejected or condemned the other profitable writings of Master Philip Melanchthon or of [John] Brenz, Urban Rhegius, [John Bugenhagen] of Pomerania, and others, inasmuch as they are in agreement with the norm incorporated in the [Book of] Concord." [26] The coordination of Luther's works with the Formula is significantly and pointedly absent.

248

In authorizing Bugenhagen to sign the Smalcald Articles for him in 1537, John Brenz had called Luther *praeceptor noster observandissimus*.[27] In the Formula and its Preface Luther's prestige is even higher. He is sometimes all but canonized as "Doctor Luther, of blessed and holy memory *(seliger und heiliger Gedächtnus, piae sanctaeque memoriae)*." [28] Out of special grace, a benign God restored the truth of His Word in the midst of the horrible darkness of the papacy "through the faithful service of the precious man of God, Dr. Luther."[29]

"In the Spirit this highly enlightened man foresaw" that after his death his traducers would distort his teaching.[30] He is the "foremost teacher of the Augsburg Confession." [31] He is the paradigm of Lutheran theologians: "Neither Dr. Luther nor any other sincere teacher of our pure evangelical church" ever rejected the accidental character of original sin; [32] "Luther and other pure teachers of the Augsburg Confession" interpreted "the bread that we break" of 1 Cor. 10:16 as "the distributed body of Christ" or as "the body of Christ shared in common by those that receive the broken bread." [33] He is hailed as the spiritual ancestor of the epigones.[34] His lifetime is remembered fondly as a kind of golden age when the evangelical churches and schools were well organized and carried on in a Christian fashion and in conformity with the Word of God.[35]

THE FORMULA OF CONCORD: OF THE SUMMARY CONCEPT

The Lutheran particular creeds — or at least the Smalcald Articles and the Catechisms — are cited as the summary and paradigm *(Summa und Fürbild; compendiaria hypotyposis)* of the Biblically based teaching which Luther had set forth extensively in his polemical writings against the papacy and the sects, that is, the Swiss Reformers and the Anabaptists. It proceeds to appeal to these extensive explications in Luther's polemical and doctrinal writings as a commentary on the Lutheran particular creeds in the Book of Concord. It does so, however, with a qualification, which it attributes to Luther himself in the Latin preface that he wrote in 1545 to the first volume of the Wittenberg edition of his collected Latin works. Here he is made to say that the Word of God is to be the only standard and rule *(Richtschnur und Regel; regula et norma)* of all teaching, to which everything is to be subordinated, and on a par with which no human being's writings are to be placed.[36] (The authors of the Formula here betray a lapse of memory. No statement like the one cited occurs in the Preface.)

But we are still far from the standard patterns of Luther adulation that we find in the 17th century.

The section in "Of the Summary Concept" on the function of antitheses in the discussion of controverted doctrines cites a Luther utterance without specifying its source: "Faithful shepherds should do both, pasture or feed the lambs and guard against wolves." [37]

THE FORMULA OF CONCORD: ARTICLE 1

In the discussion of original sin both the Epitome [38] and the Solid Declaration cite Luther. The Solid Declaration observes that Luther called original sin a "nature-sin" or a "person-sin," not to imply that human nature or the human person is identical with original sin thought of as some kind of substance, but in order to indicate the penetration of our innate sinfulness like a spiritual leprosy into every aspect of human nature and of the individual person, so that human beings are "by nature the children of wrath." [39] The point is taken up again in a later paragraph. [40] Luther, the Formula asserts, calls original sin "a spiritual poison and leprosy." [41]

The issue under discussion was the heretical assertion attributed to Vlacic and his supporters that since the fall original sin, which they conceived of as a substance, was identical with the human rational soul. The bulk of the Lutheran theologians of all parties denied both the substantial nature of original sin and its identification with the human rational soul. Both sides appealed to Luther, and at least five books of citations had been published to prove that he took the view of the respective side. [42] Luther, Art. I says, declared that sin and sinning *(Sünde und sündigen; peccatum et peccare)* are the disposition and nature *(Art und Natur)* of man. [43] Then he is quoted as saying: "Your birth, your nature, and your whole being is sin [that is, sinful], and unclean." [44]

By nature-sin, person-sin, essential sin Luther by his own declaration, according to the Solid Declaration, [45] means not only that our human words, thoughts, and works are sin but that original sin has fundamentally corrupted man's entire nature, person, and being in its totality. [46]

Luther's lectures on Genesis 3 [47] are cited as evidence that the description of original sin as an accident in the Aristotelian sense implies no depreciation of the gravity of original sin but merely differentiates between human nature as God's creature and sin as the work of the devil, a work that has deeply infected the creature that God made and makes. [48] Luther's use of the terms "accident" [49] and "quality" [50] is documented with quotations from Luther's *Enarratio Psalmi XC* [51] and his commentary on Genesis 3.[52] The present text [53] is a radical reworking of an earlier draft in response to a number of objections.[54] The original draft had merely observed that Luther did not reject the description of original sin as a "quality," even though the term does not do full justice to the gravity of original sin. When he used the term, he qualified it with an appropriate explanation; his *Enarratio Psalmi XC* is a case in point. The new text begins by asserting that neither Luther nor any sincere teacher of the pure evangelical churches ever condemned the application of "accident" to original sin [55] and proceeds to spell out Luther's and the orthodox Lutheran carefully mediating position in detail.

THE FORMULA OF CONCORD: ARTICLE 2

The original draft of Article 2 [56] quoted from Luther's *Vom Abendmahl Christi, Bekenntnis* (1528).[57] After a tentative reworking of part of the quotation the authors of the Formula lined out the whole passage at that point and resumed it later.[58]

One of the knottiest passages of Luther documentation in the whole Formula occurs when Luther is quoted as having declared in his commentary on Psalm 90 (sic) that in mundane and external matters human beings are intelligent, rational, and active, but in spiritual and divine affairs man is like a pillar of salt, like Lot's wife, like a log or stone, like a lifeless statue, who does not recognize God's wrath over sin until it is too late.[59] The alleged quotation does not occur in the cited form in the *Enarratio Psalmi XC*. It is cited in the Weimar Disputation that engaged Vlacic and Victorine Strigel in August 1560. The most that can be said for the "quotation" is that it is an expanded and adapted paraphrase of a passage in the *Enarratio Psalmi XC*.[60]

The embarrassment of the editors of the Book of Concord at this dubious documentation is reflected in the marginal supplementary note of the 1580 German edition and the 1584 Latin translation: "Dr. Luther on the 6th chapter of Hosea, as well as in the *Kirchenpostille* [in the sermons on] the Epistle for Christmas Day, Titus 3, and on the Gospel of the Third Sunday after the Epiphany." Actually, however, it is far from clear what passages the editors of the Book of Concord may have had in mind in these additional references.[61]

At the end of a quotation from the 1519 work, *Contra malignum Johannis Eccii judicium Martini Lutheri defensio*,[62] Luther's meaning is explained when he speaks of *capacitas libertatis*.[63] This reference was the center of considerable debate. In the archival copy of the

251

Formula that was deposited in the University of Helmstedt the words
non activam sed passivam appear in the margin; there is evidence that
in some copies of the Formula these words appeared in the text after
capacitatem. Andreae's Swabian Concordia has the words, and Chemnitz's Saxon-Swabian Concordia and the Torgau Book phase of the
Formula retain them. Someone struck them from the Torgau Book
copy that was used as the basis of the Bergen Book; they were written
back into the margin, then struck again.[64] Polycarp Leyser, who was
present at Bergen Abbey, states that the words were deleted to comply
with the wish of Elector August that as far as possible the text should
use the vernacular and avoid terminology in Latin. Leyser goes on to
say that the words of the previous sentence,[65] which assert that human
nature becomes capable of receiving everlasting life "not out of its
own, natural, and actual aptitude, competence, or capacity — because
it is a rebellious enmity against God — but of pure grace, through the
gracious and efficacious working of the Holy Spirit," clearly identify
man's capacity as passive and not active. The official Latin translation
of 1584 repeats the controverted words in the text.[66]

Reference has already been made [67] to an extensive quotation [68]
from Luther's personal credo appended as Part Three to his *Vom
Abendmahl Christi, Bekenntnis* (1528), in which he rejects and condemns as utter error any doctrine which lauds the freedom of the
unreborn human will in spiritual matters.[69]

The Formula also invites the attention of all readers [70] to the main
thrust and thesis of Luther's *De servo arbitrio* (1524),[71] the monergism
of divine grace in the conversion of the sinner. With commendable
prudence and in an apparent effort to obviate the misunderstanding
of *De servo arbitrio* as if it affirmed a rigid early Reformed deter-
minism, the Torgau Book phase of the Formula simultaneously directs
the reader to the pertinent passage of Luther's commentary on Genesis 26.[72] Lest anyone miss the point, the final version of the Formula,
at the suggestion of the Brunswick theologians assembled at Riddagshausen Abbey,[73] stresses that in his interpretation of Genesis 26
Luther had made a careful point of explaining it in such a way as to
preclude the misunderstanding and misrepresentation of what Luther
really had meant by certain terms that he used because Erasmus had
introduced them into the debate about the freedom of will, such as
"absolute necessity" and so on.

The Formula also addresses itself to another perversion of Luther's
position,[74] that is, false implications of his assertion that in conversion
man behaves himself in a purely passive fashion.[75] Some read this

formula as implying that in the process of conversion the Holy Spirit does not create any new spiritual movements or initiate any spiritual effects, or that the human being in question merely suffers something to happen to him as if he were a statue hewn in stone or a piece of wax upon which a seal is imprinted without the wax feeling or willing anything.[76] On the contrary, it is only designed to affirm that an unreborn human being contributes nothing to his conversion and that his conversion is not only partially but wholly the work and gift of the Holy Spirit operating through the divine Word.

THE FORMULA OF CONCORD: ARTICLES 3—6

The Solid Declaration also quotes a sentence [77] from Luther's *Der 117. Psalm ausgelegt* (1530), which links the purity of the teaching about justification with the unity of the church and its freedom from schisms.[78]

It proposes to illustrate both from Luther's *Von den Konziliis und Kirchen* (1539) and from his other writings the Reformer's use of *vivificatio* [79] as a synonym for the sanctification that follows justification through faith.[80]

The same article brings a quotation,[81] abbreviated at some points, expanded at others, from Luther's commentary on Galatians (1535) in which he insists that there is a proper and necessary place for teaching about good works, but that if the question at issue is how a sinner becomes righteous before God and is saved, we must rigidly insist that justification is only and exclusively through faith.[82]

In similar fashion it quotes Luther again [83] to illustrate that for him faith and works belong together beautifully, but that it is faith alone that lays hold of the blessing, even though it is at no time alone.[84]

The article closes by pointing the reader to Luther's commentary on Galatians [85] for a fuller exposition of the teaching on justification before God.[86] A somewhat pedestrian statement in the Torgau Book [87] to the effect that a living and saving faith is always preceded by repentance and followed by love,[88] is replaced with Luther's well-known description of faith in his Preface to Romans [89] as a divine work in us that transforms us and begets us anew out of God, slays the old Adam, makes us completely different people as far as our heart, our spirit, our mind, and all our powers are concerned, and brings the Holy Spirit with it.[90]

The theses that good works are necessary for salvation and that it is impossible to be saved without good works, it is noted,[91] were

253

rejected by Luther in the case of the false prophets among the Galatians.[92] In the case of the followers of the pope, Luther rejected these theses in a great many places in his writings.[93] He also did so in the case of the Anabaptists when they explained that one should not base one's faith on meritorious works, but that one still needs them as things necessary for salvation.[94] Fourth, in his commentary on Genesis 22 he rejected these theses in the case of certain of his own followers, who wanted these theses understood in this way: Although we require works as necessary for salvation, we do not teach that one should put his trust in such works.[95]

The authors of the Formula also quote [96] (with minor variations) one of Luther's classic descriptions of the Law (as he uses the term in the Law-Gospel polarity), a passage in a sermon on the Gospel for the Fifth Sunday after Trinity first preached in 1528 and incorporated in Cruciger's *Sommerpostille* of 1544.[97] They follow this up immediately [98] with another statement of Luther on the Holy Spirit's action in convincing the world of sin through the explication of the Law, taken from *Ein Sendbrief Herrn Wolfen von Salhausen an Doctor Martinus und Antwort Martini Luthers* (1524).[99] They also cite [100] a statement of Luther directed against the Antinomians: "Everything that rebukes sin is and belongs to the Law, the proper function of which is to condemn sin and to lead to a knowledge of sin." [101]

The opinion of the Brandenburg theologians urged that for a better explanation of the difference between the Law and the Gospel a section of Luther's *Auslegung des ersten und zweiten Kapitels Johannis* (1537–1538) [102] should be included.[103] Luther is cited as stressing in almost all his writings that the knowledge of God that comes from the Gospel is far different from the natural knowledge of God that comes through Law.[104]

In another instance [105] the editors cite Luther's sermon on the Epistle (the Latin translation tacitly corrects it to Gospel) for the Nineteenth Sunday after Trinity on the punishments consequent upon sin, of which God's children have need because of the sinful desires that still inhere in their flesh.[106]

THE FORMULA OF CONCORD: ARTICLES 7 AND 8

The Luther references in Articles 7 and 8 are relatively numerous. This is understandable. These articles intended to resolve the intra-Lutheran debate between "normal" Lutheran theology and that of the "Crypto-Calvinist" party on the Sacrament of the Altar and on the soteriologically important issue of the person of Christ.

They appeal [107] to the Wittenberg Concord of 1536.[108] The document is misnamed; it is not a "concord" between the Lutherans and the Strasbourg theologians but a memorandum for record drafted by the Lutherans — Luther's is the first signature, and so the document becomes relevant for this inquiry — and signed by both the Lutherans and the Strasbourg theologians. In it the Lutherans set forth their understanding of the position that the Strasbourg theologians take on the matters at issue, and the Strasbourg theologians sign it as evidence that the Lutherans have correctly apprehended the Strasbourg position.[109] The agreement was short-lived; the Strasbourg party soon receded from the concessions they had made in the hope of achieving intercommunion with the Lutherans.

Article 7 notes [110] of Luther's prescient conviction that his traducers would make an effort after his death to distort and water down his fervent belief that in the Sacrament of the Altar the consecrated bread is the body of Christ and the consecrated wine His blood, eaten and drunk with the mouth of the body by believing and unbelieving communicants alike. They quote at length from two pertinent portions of his personal credo that makes up the brief third part of his *Vom Abendmahl Christi, Bekenntnis* (1528).[111]

They credit Luther with a preeminent knowledge of the real and authentic meaning of the Augsburg Confession on this point.[112] As evidence that he did not change his mind shortly before his death [113] they quote Luther's comprehensive condemnation in his Little Confession of 1544 of all those who will not believe that "the Lord's bread in the Communion is His true, natural body, which the godless person or Judas received orally no less than St. Peter and all holy persons." [114]

The editors also cite the Wittenberg Concord [115] to document the term "sacramental union" for the designation of the specific Lutheran position on the coexistent relation of the heavenly and mundane elements in the Sacrament of the Altar as a sacramental analogy to the hypostatic union of the Godhead and the humanity of our Lord in His incarnation.[116]

They appeal [117] to Luther's *Vom Abendmahl Christi, Bekenntnis* (1528) [118] and the Little Confession (1544) [119] as evidence of determination to talk about the Sacrament of the Altar as the words of institution do.[120] They declare that Luther is "rightly to be regarded as the most eminent teacher of the churches which adhere to the Augsburg Confession and as the person whose entire doctrine in sum and content was comprehended in the articles" of the version presented to the Holy Roman Emperor in 1530. For that reason, it argues, "the true meaning and intention of the Augsburg Confession cannot be derived more correctly or better from any other source than from Dr. Luther's doctrinal and polemical writings." [121]

They quote Luther's *Von der Winkelmesse und Pfaffenweihe* (1533) [122] and *Vom Abendmahl Christi, Bekenntnis* (1528) [123] in support of the position that our Lord's words of institution, spoken by the celebrant, to whose speaking and action Christ has bound Himself, make *(machet, efficiunt)* the bread in the sacrament of the altar to be Christ's body and the wine to be His blood.[124]

They cite Luther's own explanation of the principle *(Regel und Richtschnur)* that Melanchthon had devised in the late 1530s: "Nothing has the character *(rationem)* of a sacrament outside the use that Christ instituted," [125] but give an incorrect reference.[126]

They set up a canon of Luther's eucharistic writings [127] which confound the "sacramentarian" rejection of the sacramental union on the basis of the properties of a human body and of the effect of Christ's ascension and His alleged absence from the world: *Wider die himmlischen Propheten* (1525); [128] *Dass diese Worte, Das ist mein Leib usw., noch fest stehen wider die Schwarmgeister* (1527); [129] *Vom Abendmahl Christi, Bekenntnis* (1528); [130] and the *Kurzes Bekenntnis vom Sakrament* (1544).[131]

They quote [132] the theological reflections with which Luther supported his realistic interpretation of the words of institution, that Jesus Christ is God and man in a single indivisible and inseparable person; that "the right hand of God" is everywhere; that a word of God is not false nor deceitful; and that God has a variety of ways of being present at a place in addition to the one that metaphysicians call local. Thus our Lord's body can be present at a place in at least three different modes: (1) the tangible and bodily mode; (2) the intangible and spiritual mode; and (3) the divine and heavenly mode.[133] Christ's birth (it is held), His resurrection and His resurrection appearances, and His presence in the bread and wine of the Sacrament of the Altar are according to the second mode.[134]

They also explain [135] the meaning that Luther and the Lutherans attach to the word "spiritually." [136] Somewhat inconsistently and confusedly it relates the vocable to both the second and third modes of the presence of Christ's body: "We have in mind the spiritual, supernatural, heavenly mode according to which Christ is present in the Holy Communion, not only to work comfort and life in believers but also to wreak judgment on unbelievers. . . . In this sense too we use the word 'spiritually' when we say that the body and blood of Christ in the Holy Communion are received, eaten, and drunk spiritually, for although such eating occurs with the mouth, the mode is spiritual." [137]

The Formula and the Preface to the Book of Concord stress that Luther and his associates reluctantly entered into the second, Christological phase of the debate with the "Sacramentarians" that had begun with the Lutheran defense of a realistic interpretation of the words of institution of the Sacrament of the Altar.[138]

The Epitome cites the principle that Luther derives from the Creed in the Catechism that Christ imparts to the communicants His authentic body and blood, present in the Sacrament of the Altar, according to the mode and property not of His human nature but of His divine nature.[139] It rejects the Nestorian solution of the mystery of the hypostatic union of the two natures in Christ [140] as Luther described it in *Von den Konziliis und Kirchen* (1539).[141]

The Solid Declaration commits the signers of the Formula in the article of the person of Christ [142] to Luther's polemical works on the Sacrament of the Altar as well as to his doctrinal works, without specifying titles.[143] The same article [144] quotes Luther in *Vom Abendmahl Christi, Bekenntnis* (1528) as asserting that we combine the two distinct natures of Christ in a single person: "Wir mengen die zwo unterschiedliche natur in ein einige person." [145] It quotes [146] the same work [147] against Zwingli's interpretation of the Biblical evidence in terms of an *alloeosis*.[148] Furthermore, it cites [149] Luther's *Von den letzten Worten Davids* (1543) for the thesis that our Lord during the state of His "humiliation" normally concealed the divine majesty that had been communicated to His humanity at the moment of His conception and also reproduces [150] the passage in context.[151] It endorses [152] Luther's position that Christ's human nature is present upon earth after the Ascension not in a mundane fashion but according to the mode of God's right hand, which is nothing else than the almighty power of God that fills heaven and earth.[153]

Once more it quotes [154] extensively from *Vom Abendmahl Christi, Bekenntnis* (1528) against Zwingli's *alloeosis*.[155] In condemning the idea that statements like "God died, God's suffering, God's blood, God's death" are mere figures of speech (*praedicatio verbalis*),[156] it quotes Luther's *Von den Konziliis und Kirchen* (1539).[157] In the same way it quotes [158] from *Vom Abendmahl Christi, Bekenntnis* (1528) [159] and from *Von den letzten Worten Davids* (1543)[160] on behalf of the indivisible unity of the Godhead and the humanity in the person of Christ. It notes [161] that this is the constant tenor of Luther's writings, and it cites and commits the signers of the Formula specifically to the

257

statements of *Dass diese Worte, Das ist mein Leib usw., noch fest stehen* (1527) [162] and *Vom Abendmahl Christi, Bekenntnis* (1528) [163] on this point.

THE FORMULA OF CONCORD: ARTICLES 9—11

The article on the descent of Christ into the netherworld entered the Formula only in the Torgau Book phase. Andreae's Epitome differs somewhat in its formulation and emphases from the Solid Declaration. Both describe as a paradigmatic discussion of the question a portion of a sermon delivered by Luther in the chapel of the electoral residence at Torgau.[164] Although the Formula gives 1533 as the date, the evidence is overwhelmingly persuasive that Luther actually preached it in February 1532 during the elector's grave illness. The sermon is interesting for its approval of the medieval pictorial and dramatic representations of the harrowing of hell; for its stipulation that the descent took place while our Lord still lay in the grave; for its repeated insistence that the descent did not take place bodily ("es ist freilich nicht leiblich noch greiflich zugangen"); for the Biblical passages that it cites (Ps. 16:10; Matt. 16:18b, but not 1 Peter 3:18-20!); for its insight that in the Sacred Scriptures the words translated with "soul" do not describe a being separated from a body, but the total person; for its stress on the necessity of the resurrection for our salvation; and for its assertion that a Christian need not fear the flames of hell because Christ has put them out, so that when the Christian goes there he will not suffer the pains of hell, just as through Christ he does not taste death, but penetrates through death and hell to everlasting life.

The tenth article, on indifferent ceremonies, was another sticky intra-Lutheran issue. In it is cited [165] Luther's *Bericht an einen guten Freund von beider Gestalt des Sakraments aufs Bischofs zu Meissen Mandat* (1528) [166] and his reminders to "the church of God" contained in Volume V of the Jena Edition of his works.[167]

In the article on God's eternal prescience and choice Luther's counsel in the Preface to Romans [168] is quoted [169] to follow the order of St. Paul in this letter by beginning with the Gospel and the war against sin in chapters 1 through 8, and then amid temptations and suffering to learn from chapters 9 through 11 how comforting the divine prescience is.

SUMMARY

By way of summary: The astonishing thing is not how frequently the Lutheran symbolical books quote Luther's nonsymbolical works but how infrequently (speaking relatively) they do so, not how often they appeal to his great magisterial authority but how rarely. Of interest too are the works that they cite most often — his commentaries on Genesis, Galatians, and Psalm 90; his four polemic-didactic treatises on the Sacrament of the Altar (especially *Vom Abendmahl Christi, Bekenntnis*); *Von den Konziliis und Kirchen;* plus appeals to *De votis monasticis iudicium, De servo arbitrio,* and certain sermons. The documents that the church historians acclaim — the writings of 1520, for instance, *De captivitate Babylonica ecclesiae preludium,* the *Tractatus de libertate Christiana,* and *An den christlichen Adel deutscher Nation* — are not so much as alluded to. There is no one-for-one equation of Luther's teaching and the divine self-disclosure.[170] Luther emerges in the Lutheran symbolical books as one to whom the universal church might well listen as a doctor, but primarily as one of God's great gifts to that part of the one, holy, catholic, and apostolic church that adheres to the Augsburg Confession. By 1577 and 1580 some of the apocalyptic certainty that had characterized Luther's own approach had evaporated, but the ambient atmosphere in which even the last generation of authors of the Lutheran symbolical books lived was still charged with eschatological expectation. Accordingly they probably did not think too much in terms of the centuries to come as they wrote. But they knew where they stood in their own time — with Luther in the catholic tradition under the Word of God — and with that knowledge they were content.

NOTES

1. Formula of Concord, Solid Declaration, Summary Concept, 4 Latin, in Hans Lietzmann, ed., *Die Bekenntnisschriften der evangelisch-lutherischen Kirche herausgegeben im Gedenkjahr der Augsburgischen Konfession 1930,* 5th ed., by Ernst Wolf (Göttingen: Vandenhoeck & Ruprecht, 1963—64). Hereafter cited as *Bekenntnisschriften.* FC SD is the abbreviation used for the Formula of Concord, Solid Declaration.
2. FC SD Summary Concept, 5.
3. FC SD Summary Concept, 12, Ernst Walter Zeeden, *Martin Luther und die Reformation im Urteil des deutschen Luthertums: Studien zum Selbstverständnis des lutherischen Protestantismus von Luthers Tode bis zum Beginn der Goethezeit,* (Freiburg: Verlag Herder, 1950), I, 67, gives a misleading impression of the scope and contents of the Book of Concord when he makes no specific mention of the Apology of the Augsburg Confession, the Treatise on the Authority and Primacy of the Pope, the Formula of Concord, and the Preface to the Book of Concord, and says that the Book of Concord "raised, among other items, the two Catechisms of Luther, his Smalcald Articles and the Augsburg Confession, along with the three ancient Christian creeds (the

Apostolicum, the Nicaenum, and the Athanasianum) to the level of the official evangelical confession, with dogmatic validity."

4. Three of Melanchthon's drafts of prefaces to the Augsburg Confession have survived. They are reproduced in *Bekenntnisschriften*, pp. 35—43. The first and longest has no reference to Luther. In the second — a mere fragment — Luther's name appears four times. The third draft — still under active consideration as late as 31 May 1530 — has six references to Luther by name. Both the second and the third draft describe Luther's reluctant involvement in the work of reformation and argue that the explosion would have come without him. The third preface draft exculpates Luther from the charge that his doctrine was responsible for the ultraism of the revolutionary reforming movements. But the preface that the Lutheran estates finally ordered prefixed to the Augsburg Confession and that thus became part of the Book of Concord version makes no reference to the Wittenberg Reformer. On Luther's direct and indirect contribution to the Augsburg Confession see Johann Meyer, "Luthers Anteil an der Augsburgischen Konfession," in *Allgemeine evangelisch-lutherische Kirchenzeitung*, 1930, Nos. 19—21. Fuller and still the best treatment, although it needs some correction in the light of more recent research, is Wilhelm Ernst Nagel, *Luthers Anteil an der Confessio Augustana: Eine historische Untersuchung* (Gütersloh: C. Bertelsmann, 1930); the bibliography is very useful.

5. Reproduced in Henricus Denzinger, *Enchiridion symbolorum, definitionum et declarationum de rebus fidei et morum*, 32d ed. by Adolphus Schönmetzer (Barcelona: Herder, 1963; hereafter cited as Denzinger-Schönmetzer), No. 1452: "In puero post baptismum negare remanet peccatum, est Paulum et Christum simul conculcare" (second of the *errores Martini Lutheri*).

6. Ap[ology] 2, 35-45. The final form of the Apology develops an idea that the original draft had set forth already in 1530 as part of the defense of the authentic catholicity of the Lutheran doctrine of original sin. *Bekenntnisschriften*, p. 148, 32-48.

7. Ap 4, 397.

8. Denzinger-Schönmetzer, No. 1461: "Nullo modo confidas absolvi propter tuam contritionem, sed propter verbum Christi: 'Quodcumque solveris etc.' Hinc, inquam, confide, si sacerdotis obtinueris absolutionem et crede fortiter te absolutum, et absolutus vere eris, quidquid sit de contritione" (11th of the *errores Martini Lutheri*).

9. Ap 11, 2.

10. Ap 12, 4.

11. Ap 12, 67.

12. Denzinger-Schönmetzer, No. 1465: "Magnus est error eorum, qui ad sacramenta Eucharistiae accedunt huic innixi, quod sint confessi, quod non sint sibi conscii alicuius peccati mortalis, quod praemiserint orationes suas et praeparatoria: omnes illi iudicium sibi manducant et bibunt. Sed si credant et confidant, se gratiam ibi consecuturos, haec sola fides facit eos puros et dignos" (15th of the *errores Martini Lutheri*).

13. Ap 21, 41.

14. Ap. 27, 3.

15. Ap 28, 22-24.

16. WA VIII, 573-669. A modern evaluation of this treatise, with a good bibliography, is that of René H. Esnault, *Luther et le monachisme aujourd'hui:*

Lecture actuelle du "De votis monasticis judicium" (Geneva: Labor et Fides, 1964).

17. Ap 27, 9-10.
18. Ap 27, 11-57.
19. Nevertheless, John Bugenhagen saw to the general circulation of the Smalcald Articles among the theologians. At a meeting on 24 Feb. 1537 the theologians were invited to subscribe the articles unofficially as an expression of personal conviction; five refused and the signature of a sixth, Denys Melander, is in actuality a defiant commitment to "the [Augsburg] Confession, the Apology and the [1536 Wittenberg] Concord on the subject of the Eucharist" rather than to the Smalcald Articles, *Bekenntnisschriften,* p. 466, 5-6.
20. Ibid., p. xxxiv.
21. Quoted ibid., p. 837, n. 1. See also pp. 1221-22.
22. Quoted in Franz Hermann Reinhold Frank, *Die Theologie der Concordienformel* (Erlangen: Theodor Blaesing, 1858), I, 45, n. 55.
23. "So auch iemand von wegen der Lehre von der Gerechtfertigung des Menschen für Gott wil die herrliche tröstliche *explicationem epistolae Pauli ad Galatas à D. Luthero, sanctae memoriae, editam,* darzu thun, sind wir mit demselben gantz und gar gleichstimmig. Denn wir keines wegs gemeinet, die *proposition* von Nothwendigkeit guter Werck zur Seligkeit zu *defendirn.*" "Bedencken der zu Liechtenberg versamleten Theologen," quoted in Leonhartus Hutterus, *Concordia concors: De origine et progressu Formulae Concordiae ecclesiarum Confessionis Augustanae liber unus, editio novissima* (Frankfurt and Leipzig: Johannes Christophorus Föllginer, 1690), p. 282. See likewise FC SD 3, 67.
24. Hutterus, p. 407.
25. *Bekenntnisschriften,* p. 752, n. 3.
26. Ibid., p. 752, 19-24.
27. Ibid., p. 466, n. 3.
28. FC SD Pref 1; 2, 44. FC SD 8, 80 has the simple *Lutherus seliger* in the German, comparable to a contemporary reference to a departed Christian as "the sainted." The Latin at this point reads *sanctae memoriae,* "of holy memory."
29. FC SD Summary Concept, 5.
30. FC SD 7, 28. Compare FC SD 2, 45: "dieses fürtrefflichen, hocherleuchteten Theologen Schriften." See also the Preface to the Book of Concord, *Bekenntnisschriften,* p. 742, 16-18; 761, 9-12.
31. FC SD 7, 34, 41.
32. FC SD 1, 56.
33. FC SD 7, 58.
34. FC SD 7, 58: "unsere liebe Väter und Vorfahren, als Lutherus und andere reine Lehrer Augsburgischer Confession."
35. Preface to the Book of Concord, *Bekenntnisschriften,* p. 743, 25-26. The reference to Luther's "Christian death," ibid., p. 742, 16-17, may be a polemic rejection of the lurid account of his suicidal end that the opponents of the Lutheran movement were diligently propagating.
36. FC SD Summary Concept, 9. The Latin preface referred to is printed in WA LIV, 179-87.
37. FC SD Summary Concept, 14. The Lübeck-Hamburg-Lüneburg theological

opinion points out that "the dictum of Luther has been corrupted by a copyist's error; it should read: 'die Schäflein nähren und den Wolf wehren.'" See the sermon on the Gospel for Misericordias Domini (1522) in Roth's *Sommerpostille* 1526: "Es ist nicht gnug, das man recht predige, welchs die miedling auch thun künnen, sonder bey den scheflyn wachen, das nicht wolffe, falsche lerer, einreyssen und für die scheflin wider die wölffe mit dem wort Gottes fechten und das leben darüber lassen," WA X/1², 243, 22-25; *Bekenntnisschriften*, p. 839, n. 4; p. 1222.

38. The Luther quotations, citations, and references in the Epitome of the Formula of Concord, drafted by James Andreae on the basis of the Torgau Book phase of the Formula of Concord in 1576 and revised on the basis of the Bergen Book in 1577, will be discussed under the corresponding passages of the Solid Declaration.

39. FC SD 1, 6. *Bekenntnisschriften*, p. 846, cites a number of illustrative passages: In *Das XVI. Kapitel S. Johannis* (1539) we have "der stam und die wurtzel aller ander sunde," WA XLVI, 39, 28; "stam, wurtzel und quell des bösen," 40, 2; and "die sunde, welche inwendig in der Natur steckt und die rechte Heubt sunde ist," 40, 10-11. In Luther's *An die Pfarrherrn wider den Wucher zu predigen* (1540) there is a reference to "die Erbsünde, die quelle aller sünden," WA LI, 354, 20-21. The references to the Erlangen Edition in the *Bekenntnisschriften* are apparently to the second Erlangen Edition (1862-85), which was not accessible to the present writer.

40. FC SD 1, 33.

41. The passages cited in *Bekenntnisschriften*, p. 854, require some revision. In WA XXXVI, 682, 19 (from a sermon that Luther preached in 1532 on 1 Cor. 15:54-55), the word "Gifft" has a different bearing; WA XXXVI, 682, 21-26, 29, 37, and 683, 16, 18, 22, 26, 27 might be cited instead. In his lectures on Genesis (1535-45) passages like this occur: "Haec sic in carnem nostram sunt implantata, hoc venenum sic late per carnem, corpus, animam, nervos, sanguinem, per ossa et medullas ipsas in voluntate, in intellectu, in ratione diffusum est, ut non solum eximi plene non possit, sed ne quidem agnoscatur peccatum esse," WA XLII, 125, 1-5; "sic haeret in nobis malum originis contractum in paradyso, fermentum illud Diaboli," WA XLIV, 472, 30-31; "ut igitur medeatur Joseph tantis malis non temporalibus sed infernali et originali veneno utitur purgatione vehementiore per periculum et timorem mortis ac inferni," WA XLIV, 489, 18-20; "memorabilis descriptio est horribilis istius mali seu peccati, quod est profundum venenum in anima et corpore," WA XLIV, 506, 13-15. This writer would add as documentation for "leprosy," WA XLII, 126, 3-4: "Ita post peccatum lepra libidinis hanc corporis partem invasit."

42. Cyriak Spangenberg, *Warhafftige, gewisse, bestendige, der H. Schrifft gemesse und in Gottes Wort gegründete Lere von der Erbsünde Dr. M. Luthers, daraus klar zu sehen, dass dieselbige nicht sey ein Accidens* (Eisleben, 1572); Christophorus Irenaeus, *Erklerung aus D. Luthers Schrifften, was für ein Unterscheid sey zwischen Gottes und des Teuffels Werk im Menschen* (1573); Matthias Flacius, *Etliche klare und treffliche Zeugnusse M. Luthers von dem bösen Wesen, essentia, Bild, Form oder Gestalt des irdischen toten Adams und von der wesentlichen Verwandlung des Menschen* (1574); Tilemann Hesshusius, *Klare und helle Zeugnissen Doctoris Martini Lutheri, das die Erbsünde nicht sey das Wesen des Menschen* (Jena, 1572); Johan Hugo, *Gründtlicher und klarer Bericht von der Erbsünde . . . aus . . . D. Luthers Schrifften gezogen* (Eisleben, 1573); *Bekenntnisschriften*, p. 844, n. 1; p. 854, n. 1; p. 1222.

43. FC SD 1, 51.

44. This is documented in Luther's sermon on New Year's Day, 1523: "Dein geburt, dein natur und gantzes wesen ist sünd," WA XII, 403, 9. The parallels from the *Enarratio Psalmi LI* (1532/38) cited in *Bekenntnisschriften*, p. 860, are less explicit: "Quin tu sic defini secundum hunc Psalmum, Peccatum esse hoc totum, quod est natum ex patre et matre, antequam homo possit per aetatem aliquid dicere, facere aut cogitare," WA XL, 2, 322, 20-23; "Peccatum nostrum est, quod in peccatis nati sumus et concepti," 325, 32; "Ideo adulterium, ideo caedem commisi, quia sum peccator natus, imo conceptus et formatus in utero," 380, 31-33. The archival copy of the Formula formerly in the University of Helmstedt and now at Wolfenbüttel cites two references. (1) *Ein Sermon von dem Sakrament der Taufe* (1519): "Dan die sund horet nit gantz auff, die weyl disser leyb lebt, der sso gantz yn sunden empfangen ist, das sund seyn natur ist," WA II, 728, 23-24. (2) The 1525 reworking of *Die sieben Busspsalmen:* "Sihe, so war ists, das ich fur dir ein sunder bin, das auch sunde mein natur, mein anhebendes wesen, mein empfengnis ist," WA XVIII, 501, 31-32.

45. FC SD 1, 53.

46. The reference to WA X/1[1], 508, 2 ff., in *Bekenntnisschriften*, p. 861, is an error for 20-21, where Luther refers to "die erbsund, odder natursund, odder personsund, die rechte hewbtsund" in a sermon on the Gospel for New Year's Day contained in the 1522 *Kirchenpostille*. The *Enarratio Psalmi LI* (1532/38) has these passages: "Theologus . . . disputat de homine PECCATORE. Haec hominis substantia est in Theologia et hoc a Theologo agitur, ut hanc suam naturam peccatis corruptam homo sentiat," WA XL/2, 327, 20-22; "Manet voluntas in diabolo, manet in haereticis, hoc fateor esse naturale, Sed ea voluntas non est bona neque intellectus rectus aut illuminatus manet. Ergo si vere volumus de Naturalibus loqui secundum hunc Psalmum et secundum Spiritus Sancti modum, tunc vocemus Naturalia hoc ipsum, quod in peccatis et morte sumus, quod corrupta et mala volumus, intelligimus et expetimus," WA XL/2, 385, 15-20.

47. The section of Ch. 3 which applies is in WA XLII, 122, 20—127, 5. The authors of the Formula appear to have no specific passage in mind.

48. FC SD 1, 61.

49. The opinion of the Brunswick theologians on the Formula at this point observed that Luther wrote a highly commendatory preface to a work of Urban Rhegius against the Münster Anabaptists in which the latter declares: "Sin is an accidental thing, indeed a damnable defect of human nature, but it does not belong to the substance of human nature," Hutterus, p. 404.

50. FC SD 1, 62.

51. WA XL/3, 571, 18-20.

52. WA XLII, 122, 38-39. The second reference had originally been included in the preceding paragraph. *Bekenntnisschriften*, p. 865, first apparatus to line 11.

53. FC SD 1, 56-62.

54. *Bekenntnisschriften*, p. 863, first apparatus on line 9.

55. FC SD 1, 56.

56. FC SD 2, 11.

57. WA XXVI, 502, 35-503, 24. *Bekenntnisschriften*, p. 876, first apparatus on line 3.

58. FC SD 2, 43.

59. FC SD 2, 20.

60. *Enarratio Psalmi XC* (1534-35/1541), on v. 11: "Philosophi hominem definiunt esse animal rationale. Sed hoc quis dicet in Theologia esse verum? Ibi enim vere homo est 'statua salis,' Sicut uxor Lot, Quia illam magnam iram Dei non intelligit et ruit imprudens in mille pericula mortis, Imo saepe volens et sciens. Hanc calamitatem nostram Moses hic nobis ob oculos ponit, quod simus coram Deo accusati et damnati, ut aperiamus oculos et credentes hoc exuamus securitatem et oremus pro liberatione, siquidem sic oppressi sumus morte aeterna et peccatis et tamen id non sentimus, nisi admoneamur, admoniti autem non credamus. Nam cum temporalia illa de calamitatibus huius vitae non intelligamus nec credamus, Quanto credemus minus spiritualia de aeterna morte et aeterna vita?" WA XL/3, 566, 25—567, 20.

61. The reference to the Hosea commentary may hinge on the connection between *dolavi* ("I have hewn with an axe," with a rough log as the implied object) in the Vulgate of v. 5 and the *Klotz* of the citation. *Praelectiones in prophetas minores* (1524 ff.): "Dolavi, gehobelt, per prophetas, q. d. hoc quod egi per prophetas, huc pertinet ut iudicarem vos occisos et dolandos, ut redigam vos in formam, ut doceam vos esse peccatores et faciam resipiscere sed nihil effectum est," WA XIII, 28, 18-21. In the sermon on the Epistle for Christmas Day in 1522 *Weihnachtspostille* we have a possible point of contact in "gleych alss wenn gott auss eynem dorren bloch eyn newen grunenden baum mechte," WA X/1¹, 114, 19-20, and "Darumb wirk hynn, wirck her, den menschen tzuvor newen unnd die person endernn, ist nit muglich, denn durch das badt der widdergepurt, des heyligen geistis," WA X/1¹, 116, 13-18. Purely illustrative, since it has survived only in *Nachschriften*, is a sermon of 1544, cited in *Bekenntnisschriften*, p. 879, with Rörer's notes reading at one point: "Econtra die holtzböck, Münch, Nonnen, qui putarunt se von leuten thun," WA XLIX, 639, 14-15, and Stoltz's notes reading: "Widerumb die Nunnen, holtz, stein, Monchen, die meineten das gottlich leben sey sich der leut entschlahen," ibid., 34-35. In connection with the sermon on the Gospel for the Third Sunday after Epiphany the following come into consideration: (a) In the *Fastenpostille* of 1525, WA XVII/2, 72-88; (b) in the *Winterpostille* of 1528, WA XXI, 74-83; (c) in the *Hauspostille* of 1544, WA LII, 116-22. None have a high degree of specific relevance to the citation.

62. WA II, 647, 28-31. Andreae erroneously attributed this passage to Luther's *De servo arbitrio* at the Quedlinburg Assembly of 1583, Hutterus, p. 1057. He may have had in mind Luther's words in *De servo arbitrio:* "At si vim liberi arbitrii eam diceremus, qua homo aptus est rapi spiritu et imbui gratia Dei, ut qui sit creatus ad vitam vel mortem aeternam, recte diceretur; hanc enim vim, hoc est, aptitudinem, seu ut Sophistae loquuntur dispositivam qualitatem et passivam aptitudinem et nos confitemur, quam non arboribus neque bestiis inditam esse, quis est qui nesciat? neque enim pro anseribus (ut dicitur) coelum creavit," WA XVIII, 636, 16-22.

63. FC SD 2, 22.

64. *Bekenntnisschriften*, pp. 880-81, n. 2, suggests that Andreae was responsible, although at Quedlinburg in 1583 he asserted that "with a good conscience as in the sight of God he did not know how the words were expunged and could only assume that it had happened by mistake in the preparation of the copies," Hutterus, p. 1056.

65. They were already in the Saxon-Swabian Concordia.

66. *Bekenntnisschriften*, pp. 880-81, n. 2.

67. See p. 251 and notes 57 and 58.

68. FC SD 2, 43.

69. WA XXVI, 502, 35—503, 24.

70. FC SD 2, 44.

71. WA XVIII, 600-787.

72. WA XLIII, 457, 32—463, 17.

73. Hutterus, p. 404.

74. FC SD 2, 89.

75. The Formula cites no passages. It may have in mind a statement in *Resolutiones Lutherianae super propositionibus suis Lipsiae disputatis* (1519):
"Ex his etiam infertur liberum arbitrium esse mere passivum in omni actu
suo, qui velle vocatur," WA II, 421, 7-8. Another possibility is *De servo
arbitrio* (1524): "Hic homo mere passive (ut dicitur) sese habet, nec fuit
quippiam, sed fit totus," WA XVIII, 697, 28.

76. Chemnitz' words in par. 8, Locus VII *de libero arbitrio*, Part One of his
Examen Concilii Tridentini, ed. Ed. Preuss (Berlin: Gustavus Schlawitz,
1861), p. 144, are apposite: "Exagitant etiam illud quod Lutherus dicit,
hominem ad regenerationem, renovationem, seu conversionem habere se mere
passive. Et sane hac phrasi offendi posset aliquis, qui non est assuetus modis
loquendi, qui Scholasticis Scriptoribus usitati sunt, quasi sensus sit, Spiritum
Sanctum ita operari conversionem, ut in voluntate quae renovari coepit, nulli
omnino sequantur novi motus, sed plane sit otiosa et iners, et tantum bruta
agitatione percellatur et protrudatur. Quod Luthero nunquam in mentem
venit."

77. FC SD 3, 6.

78. WA XXXI/1, 255, 5-7, 9-10.

79. Not *regeneratio*, as the Latin translation would have it, FC SD 3, 21.

80. WA L, 599, 26-27: "Sie predigen nichts de sanctificatione & vivificatione
Spiritus sancti, von der heiligung des Heiligen Geists." WA L, 625, 25-26:
"per vivificationem et sanctificationem, durch teglich ausfegen der sunden
und erneuerung des lebens," WA L, 626, 32-34: "Der Heilige geist . . . heisst
darumb Sanctificator oder vivificator." WA L, 627, 10-11, referred to in
Bekenntnisschriften, is less applicable: "Der heilige Geist, der heiliget und
erwecket auch den Leib zu solchem neuen leben."

81. FC SD 3, 28-29.

82. WA XL/1, 240, 17-26.

83. FC SD 3, 41.

84. *Lectures on Galatians* (1531/35): "Quare fides perpetuo iustificat et vivificat
et tamen non manet sola, id est, otiosa. Non quod non sola in suo gradu et
officio maneat, quia perpetuo sola iustificat, sed incarnatur et fit homo, hoc
est, non est et manet otiosa vel sine charitate," WA XL/1, 427, 11-14. *Lectures on Genesis* (1535-45): "Retinenda igitur distinctio haec est, quod
fides, quae agit cum Deo promittente et eius promissionem accipit, haec sola
iustificat," WA XLII, 566, 13-14; "Scimus quidem quod fides numquam est
sola, sed affert secum charitatem et alia multiplicia dona," ibid., 35-36; "sunt
connexa inseparabiliter fides et opera. Sed sola fides est, quae apprehendit
benedictionem. Ideo solam fidem iustificantem praedicamus, quia sola bene-
dicitur," WA XLIII, 255, 38-40.

85. WA XL/1-2, 184.

86. FC SD 3, 67.

87. In FC SD 4, 10-12. See Article 4 of the Torgau Book.

88. *Bekenntnisschriften,* p. 941, first apparatus on line 11.

89. WA, DB VII, 11, 6-23.

90. The change was probably inspired by the Prussian theologians' opinion on the Torgau Book, *Bekenntnisschriften,* p. 941, n. 2.

91. FC SD 4, 25.

92. This is not necessarily a reference to either of Luther's commentaries on the Letter to the Galatians, although passages occur in both that would qualify.

93. FC SD 4, 26.

94. FC SD 4, 27.

95. FC SD 4, 28. *Bekenntnisschriften,* p. 946, has probably identified correctly the passage that the editors of the Formula have in mind, WA XLIII, 253-61, especially 254, 5-6. The editors of the Formula have, however, mistaken the thrust of these passages. Luther does not have "certain of his own followers in mind," but he clearly and repeatedly indicates (254, 37; 255, 37; 256, 15, for instance) that he is directing his polemics against those followers of the Pope who no longer teach a rank Pelagianism, but who still insist that good works are necessary for salvation even though one ought not to put one's trust in them.

96. FC SD 5, 11-12.

97. WA XXII, 87, 3-18.

98. FC SD 5, 13.

99. WA XV, 228, 15-17. The Brunswick theologians meeting at Riddagshausen Abbey proposed this addition, Hutterus, p. 405, incorrectly numbered 505.

100. FC SD 5, 17.

101. *Bekenntnisschriften,* p. 957, n. 1; p. 1224, sees two possible sets of passages in Luther's works to which the authors of the Formula may be referring. The first set is in the second series of theses against the Antinomians (1537): "18. Quicquid ostendit peccatum, iram seu mortem, id exercet officium legis, sive fiat in vetere sive in novo testamento. 19. Revelare enim peccatum est aliud nihil nec aliud esse potest, quam esse legem, seu effectum et vim legis propriissimam," WA XXXIX/1, 348, 25-38. The second is in the commentary on Galatians (1531/35): "Verum officium et principalis ac proprius usus legis est, quod revelat homini suum peccatum, caecitatem, miseriam, impietatem, ignorantiam, odium, contemptum Dei, mortem, infernum, iudicium et commeritam iram apud Deum," WA XL/1, 481, 13-16. "Lex civiliter et Theologice carcer est. Primum enim civiliter cohibet et concludit impios, ne pro libidine sua praecipites ferri possint in omnia scelera. Deinde Spiritualiter ostendit nobis peccatum, perterrefacit et humiliat nos, ut sic pavefacti agnoscamus miseriam et damnationem nostram," WA XL/1, 520, 17-21.

102. WA XLVI, 667, 7—673, 30.

103. The editors of the Formula first considered an addition after what is now FC SD 5, 18, and finally incorporated a sentence at the end of FC SD 5, 22, *Bekenntnischriften,* p. 957, first apparatus on line 33.

104. Ibid., p. 955, n. 4; p. 957, n. 3; p. 959, n. 3. The last note sees the editors of the Formula as having had the long discussion of the two kinds of knowledge of God in WA XLVI, 667, 7—673, 30 (sic), in mind.

105. FC SD 6, 9.

106. On the Gospel: In Roth's *Sommerpostille* of 1526, WA X/1², 410, and WA XV, 696-712; in Cruciger's *Sommerpostille* of 1544, WA XXII, 322-24. *Bekenntnisschriften,* p. 965, n. 3, invites comparison with a sermon that Luther preached on 7 Oct. 1537, WA XLV, 161-64. (None of these are very

relevant.) On the Epistle: In Cruciger's *Sommerpostille* of 1544, WA XXII, 311-22 (which is irrelevant). The opinion of the Brandenburg theologians had called for the insertion of a section of Luther's sermon on the Epistle for the Sunday after Christmas in the *Weinachtspostille* of 1522, reproduced in WA X/1¹, 359, 21—363, 5, either in FC SD 6, 18, or after FC SD 6, 19; *Bekenntnisschriften*, p. 965, n. 3.

107. FC SD 7, 12-15.

108. C[orpus] R[eformatorum] III, 75-76. The present writer plans an early republication of the Wittenberg Concord (with English translation) on the basis of the 16th-century manuscripts in the Strasbourg and Weimar archives.

109. Walther Köhler, *Zwingli und Luther: Ihr Streit über das Abendmahl nach seinen politischen und religiösen Beziehungen*, eds. Ernst Kohlmeyer and Heinrich Bornkamm II (Gütersloh: C. Bertelsmann Verlag, 1953), Chs. 11 and 12; Hermann Sasse, *This Is My Body: Luther's Contention for the Real Presence in the Sacrament of the Altar* (Minneapolis: Augsburg Publishing House, 1959), pp. 301-11; Hans Grass, *Die Abendmahlslehre bei Luther und Calvin: Eine kritische Untersuchung* (Gütersloh: C. Bertelsmann Verlag, 1954), pp. 129-65.

110. FC SD 7, 28-32.

111. WA XXVI, 499, 15—500, 26; 506, 21-29.

112. FC SD 7, 33.

113. Against the "Heidelberg Canard" (*Heidelberger Landlüge*) that Albert Hardenberg (Rizaeus) and others had spread and Joachim Mörlin had promptly scotched, according to which Luther allegedly "confessed to Melanchthon that he had gone too far and overdone the matter in his controversy against the Sacramentarians; that he, however, did not want to retract his doctrine concerning the Lord's Supper himself, because that would cast suspicion on his whole teaching, that therefore after his death the younger theologians might make amends for it and settle the matter." Friedrich Bente, "Historical Introductions to the Symbolical Books of the Evangelical Lutheran Church," in *Concordia Triglotta* (St. Louis: Concordia Publishing House, 1921), pp. 184-85. Luther's alleged praise of John Calvin's *Traité de la Sainte Cène* is based on a source "that does not deserve unqualified credence," Grass, p. 195. Jürgen Diestelmann, *Konsekration: Luthers Abendmahlsglaube in dogmatisch-liturgischer Sicht an Hand von Quellenauszügen dargestellt* (Berlin: Lutherisches Verlagshaus, 1960), pp. 52—56, makes the interesting suggestion that the Heidelberg Canard may have as a germ of truth a change of heart on Luther's part with reference not to the Reformed party but with reference to the unfortunate curate Adam Besserer of Friessnitz. The evidence for this theory is, however, purely circumstantial.

114. WA LIV, 155, 29—156, 5.

115. CR III, 75.

116. FC SD 7, 38.

117. FC SD 7, 40.

118. WA XXVI, 261-509.

119. WA LIV, 141-167.

120. The references in *Bekenntnisschriften*, p. 984, to WA XXVI, 271 ff., 379 ff., are at best illustrative. The entire first two parts of the treatise are one sustained defense of a realistic interpretation of the words of institution of the Sacrament of the Altar in all four accounts.

121. The concrete reference of this statement to the doctrine of the Sacrament of

the Altar must not be overlooked. Strictly, of course, the Augsburg Confession could embody Luther's position only as it had developed and found expression up to 1530. In fact, the only work of a later date that is frequently cited is the *Little Confession* of 1544. It may be that Horst Stephan has this paragraph in mind when he makes the undocumented — and incorrect — statement: "[Orthodoxy] utilized [Luther's] doctrines as a corrective even with reference to the Augsburg Confession *(as the Formula of Concord had already done)"* (emphasis added), *Luther in den Wandlungen seiner Kirche,* 2d ed. (Berlin: Alfred Töpelmann, 1951), p. 17.

122. WA XXXVIII, 240, 8-14.

123. WA XXVI, 285, 13-18.

124. FC SD 7, 77-78.

125. FC SD 7, 87.

126. The Formula refers to Vol. IV of the Jena Edition of Luther's works; this volume contains writings from the year 1529, almost a decade too early. *Bekenntnisschriften,* p. 1001, refers mistakenly to a draft of part of the *Vermahnung an die Geistlichen versammelt auf dem Reichstag zu Augsburg* (1530), WA XXX/2, 254-55, and *Von den Schlüsseln* (1530), WA XXX/2, 462, 9. Both of these are likewise too early. One of the most explicit passages in which Luther interprets this principle is in his letter of 20 July 1543 to Simon Wolferinus, WA, Br X, 348, 13—349, 38, No. 3894, to be read in the light of 340-41, No. 3888. In this interpretation he is followed by Chemnitz, *Examen Concilii Tridentini,* Part Two, locus IV, section iii, pars. 12-14, ed. Preuss, p. 310; section vii, par. 12, p. 329; par 14, p. 330. It seems — Luther to the contrary notwithstanding — that Luther and Melanchthon understood this principle differently. Luther's view of the Sacrament, while dynamic, had a considerable ontological component. Melanchthon's view was exclusively dynamic. It may quite well be that the real difference between Luther's view of the Sacrament of the Altar and Melanchthon's view lies here rather than in an alleged declension of Melanchthon from his earlier position that "the true body and blood of Christ are genuinely present in the holy communion under the form of bread and wine," Augsburg Confession, 10, 1.

127. FC SD, 7, 91.

128. WA XVIII, 62-214.

129. WA XXIII, 64-283.

130. WA XXVI, 261-509.

131. WA LIV, 141-67. *Bekenntnisschriften,* p. 1005, also calls attention to the *Sermon von dem Sakrament des Leibes und Blutes Christi wider die Schwarmgeister* (1526), WA XIX, 482-523, and *Vermahnung zum Sakrament des Leibes und Blutes des Herrn* (1530), WA XXX/2, 595-626.

132. FC SD 7, 93-103.

133. The three modes correspond to the circumscriptive, definitive or diffinitive, and repletive modes of the Schoolmen. These theological considerations likewise sparked the debate about the omnipresence (Luther's opponents called it the "ubiquity") of the humanity of our Lord, which played a significant role in Luther's thinking for only a relatively short time and never had the importance for him that it acquired in the intra-Lutheran and interconfessional polemics of the late 16th and 17th centuries.

134. WA XXVI, 326, 29—327, 20; 335, 29—336, 27. WA XXVI, 326, 29—327, 20, is quoted in FC Ep 7, 10-14 with slight variations.

135. FC SD 7, 105.

136. *Bekenntnisschriften*, p. 1009, lists the following passages from *Dass diese Worte, Dass ist mein Leib usw., noch fest stehen* (1527) as illustrative of Luther's use of *geistlich:* "Wenn ich Christus fleisch ym abendmal leiblich esse, also das ich es zu gleich auch geistlich esse," WA XXIII, 179, 7-8; "das hertze . . . fasset die wort und isset das geistlich, welchs der mund leiblich isset," WA XXIII, 181, 10-11; "ym abendmal ist ein geistlich essen von Christo eingesetzt neben dem leiblichen," WA XXIII, 183, 5-6; "wenn Gotts wort dazu kompt und durch den glauben geschicht, so ists und heisst geistlich geschehen . . . es wird geistlich wo es ym wort und glauben gehet, Das geistlich nicht anders ist Denn was durch den geist und glauben ynn und durch uns geschicht, Gott gebe, das ding, da mit wir umb gehen, sey leiblich odder geistlich. Scilicet in usu, non in obiecto spiritus est. . . . Thut ers aber geistlich, das ist, so es sein hertz thut aus dem glauben ynn Gotts wort," WA XXIII, 189, 9-18.

137. One might argue that formally at least the Formula undertakes to correct Luther on one point. Andreae's Epitome, 7, 42, asserts that the Lutherans "condemn without any qualification the Capernaitic eating of the body of Christ as though one rent Christ's flesh with one's teeth and digested it like other food." In *Vom Abendmahl Christi, Bekenntnis* (1528) Luther had declared: "The fanatics are wrong, as well as the gloss in Canon Law, if they criticize Pope Nicholas for having forced Berengar [of Tours] to confess that the true body of Christ is crushed and ground with the teeth. Would to God that all popes had acted in so Christian a fashion in all other matters as this pope did with Berengar in forcing this confession. For this is undoubtedly the meaning, that he who eats and chews this bread eats and chews that which is the genuine, true body of Christ and not mere ordinary bread, as Wycliff teaches. For this bread is truly the body of Christ," WA XXVI, 442-43; translation from LW XXXVII, 300-1. The "correction" is more apparent than real; Andreae, as FC SD 7, 127, which he is expanding, indicates, is polemicizing against "all presumptuous, scoffing, and blasphemous questions and expressions which are advanced in a coarse, fleshly, Capernaitic way about the supernatural and heavenly mysteries of this supper."

138. FC Ep 8, 3; SD 8, 2-4; Preface, *Bekenntnisschriften*, p. 753, 1-6. See likewise the statements of the authors of the Formula of Concord at Tangermünde in 1578, Hutterus, pp. 633-41, and the Smalcald *Abschied* of the same year, Hutterus, pp. 660-65, 671-81, 687-89.

139. FC Ep 8, 17. *Bekenntnisschriften*, p. 808, n. 4, refers to *Dass diese Worte, Das ist mein Leib usw., noch fest stehen* (1527), WA XXIII, 131, [7—143, 22], and *Vom Abendmahl Christi, Bekenntnis* (1528), WA XXVI 326, [29—332, 11].

140. FC Ep 8, 18.

141. WA L, 582, 1—592, 15.

142. FC SD 8, 3.

143. *Bekenntnisschriften*, p. 1018, suggests the *Sermon von dem Sakrament des Leibes und Blutes Christi, wider die Schwarmgeister* (1526), WA XIX, 482-523; *Dass diese Worte, Das ist mein Leib usw., noch fest stehen* (1527), WA XXIII, 64-283; and *Vom Abendmahl Christi, Bekenntnis* (1528), WA XXVI, 261-509.

144. FC SD 8, 17.

145. WA XXVI, 324, 22-23.

146. FC SD 8, 21.

147. WA XXVI, 317, 19—325, 32.

148. On the classic and patristic Greek uses of *alloioō* and *alloiōsis* see Henry George Liddell and Robert Scott, *A Greek-English Lexicon,* eds. Henry Stuart Jones and Roderick McKenzie (Oxford: Clarendon Press, 1961), pp. 69-70, and G. W. H. Lampe, *A Patristic Greek Lexicon,* fascicle 1 (Oxford: Clarendon Press, 1961), pp. 76-77. For Zwingli *alloeosis* is a rhetorical figure.

149. FC SD 8, 26.

150. FC SD 8, 85.

151. WA LIV, 49, 33—50, 11.

152. FC SD 8, 28.

153. *Bekenntnisschriften,* p. 1026, suggests as documentation *Dass diese Worte, Das ist mein Leib usw., noch fest stehen* (1527), WA XXIII, 133, 19 [—137, 19], and 143, 10 [—147, 27]. It also suggests *Vom Abendmahl Christi, Bekenntnis* (1528), WA XXVI, 340, 8 ff.; this is a poor reference and might well be replaced, for instance, by WA XXVI, 339, 33—340, 2.

154. FC SD 8, 39-43.

155. WA XXVI, 319, 29-40; 321, 19-28; 322, 20-22; 324, 25-35.

156. FC SD 8, 44.

157. WA L, 590, 11-22.

158. FC SD 8, 81-84 and 85.

159. WA XXVI, 332, 18—333, 9.

160. WA LIV, 49, 33—50, 11.

161. FC SD 8, 86.

162. *Bekenntnisschriften,* p. 1046, suggests as a specific passage WA XXIII, 139, [24—153, 14].

163. *Bekenntnisschriften,* p. 1046, suggests as a specific passage WA XXVI, 332, [12—335, 28].

164. WA XXXVII, 62, 30—67, 2. The extensive quotation contained in the Bergen Book draft of the Formula was struck, but it is reproduced in *Bekenntnisschriften,* pp. 1050-52.

165. FC SD 10, 24.

166. WA XXVI, 560-618.

167. The Maulbronn Formula identifies these as Luther's letters to the Lutheran theologians attending the Diet of Augsburg in 1530, especially Melanchthon, George Spalatin, Justus Jonas, and John Brenz, WA, Br V, 345-630, Nos. 1580 to 1722 passim, and his more general *Vermahnung an die Geistlichen versammelt auf dem Reichstag zu Augsburg* (1530), WA XXX/2, 268-356. *Bekenntnisschriften,* p. 1062 invites comparison with *Ob die Fürsten recht daran getan, dass sie nicht haben das Klosterleben und die Messe dulden wollen (Bedenken . . . über . . . äusserliche Vergleichung)* (1530), WA, Br V, 614-16 and Luther's *Bedenken an den Churfürst Johann* (1530), WA, Br V, 258-61.

168. FC SD 11, 33.

169. WA, DB VII, 25, 1-6 with slight variations.

170. It was Elector Joachim II of Brandenburg, the patron of the antinomian John Agricola and one of the princely architects of the Augsburg Interim of 1548, who in 1564 had the medal minted that bore the legend: "Gottes Wort und Luthers Lehr wird vergehen nimmermehr," Zeeden, I, 66.

11

ECCLESIA REFORMATA SEMPER REFORMANDA

James Atkinson

1. RESPONSIBLE REFORMATION IN THE 16TH CENTURY

THE REFORMATION was not definitive but corrective.
The Reformers were renovators, never innovators, as the Anglican
Bishop Jewel (1522–1571) expressed it. It is natural for historians
and churchmen studying this movement to describe it in the terms in
which the Reformers expressed it and in the confessional statements
which their churches hammered out in controversy. Nevertheless, the
Reformers never attempted to offer the church anything save to show
her what she already possessed. Their theology and their churches'
confessional statements sought less to define the church's theology and
more to correct it in terms of Scripture, creedal statements, patristic
tradition, and sound reason — the whole in relation to a world in a vortex of social, political, economic, and intellectual revolutions.

The same is true of all religious revival. No genuine religious
revival has ever been a wholly new departure. Man has never made
proper religious advance by turning his back on the past. Religious
revivalists open men's minds to what they already have. Though men
crave for what is novel or modern, responsible reformers offer them

what is eternal. Old Testament prophets recalled men to the promises and the hope of that which God had centuries before given them in the Law and away from the corrupt idolatry that passed for worship and religion. "Is it not even thus, O ye children of Israel," appealed Amos.[1] Isaiah cried to a people who had forsaken God and had gone backward.[2] "The prophets prophesy falsely, and the priests bear rule by their means; and my people love to have it so; and what will ye do in the end thereof?" was the analysis of the situation as given to Jeremiah,[3] and the only hope was the fresh writing of the old covenant in their hearts.[4] To a people who had rejected God and were as sheep lost on the mountains,[5] to a people who had forsaken the fountain of living waters and hewed them out cisterns, broken cisterns that can hold no water,[6] there was finally offered the hope that they would once again ask their way homeward,[7] be restored to their own habitation,[8] and join themselves "to the Lord in a perpetual covenant that shall not be forgotten."[9] Christ himself identified His mission and message with God's divine activity in history. He himself came not to destroy the Law or the Prophets, but to fulfill them,[10] and every disciple was like a wise householder bringing out things new and old.[11] The apostles, notably John and Paul, saw the clear divine fulfillment of the Law in the Gospel. All the Reformers saw this with crystal clarity. They were simply pointing men to what was already there, clearing away all the spiritual trinkets and ecclesiastical bric-a-brac in the process. They sought only to redeem the church and set it on its only spiritual basis, to awaken men to the reality of the Holy Spirit calling the church to be the church and to fulfill in the world the mission God was demanding of her. In other words, God is the Great Reformer who called and calls His church to reform.

Everyone is aware that there is theological ferment today. (The world is in a crisis of economic and political rethinking, to say nothing of our cultural and philosophical upheaval, movements which most men would say are more serious than any crisis in theology. I am limiting the enquiry to the area of theological reform as a contribution to a better understanding of the whole nexus of problems in which we are all responsibly involved.) This theological ferment is of news value even in the secular press and in secular journals. Loud calls demanding a new reformation are heard on all sides. It is now of some urgency that we collectively clarify our minds and open ourselves to the meaning of reformation.

Many of the current reform movements seek a fresh theology in terms of contemporary ideologies expressed in a way contemporary

272

man can understand and is prepared to accept. The motive for reaching secular man is commendable, but the present outcry seeks to modify the approach of traditional Christianity, to begin with man rather than with God, to find truth in the depth of man's own being rather than in the God who addresses man. This may well end in a faith without foundations. Certainly, what the 16th-century Reformers offered was a Reformation that gave a greater and deeper fullness of the traditional faith; they offered more, not less. They never questioned that reformation must proceed within the framework of Christendom's historical development. They were men humbly aware that Christian truth is infinitely greater than the pronouncement of any council, any church doctor, any pope, any reformer. They could never concede infallibility to any authority other than the objective revelation of God in His Word.

Torrance parallels the present problem of opening ourselves up to a legitimate reformation to the movements in the church of the fourth and 16th centuries.[12] He sees modern "reformers" demanding the discarding of the fundamental Christian framework bound up as it is with an obsolete cosmology, and in place of these objective forms seeking to find new forms congenial to modern man's development. He argues that Athanasius faced a similar situation and solved it for the church, for he saw the basic difficulty not in the cosmology in which the Biblical theology was expressed but in the unbiblical element of the then contemporary thought. This fourth-century system made of Christ and the Holy Spirit creatures and identified Christianity with Arian and Gnostic tendencies. It argued that God does not intervene in men's lives, that any redemption is to be conceived mythologically or subjectively because it never *happened* in the true historical sense of that word, but *happens* only as a kind of cathartic, existential experience. Furthermore, it said, the Word of God revealed in Christ is not grounded in the Being of God but is separate, creaturely. They discussed Christian orthodoxy as provincial and naive (Celsus). This set all Christian imagery and conceptuality as correlative to creaturely existence. The church's answer was the *homoousion*. Christ (and later the Holy Spirit) were set once and for all on the divine and not the human side. Athanasius drew the line that no man can cross and be saved. All pagan ideas of salvation were rejected, and the relevance of the Incarnation for man's salvation was shown for all time. Christ was not a man-fashioned but a divinely provided form.

This is paralleled in what Luther rediscovered. He knew at first

273

hand that the church of his day had gradually fallen into a semi-Pelagian, sometimes a semi-Judaic, position. Its doctrine of salvation was almost irretrievably lost in a human-centered scheme of merit-earning. The greatest thing Luther did was to restore a New Testament Christology, salvation by grace in Christ alone.

Surely Torrance is right in finding a parallel between the work of Athanasius and the work of Luther. This is verified by Luther's close interest in the Greek Fathers, and by no less a person than Harnack, who said that Luther joined hands with Athanasius across the centuries.[13] The early church, however, did not carry through its Christological work into the whole realm of the church's thinking and living and worshiping. This is exactly what Luther attempted to do, a work carried further by the later Calvin. Luther argued that in Christ God had done all that He could, that in Christ God in His entirety was at work. This theology galvanized current doctrines of grace. For too long, since Ignatius in fact, the church had been too ready to conceive grace in terms of a "thing," the medicine of immortality, the bread of life. The poetry of these images had served to estrange men from the Reality who gave them their meaning. Luther took the *homoousion* theology into this realm of grace. He argued that grace was not *something* God communicated, which took different forms, but that it was none other than the living, active, working Christ, no less than God communicating Himself to us.[14] In turn this effected a transition from static, conceptual, propositional, intellectual theology to a theology that was dynamic, personal, and Biblical, a theology that in its real objectivity stood over against man and the church as a challenge, almost a threat. This conception of God who intervenes in history as its Creator and its Redeemer was an immense and disturbing challenge both to the Renaissance men in their intellectual self-sufficiency and to Roman Catholics, who identified truth with the church and its definition of it.

The Reformation movement was a movement in men's thinking that shifted the center of gravity away from the priority of thought to the priority of being, that is, to truth as objectively experienced in history and life. Rome sought the certainty and security of identifying truth with her own interpretation of it, and this caused a steady undercurrent in the movement of Rome away from the Reformation. Still more, Luther argued that the unredeemed man must be converted before he can see and know; man had to be freed from himself and his own interests, from his own prejudgments and presuppositions before he could know the truth in itself, as it comes to him and makes

274

itself known to him. True knowledge of this kind requires obedience to God and total submission to the ways He has revealed Himself to us in history. Luther's theology was shattering to the church precisely because he carried through his theological perceptions into the sphere of church practice and everyday living. He set Christ in the center in the theological schools, Christ in the center of man's everyday life. Had his Christology remained a debate among schoolmen, Luther would have had no more significance than any other of the many contemporary German professors. By pursuing it to its proper end he lifted Christianity off its hinges and rehung it.

With this recovery of the New Testament creedal, patristic doctrine of Christ there was given a deeper doctrine of the Spirit, exactly parallel to the church's struggle with Macedonianism after Nicaea.[15] With a fresh doctrine of the Spirit there followed the corollary of a recovery of the doctrine of the church, seen as a community of believing men united with Christ through the Holy Spirit.

> There is a small, holy flock or community on earth, consisting of holy persons only, under one Head, Christ, called together by the Holy Spirit in one faith and understanding; possessing many gifts, but one in love, without sect or schism. Of it I too form a part, and am a member, a sharer and participator in all its blessings through the Holy Spirit, called thereto and incorporated with it because I have heard and believe in God's Word, which is the first step towards entering it.[16]

Luther argued that his understanding of the church was the true, catholic interpretation, reaching back to the Bible and the old Greek and Latin Fathers.[17] On the claim to be the living, dynamic continuation of the true catholic church he wrote:

> We ask: What became of all those Christians who lived and died after the apostolic era and before the rise of the papacy? No teacher of the church taught better than Augustine. We ask: Was he subject to the pope? It would be too bad if we did not have Augustine; then the other church fathers would leave us in the lurch terribly. Augustine taught and guided us better than the pope with all his decretals. He leads me to Christ, not away from Him. The pope did not know a word about this when Augustine was Bishop of Hippo. The pope estranges the dear people from Christ, the Head of the church, saying: "Baptism, absolution, Holy Communion, and Gospel will not benefit you unless you receive it from me." How do you suppose Augustine will react to this? He will reply: "I and the other bishops administered Holy Communion, and we preached without the pope's permission and authorization." Then why do you, pope, raise the

275

hue and the cry that we are alienating Christendom from you, or that we do not consult you with regard to the administration of the Sacraments? If your claims are granted, then all would be viewed as rebels — Ambrose and Augustine, also the bishops in Greece and all others in the world who did not direct the people to the pope but to Christ, saying: "Christ baptizes you; He teaches you the Gospel and also remits your sin." This is still our proclamation today. Consequently, we are not schismatics. The fact that we ignore the pope has no bearing on the question. . . . If I follow in the footsteps of the holy bishops and martyrs, I am content; for they follow the dear apostles.[18]

In his important work *On the Councils and the Church* he argues for a careful understanding of the church in its beginning and for its continuity through all time.

Ecclesia, however, should mean the holy Christian people, not only of the days of the apostles, who are long since dead, but to the end of the world, so that there is always a holy Christian people on earth, in whom Christ lives, works, and rules, *per redemptionem,* "through grace and the remission of sin," and the Holy Spirit, *per vivificationem et sanctificationem,* "through daily purging of sin and renewal of life," so that we do not remain in sin but are enabled and obliged to lead a new life, abounding in all kinds of good works, as the Ten Commandments or the two tables of Moses' law command, and not in old, evil works.[19]

He also said:

We need the Decalogue not only to apprise us of our lawful obligations, but we also need it to discern how far the Holy Spirit has advanced us in his work of sanctification and by how much we still fall short of the goal, lest we become secure and imagine that we have now done all that is required. Thus we must constantly grow in sanctification and always become new creatures in Christ. This means "grow" and "do so more and more" [2 Pet. 3:18].[20]

In this same connection he wrote:

But we constantly strive to attain the goal, under his redemption or remission of sin, until we too shall one day become perfectly holy and no longer stand in need of forgiveness.[21]

His contention was that the Holy Spirit sanctifies and completes this sanctification in the life to come.

Now there are many peoples in the world; the Christians, however, are a people with a special call and are therefore called not just *ecclesia,* "church," or "people," but *sancta catholica Christiana,* that is, "a Christian holy people" who believe in Christ. That is why they

276

are called Christian people and have the Holy Spirit, who sanctifies them daily, not only through the forgiveness of sin acquired for them by Christ (as the Antinomians foolishly believe), but also through the abolition, the purging, and the mortification of sins, on the basis of which they are called a holy people. Thus the "holy Christian church" is synonymous with a Christian and holy people, or as one is also wont to express it, with "holy Christendom," or "whole Christendom." [22]

Luther's doctrine of the church was that of a church in direct inheritance of all the promises of the children of Israel. They were the people of God held together not by the outward signs of Law, circumcision, and temple but by God's work in Christ's life, death, and resurrection, acts of God not clearly seen by the world but revealed in faith to those called. To Luther the holiness of the church is rooted in the Word of God and in true faith and bears witness of this in love. This was a direct, even a penitent return home to the Father's house of the New Testament. The church was the people of God living and growing in the Word of God, and therefore looked not merely to her origins but to her destiny. It was not only a matter of what she was but more what she was to become. There was no guarantee that the church at any time is the body of Christ. She may have apostolic succession, a proper hierarchy, real forms of worship, she may possess all the creeds and confessions and show all signs of good works, and yet be dead. She cannot rest content with herself, she is truly *ecclesia non in esse sed in fieri*. It is less that the church is a church and more that it may become a church in a believing response to God's call. And in the direction of its goal, the becoming of a true church, the churches must see that their prime task is to proclaim the Gospel to a secularized world and to the tasks of the secular world.

Closely integrated with this doctrine of the church was Luther's theology of the cross. The church was never to be conceived in the terms of this world, with its glories, privileges, and pretensions. It was to be conceived as Christ Himself — mocked, rejected, killed, ignored. "I am among you as he that serveth." [23] Luther battled stiffly against the Roman idea of a triumphant church, governing and ruling the world, commanding princes and prelates. This was not the discipleship Christ intended, nor was it the church He founded. Vogelsang summarized Luther's thought:

Christus herrscht nicht durch zerstörende und strafende Gewalt, überhaupt in keinem Glanz und Prunk, in keiner Selbstherrlichkeit und Tyrannei, sondern allein durch die wahrhafte Macht des Heilens und Rettens, durch die herbe Liebe der Zucht und des Opfers, ge-

wirkt durch die Gewalt des Wortes, des Geistes und des Glaubens.
... Die Kirche bleibt auf Erden Kirche des Kreuzes, nicht Kirche
der Herrlichkeit oder vielmehr: eben unter der Schmach und
Schwäche der Kirche ist ihre Herrlichkeit und Macht verborgen
(absconditum). Das ist der tiefe Sinn, den Luther in die überlieferte
Anschauung legt, dass Christus Herr der Kirche ist nach seiner
Menschheit, d. h. nach seiner Kreuzesgestalt.[24]

This outline of Luther's doctrine of the church makes it clear that
he had forged this doctrine for himself before he faced Cajetan
at Augsburg in 1518 or Eck at Leipzig in 1519. It is equally clear
that he held it to his dying day. This breakthrough, almost break-
away, to the doctrine of the early church was an enormous liberation
from the contemporary, secularized view of a lordly church which
Catholicism had carved out for itself. Luther saw this New Testament
doctrine of the church broken from the time of Augustine (d. 430)
onwards. Augustine held the New Testament doctrine, but alongside
it made room for what was later to be the Catholic view, that the
Catholic Church with its visible structure of bishops, sacraments, and
theology was the one and holy church. Augustine did not resolve —
perhaps had not the occasion to resolve — the problem of holding
these two doctrines together. Certainly, Catholicism took over the
latter, when the Roman Empire was crumbling, baptized it, and made
it her own. So it remained for a thousand years never effectively
challenged until Luther questioned it. To Luther it was less a mighty
worldwide visible organization and more a true communion of saints
created by God, not readily recognizable and certainly not coterminous
with the visible structure. It was less the glorious *successio episcopo-
rum* and more the thin, unbroken, unpretentious line of *successio
fidelium.*

Luther's evangelical theology was wrought slowly and at much
cost to himself:

I relate these things, good reader, so that, if you are a reader of
my puny works, you may keep in mind, that, as I said above, I was
all alone and one of those who, as Augustine says of himself, have
become proficient by writing and teaching. I was not one of those
who from nothing suddenly become the topmost, though they are
nothing, neither have labored, nor been tempted, nor become experienced, but have with one look at the Scriptures exhausted their
entire spirit.[25]

In those early years at Wittenberg (1512–1515) his studies had
taught him that man wins pardon by the free grace of God and not

278

by much striving after holiness. When man lays hold of God's promise of pardon he becomes a new creature. This sense of pardon was the beginning of a new life of sanctification. Luther was now clearly discriminating between the Gospel as salvation and Law as salvation, and already drawing clear distinctions between the visible and the invisible church.

After a closer study of St. Augustine he began to question the validity of contemporary scholastic theology. He grew increasingly disquieted with the monastic discipline as a way of salvation and more drawn toward the great doctrines of predestination and salvation by free, unmerited grace. In 1516 he preached against indulgences.[26] In 1517 he wrote against the scholastic theology of Scotus, Biel, Ockham, and d'Ailly, which then dominated the schools, particularly their Aristotleisms, and in his disputation criticized it on three essential points: (a) It was Pelagian at heart and had lost the Augustinian doctrine of grace; (b) it neglected to teach the value of faith and inward righteousness; (c) it encouraged men to see how to escape the consequences of sin when it ought to have turned men's minds to the meaning of sin and God's answer in Christ to this problem.[27]

That same year saw his Ninety-five Theses and the controversy that is still with us 450 years later. The controversy resolved itself into the question whether papal authority was final and infallible or subject to correction by Scripture and a general council. Luther argued the latter view but protested that he was no heretic and that he taught nothing contrary to the Scriptures, the ancient Fathers, the ecumenical councils, and the decrees of the popes.

In the midst of this controversy Luther was summoned to a meeting of the Augustinian monks at Heidelberg where he defended 40 theses on natural depravity, slavery of the will, regenerating grace, faith, and good works, all on Augustinian and Pauline lines. Specially significant at this hour were his advocacy of the *theologia crucis* over against the *theologia gloriae,* his contrast of the Law and Gospel in the sense of God's *opus alienum* and *opus proprium,* and his uncompromising attack on the baleful influence of the Aristotelian ethic on the Christian doctrine of salvation.[28]

On the authority of Leo X, Prierias descended on Luther with the intent to crush him by the sheer weight of papal authority. The pope, he declared, was "the infallible judge of all controversies, the head of all spiritual, the father of all secular princes, the head of the church and of the whole universe." [29] Before Cajetan at Augsburg

279

in 1518 Luther maintained his position that the papacy had no authority over council, church, and Scripture.[30]

It was at this stage that his historical studies made him aware that there was no papal authority in the early centuries and none in the great Orthodox Church; his studies also convinced him of the truth of Valla's researches that the Isidorian Papal Decretals and the Donation of Constantine were forgeries. These studies prepared him for his great debate with Eck at Leipzig in 1519.

Against the papal pretensions Luther maintained the history of the church, the authority of Nicaea, and the testimony of Scripture. Luther argued that the church existed not within the Roman fold but only where the Word of God is preached and believed — this he described as the communion of saints. He admitted the external and practical authority of the papacy. The argument centered around the authority of the Pope and the infallibility of the church. Here Luther publicly denied the divine right and origin of the papacy and the infallibility of a general council.[31] He based his authority on Scripture and the power of a man of faith to discern its truth.

When he stood his ground at Worms in April 1521 and refused to recant,[32] he had won for all time and for all men the victory of the Word of God over all traditions of men and the liberty of a good conscience over the tyranny of authority. Luther was now certain that the church had taken the wrong fork when the great Greek Fathers and Augustine had passed from the scene. He therefore sought to restore the church to her New Testament foundations. He wanted the church to be truly Catholic as she purified her present theology. She should discard the corruptions and accretions entrenched behind popular piety. Luther also provided the criteria and norm for her future development.

To Luther the church had lost the Gospel and had grown into a secular institution. It was not the papacy nor the abuses Luther attacked but the wrong theology entrenched in both: *Non propter personam sed propter Deum*. Luther did not object to the idea of the pope as the chief pastor, and always realized that all churches, both Protestant and Catholic, were errant.

First, Luther opened the eyes of the church to what it meant to believe in Christ alone apart from works and merit for salvation. The church had too long given easy credence to the view that man could by his own morality, his own intellect, his own spirituality get himself near to God, near enough to be accepted. Luther tore this into shreds. Such theology was *hominem praedicare*, to preach man. Luther diagnosed the malaise of Christendom in his own soul, and in his total breakdown realized the saving truth of what God had done for frail and sinful man in sending Christ. "Here God pours out not sun or moon, nor heaven and earth, but his own heart and his dearest Son." [33] He saw all the scandals and abuses of Christendom as consequences of the rejection of the truth of salvation in Christ alone in favor of a works religion. "It is not of him that willeth, nor of him that runneth, but of God that sheweth mercy." [34]

It was the steady realization of this primal truth that caused the erosion of the priestly office. Sacramental grace, mediated only by a priest, was central to the late medieval practice. It was therefore the priesthood (and behind that the papacy) that bore the brunt of the impact of the first truth, salvation in Christ only. The Mass, and with it purgatory, crumbled everywhere, and with them indulgences. The Mass and the doctrine of transubstantiation gave way to Holy Communion and the Real Presence; paid Masses vanished; purgatory and indulgences fell aside as spiritual dross. It could never be the same again. The priest was now replaced in Protestantism by a minister of the Word and a pastor.

If the first principle of salvation in Christ alone apart from any works or merits of man meant the collapse of the mediatorial priest, then together these two principles meant justification by faith alone. A man was justified not by what he did but by what God did in Christ. This was no catchword to Luther, but the norm of all Christian belief, evangelical or catholic. It was the article by which the church stands or falls. Protestantism has been right in making this the center of its theology. It knocked the bottom out of the popular cultus, saint worship, pilgrimages, penances, pardons, indulgences, paid Masses, trinkets, shrines, images. They all seemed pointless when a man believed in Christ's merits.

This kind of thinking turned men away from the *magisterium* of the church to the final authority of Scripture. The church for too long had put the Fathers, the councils, the popes, in sum, the church, between believing man and his Bible in the way they had put the priest midway between man and God. Luther set the Word of God as foundational to Christianity. God's Word was sufficient and final, and the church was not its master but its servant. When men heard again the Word of God and listened to the internal testimony of the Holy Spirit, they knew that Luther was right. They knew they could never go back on this. Forward, yes, but backward was unthinkable.

The prime experience of salvation in Christ only led Luther to a dramatic New Testament Christology. "In Christ I have the Father's heart and will," [35] he cried. Christ filled the whole sphere of his being. He was Christ-centered and Christ-mastered. It was this total conversion that made him a theologian, for in Christ he saw the Truth of God which God was seeking to declare. This the natural man cannot see. This gave Luther his remarkable insights into the Bible and allowed him to handle Paul and John unerringly. His Christology gave him a sound sacramental authority. No longer were the sacraments media of mysterious grace but the ever-present Christ speaking to the faithful. They became a preached visible word.

Not least in its difference was Luther's doctrine of the church. The church was the communion of saints called into existence by God's Word, maintained by that Word, marked by love one to another, whose task it was to go on for all time preaching that Word with faithfulness and relevance to a lost and dying world.

Now these emphases of Luther are true enough in themselves and can be demonstrated as such, and eventually the evangelical church worked them over into a confessional position owing to historical necessity. The question raised here is whether this should not be seen as a polemical and provisional position, necessary at the time, but one that is always due for reconsideration and development. To the Reformers the Reformation was a movement and not a position; it was a movement from God to renew the church. One reason Luther grew so bitter toward the end of his life and actually threatened to leave Wittenberg and be done with the Reformation altogether was that men had not seen the urgency and immediacy of God's intervention in the 16th century and were lapsing back into their old ways. To set one's hand to reformation, to realize that the church needs reformation, is to realize that once this begins, a process is under way no man can stop, for no man began it. To add the adjective *reformata* to *ecclesia* connotes *et reformanda*.

Luther did not succeed in his task, namely, to reform Christendom with respect to its theology and morals on a New Testament basis and at the same time to preserve its outward unity. His way forward became a way out. Nor did the distinguished company of fellow reformers throughout Europe effect this very desirable end; but Europe hardened into a divided Christendom.

At first Luther thought that the church would thank him for the great disclosures given him by God, but in 1519 when he returned from the Leipzig Debate he realized that Christendom was actually now divided, that he was the cause, and his would be the responsibility for that part that reformed itself. Neither Luther nor the immense following that supported him would go against the plain meaning of the New Testament and their own conscience. The Reformation was therefore put in a false position of independency or separateness; and this was worsened because all the reforming movements had to evolve one or more confessional statements and to seek the protection of the state. These statements always argued the falsity of the now *Roman* Catholic position, declaring their own in relation to this. Yet no confessional position was a new position (in the sense, say, that the American Constitution was new). It was a restatement of the original and the concomitant discrediting of the false Roman position. The protection of the civil power meant in the long run the despiritualization of the Christian folk and the insidious identification of the church with the state and later with the prevailing culture.

This produced a position, accepted by today's Protestantism though never intended by the early Reformers, of two rival camps, and furthermore, two camps which have undergone far-reaching internal developments. These two are not always opposed, yet they are estranged and separate; each developed its own ethos. While Lutherans and Reformed were developing confessional statements, the Roman Catholic Church finally called a council from which Protestantism was excluded. At Trent Protestantism was anathematized; Rome purged herself of gross immoralities and formulated theological pronouncements.

The Reformers intended only to reform the one, holy, catholic church and to keep it one and reformed. The subsequent problems of Christendom sprang primarily from the refusal of the Roman Church to listen, and the refusal of the Reformers to deny the truth. History bears witness to the claim. So far from them was the idea of schism that their very name Protestant, for a real name they never had and never sought, was an accident of history.

When Germany was divided between those who were to go forward with Luther and those prepared to submit to Rome, men realized that some *modus vivendi* must be sought. The only way forward, for there was no democratic vote in those days, was to allow each prince to determine how his country was to live. This was adopted in Augsburg in 1555. It had been foreshadowed at Speier in 1526, but at a subsequent Diet of Speier in 1529, when discriminative legislation was attempted, six princes and 14 free cities entered a *protestatio* in defense of evangelical rights. Since then the name has stuck, but it is unsatisfactory and misleading. Luther was following in the wake of Wyclif (d. 1384) and Hus (d. 1415), voices whom many heeded.

Europe knew that the papacy was sick. England had made many moves against the papacy under Edward I and Edward III. France had rebelled against the papacy in 1438 in the Pragmatic Sanction of Bourges. The Great Schism opened many eyes, and the collapse of the Council of Basel in 1449 with the tragic failure of the conciliarist movement caused many to despair. Christendom needed a Luther who would analyze the malaise theologically and point the way forward. But what can any doctor, even a Doctor Luther, do if the patient refuses his help and prefers to stagger along without help?

2. RESPONSIBLE REFORMATION IN THE 20TH CENTURY

When the Roman Church opposed the Reformation and the Protestants determined to accept the Reformation and its consequences, Christendom hardened into two theological areas, as stated above. A reformation movement has again begun to stir both parts of Christendom, but it is no longer simply 16th-century Protestantism nor 16th-century Catholicism under discussion. A great deal has happened to both Catholicism and Protestantism in the 450 years since the break.

Protestantism has been faulted for its fissiparous and sectarian tendencies, its involvement or even identification with political, cultural, and intellectual movements of the day, the steady erosion of its theological and spiritual tradition, culminating in theological penury, intellectual uncertainty, and spiritual torpor. Roman Catholicism has been lauded for a striking rebirth, a theological and spiritual renewal, for studying fearlessly (even if 450 years late) the nature of the Reformation and its subsequent history. She is seen strengthening the faithful and facing afresh her mission to the world.

It would be naive to imagine that when Roman Catholicism has sufficiently reformed and removed the stumbling blocks to Protestants that Reformation theology will wither away. It is equally naive to imagine that Protestantism needs only to reaffirm her old Reformation principles in all their nakedness, true though these principles are. They must confront a changed Protestantism and a fast-changing, reforming Catholicism on the one hand and a world wholly different culturally, economically, politically, intellectually, on the other hand. Protestantism began to set in motion a reform of the Reformation half a century ago owing to theological necessity within and secular necessity without. This unexpected movement arose in the form of pressure

284

from the missionaries. It was the first clear sign since the 17th century that the Reformation was a continuing movement and not a settlement.

The 1910 meeting of the World Missionary Council was crucial for the Ecumenical Movement (which had virtually died with Calvin and Bucer and Cranmer and Melanchthon).[36] The devastation of the First World War caused the churches to realize more keenly what the unity of the church might mean. When Karl Barth in 1918 wrote his commentary *The Epistle to the Romans,* the death knell of pietistic morality and liberalism in the form of a shallow acceptance of a Christian culture was sounded. There reverberated through the world once again the great Reformation doctrine of *sola gratia* and the reality of Christ's judgment. Then the Nazi movement captured the synodal regional churches of Germany, and the Confessional Church took its existence in 1934 in protest. This militant confessional movement attacked the new association with the secular authorities (Naziism) and refused to recognize any authority other than the Word of God and the living Christ in the midst of believing men. Already we had the new reformation. Yet many opposed this movement, and when after the devastation of the Second World War the United Evangelical Lutheran Church refederated itself into regional churches, the movement suffered a setback. Karl Barth is right in suggesting (Easter 1966) that Protestant leaders show too much concern for the preservation of traditional positions in criticizing Vatican II. They ought to concern themselves with the meaning of Vatican II in terms of a dialog with the Word of God. He is reminding us of what we too easily forget. The Reformation is a continuum into which the church is set; it belongs to the whole of Christendom.

A forward step in the Ecumenical Movement was taken with the founding of the World Council of Churches in 1948. The member churches accepted responsibility both for the disunity of Christendom as well as for the failure to bear the Christian message to a world torn with wars, racial hatred, social and economic inequality, and uncertainty. History may well describe this as an act of penitence rather than theological reformation, yet the germ of reformation is there. Nevertheless, the Protestant churches are largely in a state of theological paralysis or uncertainty and have neither the strength nor the confidence to make any certain theological move, much less reformation.

In the meantime Rome is undergoing a self-renewal; the next stage, responsible theological dialog between Rome and some or all of the churches of the Reformation, has begun.

285

What points can Protestant theologians discuss with their Roman Catholic counterparts? The reformed teaching in relation to the Roman Catholic view on Scripture coupled as it is with the *magisterium* and tradition, papal primacy, the papal claims as a teaching authority, the centrality of Mary, the additions of dogma, and other notable disagreements could be argued. Yet these issues are largely theoretical and academic, debating points for believing theologians. I do not argue that they are not true, only that they are theoretical, almost hypothetical, in relation to the current Protestant theological climate and the world in which we find ourselves.

This point must be demonstrated. For four centuries Protestantism has stood on the basis of a theology founded on the Bible and has stood over against Rome on this ground. Today some Biblical exegetes are criticizing the hitherto Biblical certainties to such an extent that the man in the pew hardly knows what he believes, or if there is any truth in what he does believe. This criticism attacks not only the natural weaknesses any church normally has, but the very doctrine of God, the nature and person of Christ, the work of the Holy Spirit, and the entire range of Christian theology and morality. Press and television have taken up the various attacks and great cries have gone up for a "New Reformation."

The protagonists of this "Reformation" argue that there is no longer any God "out there," but one who is to be identified with the ground of our being and our own experience. This amounts to a recrudescence of the ancient disjunction between God and the world, a dichotomy which destroyed (and destroys) the religious Creator-creature relationship. Theological knowledge is no longer rooted in an objective Word from God to man, but is a construct of man himself. God cannot act in history, it is said, and thereby the world is secularized, and with that, nature and religion are secularized too. God is now met in the ground of our being and in the patterns man develops as he "grows up." On these bases theological reform amounts to some mythological or human construct device by man as he seeks to understand the universe and his own existence. Such theologians argue that theological thinking is nonconceptual and only symbolic, for God cannot be known in Himself but requires to be rationalized in terms of conceptions borrowed from current science or philosophy.

Once this view is adopted, then the basic view that in Jesus Christ we have none other than the being of God Himself acting in our temporal existence is in jeopardy. This view, and in fact all theological statements, are transmuted into statements of human observation on human existence. This is precisely what is meant when these pundits argue that "God is dead." Not only is their God dead, but so is Christ and the Holy Spirit. The latter has become engulfed in man's spirit, and the great saving acts of God and the work of the Holy Spirit are now indistinguishable from man's existential decisions. This concern for an existentialist, anthropocentric, humanistic theology is a fatal retrograde movement and means for its protagonists the death of God, and for its followers eventually the death of religion.

Therefore, on this 450th anniversary of the publication of Luther's Ninety-five Theses we would remind ourselves that the Reformation neither started nor ended with Luther; it is a continuing discipline within the true church. Luther only prodded his own church in her sleep, to wake her up from her drowsiness. He merely pointed out the Biblical foundations; he sketched the lines along which the great Church Fathers of East and West had worked; thereby he uncovered the gross corruptions and accretions of a secularized, despiritualized church.

The call is not other today, but it is set in a more complex intellectual situation. The new reformation must free itself from its own deadly subjectivity, which sees Christianity as some kind of self-expression of man. It must be committed to a complete belief in the Biblical Creator and Redeemer God, tremble again before the terrifying and startling fact of the Incarnation, strengthen itself in the great witness the Greek and Latin Fathers made, and must work out these truths face to face with totalitarian secular powers and competing religious and philosophical movements. In this new reformation we must develop a fresh theology, not out of our own proud artistic or cultural creativity but under the humbling discipline of a rigorous obedience to the reality of the Word of God made flesh in Jesus of Nazareth. The reconstructing (perhaps development) of the church's life and thought must take place on its own proper foundations. Any appropriate or permanent advance must take place within the dialog between the great historical traditions of the churches.

This argument does not imply some kind of theological reform engaged in by theologians and then offered to the churches. It would offer the full doctrine to all members of the churches and in that presentation move the churches to penitence and spiritual obedience. History is asking us now whether we know what the Gospel truly is and truly means. The answer to this question, this writer believes, will take the combined resources of all Christendom to receive from God nothing less than the penitent purification of all the people of God

287

and a Pentecostal movement that will sweep through our churches and make us all one in Christ.

Is it peering too far into the future to see the meaning of the rise of the World Council of Churches and the calling of Vatican II as a divine pressure to urge on the churches to come together penitently and conserve collectively all that God has given and preserved in our historical traditions? Protestantism and Roman Catholicism belong to one another. Can Roman Catholicism rise to the demand of the hour and reform herself sufficiently to realize that the Protestants are perhaps her noblest sons after all? Can the Protestants really stand within some new restoration of a world church and show the validity of classical Reformation theology in a new milieu, in a new way, before new demands?

Protestantism has too long suffered from its own failure to recognize the theological meaning of the Reformation. It must in penitence submit itself to its own self-renewal in terms of the Reformation doctrines which once before reformed it and may once again reform it along the lines of New Testament theology and patristic learning; it would be fatal to turn its back on its own past. Were Protestantism able to effect this, it would bring about a spiritual renewal and make her fit to enter a colloquium with Rome. She would then also be enabled to think out the stresses and strains within the faith in relation to the world now largely alienated and find again some sense of divine mission. Such a theological and spiritual revival would go far to cure the indifferentism within the fold and the absenteeism of the wandering flock.

Far too long has Protestantism's solidarity with the world been unquestioned, the world with its fads and fashions, its problems and prejudices, its creeds and cultures. We must stand within the world admittedly, but we must also stand over against the world that pays too little heed to the Gospel. The church has something very definite and authoritative to say about God, the world, sin and judgment, heaven and hell, and the meaning of life. This word is not something the church or our fathers evolved, but is a word from God that addresses man where he now is. The church must live in a continuing reforming movement, but that movement arises from the Word of God for us men and for our salvation, reaching back to the dim pasts of Abraham and through to the city of God; it does not and cannot originate in the human mind. In no part of Christendom is the continuing Reformation more urgent than it is in Protestantism. *Ecclesia reformata, semper reformanda* may well be adopted as the watchword not only of Reformed Protestantism but of Protestantism as a whole. But we must remember that it is God's church that has to be reformed, not ours; in God's way, not ours; in His time, not ours; for His purposes, not ours.

NOTES

1. Amos. 2:2.
2. Is. 1:4 et al.
3. Jer. 5:31.
4. Jer. 31:33.
5. Jer. 50:6.
6. Jer. 2:13.
7. Jer. 50:5.
8. Jer. 30:18.
9. Jer. 50:5.
10. Matt. 5:17.
11. Matt. 13:52.
12. Thomas F. Torrance, *Theology in Reconstruction* (London: SCM Press Ltd., 1965) pp. 259-83.
13. Adolf von Harnack, *Lehrbuch der Dogmengeschichte* (Darmstadt: Wissenschaftliche Buchgesellschaft), III, 814.
14. Augustine: "Non est aliud Dei sacramentum nisi Christus." MPL 38, 845.
15. Regin Prenter, *Spiritus Creator* (Philadelphia: Fortress Press, 1953), published originally in Copenhagen in 1946 in Danish, has developed this thought extensively.
16. Large Catechism, cited from *Luthers Werke in Auswahl*, ed. Otto Clemen (Berlin: A. Marcus und E. Webers Verlag, 1912 ff), IV, 58, 19-27.
17. *De servo arbitrio*, 1525, Clemen, III, 138, 25 ff. On the former point of its Biblical origins he wrote to Erasmus: "Quis igitur et nunc negare audeat, Deum sub istis principibus viris . . . in vulgo sibi servasse Ecclesiam, et illos omnes, exemplo Israelitici regni, perire permisisse? . . . Feces vero et reliquias Israel servare, ut Isaias dicit."
18. On John 4:4 (1540), LW XXII, 512-13; WA XLVIII, 217, 33 ff.
19. LW XLI, 144; WA L, 625, 21.
20. LW XLI, 166; WA L, 643, 22 ff.
21. LW XLI, 166; WA L, 642, 36 ff.
22. LW XLI, 143-44; WA L, 625, 15 ff.
23. Luke 22:27.
24. Erich Vogelsang, "Die Anfänge von Luthers Christologie nach der ersten Psalmenvorlesung," in Vol. XV of *Arbeiten zur Kirchengeschichte*, eds. Emanuel Hirsch and Hans Lietzmann (Berlin and Leipzig: Verlag von Walter de Gruyter & Co., 1929), pp. 142-44. Vogelsang's footnotes are filled with interesting and valuable quotations from Luther.
25. "Preface to the Complete Edition of Luther's Writings, Wittenberg, 1545," LW XXXIV, 338; Clemen, IV, 428, 22-27.

26. WA I, 94-99.

27. WA 1, 221-28; LW XXXI, 9-16; *Luther: Early Theological Works,* LCC XVI, 266-73.

28. WA I, 350-65; LW XXXI, 39-70; LCC XVI, 276-307.

29. See Luther's answer to Prierias, WA I, 647-86.

30. WA II, 6-26; LW XXXI, 259-92.

31. WA II, 158-61; LW XXXI, 313-25.

32. WA VII, 814-57; LW XXXII, 105-31.

33. WA XXXVI, 426-34.

34. Rom. 9:16.

35. Vogelsang, p. 134.

36. The best account is still *A History of the Oecumenical Movement,* eds. Ruth Rouse and Stephen Neill (London: S. P. C. K., 1954); see pp. 355 ff.

12

REFORMATION, RESTITUTION,
AND THE DIALOG

Franklin H. Littell

I N OCTOBER 1523 an incident occurred in Zürich, Switzerland, which foreshadowed the two different pathways the Protestants were to travel for more than four centuries. The one party, headed in Switzerland by Ulrich Zwingli, went the way of a reform of doctrine and cultic practices, with retention of the medieval parish pattern. The other party, headed by Conrad Grebel, purposed not reformation but restitution; the genius and style of life of the New Testament and the early church were to be restored after a lapse of 12 centuries. Perhaps now that we are cultivating a dialog between Roman Catholics and Protestants, the time has come when it will be useful to clarify some of the issues still tending to separate Protestants: Anglicans, Lutherans, and Continental Reformed from Baptists, Mennonites, and Disciples (among others) when matters of faith and order are at stake. The differences are not accidentals but substantive — although a growing spirit of Christian charity, combined with the common experience of religious liberty and pluralism in America, has tended to bridge the originally sharp cleavages.

The date was 26 October 1523 during the first Zurich Disputation. The issue was what was to be done concerning images and the Mass. The chief parties were the reformers and the defenders of the old order, but a spirit that led in yet a third direction broke the surface at one point. The moment came when Zwingli responded to Conrad Grebel's question what advice should be given the preachers as to what they should do with the Latin Mass. Much had been said about it, and the whole thing would be in vain if no change were made. Zwingli, later to explain that the assembly did not convene to decide things but to be informed on the issues, said that the town council would know best what to do concerning the Mass. Thereupon Simon Stumpf, of Grebel's circle and like him still a follower of Zwingli, burst out with the critical words: "Master Ulrich! You don't have the authority to put the decision in milords' hands. The decision is already fallen: the Spirit of God decides." [1]

On its surface this incident seems a striking parallel to what Martin Luther had experienced just a few months before with the so-called Zwickau prophets. Leaving his place of concealment at the Wartburg against the orders of his protector and to the consternation of his friends, Luther preached the famous Eight Sermons of 7 to 14 March 1522 to quiet the unruly spirit and the precipitate haste in which crowds were following the agitators into iconoclasm. In his "Letter to the Princes of Saxony" Luther later reported (1524):

> They themselves boast that they do not belong to us, and have learned and received nothing from us. They come from heaven, and hear God himself speaking to them as to angels. . . . "You yourself must hear the voice of God," they say, "and experience the work of God in you and feel how much your talents weigh. The Bible means nothing. It is Bible-Booble-Babel to these prophets." [2]

When challenged to state the authority by which they acted, the prophets claimed a special revelation (eine besondere Offenbarung). When the Reformer referred to the Bible, they claimed that "man must be taught by the spirit alone. For if God had intended to instruct men by scriptures, he would have sent down a Bible to us from heaven." [3]

Luther is supposed to have said, in the rough common sense that was part of his genius, that if what possessed them were the Holy Spirit, he'd "eat it feathers and all"! The encounter did not remain on that humorous level, however. Nor did it stay on the level which he fixed in his Eight Sermons:

> Summa summarum, I will preach, speak, write, but I will force no

292

one; for faith must be voluntary. . . . I did nothing, the Word did everything. . . . Do you know what the Devil thinks when he sees men use violence to propagate the gospel? . . . But when he sees the Word running and contending alone on the battle-field, then he shudders and shakes for fear. The Word is almighty, and takes captive the hearts.[4]

The Enthusiasts shifted to social revolution in the name of God. And by the time the Peasants' War and the revolt at Münster were finished, Luther had shifted to the persecutor's position. If not heresy, then blasphemy — at least — could be punished by government.

The positions represented by Simon Stumpf at Zurich and Marcus Stübner at Wittenberg were, however alike they seemed to Zwingli and Luther, fundamentally different. The tragic misunderstandings of later years were fixed by the fact that to those who were defending Christendom the challenge of the Spiritualizers and the challenge of the Biblical Anabaptists appeared to be identical. Martin Luther — and John Calvin too, for that matter — never encountered a genuine Anabaptist. And Ulrich Zwingli, who knew intimately the Swiss wing of the Anabaptist movement, was of all the reformers the least critical of intimate cooperation between church and state to serve religious aims. As a patriotic citizen of Kanton Zürich he took it for granted that the town council should make the basic decisions for church life as well as for other aspects of communal existence. Luther, who would never have consented to such an arrangement, knew only those radicals who defied order, denied the meaning of the means of grace, and saluted the arrival of the Age of the Spirit with disorderly enthusiasm.

What was Stumpf in fact saying? What his opponents heard as an assertion of individual inspiration, like the word of the Zwickau prophets, was for him and his brethren nothing of the kind. He was of course denying the right of the magistrate to interfere in decisions of faith, where authority belongs alone to Christ, the Head of the church. Luther, but not Zwingli, would have agreed — so far as positive interference was concerned. But Stumpf did not meet Luther, a fact that may have had great consequence for Protestantism. What might have happened had the great Reformer met pioneer Free Church men instead of *Schwärmer*, we can only speculate. The spirit to which Stumpf had recourse, claiming that the Spirit had already decided the matter, was no private inspiration. That spirit was not even the illumination of the Logos given to every man who comes into the world. For Stumpf, as can now be reconstructed from recently published documents, the spirit was very precisely the Holy Spirit —

293

the Spirit of truth, the Guide and Governor sent into the midst with the resurrection of Christ (John 14:16-18). He it was who enabled the early Christians to report — after a good discussion — that a decision had fallen, with the words, "It seemed good to the Holy Spirit and to us." (Acts 15:28)

To most who thought in the framework of Christendom, with its patterns of authority and obedience, the two appeals seemed the same. Yet we can see today that they were fundamentally different: the Wittenberg radicals pointed toward religious individualism and anarchy, the Zürich radicals toward a new style of church government. The two lines were distinguished by Alfred Hegler in a famous essay, and through the writings of Ernst Troeltsch they have become common currency in the sociology of religion.[5] On the one hand were the Spiritualizers (*Spiritualisten*), who in hostility to all outward forms dissolved both creeds and disciplines — and finally, among some of them, the prevailing civil order too. On the other were the *Täufer*, the forerunners of the Free Church, who obeyed the magistrate in things political but denied any authority to civil government in matters of faith and confessed the authority of the Holy Spirit in the midst of the covenant community.

The Spiritualizers, of which the Zwickau prophets were but one type, were the forerunners of the modern champions of *positives Christentum*, "religionless Christianity," and "nonsectarian religion."[6] Those who affirmed the governance of the Holy Spirit in the church were — or so they thought — restoring the apostolic style of decision-making. They were the forerunners of the Free Church line, where the various groupings have always found it more congenial to speak of the divine initiative in terms of the Holy Spirit rather than the mystical body.[7] Today, especially on the mission fields, this "Third Force" has become an important factor in the world map of the faith.

The confusion of Spiritualizers and Free Church men has continued in some circles to the present day to the detriment of dialog between two major types of Protestantism. Karl Holl is one illustration of the problem created by this misunderstanding; he considered the Enthusiasts (*Schwärmer*) who confronted Martin Luther to be the type of all later Free Church men, particularly what he called the "sect-influenced English-American."[8] He was right in seeing the importance of the principle of voluntaryism to the Free Church (*Freiwilligkeitskirche*); but he was wrong in assuming that the sociological reality necessarily implied a theological synergism. Another illustration of the confusion would be the conclusion of Joachim Wach that "the term 'free church'

294

has the double meaning of freedom from secular interference (e. g., from the side of the state) and of freedom from coercion in religious matters (e. g., compulsory discipline)."[9] Contrarywise, on the basis of voluntary church covenants the Biblical Anabaptists built up a structure of church discipline without equal in earlier generations of Protestantism. Wach, like Holl, confused two distinct wings of the radical Reformation.

It is not difficult to see how in the 16th century the mainline Reformers found it difficult to distinguish between those who disregarded all historical and institutional commitments and those who rejected the oath, church taxes, and other supports of "Christendom." Both parties were "primitivists,"[10] dating the fall with the triumph of Christianity under Constantine the Great. But even their view of the "Fall of the Church"[11] points up the essential difference between them. The Spiritualizers dated the fall with the fixing of theological concepts at the Council of Nicaea, which was said to end the pure inspiration and life of the spirit of the early church. The pioneer Free Church men dated the fall with the union of church and state, which ended the Pauline missionary method of preaching and letter writing and welded the cross to the sword. The view of the Restitution is equally revealing. For the Spiritualizers the Restitution is a return to the unchanneled and uncontrolled movement of the spirit which sectarian parties have attempted to control. True faith is "non-sectarian" (*unpartheyisch* — a word Sebastian Franck gave to the German language). For the Free Church men the Restitution involved a return to the simple Gospel, ethical and moral norms, nonresistance, and mutual aid, which had marked the true church (*die rechte Kirche*) in the age of confessors and martyrs.

In the 16th century, despite rejection and persecution by both Catholic and Protestant governments (a persecution in which only Philip of Hesse refused to participate), the Biblical Anabaptists contributed two major institutions to the established Protestant churches: church discipline and confirmation training. John Calvin added church discipline as the third mark (*tertior nota*) of the church on the basis of lessons learned from Martin Butzer's (Bucer) encounter with the Anabaptists of Hesse while he was an exile in Strasbourg, 1538–1541.[12] Confirmation, distinct in style and purpose from the Catholic *Firmung* — which was a kind of Christian puberty rite — was instituted in Strasbourg as a result of debates between city leaders and radical reformers in 1531–1533 and spread from there rapidly throughout Lutheran, Reformed, and (finally) Anglican areas.[13] In a famous series of public debates a spokesman for the radicals urged Butzer and his colleagues that if they would not end infant Baptism and introduce adult Baptism, they ought at least to have a *Ceremonie* by which, when persons came of age, they could voluntarily and as adults affirm again the vows made for them in their infancy. Butzer decided that the counsel was good, just as he later decided church discipline was Scriptural, and advised Philip of Hesse to institute it, and from that decision dates the familiar rite. Today it may be suggested that there are other points where the Anabaptist (radical Puritan) Free Church line has something to contribute to the strengthening of the whole Christian movement.

The brilliant Catholic lay theologian Michael Novak has recently published an irenic discussion of what the Free Church theory and practice can contribute to Catholic thought.[14] He is of the mind that the major points of conflict and mutuality between Catholicism and the Free Churches lie elsewhere than they do between Catholicism and the mainline Reformation. If this is true at the level of Catholic-Protestant dialog, there are certainly a number of unresolved issues between the party of the Reformation and the party of the Restitution — not the least important being a quite different understanding of "apostolicity." For Luther continuity lay in the preaching of the Word across the generations. For the Anglicans continuity may lie in a certain view of episcopal succession. For the radicals "apostolicity" meant to be true to the spirit and model of the apostles.[15]

In Novak's view the importance of the Free Church to the ecumenical dialog lies in these testimonies:

1. religious liberty;
2. the church as a covenanted community;
3. the work of the Holy Spirit in the midst;
4. consensus as a principle of church government;
5. lay participation in consultations and decisions at local level.[16]

To these I would add a second list of concerns that run throughout the history of the "Third Force":

1. normative significance accorded the New Testament and early church;
2. "separation" from the spirit of the times, enforced by moral and ethical codes;
3. restitution of the Pauline missionary methods and mood to replace coercive religion or religion limited to a single tribe;

4. accenting the general priesthood;
5. church order attained by voluntary covenants rather than decreed by government and/or defined by theologians;
6. church government based on discussion among all full members, leading to consensus ("the sense of the meeting");
7. discipline and devotion to religious obligations made voluntary and separated from all political status;
8. a new style of church action in the public forum, growing up out of the general priesthoood ("from church meeting to town meeting");
9. a common style of life developed in expectation of the fulfillment of history ("church" as an eschatological concept).[17]

No claim is made here that these concerns are uniquely the property of the Anabaptist (radical Puritan) Free Church groups. In four and a half centuries a good deal more has been learned mutually by those who stand in the line of the "magisterial Reformation"[18] and those who stand in the line of the Restitution (or Restoration, as the Disciples of Christ have preferred to call it)[19] than is commonly admitted. Quite soon after the denunciations of the Anabaptists in Articles IX, XVI, and XVII of the Augsburg Confession (1530) several of the Lutheran and Reformed territorial churches modified the harsh positions taken when the Anabaptists were mistakenly blamed for the Peasant Revolt and the Münster revolution.[20] Today, in the age of dialog, even the great ethnic religions — Buddhism, Hinduism, and Islam — are sending missionaries to vie in the open forum for men's voluntary commitment.[21] And even though areas like Saudi Arabia and Ceylon and Burma may strive to continue coercive measures, even though Marxist governments in Russia and China and their satellites endeavor to construct a new facade for the old style of sacral civilization, religious liberty is on the march. As the common folk become educated, as they claim the dignity of citizens and reject the indignities suffered by subjects, they will assert that just government is "secular" (i. e., limited in scope, modest in claims, "creaturely" in self-identity) and that true faith is based on voluntary commitment, support, and devotion. When we have passed through this time of totalitarian terror, this last age in which states attempt to define and delimit religion to serve to their own ends, a finer church — more gloriously catholic, more soundly confessional, more disciplined in service and mission — may rise phoenix-like from the ashes of Christendom.

Once the sacral pretensions of demonic political regimes have been recognized and identified for what they are — a denial of the terms of reference of just government — the key question is whether the church will have recovered that eagerness of mission, that readiness of selfless service, that acceptance of self-criticism which are the fruits of a lively faith. The men of the Free Church line, from Conrad Grebel and Menno Simons through William Penn and Oliver Cromwell to John Wesley and Alexander Campbell, have consistently affirmed their indebtedness to the great Reformer for recovering the liberating reality of justification by faith. They may, in return, serve all the churches by sharing their rich testimony to the power and presence of God the Holy Spirit.

It is informative to note that the radical Reformation has usually preferred to discuss the fullness of the Spirit present in the imagery of the work of the Third Person of the Holy Trinity rather than in the imagery of the Second Person.[22] This would be, if taken seriously, not only a useful corrective to the appalling Jesus-mysticism of latter-day Pietism but something much more important: a corrective to the misuse of the doctrine of "the body of Christ" to forestall all criticism of the church in her known and visible form. Menno Simons criticized the Roman Church of his day for so defining the organized church as an extension of the mystical body of Christ as to be guilty of recapitulating the Monophysite heresy.[23] In a striking parallel to his criticism, a contemporary Catholic scholar has recently complained of

> the unfortunate tendency of Catholic ecclesiology to assimilate the visible collective church of historical action and juridical organization directly and unconditionally into the church's eschatological essence. The historical church, here and now, is then conceived of, unconditionally, as the Kingdom, the Bride, the Mystical Body. Thus the whole dialectical situation of the church's present existence is overlooked and the church claims her eschatological essence as immediately and unconditionally one with her historical existence. The historical church is thus made sinless and perfect, and all sinfulness and imperfection are relegated to the private and individual acts of the members of the church, for which the church herself claims no responsibility. Mother Church, herself completely spotless, lends her solicitous care upon her sinful children, but never does she have to stand before her Lord and confess herself a harlot. With triumph, the historical church herself can now proclaim, "without any fault at all *(utique absque ulla labe)* the pious mother shines forth in the sacraments." [24]

If we did not know the author, we would almost certainly jump to the conclusion that here spoke a spiritual child of Martin Luther! Perhaps so, for in this age of startling openness and God-given dialog we are learning from each other constantly and in unexpected ways.

What I am suggesting is that an increased attention to the doctrine of the Holy Spirit among theological minds and an enlarged readiness to rejoice in the work of the Spirit wherever the fruits thereof are made manifest may well provide one major area where Catholic, confessional Protestant, and Free Church Christians can meet today — and in their meeting learn better to serve the Head of the church and those for whom He died.

Reading the records of the 16th-century divisions, one is struck by the degree to which the image of the fortress informed the actions of the various parties. Pope Adrian and others of the Roman party referred to Protestantism as a second Islam that threatened to tear away choice sections of Christendom as once the followers of Mohammed had overrun the ancient cities of the faith, carried away over half of the Christian world (and the best half at that), and even yet threatened Christian Europe from the south. Against this new rebellion they shored up the walls of Roman Catholic Europe and battened down the hatches with the canons and decrees of the Council of Trent. The style of Protestantism during the high tide of Protestant scholasticism and the proliferation of sectarian enclaves on the Free Church side was not greatly different. Certainly we can understand the pressures that produced this kind of response, when in our own time — in the struggle with communist and fascist attackers — the church has repeatedly been pressed *in statu confessionis*. But that is not the normal posture of Christians, and certainly we do wrong if — when the dialog is opened up — we remain transfixed, as it were, by the experience of hostility. When the floods recede and the welcome and open land again beckons, to remain lodged in the ark that carried us through the heavy waters is hardly to live the life of faith.

The Spirit and work of the modern missionary movements first brought us out of the ark (or fortress, if you will). It is the recovery of the vision of a world-spanning faith that challenges the particularism and parochialism into which we had settled in our respective camps. Even the savage attacks of totalitarian groups and ideologies bring us closer together as God uses the "rod of the Assyrian" to His glory. Christians of many different schools of thought have experienced the fellowship of *KZ* and slave labor camp. The postwar consultations of Lutherans and Catholics and of *Landeskirchen* and *Freikirchen* (both series held at the Bad Boll *Evangelische Akademie*); the cooperation of the Frankfurt ecumenical circle and the Paderborn *Kreis,* uniting Protestant and Catholic churchmen in Germany in joint theological labors; the pragmatic wisdom of the *Simultankirchen;* the common cause of *Caritas* and *Hilfswerk* and the Mennonite Central Committee — all these Christian events signal the emergence of a greater spirit, a more universal *diakonia,* and the wise conclusion that in a time of spiritual warfare with demonic powers like communism and fascism there are worse things than for Catholics and Methodists, Lutherans and Mennonites to join hands in honor to the universal Lord of the universal church. We have in this time often seen the doubtful accomplished and the impossible performed through the grace and power of Him who goes before us to open up what are, humanly speaking, the most difficult fields. Through the eyes of faith we perceive that the Creator is working in ways which, even a decade ago, were beyond our human imagining. We are learning to see again that the whole creation groans in travail for the great Redemption, standing on tiptoe, as it were, to see the sons of God coming into their own. As we leave our respective fortresses to dwell again in the tents of the covenant people, to join again the line of march of those who seek "the city which hath foundations," new forms of parish work, of joint ministry and cooperative witness open up for us. We see that He has gone before us and that the fruits of mercy and truth and righteousness are borne on occasion by the sons of the stranger as well as by those who know and openly confess the Lord's name.

Nor are we left comfortless and without a compass in the secular city, in the pluralistic setting which results from the end of sacral civilization (Christendom or its variants). There has in fact always been a pluralism of commitments; we now have been given the liberty to admit it and to draw the necessary consequences for the church's ministry and missions. We can now meet each other with the open face of truth, with no partner coerced or silenced or prevented from expressing his honest questions. And in the celebration of the age of dialog we are beginning to perceive again the truth which the Logos Fathers confessed, which we had almost forgotten in the hermetically sealed chambers of our several fortresses, that whenever truth is found we encounter the Spirit who has never, in any place, left Himself without a witness.

Nor is He an unknown God. We are met not like an accidental configuration of isolates, to fly apart again into separate orbits, wandering our solitary ways in the cold and distant stretches of outer space. He does not inspire atomized fragments, individuals with claims to

300

special revelations apart from the means of grace. The one who draws us together, who has decreed — to paraphrase Teilhard de Chardin — that the ultimate meaning of the cosmos is personal, is the Spirit who proceeds from the Father and the Son. The one who wrestles secretly with us, even as we struggle to speak and to listen and to learn from each other in the dialog, has a name above all earthly powers. His nature and His name is Love.

In the kingdom which He is bringing into being, in the church which is constantly being reformed by His truth, in the fellowship which is continually restored by His Spirit, we cannot be made whole without each other.

In his meditation on the Twenty-fifth Psalm (ca. 1537), Menno Simons affirmed the authority of the Word and the work of the Holy Spirit:

> Then if I err in some things, which by the grace of God I hope is not the case, I pray everyone for the Lord's sake, lest I be put to shame, that if anyone has stronger and more convincing truth, he through brotherly exhortation and instruction might assist me. I desire with all my heart to accept it if he is right. Deal with me according to the intention of the Spirit and Word of Christ.[25]

I believe that Luther would have understood and appreciated that doctrine of the Spirit. The pity is that the great Reformer encountered not Menno but Müntzer.

NOTES

1. Quoted and discussed in John Yoder, *Täufertum und Reformation in der Schweiz: I. Die Gespräche zwischen Täufern und Reformatoren 1523-1538* (Karlsruhe: H. Schneider Verlag, 1962), p. 20.
2. LW XL, 50.
3. Nikolaus Müller, *Die Wittenberger Bewegung, 1521 und 1522* (Leipzig: M. Heinsius Nachf., 1911), p. 143.
4. Philip Schaff, *History of the Christian Church* (New York: Charles Scribner's Sons, 1892), VI, 389.
5. Alfred Hegler, *Geist und Schrift bei Sebastian Franck* (Freiburg: J. C. B. Mohr, 1892); Ernst Troeltsch, *The Social Teaching of the Christian Churches* (New York: The Macmillan Company, 1931), II, 745 ff.
6. Franklin H. Littell, "Spiritualizers, Anabaptists, and the Church," *The Mennonite Quarterly Review*, XXIX, 1 (Jan. 1955), 34-43; "The Protestant Churches and Totalitarianism (Germany, 1933-1945)," *Totalitarianism*, ed. Carl J. Friedrich (Cambridge: Harvard University Press, 1954), pp. 108-19.
7. See "Some Free Church Remarks on the Concept, the Body of Christ," *The Church as the Body of Christ*, ed. Robert A. Pelton (Notre Dame: University of Notre Dame Press, 1963), pp. 127-38.

8. Karl Holl, *Gesammelte Aufsätze zur Kirchengeschichte* (Tübingen: J. C. B. Mohr, 1928-32), I, 466.

9. Joachim Wach, *Sociology of Religion* (Chicago: University of Chicago Press, 1944), p. 148.

10. See "Primitivismus," *Weltkirchenlexikon: Handbuch der Oekumene*, eds. Franklin H. Littell and Hans Hermann Walz (Stuttgart: Kreuz Verlag, 1960), cols. 1182-87.

11. See Franklin H. Littell, *The Origins of Sectarian Protestantism* (New York: The Macmillan Company, 1964), Ch. II.

12. See "New Light on Butzer's Significance," *Reformation Studies*, ed. Franklin H. Littell (Richmond: John Knox Press, 1962), pp. 145-67.

13. See Franklin H. Littell, *Landgraf Philipp und die Toleranz* (Bad Nauheim: Christian Verlag, 1957), p. 26.

14. Michael Novak, "The Free Churches and the Roman Church," *Journal of Ecumenical Studies*, II, 3 (Fall 1965), 426-47.

15. See Walter Lowrie, "Apostolicity and Restitution," *Ministers of Christ*, ed. Theodore O. Wedel (New York: Seabury Press, 1964), pp. 134-47.

16. Novak, pp. 445-46.

17. See Franklin H. Littell, "The Historical Free Church Tradition Defined," *Brethren Life and Thought*, IX, 4 (Autumn 1964), 78-90.

18. A typological concept introduced by George H. Williams in *The Radical Reformation* (Philadelphia: The Westminster Press, 1962), Introduction.

19. See Alfred T. DeGroot, *The Restoration Principle* (St. Louis: Bethany Press, 1960).

20. Schaff, VI, 712.

21. See Kurt Hutten and Siegfried von Kortzfleisch, eds. *Asien missioniert im Abendland* (Stuttgart: Kreuz-Verlag, 1963).

22. Supra, p. 293.

23. See *A Tribute to Menno Simons* (Scottdale, Penn.: Herald Press, 1961), p. 54.

24. Rosemary Ruether, "Is Roman Catholicism Reformable?" *The Christian Century*, LXXXII, 38 (22 Sept. 1965), 1152-54.

25. *The Complete Writings of Menno Simons* (Scottdale, Penn.: Herald Press, 1956), p. 65.

INDEX

303

Augustine 16-18, 30-1, 43-4, 70-2, 87, 111, 132, 172-99, 212, 244, 275-79, 280
Aurogallus (Goldhahn) 125
Averroes 46

Bad Boll 299
Bamberg, Bishop of 110
Baptism 19, 173, 188, 200-15, 244, 275
Baptism, Infant, Luther's defense of 200-15
Barbaro, Ermolao 46
Barbarossa, Emperor Frederick 109
Barth, Karl 200, 201, 222, 285
Basel, Council of 284
Baumgartner, Hieronymus 116
Bergen Book 252
Bernard of Clairvaux 42, 210-11
Bertram, Robert 14, 219
Bible 88, 92-7, 249, 296
  German 146
  Other vernacular 146-70
    Authorized Version 163
    Basel edition (1509) 147-69
    Vulgate 144
Biel, Gabriel 279
Bishop of Bamberg See Campeggio
Bizer, Ernst 180
Bluhm, Heinz 13, 18, 144
Boccaccio 32
Book of Concord 243, 247-8
  See also Symbolical Books
Bornkamm, Heinrich 185
Bouyar, Louis 16
Bovillus, Carolus 36
Bracciolini, Poggio 16, 33, 45
Brenz, John 116, 247, 249
Bring, Ragnar 15
Brinkel, Karl 205
Bruni, Leonardo 33, 45
Bucer, Martin 14, 255, 285, 295
Buchfürer, Michael 84
Bugenhagen, Johannes 126, 137, 242, 248, 249
Burckhardt, Jacob 23, 24, 25, 50
Burduch, Conrad 25
Butzer See Bucer

Cajetan, Thomas de Vio of Gaeta 68, 111, 278-9
Calvin, John 16, 39, 202, 274, 285, 293
Campbell, Alexander 298
Campeggio, Cardinal Legate Lorenzo 115

Cantor, Norman 57
Carlstadt, Andreas Bodenstein von 131, 132, 209
Carlyle, Thomas 23
Cassander, George 14
Catechism, Large See Luther
Catechism, Small See Luther
Celsus 273
Chardin, Teilhard de 301
Charles V 116
Charles VIII 36
Chateaubriand 48
Chemnitz, Martin 243, 247, 248
Christology 16, 173, 273-5, 282
Chrysostom 179
Church, Luther's doctrine of 277, 282
Churchill, Sir Winston 23
Chytraeus, David 243, 247
Cicero 26, 33, 36, 40, 55, 126
Clairvaux See Bernard of Clairvaux
Clemen, Otto 84
Clement of Alexandria 28
Coburg, Castle 68
Colet, John 36
Complutensian Polyglot 164, 165, 167, 169, 170
Concordia Seminary, St. Louis 13, 14, 59
Conflict, Christian's 222
Confutatio (1530) 219
Congar, Yves 16
Constance, Council of 211
Constantine, Donation of 280
Constantine, Emperor 31
Contarini, Gasparo 14
Copernicus 49
Cordatus, Conrad 57
Cornerus, Christopher 247
Covenant, and Infant Baptism 212-15
Cranmer, Thomas 14, 85
Creation 31, 36
Creeds, Catholic 243
Crispus 31
Cromwell, Oliver 298
Cruciger, Kaspar 137, 254
Cusa, Nicolas 70
Cyprian 201

Dante, Alighieri 41, 44, 49
Darwin, Charles 49
Degrees See Wittenberg, University of
Demosthenes 126
Dialog 291-301
Dictata 178
Diefenbach, Laurentius 150, 154
Diets, Imperial 112-16

Dilthey, Wilhelm 14
Disciples of Christ 297
Disputations at Universities
    Educational 126, 127
    Faculty 128
    Promotional 126, 134
Dix, Gregory 201
Dominic, St. 220
Donatists 206, 208
Donne, John 49
Donum 175, 190, 191
Dressel, Michael 69
Dürer, Albrecht 44, 54, 57, 111

Ebner, Hieronymus 111
Ecclesia reformata semper reformanda
    20, 271-89
Eck, Johannes 68, 71, 83, 90, 94, 112,
    113, 278
Ecumenical Movement 15-20, 215,
    285-9
Ehrenberg, Hans 70
Emser, Jerome 90
Enthusiasts 16, 293
Epieikeia 236
Erasmus, Desiderius 18, 36, 38, 39,
    49, 55, 72, 145, 146, 152
    Greek Testament of *1519* 147-69
    Latin Testament of *1519* 147-69
Eucharist 188
    See also Holy Communion, Lord's
        Supper, Mass
Exsurge Domini 244, 245

Faith 219-38
Faith and works, radical dialectic be-
    tween 219-38
Fathers, Greek and Latin 275, 287
Fazio, Bartolommeo 16, 33, 34-5, 36,
    48
Ferdinand, Archduke 115
Feuerbach, Ludwig 239
Ficino, Marsilio 35, 45
Flacius, Matthias Illyricus *See* Vlacic
Flesh 223-5
Formula of Concord 243, 246-59
    Article I 250-1
    Article II 251-3
    Article III & IV 253-4
    Article VII & VIII 254-8
    Article IX & X 258
    General 246-9
    Solid Declaration 250-8
    Summary Concept 249-50
Francis, St. 220

Franck, Sebastian 295
Frederick, Elector John 56, 137
Frederick the Wise, Elector 67
Free Church, The 294-9
Freud, Sigmund 49
Friends of God 70
Frost, Robert 25, 50

Galatians, Epistle to 144-71, 219-38
Galen 43
Gavin, Eugenio 42
George of Brandenburg 115, 116
Gerbelius, Nicolaus 146, 147
Gerrish, Brian 207
Gerson, John 210-11
Gide, Andre 44
Gnosticism 28, 273
Goethe, Wolfgang von 24, 54
Goldhahn, Mattaeus 125
Goldman, Eric 51
Good Works *See* Faith and works
Gospel 15, 70, 99, 175, 184, 244, 254
Grace 99, 220
Gratian 204
Grebel, Conrad 291, 292, 298
Gregory of Nazianzus 28
Gregory of Nyssa 30
Grimm, Harold J. 13, 17, 108
Guicciardini 45

Harnack, Adolph von 203, 274
Haupt, Rudolf 84
Hegel, Friedrich 23, 57
Hegler, Alfred 274
Heidegger, Martin 23
Heiler, Friedrich 210
Henry VIII 83
Hessen, Johannes 16
Heubner, Heinrich 123
Hilten, John 245
Holl, Karl 207
Holy Communion 275, 281
    See also Eucharist, Lord's Supper,
        Mass
Holy Roman Empire 244, 246
Holy Spirit 275-7, 298
Homoousion 273, 274
Humanism, Christian 18
Humility 186
Hus, John 56, 210-11, 284
Hutten, Ulrich von 24

Ignatius 274
Imitatio Christi 175, 178, 187
Indulgence 82, 90, 98, 128
Infant Baptism *See* Baptism

Reformation 120, 291-301
  17th century 120
  20th century 284-9
Reformers 54, 271, 291
Renaissance 30, 36
Renan, Ernst 53
Repentance 72
Restitution 291-301
Reuchlin, Johannes 112
Revelation 87
Rhegius, Urban 248
Righteousness 97
Romanticism 48
Rome 110
Rupp, E. Gordon 13, 15, 17, 20, 67

Sacrament 14, 15, 19, 200, 210, 213
Sacrament of Altar 254-8
Sacramentum et exemplum 18, 172-99
Salutati, Coluccio 16, 33, 45
Sanctification 19
Santayana 30
Sartre, John 50
Scheel, Otto 172
Scheurl, Christoph 111
Schism, Great 284
Schurff, Jerome 125, 126
Schwärmer 16, 293
Schwiebert, Ernest G. 13, 18, 120
Scotus, John Duns 46, 89, 279
Scriptures, or Word of God 19, 20
Seeberg, Erich 175
Selneccer, Nicholas 243, 247
Seneca 32, 39, 40, 50
Senf, Max 120
Septembertestament 144-71
Silvius, Aeneas 38
Simons, Menno 298, 301
Simul justus et peccator 19
Smalcald Articles 248, 249
Smalcald League 116
Smyth, John 201
Sola fide, sola gratia, sola Scriptura 83
Solid Declaration *See* Formula of Concord
Sophists 26, 40
Soteriology 225
Spalatin, George 69, 71
Speier, Diet of (1526) 283
Speier, Diet of (1529) 283
Spengler, Lazarus 17, 108-17
  Admonition and Instruction for a Virtuous Life 110
  Comforting Christian Prescriptions and Medicine for All Adversities 113

Confession of Faith 113
Durch Adams Fall 113
Short Excerpts from Papal Law 113
Spenlein, George 69
Spirit 225-29
Spiritualizers 294-95
Spitz, Lewis W. 13, 16, 23
Stapulensis, Faber 70, 145, 146
Statutes of 1533, Wittenberg U. 135
Statutes of 1536, Wittenberg U. 136
Stoics 26
Strasbourg 109
Staupitz, Johann von 70, 71, 72, 74, 111
Strigel, Victorine 251
Stübner, Marcus 293
Stumpf, Simon 292, 293
Swabian Concordia 252
Symbolical Books, Lutheran 242-59
  See also Augsburg Confession, Apology, Small Catechism, Large Catechism, Smalcald Articles, Formula of Concord
Szczesny, Gerhard 53

Tauler, Johann 17, 71-4, 78
Te Deum 15
Teilhard de Chardin 301
Tertullian 28, 204
Tetzel, John 68, 122
Theologia crucis 17, 20, 62-78, 173, 175, 277-8
Third Force *See* Anabaptists
Thomas a Kempis 44
Thornton, Geoffrey 201
Timon of Athens 51
Torgau Book 248, 252, 253, 258
Torrance, Frank F. 273, 274
Townsmen 108
Tradition and infant Baptism 209-11
Treatise on Authority and Primacy of the Pope 243, 246
Trent, Council of 283, 299
Tristitia 43
Troeltsch, Ernst 294
Trutvetter, Dean Jodocus 125, 132, 133
Ulrich, Duke 292
University of Leipzig 109

Valla, Lorenzo 145-6, 280
Vatican Council II 15, 16, 19, 285, 288
Vives, Juan Luis 16, 36, 48,
Vlacic, Matthias 246, 251
Vogelsang, Erich 277

INDEX TO SCRIPTURE PASSAGES

311